EZRA POUND

RADIO SPEECHES
OF WORLD WAR II

EZRA POUND
(1885-1972)

Ezra Pound was a key figure in the modernist poetry movement. Known for his innovative style, he championed other writers like T.S. Eliot and wrote the epic *Cantos*. However, his support for fascism and wartime broadcasts led to controversy. Despite this, his impact on 20th-century literature is undeniable.

Radio speeches of World War II

First published in 1978 by Greenwood Press, Inc.

Published by
Omnia Veritas Limited

OMNIA VERITAS®

www.omnia-veritas.com

© Omnia Veritas Ltd - 2025

All rights reserved. No part of this publication may be reproduced by any means without the prior permission of the publisher. The intellectual property code prohibits copies or reproductions for collective use. Any representation or reproduction in whole or in part by any means whatsoever, without the consent of the publisher, the author or their successors, is unlawful and constitutes an infringement punishable by articles of the Code of Intellectual Property.

INTRODUCTION 13

PART I 18

    110 FCC–Recorded Scripts #1 (October 2, 1941) U.S.(A43) LAST DITCH OF DEMOCRACY .. 18

    #2 (October 26, 1941) U.S.(A47) BOOKS AND MUSIC 22

    #3 (November 4, 1941) U.S.(A51) THE GOLDEN WEDDING 26

    #4 (November 6, 1941) U.S.(56) THIS WAR ON YOUTH—ON A GENERATION 31

    #5 (December 7, 1941) U.S. & U.K.(A66) THOSE PARENTHESES 36

    #6 (January 29, 1942) U.S.(A1) ON RESUMING 40

    #7 (February 3, 1942) U.S.(A2) 30 YEARS OR A HUNDRED.. 45

    #8 (February 10, 1942) U.S.(A69) THE STAGE IN AMERICA 49

    #9 (February 12, 1942) U.S.(A71) CANTO 46 52

    #10, FCC Transcript (February 17, 1942) U.S.(A72) SALE AND MANUFACTURE OF WAR 57

    #11 (February 19, 1942) U.S.(A77) POWER The President hath power. 60

    #12 (February 26, 1942) U.S.(B17) AMERICA WAS INTENTIONS 63

    #13 (March 2, 1942) U.S.(B18) NAPOLEON, ETC. 67

    #14 (March 6, 1942) U.S.(B19) WHY PICK ON THE JEW? 71

    #15 (March 8, 1942) U.K. (B15) GOLD: ENGLAND 74

    #16 (March 15, 1942) U.K.(B16) ENGLAND 79

    #17 (March 19, 1942) U.K. (B21) AND THE TIME LAG.. 83

    #18 (March 22, 1942) U.K. (B20) BUT HOW? 87

    #19 (March 23, 1942) U.S. & U.K.(B22) BUT HOW? SECOND ITEM 91

    #20 (March 26, 1942) U.S.(B23) McARTHUR 95

    #21 (March 30, 1942) U.S. & U.K.(B24) THE PATTERN 99

    #22 (April 6, 1942) U.S.(B27) DESTRUCTION 102

    #23 (April 9, 1942) U.S.(B28) INDECISION 106

#24 (April 12, 1942) U.K.(B26) COMIC RELIEF 109

#25 (April 13, 1942) U.S.(B20) QUESTION OF MOTIVE 113

#26 (April 16, 1942) U.S.(B33) CLARIFICATION 116

#27 (April 19, 1942) U.K.(B29) TO SOCIAL CREDITORS 119

#28 (April 20, 1942) U.S.(B34) ABERRATION 124

#29 (April 23, 1942) U.S.(B35) MacLEISH 127

#30 (April 26, 1942) U.K.(B31) BLAST 130

#31 (April 27, 1942) U.S.(B36) OPPORTUNITY RECOGNIZED 134

#32 (April 30, 1942) U.S.(B37) NON-JEW 138

#33 (May 4, 1942) U.S.(B38) UNIVERSALITY 142

#34 (May 9, 1942) U.S. (B39) THE DURATION 146

#35 (May 10, 1942) U.K.(B40) THE PRECARIOUS... 149

#36 (May 11, 1942) U.S.(B41) A FRENCH ACCENT 153

#37 (May 14, 1942) U.S.(B42) TO BE LATE (ESSERE IN RITARDO) 157

#38 (May 17, 1942) U.K.(B45) FREE SPEECH IN ALBION (ALIAS ENGLAND) 160

#39 (May 18, 1942) U.S.(B43) WITH PHANTOMS 164

#40 (May 21, 1942) U.S.(B49) E. E. CUMMINGS EXAMINED 168

#41 (May 24, 1942) U.K.(B47) BRAIN TRUST 173

#42 (May 28, 1942) U.S. & U.K. (B50) AS A BEGINNING 178

#43 (May 31, 1942) U.S. & U.K. (B48) BRAIN TRUST: SECOND SPASM 183

#44 (June 4, 1942) U.S.(B55) AS TO PATHOLOGY AND PSYCHOSES.............................. 187

#45 (June 8, 1942) U.S.(B56) THE KEYS OF HEAVEN 191

#46 (June 14, 1942) U.K.(B32) THE BRITISH IMPERIUM 195

#47 (June 15, 1942) U.S.(B58) VIOLENCE 200

#48 (June 19, 1942) U.S.(B59) THE FALLEN GENTLEMAN (IL SIGNOR DECADUTO)...... 204

#49 (June 25, 1942) U.S.(B62) THAT INTERVAL OF TIME 208

#50 (June 28, 1942) U.K.(B64) THE GIFTIE 212

#51 (July 2, 1942) U.S.(B65) DISBURSEMENT OF WISDOM 217

#52 (July 6, 1942) U.S.(B66) CONTINUITY 221

#53 (July 10, 1942) U.S.(B67) HOW COME 225

#54 (July 12, 1942) U.K. (B72) FREEDUMB FORUM 228

#55 (July 13, 1942) U.S.(B68) DARKNESS 232

#56 (July 17, 1942) U.S.(B69) PERFECT PHRASING 236

#57 (July 19, 1942) U. K. (B73) JULY 16TH, AN ANNIVERSARY 240

#58 (July 20, 1942) U.K.(B71) SUPERSTITION 243

#59 (July 26, 1942) U.K.(B76) AXIS PROPAGANDA 247

#60 (February 18, 1943) U.S.(C8) MORE HOMELY 251

#61 (February 19, 1943) U.S.(C9) THAT ILLUSION 255

#62 (February 21, 1943) U.K.(C5) SERVITI 259

#63 (February 23, 1943) U.S.(C10) COMPLEXITY 263

#64 (March 7, 1943) U.K.(C13) TOWARD VERACITY 267

#65 (March 9, 1943) U.S.(C17) POTS TO FRACTURE 271

#66 (March 14, 1943) U.K.(C15) ANGLOPHILIA 275

#67 (March 16, 1943) U.S.(C20) TO EXPLAIN 279

#68 (March 19, 1943) U.S.(C21) MORE NAMES 283

#69 (March 21, 1943) U.K.(C16) POGROM 287

#70 (March 25, 1943) U.S.(C22) TO RECAPITULATE 291

#71 (March 26, 1943) U.S.(C23) FINANCIAL DEFEAT: U.S. 294

#72 (March 30, 1943) U.S.(C24) USUROCRACY 297

#73 (April 4, 1943) U.K. (C30) LYRIC TENORS 300

#74 (April 6, 1943) U.S.(C27) FETISH 303

#75 (April 13, 1943) U.S.(C29) VALENTINE 306

#76 (April 17, 1943) U.S.(C31) J.G. BLAINE 309

#77 (April 1843) U.K.(C35) CANUTE 312

#78 (April 20, 1943) U.S.(C35) ZION 315

#79 (April 24, 1943) U.S.(C34) CONSCIENCE 318

#80 (April 27, 1943) U.S.(C37) ON RETIRING 321

#81 (May 2, 1943) U.K.(C36) ON THE NATURE OF TREACHERY 324

#82 (May 4, 1943) U.S.(C40) ROMANCE 327

#83 (May 8, 1943) U.S.(C42) PHILOSEMITE 330

#84 (May 9, 1943) U.K.(C39) LORD BLEEDER 333

#85 (May 11, 1943) U.S.(D1) SUMNER WELLES 336

#86 (May 15, 1943) U.S.(D2) ECONOMIC AGGRESSION 338

#87 (May 16, 1943) U.K. (C41) ADMINISTRATION 341

#88 (May 18, 1943) U.S.(D3) ECONOMIC OPPRESSION 344

#89 (May 22, 1943) U.S.(D4) IN THE WOODSHED 347

#90 (May 23, 1943) U.K.(D6) SOBERLY 350

#91, FCC Transcript (May 24, 1943) U.S.[?] [TITLE UNKNOWN] 352

#92 (May 25, 1943) U.S.(D5) AND BACK OF THE WOODSHED 355

#93 (May 29, 1943) U.S(C46) SURPRISE 358

#94 (June 1, 1943) U.S.(C47) BIG JEW 361

#95 (June 5, 1943) U.S.(C48) DEBT 364

#96, FCC Transcript (June 12, 1943) U.S.(C55) [THERAPY] 367

#97 (June 13, 1943) U.K.(C44) TO THE MEMORY 370

#98, FCC Transcript (June 15, 1943) U.S.(C58) [OBSEQUIES] 373

#99 (June 19, 1943) U.S.(C43) WAR AIMS 376

#100, FCC Transcript (June 20, 1943) U.K.(C45) [ON BRAINS OR MEDULLA]..................... 379

#101 (June 22, 1943) U.S.(C64) STALIN 382

#102 (June 26, 1943) U.S. (C65) MATERIALISM 385

#103 (June 29, 1943) U.S. (C67) COMMUNIST MILLIONAIRES.. 388

#104 (July 3, 1943) U.S.(C68) COLORING 391

#105, FCC Transcript (July 4, 1943) U.K.(C57) [TITLE UNKNOWN] 394

#106 (July 6, 1943) U.S.(C69) CREDIT: LEGALITY 397

#107 (July 17, 1943) U.S.(C71) AUDACIA/AUDACITY 400

#108 (July 20, 1943) U.S.(C77) OBJECTION (PROTESTA) 403

#109 (July 24, 1943) U.S.(C79) CIVILIZATION 406

#110 (July 25, 1943) U. K. (C74) LOST OR STOLEN (PERDUTO O RUBATO).......................... 409

PART II 412

#111 (early 1941) HOMESTEADS 412

#112 U.S. (1941) MARCH ARRIVALS 416

#113 (1941) U.S.(68) AMERICA WAS PROMISES 419

#114 (1941) U.S.(50) ARISTOTLE AND ADAMS 422

#115 (1942) U.S.(27) TO CONSOLIDATE 425

#116 (1941) U.K.(20) TO ALBION 428

#117 (1941) U.K.(65) TWO PICTURES 431

#118 (1941) U.S.[?] QUISLING 434

#119 (1943) U.S.(14) PHILOLOGY.. 438

#120 (1941) U.S.(142) CHURCH PERIL 442

ALREADY PUBLISHED...445

INTRODUCTION

The title of this book is the signature Ezra Pound almost always used at the start and sometimes at the end of each broadcast from Radio Rome in World War II. Pound himself had proposed to publish "300 Radio Speeches," containing also the texts of his "Money Pamphlets," newspaper articles published in Italian, and his translations from the Chinese: Ta Hio (*The Great Digest*) and Chung Yung (*The Unwobbling Pivot*).

Pound started to write for radio toward the end of 1940. The first scripts to be accepted were read in English by regular speakers of Radio Rome. In January 1941 he was able to record his own speeches, which were broadcast, on an average, twice a week. He wrote the texts at his home in Rapallo and on occasion in Rome where he traveled to record on discs a batch of 10 to 20 speeches. He wanted the discs to be transmitted in a particular order, but it is apparent from the discrepancies between his numbering system and the dates on which the Federal Communications Commission (FCC) recorded the speeches that the Italian officials did not always follow his plan, although in general the deviation was not great. He gathered news and information from Italian newspapers and whatever foreign papers he managed to obtain; from Italian broadcasts and any foreign station (especially the BBC) he could hear on his own radio; from conversations with friends, officials, and travelers; from letters of friends in America and other countries; and from his own library, which included back numbers of periodicals. He envied the BBC's supply of news and feature materials, since he himself had "not one disc" (July 25, 1943).

After the Fascist government fell in July 1943, Pound left Rome and eventually submitted scripts and ideas to Mussolini's Republic of Saló. No evidence exists to indicate that any of this material was ever broadcast to America in Pound's name from Radio Milan while that station remained under the regime's control.

The present collection consists of original manuscripts Pound prepared to read on Rome radio, divided into two parts:

Part 1 includes all of the available manuscripts (105) for the broadcasts recorded by the FCC: October 2, 1941, to December 7, 1941; January 29, 1942, to July 26, 1942; February 18, 1943, to July 25, 1943.

These are the speeches that have been quoted by Pound's critics, and they include those selected by American authorities who sought to press the charge of treason against him. The monitoring unit of the FCC, called the Foreign Broadcast Intelligence Service, recorded every broadcast from Radio Rome, included among which were Pound's speeches. There are egregious errors and omissions in these FCC transcripts because recording equipment in those days was crude, because atmospheric conditions interfered with the monitoring, and because, I assume, the transcribers sometimes did not recognize Pound's references. The FCC versions of Pound's speeches hitherto available, there fore, sometimes give a wrong impression. Poundians and others have noted that the French novelist Céline was transcribed as "Stalin." Other mistakes can be observed, in many instances probably resulting from the vagaries of shortwave. One illustration: Pound's sentence, "Even Lenin saw that the easiest way to debauch the capitalist system is to debauch its currency' (April 13, 1943), became "Yet even seven saw that the easiest way to divorce the capitalist system is to divorce its currency." To date, however, it has been impossible to locate five of Pound's original manuscripts; hence the FCC versions in these instances, imperfect though they are, have been substituted in this volume. In a few instances gaps in the manuscripts themselves have been filled by sections of the FCC transcripts; these substitutions are clearly indicated.

Part 2 includes 10 speeches written before the FCC monitoring unit had been established, some read by Pound and some read by others, as well as speeches either not used or not monitored. They have been selected by Mary de Rachewiltz because in her opinion they represent a fair sample of Pound's central ideas and themes.

The anonymous and pseudonymous scripts Pound also wrote are not included in this book because they merely repeat ideas already expressed in other speeches.

Most of the speeches in part 1 were intended for an audience in the United States, some for an audience in the United Kingdom, and some for both. It is known that Pound was heard in the United States by people other than the monitors of the FCC, and eventually in April 1942 the Department of Justice began an investigation through the FBI. There is no way of estimating how many persons listened to him regularly or how large his audience ever was. Certainly his broadcasts never attained great popularity. He himself in the broadcasts occasionally expressed jovial skepticism concerning the size of his audience: "I was wonderin' if anybody listened to what I said on Rome Radio" (February 19, 1943).

After January 29, 1942, Pound was introduced by a statement he had drafted: Rome Radio, acting in accordance with the fascist policy of intellectual freedom and free expression of opinion by those who are qualified to hold it, has offered Dr. Ezra Pound the use of the microphone twice a week. It is understood that he will not be asked to say anything whatsoever that goes against his conscience, or anything in compatible with his duties as a citizen of the United States of America.

Pound always referred to himself as an American.

With the exceptions already noted, therefore, the texts of the speeches come from Pound's original manuscripts, which he typed and then often amended in his not always intelligible handwriting. Editing has been kept to a minimum. Elementary misspelling has been corrected. Punctuation and paragraphing have been altered in the interest of intelligibility. Since the scripts were to be read and heard, abbreviations and initials of persons have been spelled out. Pound's penchant for achieving emphasis through capitalizing entire words has been retained. Brackets have been added when my colleagues and I were unsure of a word or phrase after studying the manuscript and after examining the FCC transcript for possible clues. The five PCC scripts have not been edited or amended. Words that cannot be de ciphered or are missing from the manuscripts or the FCC scripts are indicated by a 2-em dash.

The following information is provided at the outset of each speech:

1. To the left

a. Part 1 a consecutive numbering system based on the dates recorded by the FCC Part 2 the order is perforce arbitrary since the speeches have been selected for content and since no reliable dating or numbering system has been located.

b. In parentheses Part 1 the FCC date part 2 the estimated year in which the script was written.

2. To the right

a. When available, the target audience indicated by Pound and/or the FCC.

b. Part 1 Pound s own numbering system in parentheses actually he used three separate numbering systems that have been distinguished here by placing the letter A, B, or C before his number. Part 2: whatever number appears on the original manuscript is provided without relating that number to Pound's different numbering systems.

3. To the left, second line

The title of the speech as given by Pound.

The book has four appendices that attempt, both quantitatively and qualitatively, to provide insight into Pound and his critics. I would have preferred to provide additional information, but too many facts were obscure to express reliable judgments. Neither the Italian archives, for example, nor an examination of the papers at the Beinecke Library at Yale University have revealed why Pound ceased broadcasting between July 26, 1942, and February 18, 1943.

The glossary and index to names at the end of the book are as complete as my collaborators and I could make them, but we have not been able to identify every name to which Pound referred. Admittedly we have often been able to provide only our best guesses.

This volume, in short, seeks to offer the speeches as Pound wrote them. For the first time all of his monitored speeches and some of his other scripts are brought conveniently together. No longer will Poundians or historians be dependent upon the FCC transcripts, pirated editions of the speeches, or hit-and-miss citations to learn what Pound said over Radio Rome.

Reproducing Pound's admittedly controversial speeches over 30 years later requires justification. Why publish this volume? Why have I agreed to function as editor? Pound wrote these scripts; they are part of his legacy. He is so important in American and British literature of the twentieth century that whatever he wrote cannot be ignored. The speeches, moreover, are valuable from a historical standpoint: they reveal what one man, broadcasting from an enemy radio station during World War II, believed his countrymen should hear. On the basis of what he said, moreover, Pound was arrested and accused of treason; he spent 13 years in St. Elizabeth's Hospital (a government institution for the criminally insane in Washington, D.C.) as a result. Anyone who seeks to understand Pound or to write about him and his times cannot overlook these speeches. Although Pound's reputation will forever rest on his poetry and other writings, and not upon these scripts, the broadcasts are part of his record. Actually, the speeches should be of interest of Poundians not only because, according to Mary de Rachewiltz, they reflect his earlier writings but also because they affected his subsequent poetry.

To the second question: why have I personally undertaken this editorial role? Admittedly, I am not a Poundian in any sense, and I have read and understood very little of his poetry. I offer three reasons. First, Mary de Rachewiltz asked me originally to work with her in preparing a definitive edition because she thought my knowledge of propaganda and World War II would be helpful. During that war, I was actively engaged in psychological warfare against Italy, Germany, and Japan. I remember vaguely seeing some of the FCC transcripts of Pound's speeches at the time and dismissing them as irrelevant to my own work.

Then, secondly, I have been interested to see whether the technique of content analysis—which was useful to me during World War II and later in analyzing Goebbel's diaries—would be helpful in comprehending this vast collection of words. The analysis of the 110 speeches, the reader will note in appendices, is pitched on a modest level and simply seeks to answer a straightforward question: in how many of the broadcasts did Pound make one or more references to particular themes, persons, and countries? Finally, although I must add that my own attitudes and feelings have not been one bit changed after working with these speeches, it has been interesting to come to comprehend what Pound was trying to accomplish. His attack on the profits some men reap from wars reminded me of my experience during the summer of 1934 when I was employed by the Senate Committee then investigating "The Merchants of Death."

My own conscience is at peace on a mundane level. Compensation to my research assistants has exhausted, nay exceeded, the funds allocated to me personally in my role as one of the Pound Literary Trustees. My share of the royalties from this book will not go to me. I am grateful to the Trustees of Pound's Estate for giving Mary de Rachewiltz and me access to the original manuscripts. Others who have faithfully cooperated with us are James A. Fishback, who performed the content analysis of the 110 broadcasts; Ellen S. Schell, who worked diligently on the index and glossary; Maryrose Coiner, who prepared the data from the content analysis for the computer and provided us with printouts constituting the basis for the tables; Jane C. Olejarczyk, who heroically managed to prepare typed copies of the manuscripts; and Marjorie A. Sa'Adah, who pitched into the project whenever extra assistance was needed, which was often. Especially cordial gratitude is expressed to Olga Rudge who originally preserved Pound's manuscripts and who conveyed to me a sensitive feeling for Pound's philosophy and approach.

This volume could not have been prepared without the assistance and persistence of Mary de Rachewiltz. This is Pound's book, however, and with her help I have simply facilitated its appearance.

Part I

110 FCC–Recorded Scripts
#1 (October 2, 1941) U.S.(A43)
LAST DITCH OF DEMOCRACY

It's a DITCH all right. Democracy has been LICKED in France. The frogs were chucked into war AGAINST the Will of the people. Democracy has been licked to a frazzle in England where it never did get a look in ANY—HOW. But even pseudo-democracy breaks down when a people is chucked into war against its will, and the Brits. never VOTED Winston into the premiership. In fact WHEN DID they have an election?

Remember it is the government in England that decides WHEN to have an election. Think where we would be if Mr. Roosevelt could merely POSTPONE elections till he got ready to have one.

Well, democracy is in her last DITCH, and if she ain't saved in America. NO ONE is going to save her in her parliamentary form.

As to UNITIN' with England—taking on a lot of bad debts and new liabilities—one of the speakers on this radio was kind enough, that is, he showed respect enough for American intelligence (yes, even today, he showed respect for American intelligence) by saying only Britons were rootin' for this FEDERATION.

On close examination the Brits themselves don't seem to be so numerous in the movement toward merger.

Horeb Elisha [Hore-Belisha], well IS he English? And Victor Sassoon, ALL for the merger.

Twenty percent capital to be paid by the English.

Twenty percent PAID capital to be paid by the United States of America. The balance of 60% UNPAID to remain in the hands of the promoters, probably as PREFERRED stock, with board of directors ready to grant special bonuses to their friends at ANY and every moment.

Well, is Vic Sassoon, that Jew pseudo-parsee, head of the Shanghai rackets, opium, brothels in probability and so forth, night life of Shanghai? IS he YOUR idea of David Copperfield and Mr. Pickwick?

And Mr. Streit? And of course there are MILLIONS behind it. Any one of 86 Jew millionaires can start a publishing firm and any one of the 4,000 hired troops in the British Embassy can print all the crap he likes.

I dunno where the rugged American INDIVIDUAL is going to git FUNDS to combat'em.

BUT, on the other hand, you can annex Canada without taking on liabilities. You can annex Newfoundland, and Jamaica and all the rest of it without either paying England OR paying Sir Victor.

Why this sixty percent cut to promoters who will do NOTHING for you? Yes, I know there is all the Sulgrave Manor association, all the glamour of cousinship; but it WAS cousinship with John Bull, in the old days, not with BULLesha, or Bullstein.

And Bulistein is apparently itchin' to drop off the B and remain simple ULLstein, by means of the merger.

The MILITARY situation? Conducing to UNION? The number of troops that can be supported, and fed, and supplied by ONE line of railway from ArcAngel—from Vladivostock or via Teheran—is considerably less than the TWELVE Million which the Russians set out with.

That Slavic fatalism which induced these troops to die in large numbers has in this war appeared quite ALIEN to the sensibilities of the fighting force put in the field by Mr. Churchill and Mr. Belisha.

I don't see even Winston inventing an echelon system. I mean Tommy Atkins won't shoot Tommy Atkins in the back on SYSTEM. He would feel something after doing it once.

Doubtless Belisha's bright eye, and invigorating etc. will one day suggest that the Aussies could shoot the Sepoys and as the Pathans enjoy shooting anything, and would enjoy shooting Australians especially if invited to do so. And doubtless there could be found an even super-Slavic fatalism some where among the thousand alien races crushed by the Anglo-Jew empire. But it mightn't take a very active military form. It might just sit down with a hand loom in face of the carnage.

But in ANY case it's a question of QUANTITY. And WHAT support does the United States GET from Anglo-Judaea? Just WHOM have the British supported in this so bloody series of swindles?

They have EVERY reason NOT to waste their forces in enforcing American trade in the Orient. They have every reason to leave America to pin up the diapers of their baby.

Except of course the feeling that the United States MIGHT take a leaf out of THEIR book, and grab this or that, as they have grabbed French possessions, and shot off the remaining French combatants.

In Persia it becomes a question of QUANTITY. Walla walla, etc. Twelve Million Russians did NOT stop Von Rundstedt and Baron Keitel. They have not stopped ONE German army.

Nor have they reduced the German forces to a figure ANYwhere near the number of troops that England could maintain with SIX railways over the Caucasus.

So THAT is not exactly where the strategists expect YOU to help England win any wars. Whatever Growler, Mr. McGrump, sez on the B.B.C. liary [lie-ary].

Now when I was a kid Admiral DEWEY ... that sounds like Napoleon at Moscow?

Yes, that sounds to ME like the story about the "Fifth element MUD, said Napoleon."

There are millions of Chinamen. Many of them living on very short rations in the INTERIOR and about as much interested in Chiang Kai-Chek as they are in the White Socks and the Phillies. If there still are any Phillies. You could get more enthusiasm out of those Chinks for a Hot Dog Championship on the Northside than you could for Chiang's FOREIGN party in China.

A LOT of China is NOT pro-Kai-Chek. A lot of China is NOT FOR that gang of foreign investors.

Then, of course, you might rescue the de Gaulle interests. Namely you might go die in the GLORIOUS cause of the Bank of the Paris Union, AGAINST General Pétain, the victor of Verdun.

Do you think the French people would thank you? Listen to the FRENCH radio, that is NOT paid by London; and ASK me.

Yes, the Vichy radio is twisty, it is trying to hold onto France, and double cross the Axis, and hold ONTO FRANCE, and hold or get every inch of French soil, and hang onto every French sou it can lay eye or hold on.

BUT it is NOT working for the *famille* de Gaulle.

AND it knows that Winston wanted Paris razed to the ground, as was Rotterdam, and as Leningrad either is being or has been.

And Pierre Laval was about all that stopped Winston from attaining that so desired result. Because "we as lenders of money" would be able to intervene and LEND money for reconstruction.

A lovely ambition. But will any born Frenchman thank you for exercising that at this moment, will any FRENCHMAN thank you for exercising that kind of ambition?

The French peasant wants his field for himself. He has a healthy MISTRUST of all mortgages.

As to the DATA whereon the American government bases its "judgment" (I believe they still call it judgment). Roosevelt is reported in the Herald Tribune of New York on August 17 as being in complete agreement with Churchill and saying Russia could fight all winter.

Mebbe he meant that Siberia could remain outside German protection during that period. He did go so far as saying that "events in Crete" had delayed his meeting with England's public enemy Number 3. That was some thing but not quite enough to win the Ukraine campaign.

He might have told you that events in Russia had delayed my gettin' the Japan Times. Copy for June 19th has just come. I suppose it was sittin' at Kieff to git through. One lap writer at that time allowed like, as if Franklin was gettin' you folks into the war. But it didn't look to me as if he thought it was an act of idealism. He didn't confuse it with savin' democracy.

In the meantime do LOOK at Belisha's Anglo-Saxon face, as reproduced in P.M. and other organs of similar nature.

That is what the American branch of Sulgrave Manor Association is asked to Unite with.

#2 (October 26, 1941) U.S.(A47)
BOOKS AND MUSIC

Mr. Churchill, EVEN Mr. Churchill hasn't had the brass to tell the American people WHY he wants'em to die to save what.

He is fighting for the gold standard and MONOPOLY. Namely the power to starve the whole of mankind, and make it pay through the nose before it can eat the fruit of its own labor.

His gang, whether kike, gentile, or hybrid is not fit to govern. And the English OUGHT to be the only people ass enough, and brute enough to fight for him.

Now as to my personal habits, the few of you who know that I exist know that I have given most of my time to muggin' up kulchur, that I have writ a few books, and spent my spare time trying to learn musical composition, or else playin' tennis and floatin' round the gulf of Tigullio, in which act I make, so far as I know, a nuisance of myself to no one whatever.

And in the mornings I write letters to and read letters from the most intelligent of my contemporaries, and Mr. Churchill and that brute Rosefield, and their kike postal spies and obstructors, kikarian and/or others annoy me by cuttin' off my normal mental intercourse with my colleagues. But I am NOT going to starve, I am not going to starve mentally. The culture of the Occident came out of Europe and a LOT of it is still right here in Europe, and I don't mean archeology either.

So a few weeks ago Monotti sez: ever read Pea's Moscardino So I read it. and for the first time in your colloquitor's life he wuz tempted to TRANSLATE a novel, and did so. Ten years ago I had seen Enrico Pea passin'' along the sea front and Gino [Saviotti] sez: It's a novelist. Having seen and known POLLON

IDEN, some hundreds, or probably thousands I was not interested in its being a novelist. But the book must be good or I wouldn't be more convinced of the fact AFTER having translated it, than I was before. Of course, my act was impractical so far as you are concerned. I haven't the ghost of an idea how I am to get the manuscript to America or get it published. Pea has never made a cent out of the original. Well neither had Joyce nor Eliot when I started trying to git someone to print'em.

What's it like? Well if Tom Hardy had been born a lot later, and lived in the hills up back of Lunigiana, which is down along the coast here, and if Hardy hadn't writ what ole Fordie used to call that "sort of small town paper journalese," and if a lot of other things, includin' temperament, had been different, and so forth ... that might have been something like Pea's writin'—which I repeat is good writing—and was back in 1921 when Moscardino was printed. Moscardino is the name of the kid who is tellin' about his granpop, a nickname, like Buck.

As soon as the barriers are down I shall be sendin' a copy along for the enlightenment of the American public.

In the meantime, if any one wants to learn how to write Italian let'em read the first chapter of Forastiero, or the couple of pages on the bloke who had been 20 years in jail. This is just announcin' that Italy has a writer, and it is some time since I told anybody that ANY country on earth had a writer. Like Confucius, knocked'round and done all sorts of jobs. Writes like a man who could make a good piece of mahogany furniture.

I sent in a hurry call from the Siena music week, but I reckon it was too late, not time to get retransmittal, but I wanted the clean and decent Americans to hear the Vivaldi Oratorio Juditha Triumphans; which makes ole pop Handel look like a cold poached egg what somebody dropped on the pavement.

Of course it's not THAT kind of an oratorio, it is a musical whoop in two parts, to celebrate the retaking of Corfu from the Turks in 1715; and it was very timely and suitable as a bicentenary funeral wreath on red-head Vivaldi.

I got it once from the top centre, and once in a box hangin' over the orchestry, once for the whole and once for the details.

And I think it's O.K. brother. You'd have to hear it alternate with Johnnie Bach, say the Mathias, seven times over, at least I would, before I would think I was ready to say just HOW good it is.

There has been some good Vivaldi done for orchestra over Rome Radio, but I dunno whether it has been short-waved over to Amerika. There was some good Vivaldi done two years ago, when the Chigi organization had the sense to devote the whole of the Sienese fest to Vivaldi, but the Juditha is one up on that. Better than the Olympiade, as then presented. In fact I think it is better built up as a whole, and you don't have to be annoyed by ginks walkin' about and doin' stage actin'. Well some people like their music with that distraction. When you stop shootin' and stop pilin' up profit for kikes by conveying their guns to the god damn English who ought to be spanked and put to bed by their nurses, you might be able to come over and HEAR IT.

That would be a saner way of passin' the time than doublin' your taxes and being robbed by the American treasury. God, my god, you folks are DUMB!!!

Now as to criticism of the Juditha; I affirm that Vivaldi knew more about using the human voice than Johnnie Bach ever discovered. That may sound like heresy. Waaal, you decide after you have listened to both of'em. And I affirm that Tony Vivaldi knocks the spots off of Handel. I got no doubt on that point whatsoever. Very nice bit for viola d'amore and naturally it pleases me on account of a kink I had before I knew Vivaldi had done it. I have a high opinion of Rossini and Mozart. I.e., use of mandolin in serious orchestra. So has everyone who ain't stark ravin' goofy. But Mozart when he came down to Italy did NOT set the public crazy. And part of the reason was, as I conjecture, that the Italian had then had an earful of Tony Vivaldi. That is guess work. But there are things to set against Bach. In fact things Bach took hold of and rearranged; without as I think improvin'''em.

I had a chance to hear both together two years ago in Siena, in a good orchestral concert, one up to Casella, the way that program was built. Man named Guarnieri conductin', been doing three years now in Siena, at this summer fest. And I would by god rather hear Guarnieri conductin' Vivaldi than hear Toscanini conductin' Beethoven in Salzburg. An idea which occurred to me, dunn' the Juditha performance.

I try to tell you that Italy is carryin' ON. *La rivoluzione continua*. This is the kind of thing Italians go on doing, despite that dirty mugged bleeder and betrayer of his allies, Winston babyface Churchill.

And his gangsters. Those blighters have never done one damn thing for civilization. They have rotted their country, and should not be allowed to rot anyone elses. They didn't start the process of corruption, but they have been, everyone of'em for it, all day and every day, and for the 24 hour period.

Di Marzio is runnin' a paper. Vicari is runnin' a monthly devoted to the "narrative" nothin' but narrative or careful discussion of narrative, and how one should do it. Over in Barcelona, they are printin' a series, *Poesia en la Mano*, bilingual editions of everyone from Villon to Mallarme' and Rilke, and, I am told, your present colloquitor if they can git anyone to translate me.

EUROPE is an organic body, its life continues, its life has components and nearly every damn thing that has made your lives worth livin' up to this moment, has had its ORIGINS right here in Europe.

Yes, we HAD some colonial architecture and 30 pages of Whitman (Walt Whitman, not Whitemann) and then Whistler, and Henry James left the country. In fact it warn't no bed of roses fer authors and painters. Though my generation allus thought we ought to plant something or other, and try to git a new crop of somethin' or other. The idea of the Returnin' Native was prevalent, except possibly to Thomas S.

Eliot who saw from the start that you folks weren't episcopal enough to suit his episcopal temperament, and he somewhat looked down on my pagan and evangelical tendencies. Waaal, frankly, I allus though it would be a good thing to come back and put some sort of a college or university into shape to teach the young something. Not merely the god damn saw dust and subsitutes for learnin' and literature they git handed. However, ca hold up the whole course of civilization. If you wanna line up with bone heads, you will line up with bone heads.

And you will go on having conductors instead of composers and European authors who have resigned.

But don't get that Anglican attitude, of the old story, storm in the channel called by the English, the English channel—the straits between Calais and Dover—and the dirty old Times out with a headline "Continent isolated."

Nobody here is layin' flowers on the tomb of Columbus, not this year. But don't go and run away with the idea that Europe is no longer here, or that books aren't being written. I mean bein' WRITTEN, and that we have no painters, or writers, or musicians.

I regret the personal correspondence of a small number of writers, who mostly don't write to each other. And I would like to see what Hillaire Hiler is paintin', and to git kumrad cumminkz's last set of verses. Or to go on get tin' Kitasono's Japanese magazine. But I ain't gittin' weak and pindlin' or goin' into a pronounced and delicate melancholy fer the extinction of all human intercourse.

#3 (November 4, 1941) U.S.(A51)
THE GOLDEN WEDDING

The sight of elderly wedded couples dwelling in mutual devotion sometimes impells one to think of their early loves. In the present case the spectacle of Mr. Churchill's government wedded to Stalin's, and Mr.

Roosevelt's in violable word mixed into it; in short, this triangual Darby and Joan of the three hebraicized governments leads one to look back at the forgotten incidents of their courtship.

In particular, the love feasts between our American Reds and Moscow in vite beautific contemplation.

Our idealists loved Moscow while Mr. Churchill was still playing the bashful Swain. In fact he was scowling at Stalin, and from the incomprehension of his eternal love for the Moscovites he was being not only sulky, but insulting. So with true love. Never, Never, NEVER would he come and kiss the Russian Joan under the sickle and mistletoe.

Our own American Trade Unionists were more oncoming. They LIKED the bud of Russian promise.

Ref. Worker's Library No. 3 bearing the dim and lavender date: Sept. 9, 1927.

Jay Lovestone (né possibly Liebstein) on the first page of amorous paean inscribes the luminous words "THE establishment of the 7-hour day in Russia." Well that's far off enough and long enough before the Stakhelevites, and Mr. Lovestone is very hard on the American Federation of Labor. "Reactionary trade union bureaucrats" he call's'em.

And in that memorable day an' year our dewey-eyed workers (trade unionists and idealists) technical advisors they figger in the catalog, Brophy, R.W. [?] Dunn, C.H. Douglas, Rex Tugwell, Stuart Chase, a lot, as you see, of brawny fellows who had used either the hammer or sickle in daily life, went over to visit the Kumrad. And apart from the general, as op posed to the specific nature of the answers, the kumrad didn't do so bad. The questions being rather more nebulous and UNspecific than the answers. How could the debonair murderer get down very near to brass tacks in his answers?

After all Marx was pretty good at history and diagnosis. Nobody on the Axis side denies that Marx discovered several genuine faults in the usury system.

All we ask is a way to CURE'em. And the torture chambers in most countries where Stalin's power has reached, and in a few embassies where he had been unable to get control of the total police force, rather indicate that the Boishie system never got UNIVERSAL approval from its victims.

However, when next dining with Rabbi Lehman, or Scholem Mosestha and the rest of the international bankers, spring a few pages of the kumrad's answers between the caviar and the pheasant and see if it don't enliven the dinner.

Sure Stalin approves of Marx and Engels wantin' to take ECONOMIC, political, cultural and organizational measures. And seem' as he put'em in that order, you would expect me to fall for it?

ECONOMIC first. Of course the Bolshies didn't. Any party that comes into power, probably puts ORGANIZATIONAL measures first, and the economics belong, alas to the almost inaccessible part of culture. So FEW people seem able to grasp simple economics without, as Senator Bankhead remarked, about three centuries delay.

Three centuries, to get people to understand anything about anything havin' to do with money. An' it is now demonstrated on the corpus vilis of British reformers' hopes that very little economic reform gets into practice without precedent organizational and political measures of an almost earth shaking nature. A curious phrase about "reconstruct capitalist society" must belong to the translator. I don't want to pin that on Joseph, tho' mebbe that was part of his muddle. I am far less concerned with Joe's lacunae than with a few clear positive statements. Joe said he was aware that "a number of capitalist governments are controlled by big banks," notwithstanding the existence of "democratic" parliaments.

Not bad for a Georgian assassin. And possibly several decades ahead of the American public and professoriat. Not a single power in which the Cabinet can be formed in opposition to the will of the big financial magnates. I wonder: is that why they took Joe for a ride?

"It is sufficient to exert financial pressure to cause Cabinet Ministers to fall from their posts as if they were stunned."

Joey was talkin' of European cabinets; not of the so very different American DEMocracy (as they call it) etc. where, unless there is absolute surety that financial pressure won't be used, the blighters seldom or never get in. Joe SAID that the control of government by money-bags is inconceivable and absolutely excluded in the U.S.S.R. How different from the home life of our own DEMOCRACY (as they call it), etc. and how different from anything any British politician has ever encountered, and how different from any state of things that Churchill's group would desire.

"Narrow circle" said Joe of individuals connected in one way or another with the large banks and because of that they strive to conceal the part they play in this from the people.

What a PERFECT ally for Churchill, Morgenthau, Lehman, and the present Anglo-Jewish regimes!

Well, the starry eyed Mr. Tugwell, and the cautious Mr. Chase and Jim Maurer and Brophy took it all down hook, line and sinker. Seven hour day and the rest of it. It was a stirring occasion. The only thing is that the idealist's ideals have got going so much faster and gone so much further. The Axis side of the present hard feelings.

Here the TRADE UNIONS, with their syndic. organization, and their recognized legal status whereby they propose, formulate, and GET what they want in Italy is really of so much MORE interest for any member of ANY trade union, or for any leader of labor who cares a hang about the welfare of the led that one only hopes the American trade unionist will someday read Por, or at least read something about Italian organizational measures.

The Stalin interview is a tough piece of reading, very hard to take hold of. That was probably the secret of his hold—plenty of people who KNOW Russia have been puzzled by the gap between their effective propaganda and their local failure in solving human problems. I believe the human material they had to work on explains part of the latter. I mean why they did NOT make a paradise, but mostly a sweat shop—machines before men—men as material. But the other side, the devilish efficiency of their propaganda, is worth study.

And it seems to be a variant on the old political wheeze of sticking to general statements that each auditor interprets to mean what HE would mean IF he said it.

And now for contrast, close harmony, let us look at a recent emission from Joe's faithful companion, fellow idealist, and pledged ally, Mr. N.M. Butler. On June 3, 1941, year current, as delivered at the commencement of Columbia University, when Ole Nick was awaitin' another Waterloo, and as is common with his kind, he wasn't puttin' it in the first person singular. Nick wanted Americans to go fight for the British exploiters; so he said "THE WORLD" etc. In this case THE WORLD (meaning Nick and his pay masters). The World he sez, awaits another Waterloo. And on the fifth page it turns out he meant a defeat of Hitler!! Which might be called "metonomy" or takin' a part for the "whole," and not the better whole either.

Now the WORLD, as any college president ought to know, before the trustees pay him his fat annual salary, is spherical in form, and is composed of MORE than one continent, and not wholly and totally enraptured with the big usury central.

However let Nick Butler speak for himself, as he has never failed to do in all his oleaginous lifetime.

Several pages of the old scamp's palaver contain statements by which no right thinking man would be offended. The slabs of print, the page undivided by paragraph divisions, tends to lull the reader or auditor into security.

Mr. Butler even disapproves (mildly, of course) of the "controlling desire for gain," alias our old enemy the profit motive. Of course he keeps off the specific MEANS of gain, exercised by his owners. He then pays a delicate compliment to Lord Holy Fox, without committing himself, in fact nothing could be more downy.

The FIRST Lord Halifax, unaided by his charming and formidable Lady, said there were three hundred years ago many things that riches cannot buy. Therefore the American boys should bleed for the present Lord Holy Fox. Now Ole Nick don't go as far back as all that, he stops back in the 17th Century; before Robert Cecil was so vigorous in defense of the British OPIUM interests in Shanghai.

Victory for a moral ideal is not enough, according to Nicholas, because the "gain-seeking interest has control of so vast a proportion of mankind." That is true enough, but it ain't reduced the moral ideal to ABSOLUTE impotence. This is what was worrying Butler; but he hadn't got down to bed rock. He said there was a time, back apparently when Mark Hanna was running the United State of America, when the moral ideal was to all appearances gainin' ground.

Of course if by that he means that some empires were GAINING territory, he might have said so, only he didn't. Ole Nicholas puts the rise of the triumph, real or apparent, the IDEAL, from the McKinley to the Wealsohn administration.

Note of HOpe and progress.

In 1910, the American Congress was unanimous for the moral principle (so long as no questions were asked about the privileges of the usury central). Nic complains that the moral ideal has disappeared in all that has to do with international relations.

Which shows the state of DEEP ignorance in the WORLD; as distinct from Nicholas Butler's circle or pot.

And lookin' at dates, he must have been blurrin' this blurb the same week that a Chinaman, not of Wang Ching Wei's party, but of Chiang Kai-shek's party, and FAITHFUL to Chiang, saying what Hitler's justice in scuttling international affairs was such that the Chinese of the ANTI-JAP, anti-Wang party might accept Hitler's arbitrage.

Mr. Butler then seems to fall into incoherence. He talks of a PLEDGE as something to be kept; what price, England, Churchill, and Roosevelt? He objects to having the savings of generations swept away; he asks what has become of the influence of and guidance of the great religions; Christian, Mosel, HEBREW, and Buddhist, and begorrah, of Plato, Aristotle, St. Augustine, St. Thomas Aquinas, leaving out St. Ambrose and St. Antonio da Firenze, and graciously waivin' a hand to the captains of the mind, Spanish, Italian, French, English, German. And of course Abraham Lincoln, not quoting old Abe on the currency issue. And then barbarous brutality, without mention of Esthonia, Finland, or places occupied by the— —Bustin of churches and museums. Wot price Louvain and Cyrenaica? And all this "However dark the skies," etc. ends up with a historic parallel; the WORLD waitin' for a new Vaterloo; because Napolean BonypartY went into Russia, and if Hitler ain't licked in Europe, it will come in Asia or Africa. Well that is a bad slip, because Knox and Stimson, etc. are retching for to rape Africa. But at any rate you git a picture of Nicholas, and METONOMY or takin' a part for the HOLE. A figger of Rhetorik sez Sam Johnson, whereby one word is put for another.

Now if Butler, the old goof, wants me to give him a clean bill of health, he can use the enormous power conferred on him by his position, to get Columbia University to issue a series of volumes containing the GIST of the beliefs and knowledge of John Adams, Jefferson, Jackson, Van Buren, and Lincoln. NOT leaving out every phrase and paragraph which I, and men like me, consider vital to the understanding of American history.

#4 (November 6, 1941) U.S.(56)
THIS WAR ON YOUTH—ON A GENERATION

A consignment of the unpopular American magazines has reached me. I don't mean doctrinal magazines, but magazines in which a serious article occasionally appears. Thus I have learned that Professor I.A. Richards, one of England's few respectable high brows in America, is lecturing; yes, naturally, lecturing.

And apparently the normal effort to keep things going, goes on. Wallace Stevens, J.G. Fletcher, ole Doc Williams, and kumrad kumminkz knowing a bit more about writing than the younger men who haven't quite made up their minds whether they want to do a real job of work, and LEARN how.

And a man with a Scotch front name married a gal who would appear from the nomenclature to be Scotch, Welsh, and British. And Ted Spencer has got his dancing man into print where it ought to be, and the objections to it are as silly as one would expect them to be and mebbe the young are comin' on, as Mr. Calder Joseph; and Langston Hughes has a book in press; probably out by now, which is allus a good thing and Dr. Gogarty or goGARTY, better known to the outer world as Buck Mulligan, has got to New Jersey, and keeps writin' poems, and is accused of being engaged on a novel. [He] has written a rather fine ode for the revival of the Tailltean Games, Irish Olympics. I don't quite know why it is only published now, as the Tailtean Olympics were restored nearly 20 years ago.

Well, that's a human touch, and a relief from the noise of the American papers. We need more communication between the five continents.

And some of the younger professors appear not to have been WHOLLY hoodwinked by propaganda.

Got tired of Georgian poets and so forth.

And that brings me to the question of AGE. Can you or can you not see that this war is a war against YOUTH? That there is in England a whole generation or two generations ready to vomit at the mention of Churchill, Beaverbrook, Garvin, and Baldwin and these senilities want vengence for the lack of respect.

Back in the other war W.B. Yeats said of the old politicians: War, of course they want war, they want all the young gals for themselves.

And in one way or another—lust for power, lust, jealously of the next generation—pretended anxiety for the world as it will be in the time of their grandchildren. Hurry, for fear they won't be able to kill off the present younger generation before the IDEAS of my generation go into effect. It is NOT *necessary* to have the earth ruled by senile bleeders and swindlers. The youth of Europe has discovered that cardinal fact.

Hence the senile outcry Europa-Delenda. Europe, according to the Financial News of London, must be wiped OUT, or certain monopolies will disappear. Men will be able to eat the grain of their own fields, UNLESS Europe is blown to flinders.

HAVE you read the DETAILS of British blackmail on Chile, on the men in Chile who want to trade with the outer world? Details of Roosenstein's "freedom of the seas," NAVICERT, that was what they tried on Italy and Italy came in on the German side.

If Chile don't, that merely means that every man in Chile who is black mailed into signing those papers will store up a silent hate against every thing English, and against any nation that participates in such a policy.

STARVE'em out. Will YOU separate the starvers from the producers, the growers, the makers?

Look at Hank Wallace, good guy, nice presence, led down one garden path after another. Perfect Hampton Court maze, Lord Halifax. First you are asked to reduce production, plow under, then after a few years you are threatened with rationing.

RATIONING!

In the United States of America, the land of abundance, the land the Loeb chart showed beyond any possible shadow of doubt whatsoever to *be* the land of abundance. Every family of four COULD have had then a standard of living equal to what then cost 4000 dollar a year. Needed monetary reform, of course, had to have honest national money to get it.

The United States of America needed INTERNAL reform, not a war in Africa or in Asia. Not a war for the mine owners AGAINST the farmers of Rhodesia, not a war for the opium of Shanghai and Singapore. From IN TERNAL reform could have come collaboration with the other four continents. AND freedom of the seas, the KIND that will permit Chile and the Argentine to trade with France, Spain, and Sweden, and Switzerland and will let ole Hoover tote food into Belgium.

Will you look at the AGE of the chief war pimps? Roosevelt now says he saw war coming in 1937. In 1937 there was NO necessity of War. Roosevelt did all he could to make it inevitable. There is no record of any single act of Roosevelt aimed sincerely at staving off war. Ignorance of Europe, government in charge of hicks, all the outer world thinks Roosevelt took orders from the worst gang in Europe.

Don't say I affirm that he did, what I affirm is that he never showed the faintest inclination to learn the facts and come out for a JUST solution. That is a fairly conservative statement. He has NEVER been neutral. But get down to this one point of AGE How old are these blokes who are trying to throw America into the conflict? What is their business? What is their civic record? What is, or ever has been, their desire to let YOU get the facts?

Have any of 'em ever come out for the JUST PRICE? Which is basic in all economics.

Even the old laissez-faire or Whig economics believed at the start that free competition led to the just price.

The wheeze against it was worked partly by faking the FREEDOM of that competition.

If you start a ten years war? Yes, IF you start a ten years war. None of these old swine will be there at the end of it. It won't be their world, it may be your ruin.

As to RUIN. What about Petrograd? No military purpose in its destruction.

Laval saved Paris. Churchill would have had 'em lay Paris flat, to gain three days time that would have had NO effect whatsoever on the result of the German campaign in France. What causes that? Criminality?

Imbecility? Or what Napoleon would have called lack of imagination, meaning incapacity to form a picture in the mind's eye of what the TOTAL destruction of Paris would mean.

Those of you who want to see Paris again will owe it to Pierre Laval whom the British tried to have murdered.

Those of you who ever do see Paris either for the first time or again will not owe it to Mr. Churchill.

Had that criminal ape got his way, there would have been absolutely NO PARIS there.

Yes, we were once young or younger, and many of us fell for the Russian Red Revolution. Because the Marxist diagnosis was pretty near right. The remedy did NOT work. AND the revolution was betrayed.

Another revolution, a youth, has NOT been betrayed. It is moving, it is moving toward what the decent Reds wanted.

A lot of'em saw no further, wanted no more than the end of certain abuses. The fools got control.

Now YOU are NOT communists. The United States of America and France and every other nation East of the Volga WANTS the homestead. The French peasant wants his own bit of land, without the dead hand over him; without mortgage. The working man does NOT want to govern; he wants good government.

You Americans and the English want government to be good without ANY effort on your part whatsoever. You don't even look at what is done by your governments. Takes an awful heave to get ANY of your attention turned onto the vital facts of a government policy. Most men want certain things IN their own lives, largely in or inside the sphere of their own trade or business. Very few analyze that want or carry their thought thru into the realization of what they want with a practical system of government.

Our system was O.K. for the open and unsettled continent, etc. The frontier, individualism in a state of things where man who couldn't stand on his own feet in the forest and live on the plain and live, possibly on horseback, merely died off.

First intellectual reaction to mere approach of industrialization Thoreau tried to see how little he need bother about other humanity Amateur move.

COHABITATION with other men. POLIS, a city, politics, right way for people to live together in a city. Greek cities very small; Aristotle bothering about a system for 5000 citizens, etc.

Five million, 130 million, bit more of a job; better regulations needed.

Great swindle, money issue, the exchangeable measured titles to goods.

AS our Constitution got well out in front, was for more than a century, in fact for 130 years, far and away the BEST on earth. I had allus thought we could get all the social justice we need, by a few sane reforms of money, such as Adams and Lincoln would have thought honest AND CONSTITUTIONAL The grafters would rather throw you into a ten years war and kill off five or ten million YOUNG men than even let the discussion of monetary reform flower on the front pages of the American papers What causes that? Dirtiness causes it; greed, lust, avarice, petty vindictiveness and senile swank cause it

Europe with systems of government less modern than ours, Germany and Italy with the leftovers of earlier centuries especially Germany saw revolutions Worked out a new system suited to EUROPE It is NOT our

American affair. We could with honor advocate freedom of the seas. For EUROPE as well as for a few Jew controlled shipping firms. We could, with honor advocate NATURAL commerce; that is, a commerce wherein each nation would exchange what it has, what is has in superfluity or abundance, with what other nations can or will spare.

We could stand for that sort of commerce instead of trying to throttle it Why do we NOT?

Why should all men under forty be expected to die or be maimed in sup port of flagrant injustice, monopoly and a dirty attempt to strangle and starve out 30 nations?

For whom?

It is NOT even for the people of England, to whom a ten years war means death by starvation.

#5 (December 7, 1941) U.S. & U.K.(A66)
THOSE PARENTHESES

Europe callin', Pound speakin'. Ezry Pound speakin'. And I think I am perhaps still speakin' a bit more TO England than to the United States of America but you folks may as well hear it. They say an Englishman's head's made of wood, and the American head made of watermelon. Easier to git something INTO the American head, but nigh impossible to make it stick there for ten minutes.

Of course I don't know what GOOD I am doin', I mean what IMME DIATE good. But something you folks on both side of the wretched ocean will have to learn, war or no war, sooner or later.

Now what I had to say about the state of MIND in England in 1919, I said in my Cantos (14 and 15).

Some of your theosophists and fancy thinkers would have called it the spiritual state of England. I am content to say state of mind.

I can't say my remarks were heeded. I thought I had got'em simple enough. Words short and simple enough. In fact some people complained that several of'em contained no more than 4 or 5 letters (some less).

Now I hold NO Catholic has ever been or ever will be puzzled by what I said in those Cantos. I have, however, never asked for sympathy when misunderstood. I go on trying to make my meanin' clear and then clearer. And in the LONG run people who listen to me (very few do, but members of that small and SElect minority) do know more in the long run, than those who listen to Mr. H.G. chubby Wells and the liberal stooges.

What I am gitting at is, a friend said to me the other day that he was glad I had the politics I have got, but that HE didn't understand how I, as a North American, United Stateser could have it.

Well that looks simple to me. Things OFTEN DO look simple to me. On the CONfucian system that if you start right, and then go on, start at the root and move upward, the pattern often is simple, whereas if you start constructin' from the twig downward, you get into a muddle.

My politics seem to me SIMPLE. My idea of a state OR an empire is more like a hedge hog or porcupine, chunky and well defended. I don't cotton to the idea of my country being an octopus WEAK in the tentacles and sufferin' from stomach ulcers and chronic gastritis.

I wish Brother Hoover had spilled his facts about the stinking and rotten Treaty of Versailles while he was still in the White House. But I am glad he has done so now. Tho' he could also confess his OWN errors and aid even now to acceleratin' the United States of America welfare.

Anyhow, I have, in principle, NO objection to the U.S. absorbin' Canada and the whole NORTH American continent.

The rot of the British Empire is from inside, and if the whole of that syphilitic organization, headed by Montagu Skinner Norman, makes war on Canada, or Alberta, I see no reason for Canada not making war on the Jews in London. Whether they are born Jews, or have taken to Jewry by predilection.

What I am ready to fight AGAINST is havin' ex-European Jews making another peace worse than Versailles, with a new two dozen Danzigs. Namely the United States bein' left with war baby bases in Aberdeen, Singapore, Dakar, South Africa, and the Indian Ocean! All draggin' the tail of their coat, and making dead mathematically sure of another war for Dupont, Vickers, Mond, Melchett, Beit, Ellermann in ten or fifteen years after the present one (present war). And to that end Roosevelt, Morgenthau, Lehman are working, day and night, not to mention the Warburgs. And precisely on the subject of Warburgs, I wish Herb Hoover would say MORE about the stink of Versailles.

God knows I have loathed Woodie Wilson, and I don't want to see more evil done to humanity than was done by Woodrow codface. And the sooner all America and ALL England wake up to what the Warburgs and Roosevelt are up to, the better for the next generation and this one.

And as an American I do NOT want to see my country annihilatin' the population of Iceland, as the British annihilated the Maoris. And as for the Australians, they deserve a Nippo-Chinese invasion.

Criminals were their granddads, and their contribution to civilization is not such as to merit even a Jewish medal. Why the heck the Chinese and Japs don't combine and drive that dirt out of Australia, and set up a bit of civilization in those parts, is for me part of the mystery of the orient.

And in any case I do NOT want my compatriots from the ages of 20 to 40 to go git slaughtered to keep up the Sassoon and other British Jew rackets in Singapore and in Shanghai. That is not my idea of American patriotism. We are gittin' on for the centenary of the opium war, that never did any good to the lads of Lancashire or of Sussex, and that brought no prosperity in Dorset or Gloucester.

Hardy's England, aye, aye sir, where is it? Did Rothschild save it? He did not. Did the Goldsmid save it? He did not. Does Churchill endeavor to save it? He does NOT. I repeat the rot and stink of England, and the danger to her empire is inside, and has been: from the time of Cobbett.

And NO number of Rabbis and bank touts in Wall Street and in Washington can do one damn thing for England, save let her alone. And a damn pity they didn't start doin' sooner. That is a pity for England.

And a peace with American war bases all over the whole of the planet would be no more a real peace than Versailles was. And as to all visible signs Roosevelt is MORE in the Jew's hands than Wilson was in 1919. I am against havin' him mixin' into ANY post-war matters whatever. This objectin' being academic.

An' I think it would be well for ALL men, from China to Capetown to SEE as soon as possible what Franklin is up to. Let him keep his paws on the North American continent. Even if it means DIMinished gun sales for all his pals, and for all gold-bugs.

Eight years ago he was sayin' "nothin to fear but fear." Well what has become of THAT Roosevelt?

What has he done for three years but try to work up a hysteria on that basis? He got his face into a paper called Life, eight or ten photographs. Jim Farley would have been less nuisance in the White House than snob Delano, who objected to Farley NOT on moral or ethical grounds, but PURELY as snobism; didn't want a mere henchman to succeed him.

And as to American labor. When will American labor start lookin' into the currency question?

"Question," of course there ought not to be any INTERROGATIVE element in it. Even a hod carrier OUGHT to be able to learn why interest payin' debt is NOT so good a basis for money as is productive labor.

But will they? Will the American hod carrier and skilled engineer (includin' Mr. Hoover) ever git round to the currency issue? (I call it issue, not question.) And will the American big employer or financier, except Baruch, ever start studyin' the solution of HIS problem, which is a corporate solution, in the sense of that word now current in Europe?

A CORPORATE problem, or issue, which does NOT mean starving the workman, or breakin' him up by scab mobs.

Lord knows I don't SEE how America can have fascism without years of previous trainin'. Looks to me, even now as if the currency problem was the place to start savin' America. As I have been sayin' for some time back, call it ten years or call it twenty. At this moment it looks like as if John

Lewis would take just as long to git round about feedin' my books to his troops, as it would take the Harvard faculty to git Mr. William G. Morse's permission to use'em in Harvard (Economics Department).

Both sides will have to come to it.

#6 (January 29, 1942) U.S.(A1)
ON RESUMING

On Arbour Day, Pearl Arbour Day, at 12 o'clock noon I retired from the capital of the old Roman Empire to Rapallo to seek wisdom from the ancients.

I wanted to figure things out. I had a perfectly good alibi, if I wanted to play things safe. I was and am officially occupied with a new translation of the Ta S'eu of Confucius. I have in Rapallo the text of Confucius, and of Mencius, the text of the world's finest anthology, namely that which Confucius compiled from earlier authors, and I have in reach the text of a book which bears on its front page the title Li Ki (which the head of the Chinese Department in our Congressional Library tells me proper minded Chi Sinologues now think is pronounced Lee Gee). And I have six volumes of the late Dr. Morrison's Dictionary, not the most up to date dictionary of Chinese Ideograms, but nevertheless good enough.

That is, I have WORK thaaar for some years, if I don't die before I git to the middle.

The Odes are to me very difficult. They are of extreme beauty. Thousands of poets have looked at those odes and despaired. There are points at which some simple ideogram (that is, Chinese picture word) is so used as to be eternal, insofar as our human sense of eternity can reach. There is one of the sunrise that I despair of ever getting translated.

There was to face this, the SITUATION. That is to say the United States had been for months ILLEGALLY at war, through what I considered to be the criminal acts of a President whose mental condition was NOT, as far as I could see, all that could or should be desired of a man in so responsible a position or office.

He had, so far as evidence available to me showed, broken his promises to the electorate; he had to my mind violated his oath of office. He had to my mind violated the oath of allegiance to the United States Constitution which even the ordinary American citizen is expected to take every time he gets a new passport.

It was obviously a mere question of hours, between that day and hour, and the time when the United States of America would be legally at war with the Axis.

I spent a month tryin' to figure things out, well did I, perhaps I concluded sooner. At any rate I had a month clear to make up my mind about some things. I had Confucius and Mencius, both of whom had been up against similar problems. Both of whom had seen empires fallin'. Both of whom had seen deeper into the causes of human confusion than most men even think of lookin'.

Then there was my old dad in bed with a broken hip; Lord knows who is going to mend it or whether it will mend. So—I read him a few pages of Aristotle in the Loeb Classical Library, English version, to take his mind off it. Also to keep my own work in progress.

Because for some time I have had in mind the need of comparing the terminology of Chinese and Greek philosphy, and also comparing that with the terminology of mediaevil Catholic theology.

No. For a man cut off from all his NORMAL contacts with the non-European world, I can't say I was destitute—mentally—there was plenty lyin' there for me to be busy about, if I had wanted to "contract OUT." If I had wanted to go into a funk hole, I had a nice sizeable funk hole. About as good as an endowed professorship in one of our otiose or veiled, shall we say veiled universities, or even Oxford or Cambridge. Plenty of muckers down there settin' pretty, and drawin' 5000 dollars or ten thousand a year for not tellin'. I reckon it is Mencius who thought that "the true sage seeks not repose."

It is not a claustral motto. I began figurin' out that a COMPLETE severance of communication between the calm and sentient men is not to be desired.

I have before now pointed out that England was CUT off from the current of European thought during and BY the Napoleonic Wars, and that she never got ketched up again, not during all the damned nasty and 19th century. Always laggin' behind. Perhaps she allus WAS laggin' behind. I have pointed out the difference of up-to-dateness between Voltaire and Mr. Samuel Johnson.

At any rate it is NO GOOD.

The United States has been MISinformed. The United States has been led down the garden path, and may be down under the daisies. All thru shuttin' out news.

There is no end to the amount of shuttin' out news that the sons of Blood who started this war, and wanted this war, and monkeyed round to git a war started and monkeyed round to keep the war goin', and spreadin'. There is NO end to the shuttin' out and perversions of news that these blighters ain't up to, and that they haven't, and aren't still trying to com pass. Whatever happens it is NOT going to do the United States any good to be as cut off from all news, and all NEWS of CONTEMPORARY thought like the damn fools and utterly decadent Britons have got themselves cut off from.

As you can HEAR from the British Blurb Corporation any Monday and Tuesday evening, and any Wednesday, Thursday, Friday, Saturday and Sunday evening that you choose to listen in to their phenomenal hogwash.

That's where they've got to. And for their bein' there neither I nor any man I shake hands with, is to blame in any way whatsoever. Every English friend I got in the world, has done his damnest to keep England from makin' such a thunderin' and abysmal ass of herself.

As for my American friends, Senator Borah is dead, not that I knew him much save by letter; but I can still feel his hand on my shoulder as just before he was getting into an elevator in the Senate building, and I can still hear him sayin':

"Well, I'm sure I don't know what a man like you would find to DO here."

That was a few days sooner, mebbe the first time I met him. Neither he, nor William J. Bryan lived to hear Senator Wallace tellin' the world there would be no peace till the nations of the world knocked under and bowed down to the GOLD standard. Bowed down like drunken and abject fools and said, let gold rule humanity, let all human exchange of goods be bottle necked and ask permission from a few bloodthirsty kikes who OWN gold. Bow down and say monopoly is God over all men; and this from a man, said to be, or to HAVE BEEN, interested in farmers, and farmer's welfare. This after all the lies from the London gold ring, this after 20 years of evasion, this in fact after 20 years' attempt to conceal from the English people that they were being asked to go out and DIE for gold, for the monopoly of the owners and brokers; owners of gold mines, brokers, and owners of gold.

Back in December I had never expected such a confession from anyone as high in office.

Yaaas, I knew that was what the war was about: gold, usury and monopoly. I had said as much when I was last in America. I had then said: IF a war is pushed onto us. So now we have got pushed out of Guam, and Wake, and I suppose out of the Philippines, and a 30 years war is in process? Is it? Is a 30 years war what the American citizen thinks will do most good to the United States of America?

Or has someone been MiSinformed? and IF so, who misinformed him? Accordin' to the reports of the American press now available to the aver age European, someone in charge of American destiny miscalculated somethin' or other.

An "inquiry" is in progress, at least as they print here. It bein' my private belief that I could have avoided a war with Japan, if anybody had had the unlikely idea of sending me out there, with any sort of official powers.

The Japanese have a past. Of course when I talk to'em now, they are apt to remind me that they have ALSO a presertt.

They have not mentioned the future in our conversations.

The last American journalist I saw, and that was the night before Arbour Day, told me the Japs would never etc., etc.

A nation evolves by process of history. Japan to me consists in part of what I learned from a sort of half trunk full of the late Ernest Fenollosa's papers. Anybody who has read the plays entitled Kumasaka and Kagekiyo, would have AVOIDED the sort of bilge printed in Time and the American press, and the sort of fetid imbecility I heard a few nights ago from the British Broadcasting Company.

There are certain depths of ignorance that can be fatal to a man or a nation. When these are conjoined with malice and baseness of spirit, it seems almost useless to mention them.

A BBC commentator somewhere about January 8 was telling his presumably music hall audience that the Japs were jackals, and that they had just recently, I think he said, within living men's lifetime, emerged from barbarism. I don't know what patriotic end you think, or he thinks, or the British authorities think (if that is the verb), is served by such fetid ignorance.

A glance at Japanese sword guards, a glance at Jimmy Whistler's remarks about Hokusai, or, as I indicated a minute ago, a familiarity with the Awoi no Uye, Kumasaka, Nishikigi, or Funa-Benkei. These are Japanese classical plays, and would convince any man with more sense than a pea hen, of the degree of Japanese civilization; let alone what they conserved when China was, as Fenollosa tells us, incapable of preserving her own cultural heritage.

China lettin' Confucius go OUT of the schools, for example.

And you needn't sniff, the Bostonians kulturbund needn't sniff and say the British Broadcasting Company, the Bloody Boobs Corporation, is over in vulgar London, such things couldn't happen in Boston.

Almost equal imbecility was attained by Time weekly magazine in November of 1941.

Someone had apparently blundered, as Lord Tennyson wrote of the charge at Balaclava. And blundered, we think, considerably worse. Waaal now who blundered. A commission has been appointed—possibly to white wash who blundered. I don't know that it is in the citizen's duty to white wash who blundered.

I think the United States and even her British Allies might do well to keep more in touch with continental opinion.

I don't think anybody is going to whitewash who blundered into the alliance with Russia.

I think there are some crimes that nothing will whitewash.

I don't think an alliance with Stalin's Russia is lucky. I don't think the crime of even going thru the motions of invitin' Russia into slaughter and kill all eastern Europe is a NECESSARY part of the program; program of defense, program of offense. I don't think this horror was NECESSARY.

I don't think it is the function, even of the Commander-in-Chief of the United States American Army, to dictate the citizens' politics; NOT to the point of invitin' Bolshevik Russia to kill off the whole east half of Europe!

I don't think it is a lucky move. EVEN if Eden hopes to doublecross Russia, which nothing indicates that he does hope.

The day Hitler went into Russia, England had her chance to pull out. She had her chance to say, let bygones be bygones. If you can stop the Moscovite horror, we will let bygones be bygones. We will try to see at least HALF of your argument.

Instead of which Hank Wallace comes out—no peace till the world accepts the gold standard.

Quem Deus vult perdere.

Does look like there was a weakness of mind in some quarters. Whom God would destroy, he first sends to the bug house.

#7 (February 3, 1942) U.S.(A2)
30 YEARS OR A HUNDRED

The prospect of a 30 years war is not one to arouse mirth and hilarity even in a flighty, chicken headed and irresponsible people such as the United States of Americans.

You are in it, and Lord knows, who is a goin' to git you out. The late Lord Rothermere, whose culture was nothin', as you might say, to write home about, finally decided that the English public was wholly unteachable. I don't know whether you can learn ANYTHING from history, I don't know whether you are even yet in the state of mind where you want to learn any thing from history or from any other source whatsoever.

A way to get yourselves OUT, might be discoverable, it might be more discoverable if you first had the faint inkling of a curiosity as to how you got yourselves IN.

Now whether you can learn anything from the disasters of England, I do not know. But I would about lay it down as an axiom that empires do not get knocked apart from outside until they are plum gone to rot in the middle.

The laws of right government have been known since the days of Yao and Shun, ole Chinese emperors, and from the time of Shun to King Wen was a 1000 years, and from Wen to Confucius 500.

And they say when the policies of Shun and of Wan were set together (compared), they were as the two halves of a seal, or it might be of a tally stick.

And for nigh onto 4000 years I think no one has dodged the facts of these policies. And from the time of Confucius every dynasty in China that has lasted 300 years has been founded on the law of Confucius, a man or a group, seem' the horse sense of government, as learned by Confucius, I mean he learned it looking at history, talking of Shun and Wan and after him whenever a great man learned it he started or upheld some sort of imperial order.

And for that reason I am distinctly unimpressed by the bombastic lies of Mr. Winston Churchill or the dirt of Mr. Anthony Eden.

And if the United States was going to have a foreign alliance, I would have preferred it to be with some other kind of a government than Eden and Churchill. There are worse things than a biff on the jaw.

Get slugged on the jaw, you can mebbe get up and fight, but a long term of syphilis weakens the constitution.

No, the United States has, politically and economically speaking, had economic political syphilis for the past 80 years. Ever since 1863. And England has had economic syphilis for 240 years, so now she is a moultin' and droppin', Hong Kong, Singapore, Canada, and Australia. Seems like it is tertiary.

Well, as Lord Rothermere said: they are unteachable. I don't know how much more they reckon to drop before they get ready for physic. I have said on this radio before now that along about 1695 or 94 the Bank of England was put together, and in 1750 they shut down on the Pennsylvania colony money, and the system of lending paper out to the farmers. And in 1776 the natural consequences of that dirty London policy of starvin' and cheatin' became, as they say, more apparent. And a year or two later Johnnie Adams said to the British commander: They were havin' a parley, sez John Adams. "I don't care what capacity I am received in, receive me in any capacity you like except that of a British subject." So the first large scale effect of the London cheatin', and money monopoly was the loss of the American colonies. The Chinese have a method of countin' cycles of 80 years. I don't know that there is much in it, but it seems to work sometimes. Eighty years, from the bank to the American Revolution. About 80 years from startin the American government to the great betrayal of 1863. Think it over And from 63 to the present OUR rise as a state thru three or four major, but POSITIVE convulsions, like Jefferson's revolt against Hamilton's dirtiness, the Jackson-Van Buren war for the liberation of the American Treasury. Lincoln's sayin', "gave to this people the greatest blessin' they ever had, their own paper to pay their own debt." And then the assassination of Lincoln.

And then another 80 years: to the END, and absolute collapse of the American system of government.

Can we revive it?

Has the country got the guts for the climb? Is there, as I am sayin' this, the faintest stirring of a desire INside the United States for any healthy new structure? Or are we the gadarine swine taken with collective hysteria? Are there ten men in America ready calmly to go back over the events of the past few years, in America and in England? Is there the faintest stirring of American curiosity as to how a sane government could be built up? Or at any rate any nucleus or group ready to go back and learn how we were built up from the beginning?

Adams, Jefferson, and Van Buren to read and digest. You can't talk it over with me; because none of you can get to a radio. You can't print stuff like this in your papers, cause the newspapers are NOT there to inform the people. You have got to talk to each other, you have got to write letters one to another.

The texts and the guides you have got, that is, in a way you have got'em, sprawled out, in big sets of unhandy volumes. Our publishers don't print handy compendiums. Your professors don't analyze, that is, not very much. I don't know what has become of Claude Bowers. He did a bit of digging about. You have a half-dozen historians but not all of'em, by any means, able to take out the facts and show how they hitch together.

I dunno how you think you are going to assist in a war by a money system which, as Jefferson already saw, "charges the public TWO dollars for every dollar spent by the government," just automatically and independent of any particular grafting and swindling.

Thirty years war, 30 years paradise for Army contractors, may not be what you voted for. In fact, Mr. Franklin D. Roosevelt on that score is manifestly what they called him here the other day: the boy that fell down on his assignment. And when you think, if you do think, of the BILLIONS that have been lifted by the Morgenthau treasury policy during the past nine years of peace time. God knows.

God knows what it will be during warfare, or by the end, shall we say, thirty years? Well, you are now IN, and nobody in Europe can now get you out. Inspired (shall we say) by the principle of self-determination of peoples, oppressed peoples? Illustratin' it by the determination to keep Mr. Aguinaldo out of his native Manila you have chucked away our national cultural heritage.

Relatively speakin' that heritage was the determination of our forebears to set up and maintain in the North American continent a government better than any other.

The determination to govern ourselves INternally, better than any other nation on earth. The idea of Washington, Jefferson, Monroe, to keep out of foreign shindies.

Well, you have chucked that idea, or ideal onto the dung heap. And you have insulted the most highly tempered people on earth. With unspeakable vulgarity you have insulted the most finely tempered people on earth, threatenin''em with starvation, threatenin''em with encirclement and tellin''em they were too low down to fight.

You are at war for the duration of the Tenno's pleasure. Nothin' in the Western World; nothin' in the whole of our Occident can help you to dodge that. Nothin' can help you dodge it.

I could go along on this line for some time, but mebbe I said enough for one evenin'.

#8 (February 10, 1942) U.S.(A69)
THE STAGE IN AMERICA

Well perhaps I won't stick to my title very closely, but to start off with, when I was in New York a while back I saw Katharine Cornell in a play, that was a bit soft, and the little sermon she gave from the stage, not quite part of the piece sounded THEN a bit sentimental. I have no doubt that vague language is used on both sides of the present discussion. We can't all be stylists.

I am chasm' the METHOD of war scares, the method used for gettin' people worked into hysteria.

And part of it, is attackin' one wrong, appealin' to the soft heart and then by false dilemma offering the hearer a bit of sheer buncombe, i.e., offering him an alternative and doing a hat trick to make him think it is the ONLY alternative; false dilemma, you call that in a logic class.

Thus with the stink of Russia NO ONE with any thought in Europe or North or South America believes in the abolition of ownership of every thing.

East Europe and North America believe in the homestead, from A to Z, and from bedrock to roof tree the American people believe in the homestead.

The members of the floating population, to which the top crust has been REDUCED, are beliefless, they got no belief, they want this, that or tother, tinsel and limelight. The young, I ain't the first to notice it, the young WANT this, that, or tother, often they want something different over two weeks. The stronger ones CIT it. After they git to be fifty, a few of'em try to see what all the fuss was about.

Lord knows j'ai roulÂ©e ma bosse. I wanted metropolitan life, etc. But you can't run a whole state or nation on the predilections of a few writers and artists. WHEN they ripen, as take the case of William Shakespeare, they git to hear of the homestead.

The WHOLE and total best of civilization, Chinese or Western, is based on the homestead. It is not based on nomadic tribes, and destructions.

Being DISGUSTED as 98% of all decent men were with the results of usuriocracy, money lenders' decivilization, money lenders' RUIN of the good life in the Occident and everywhere else they could get their dirty hooks onto, a lot of us fell for ANY alternative, jumpin' the part we didn't look at very closely, never stoppin' to ask: DO we believe Marx and Lenin? Hence PART of the red and pink beano. When their hair begins to lose its adolescent hue, a few men begin to think of a SYSTEM, a working system, a base and BASIS for human living together. And the answer comes out the same, a house GOOD enough for the ordinary folk to go on livin' in from one generation to the fourth and fifth generation. And you get relief classically in the Wanderjahre. Run around and look at the world [the kikes and Frank Roosevelt and Hill Billy Hull and Welles are doin' their worst to clamp down on. DON'T want any witnesses, any free and independent witnesses, to tell what IS goin' on elsewhere. In the ole days it was the fatheads with privilege; or mediocre writers and architects and artists that did not WANT criticism. [FCC transcript: Every decent idea was to go around, see the best, and then come home and do better. That is the way the good life is built. The so-called stifling air of the provinces et cetera was due to fear, due to shunning comparisons. While, if every American would get up tomorrow morning and ask himself what he really wants, there would be an end to the Roosevelt hysteria. That is to say, it would not spread like a pest throughout the American nation.] If the citizen, after having asked himself that, would then go on to the ole Rights of Man, and say how much of it can I git without doing dirt to my neighbor, the good life would approach very rapidly, more rapidly than it usually does; if we can trust to the human record.

Yes, I know what the decent English are resistin' and what they were even ready to fight to resist. And if they had any clear headedness, that would be dandy. They want their cultural heritage, they think the English once had nice manners.

Well I was talkin' to a friend of mine, and she was born with a name sacr'd to every man who cares for poetry written in English, Rossetti. And she said, "The worst manners come from people trying to be nasty to people whom they consider inferior. Matter of class. And the Nazis have wiped out that feeling, and wiped out bad manners in Germany."

The New Europe goes ON NOW doing what American democracy, in the clean sense of that word, started doin' when it made a DECLARATION of Independence, but failed to define all the words used, or compromised on the wording, struck out Jefferson's original sentences about abolition of slavery, and for the sake of a vote, omitted to specify that "equal" means equal in the courts of law, no man having privilege over any other, to be let off certain penalties cause he was the son of his papa, or had been to a university.

I told my rare and precious readers ten years ago that there was an ANTI snob movement in Italy. Of course no one paid any attention to that sentence, so I repeat it.

Some things you are learning 30 years late, some things 20 and ten years. And in others you swallow goof like Mr. Donovan, Colonel Donovan, or you merely get hooked with press lies contradicted two days or ten days later. I have a weakness for newspaper writers, ever since a fellow named Monsier turned up in London in 1915 or some such, and later when there weren't any new book writers, I took to my newspaper colleague, who of course allus looked down on the outsider, but a few of'em were kindly and tolerant, regardin' me as an amateur, who didn't menace their pay cheque. And I finally took to noticin' the waves of credulity that pass over'em. They know that most of what they can print is all horse. But they believe certain unprinted rumors. Sure, we were set to invade Dakar. Well, I don't deny it. Sometimes their tips are straight. But we do almightily need a better system of communication. We need a greater honesty?

Naturally, and I don't mean merely about stealing and graft. I mean inside the individual head. A greater resistance to these waves of hoakum.

Do you want the destruction of the people of Iceland? Is Finland a menace to anyone save a few kike owners of nickel mines? Do the Beits and Sassoons and their delegates represent the best English tradition?

If the United States is to steal and embezzle, wouldn't it be wiser to stick to French, English, and Dutch dependencies in the American hemisphere? And wouldn't it be honester to get same by purchase, even if it meant fewer IMMEDIATE profits to the tinned meat and armament rackets?

#9 (February 12, 1942) U.S.(A71) CANTO 46

I am readin' you now another Canto for diverse reasons. It contains things or at least hints at things that you will have to know sooner or later. Berle or no Berle, war or no war.

And as I stated last time, I am feedin' you the footnotes first in case there is any possible word that might not be easily comprehended. The Decennio, and decennio exposition was the exhibition in Rome at the end of the first ten years of the Fascist regime. Mussolini's fascist regime. They set up the office of the old Popolo d'Italia, very like what had been the New Age Office in London. Except that Orage's office contained a couple of drawings by Max Beerbohm which have never been published.

John Marmaduke is a pseudonym, the rest of the names in the Canto are real. The MacMillan Commission sat after the other war to look into the sins of the British Financial system.

Antoninus Pius, a Roman emperor; lex Rhodi the law of Rhodes, well I say that in the Canto. The Latin phrase: Aurum est commune sepulchrum, gold the common sepulchre. Parallels: Troy the common grave, I think it is a part of a line by Propertius. But it don't matter who it is quoted from. And the Greek: helandros, kai heleptolis kai helarxe [usary destroyer of] men and cities and governments. HELARXE more or less twisted from a line of Aeschylus; about Helen of Troy destroyer of men, and cities. Geryon, Geryone; allegorical beast in Dante's hell, symbol of fraud and all dirtiness. *Hic Geryon est*, is a Latin tag meaning, with the other phrase, *Hic hyperu sura*: this is extra strong usury. Super usury. All right, now I am going on with Canto 46.

XLVI

And if you will say that this tale teaches ...
a lesson, or that the Reverend Eliot
has found a more natural language ... you who think
you will
get through hell in a hurry ...
That day there was cloud over Zoagli
And for three days snow cloud over the sea
Banked like a line of mountains.
Snow fell. Or rain fell stolid, a wall of lines

So that you could see where the air stopped open
and where the rain fell beside it
Or the snow fell beside it. Seventeen
Years on this case, nineteen years, ninety years
on this case
An' the fuzzy bloke sez (legs no pants ever wd. fit)'IF
that is so, any government worth a damn can
pay dividends?'
The major chewed it a bit and sez:'Y—es, eh ...
You mean instead of collectin' taxes?''
Instead of collecting taxes.' That office?
Didja see the Decennio?
?
Decennio exposition, reconstructed office of Il Popolo, Waal, ours waz
like that, minus the Mills bomb an' the teapot, heavy lipped chap at the desk,
One half green eye and one brown one, nineteen
Years on this case, CRIME
Ov two CENturies, 5 millions bein' killed off
to 1919, and before that
Debts of the South to New York, that is to the
banks of the city, two hundred million,
war, I don't think (or have it your own way ...)
about slavery?
Five million being killed off... couple of Max's drawings, one of Balfour
and a camel, an'
one w'ich fer oBviOus reasons haz
never been published, ole Johnny Bull with a'ankerchief.
It has never been published..
'He ain't got an opinion.'
Sez Orage about G.B.S. sez Orage about Mr. Xtertn.
Sez Orage about Mr. Wells,'he wont HAVE an opinion
trouble iz that you mean it, you never will be a journalist.
19 years on this case, suburban garden,
'Greeks!' sez John Marmaduke'a couple of art tricks!
What else? never could set up a NATION!'
Wouldn't convert me, dwn't HAVE me converted,
'Said "I know I didn't *ask* you, your father sent you here
"to be trained. I know what I'd feel.
"send my son to England and have him come back a christian!
"what wd. I feel?"'Suburban garden
Said Abdul Baha: "I said'let us speak of religion.'
"Camel driver said: I must milk my camel.
"So when he had milked his camel I said'let us speak of religion.'

And the camel driver said: It is time to drink milk.
Will you have some?' For politeness I tried to join him.
Have you ever tasted milk from a camel?
I was unable to drink camel's milk. I have *never* been able.
So he drank all of the milk, and I said: let us speak of religion.
'I have drunk my milk. I must dance.' said the driver.
We did not speak of religion." Thus Abdul Baha
Third vice-gerent of the First Abdul or Whatever Baha, the Sage, the Uniter, the founder of a religion,
in a garden at Uberton, Gubberton, or mebbe it was some other damned suburb, but at any rate a suburban suburb amid a flutter of teacups, said Mr Marmaduke:
"Never will understand us. They lie. I mean personally
"They are mendacious, but if the tribe gets together
"the tribal word will be kept, hence perpetual misunderstanding.
"Englishman goes there, lives honest, word is reliable,
"ten years, they believe him, then he signs terms for his government.
"and naturally, the treaty is broken, Mohammedans,
"Nomads, will never understand how we do this."
17 years on this case, and we not the first lot!
Said Paterson:
Hath benefit of interest on all
the moneys which it, the bank, creates out of nothing
Semi-private inducement Said
Mr Roth-schild, hell knows which Roth-schild
1861,'64 or there sometime, "very few people
"will understand this. Those who do will be occupied
"getting profits. The general public will probably not
"see it's against their interest."
Seventeen years on the case; here
Gents, is/are the confession.
"Can we take this into court?
'Will any jury convict on this evidence?
1694 anno domini, on through the ages of usury
On, right on, into hair-cloth, right on into rotten building, Right on into London houses, ground rents, foetid brick work, Will any jury convict'um? The Foundation of Regius Professors Was made to spread lies and teach Whiggery, will any
JURY convict'um?
The Macmillan Commission about two hundred and forty years
LATE
with great difficulty got back to Paterson's
The bank makes it *ex nihil*
Denied by five thousand professors, will any

Jury convict'um? This case, and with it
the first part, draws to a conclusion,
of the first phase of this opus, Mr Marx, Karl, did not foresee this
conclusion, you have seen a good deal of
the evidence, not knowing it evidence, is monumentum
look about you, look, if you can, at St Peter's
Look at the Manchester slums, look at Brazilian coffee or Chilean
nitrates. This case is the first case
Si requieres monumentum?
This case is not the last case or the whole case, we ask a REVISION, we ask for enlightenment in a case
moving concurrent, but this case is the first case:
Bank creates it ex nihil. Creates it to meet a need,
Hic est hyper-usura. Mr. Jefferson met it:
No man hath natural right to exercise profession
of lender, save him who hath it to lend.
Replevin, estopple, what wangle which wangle, VanBuren met it.
Before that was tea dumped into harbour, before that was a great deal still
in the school books, placed there
NOT as evidence. Placed there to distract idle minds,
Murder, starvation and bloodshed, seventy four red revolutions Ten
empires fell on this grease spot.
'I rule the Earth' said Antoninus 'but LAW rules the sea'
meaning, we take it, lex Rhodi, the Law Maritime
of sea lawyers.
usura and sea insurance
wherefrom no State was erected greater than Athens.
Wanting TAXES to build St Peter's, thought Luther beneath civil notice,
1527. Thereafter art thickened. Thereafter design went to hell, Thereafter
barocco, thereafter stone-cutting desisted.
'Hic nefas' (narrator)'commune sepulchrum.'
19 years on this case/first case. I have set down part of The Evidence.
Part/commune sepulchrum
Aurum est commune sepulchrum. Usura, commune sepulchrum.
helandros kai heleptolis kai helarxe.
Hic Geryon est. Hic hyperusura.
FIVE million youths without jobs
FOUR million adult illiterates
15 million 'vocational misfits', that is with small chance for jobs NINE
million persons annual, injured in preventable industrial accidents
One hundred thousand violent crimes. The Eunited States ov America
3rd year of the reign of F. Roosevelt, signed F. Delano, his uncle.
CASE for the prosecution. That is one case, minor case in the
series/Eunited States of America, a.d. 1935

England a worse case, France under a foetor of regents.
'Mr Cummings wants Farley's job' headline in current paper.

E.P. speaking. That's the end of Canto 46.

#10, FCC Transcript (February 17, 1942) U.S.(A72)
SALE AND MANUFACTURE OF WAR

This challenge is a chance to— —about the sale and manufacture of war. This war is part of a profit. The present phase of that profit began at the end of the 17th Century. By 1750 a corrupt and avaricious government in England, working for British monopolies, was shutting down on the Pennsylvania colony's issue of money, paper money, money issued against land, work and the industrious and sane nature of the Pennsylvania colonists.

I have given between 70 and 100 talks on the radio and if I come back to the microphone 100 or 200 times more, I could start every talk with that statement. Until you see this war as an incident in a series, you cannot understand it or judge it or qualify yourselves as judges of the rights and wrongs of the present act in the story.

Will men of my generation in America stop to consider what is not printed? Will Americans between the age of 50 and 60 look back honestly over their own reading over what they have read during the past 50 years? Note the vague dissatisfaction, the sense of bafflement, especially for the man who reads after working hours.

Now take the current issues of supposedly serious magazines, magazines that are certainly authoritative in a twisted sense, authoritative and influential. I believe one of them nominated Willkie and by now perhaps that fact needs no comment whatever. I've been accused in these talks but, if anyone has seriously answered any of my statements, they have been unable to do so in any form that reaches me.

Well, I ask my compatriots of my own age to note that the very high percentage of articles printed in American magazines contains a joker, that is a silent point, a basically false assumption. I don't mean they all contain the same false assumption. I point k out that there is no public medium in the United States for serious discussion.

Every [one?] of these publications has subjects which its policy forbids it to mention or to mention without falsification. And I ask the men in my generation to consider the effects, the cumulative effect of this state of things which does not date from September, 1941, but has been going on ever since we can remember.

The progressive falsification of America has been going on for 80 years at least and we have lived through half of it. I mean as conscious leaders, we have had 40 years of ill-intentional and of semi-conscious befuddlement to contend with and it is time to come to the cumulative effect of that profit.

Baruch, Berle, Best?—to take three names starred in American publicity, one pronouncement and two headlined articles are before me. All of these men writing and speaking with authority of a sort official positions, dominant in national affairs and with such views that no man under 40 can possibly untangle their cobwebs.

In normal times, qualified readers wouldn't try. They would let it go at that. They would be busy on constructive work. The old are indifferent, the experienced are indifferent and a cautious son of a New York editor, now in his 70th year, I mean the son in his 70th year, remembered his father's——. He shrugged his shoulders, or did when I saw him last autumn, who is he to impede human carnage? The folly of all mankind ain't nothing, but human imbecility gives us an idea of the infinite. And in a way, as he said, do nothing about it.

Well, there is still time to learn something about it, still time to fight against a peace that can be no peace, still time to fight against widespread efforts to prevent the end of the slaughter, which efforts are being made. I mean people are now trying to prevent the war from ending. People have already planned for a peace like the last, a mere parenthesis, a mere slow-up of munition sales, a mere disequilibrium that will keep the world on tenterhooks between the end of this war and the start of the next one.

You cannot sit in Ohio and judge the Balkans. You cannot judge China from Omaha. You could read, and perhaps some American will some day make a vow to read one old paper or magazine once a month, by all means say three or six months old, and once a year read a still older one. That might give you a perspective.

Unless you know at least as much about the past 20 years of Italian history as is contained in old— —volume on "Italian Socio-Economic Policy," you will not be able to observe how much of old programs has been recently endorsed by Barney Baruch. Nor will you be able to see the price of confidence was— —article in October Fortune, A.A. Berle, Assistant Secretary of State.

Well, when I was in Washington, a member of the Cabinet told me that so far as he knew Barney was a patriotic gentleman.

Baruch now came out for a constituted price, a price in accord with— —, a price that would guarantee just recompense to everyone who collaborates in a final product.

I will be ready to consider Baruch's a patriot when he comes out seriously for abolition of the national debt. He is far in— —that lives in the new economics.

Now Berle's article is very nice in the second half. It— —.

#11 (February 19, 1942) U.S.(A77) POWER
The President hath power.

The President has NO LEGAL power to enter into devious and secret agreements with foreign powers. He has no legal power to cook up policies with the late Johnnie Buchan and sign the nation's name on the document.

United States Treaties are valid when ratified by the Senate and not before. The President has no legal power to enter into condominiums with foreign governments, for the misconduct of scandalous islands off the China coast or in proximity to distant oriental, or any other damn harbors.

The President has no more legal right to do these infamies than you have to sign my name on a cheque, or I yours.

There is no darkness save ignorance.

The labile, that is to say slidy and weak memory of past events is no asset to a nation or statesman.

Looking back to an unsavory part of our American past we find it more savory than the present. Whether Roosevelt has mental stamina enough left to learn anything from his nasty forerunner and foreslider, Woodrow the codface: I know not. But men of mental capacity above that of a wart hog ought to be able to look back as far as 1914 and 1919. Woodrow resisted clamor to get us into that war. When he came in, he was in accord with the will of the people, a will which he had not faked or concocted. The Allies won that war, and then cheated Italy. It was an error. The cheating of Italy was an error, and Lloyd George ought to know it by now. The cheating of Italy was an error.

When Wilson further signed or tried to sign the United States name to a rascally agreement, he was NOT expressing the will of the nation. He had already wormed and wriggled out of the proper functions of his office. He had already wormed and wriggled, KNOWING that he opposed the will of the people.

There is a limit or orbit to power. There is a limit or orbit to the practical effects of illegality. The error of old codface, sorefoot, was his own. But he was abetted. In fact he was buttered, caressed, inoculated, and led down the garden path, by his accomplices. They were warned and even had they not been warned it was their duty to ascertain what Woodrow's real powers were. The position of the Warburgs and Lloyd George at Versailles was that of crooks who accept a forged cheque in the hope of passing it on to some one else.

The dirt and grease of the Versailles scoundrels, Jews, sub-Jews and Gen tiles alike, was that having concocted Wilson, having passed him off on their brutalized and stupefied peoples as the United States of America, they proceeded to offer his forged cheque to their people.

The League stank from the beginning. It stank of the Bank of Basel, the Warburgs, the Regents of the Banque de France and the ulcer of England. Not all Roosevelt's actions are infamous. As there is no criticism of music till you can judge the relative merits of different works by the same com poser, so there is no political or ethical criticism till you can measure and judge the different political acts of the same political criminal, gangster, or statesman.

When the President acts within his powers, he has NO NEED to do violence to the laws. His powers are executive, that is, he is legally there to PUT INTO effect the will of the nation and the laws made by the representatives of the People. When he violates and passes beyond his legal powers, he acts TOWARD the destruction of ALL legal government of the United States of America, all government by law and by the laws.

I mean by ANY law, he moves toward a total illegality. This is evil, this is extremely dangerous in the long run, it is myopic, it is short-sighted. In fact, the man is an ass. No good American objects to the U.S.A. assuring the tranquility of the Caribbean.

There is no need to violate the mandate of the people in making QUITE sure that there be no submarine bases, poison factories, etc. immediately off the coast of Florida or in easy reach of Georgia, Alabama, and the mouth of the Mississippi. There are even ways [for] America [to] occupy foreign territory after at least attempting to do it legally.

One can offer to buy, even if one thinks one will have to take over, and make reparations later. I do not think Congress would have objected to the taking over of ALL Guiana, not merely the gotterdamn Dutch part. When a politician's WHOLE policy has been indirect, when his whole political strategy has consisted in indirectness, in the carom shot (not the straight shot), it is unwise to accept any act of his at its face value.

If Roosevelt's aim had been Dutch Guiana, he would probably have turned public attention elsewhere.

It is reasonable to assume, on the basis of Roosevelt's public career since the end of his second year in the White House, that his aim in this case was NOT Dutch Guiana.

It is legitimate at least to suspect that his MAIN purpose was to grab yet more ILLEGAL power, to put a hot one over such fools as Senator Pepper and the other fools in the Senate and Congress. Like balloon-faced bumbustuous Churchill, Roosevelt follows every error by a demand for more personal power.

We should be very careful in arriving at [a] judgment of his Caribbean policy. It may be another mere grab. His interest in international politics is considerable. His hate and loathing of legitimate action, of reasoned action, is extreme. His intolerance of all real collaboration either is, or ought to be known to men who share the responsibility for the governing of the United States of America. I should desire an open mind in considering the Caribbean policy, which is O.K. insofar as it aims at peace and security. The question of how far Brazil should agree [with] our IDEAS of peace and security is a hemisphere question.

All this is a matter of the American hemisphere. And as I said in opening, we will have no criticism of our *own* politics, no criticism of it worth the name, till we can judge between one act of our blowy rhinoceros and another. The policy for the western hemisphere is one thing, Asian affairs are another.

England's conduct in China has been for the most part an infamy. Let some bloody-minded betrayer of the British people get up in their grimy assembly and tell the world of their kind acts in the Orient. From the sacking of the Imperial Palace in Peking to the Jewsoons', Sassoons' century of infamy and of opium with Robert Cecil their advocate. That is their dirt, why make it ours? In any case secret agreements between an usurious nature faker whether in or out of the White House are ILLEGAL. And a foreign government which presents these secret pledges to ITS people as acts of the United States of America participates (and naturally HAS participated) in the swindle. We should leave this trash to its own people, human— —. If this people hasn't the manhood and sense to spew out their Churchills, Baidwins, Buchans, and lesser vermin, that is their own affair, and they will presumably pay the penalty for their own flaccidity and mistaken toler ance. They will slang us for THEIR errors all right. But that any sub-Jew in the White House should send American lads to die for their Jewsoons and Sassoons and the private interest of the skum of the English earth, and the still lower dregs of the Parsee and Levantine importations is an outrage: and that ends it. To send boys from Omaha to Singapore to die for British monopoly and brutality is not the act of an American patriot.

#12 (February 26, 1942) U.S.(B17)
AMERICA WAS INTENTIONS

The Honor of the United States of America is NOT concerned with becoming an arsenal.

The men who wintered at Valley Forge did not suffer those months of intense cold and hunger with the design, or in the hope that Pennsylvania, Massachusetts, Virginia, the union of the colonies would one day be able to stir up wars between other countries in order to sell them munitions.

I don't want, the last thing I want, is that any harm should come to Uncle Sam's Army and Navy. The Navy is, some, of it, gone where I can't much help it. The Army can get on all right if it stays where it ought to be, namely on the North American continent.

I certainly do NOT want American's young blood shed in an assinine attempt to wreck all European civilization. I don't want it Dunkirked, and I would like for Mr. C. Gessler to go on getting his bath at Waikiki, if it ain't too late to mention the subject. I have heard said that Aguinaldo had and has as good a right to the Island of Luzon as George Washington had to Virginia. I am not a Philippine specialist. I have read on fair authority, namely on that of at least one participant, that the British troops after the last war were about fed up with some features of English government.

Dunkirk is one way to keep troops from showing their feelings. Whether American air destroys the memory, I am not prepared to state. John Devey kept his till ripe old age; and I am reminded of his quotation from Burke on the penal laws, "an elaborate contrivance as well fitted for the expression, impoverishment and degradation of a people, and the debasement in them of human nature itself as ever preceded from the perverted ingenuity of man."

Well, as Prattling Nelson is telling you, you haven't seen anything YET. And it has been forgotten that the 18 years of Irish Parliament, 1782–1800, followed close on our American revolution, preceding the French [of] 89. That is, if it isn't rank pretense that any non-Irish American knows it, save by odd chance.

For indeed is there much analogy in it for North America? There is for South American countries. Our South American policy hasn't yet got as far as the Times. A Celt will soon be as rare in Ireland as a Red Indian on the shores of Manhattan.

Perhaps it would be unwise to see too deep for analogies. Palmerston, Lord John Russell and the Times, intending their utterance to apply only to the Pope and the King of Naples, had been advocating the right of every people to choose their own rulers. [By that allusion, I mean short, that they] had a word for it before the Atlantic Conference.

What am I getting at with all this which what, what which? Well, the moral behind any reference to John Devey is that Oireland kept hold of something. Call it the soul of the Irish nation. Kept hold of it thru 700 years of oppression, bloody oppression, not tea party conversation.

And the Americans, the U.S'ers, have started a fine government in 1776. Couldn't keep it a century and have now plum forgotten it ever existed.

It is to be supposed that you are all running round hot and bothered, like headless chickens, no man understanding another. And the pathological brainstorm in the White House after years of robbing the country dipping into the Treasury, years of frothing at the mouth about Mussolini and Hitler, in mid January comes out with a discourse and EVERY single item in it that has a trace of sanity is IMITATED from Mussolini or Hitler.

After 20 years [of] judaic propaganda Lenin Trotsky stuff crowding American history out of the schools, wild inferiority hate against Europe, here old Delano comes out with a mixed bag, in which two thirds of the program is fascist. With, of course, the essential parts missing.

Well now what causes this? Twenty years late, just 20 years late as Amerikanishly usual. The same old American time lag, leading the world from the back seat as usual.

Amid all which flurry there is much that I am sure of.

This war is part of a process that has been going on for some time. And Roosevelt never lied with mere typically Rooseveltian fluency than when he bleated out his sick blah about wanting to keep YOU (that is you, the American people, and your children and your grandchildren) out of war.

A clean man would have been content to keep peace in his own time and trust his children to follow example. By continued bosh about Europe, which his mental and ethical level is much too low to reach he tipped you into war with the Jew Asia and you are most of you his accomplices Nevertheless I am convinced of at least one thing. The present war should NOT be allowed to degenerate into a 30 years or even ten years beano for Knudson and the other sustainers of speed-ups and sweating, chain table.

Work'em up in six years, was the old Jamaica slave owners system. Do the young men, and only young men can stand it, last SIX years at the Knudson band assembly systems? Jews paid by Schiff in New York got hold of Russia and turned the whole land into a sweat shop. Watch your step, brother, it CAN happen to you.

Nothing here about winning the war or not winning it. Wars are not won by sweat shops alone. They are not won by profiteers ONLY. I mean the profiteers win PROFITS, but they do NOT win wars. They start war, but they do not start them in order that any particular nation shall win them.

You can swipe all South America and end up ruined. You can end up with your farms ALL ruined by South American competition INSIDE a customs ring. Dumping of cheaper products is not stopped by mere LACK of customs wall.

If there are any New Englanders, if there are any Americans who have BEEN American for three centuries, or two centuries, or one century, any whose forebears constructed the nation, it is time for'em to get together and think. It is time for them to break the spell of the Knudson and Stimson slop.

Army [regulations] make it unethical to assert that a plane can not be in two places at once. That is the Knox, Stimson, Roosevelt coherence. Possibly new arms manuals will be issued. It seems unlikely that Stimson will bring luck to an army. Military honor has existed. Stimson is unaware of ANY such component in the life of an army. I don't think Henry is a very good bet.

I refer to his absolute and TOTAL lack of any sense of honor whatsoever, let alone the fine honor that has in the past inhered in the concept of the solider and officer. Three generations of c[h]anting parsons are back of that fishface. As to Knox, well your worst enemies hope you will keep him. A child of four [?]. I am making these rather gross allusions with a purpose. That is the faint wavering hope that something will wake you. That some phrase will penetrate the hypnotic or dope trance. These two men were distinctly NOT chosen by the people. No member of the Democratic Party would do particular dirts. Some [of] these decrepit hacks are chosen as instrument.

That is O.K. from one point of view, point of view of tyranny. The over lord or autocrat must be served. If his own party will NOT follow him into certain messes, he must go outside his own party.

Why not lay a wreath on the grave of the elective system?

"Here lies John Jones, he is not dead but sleepeth." Or here lies democracy.

By God if I was dead, I think I'd admit it.

The question is, if two or three sane men, in the bog of Rooseveltian fuddlement can ANYwhere meet and cohere, and clarify their mental perceptions, they should or could, could or should, begin to wonder WHERE the country is coming OUT, "coming out AT" is, I believe, the phrase current.

Are you headed for a CHEAP, ten cent kike, Blumstein, Blumenstein, Zukor, tawdry imitation of nazism, or say for the moment, of fascism? VOID of all vital content. And if you mean to imitate it, are you going to emulate, or to vie? Are you going to try to have as GOOD a brand of the corporate State as is now provided in Europe? If not, why not?

You have the least desirable member of the teempin [?] North American population now at the head of it.

The people have been lied to, betrayed, hog swoggled, and you can't just rub all that out. The question is WHAT of tomorrow morning? Where do you go from HERE?

Thirty years intensive production of synthetic products in order to attack the Japanese colony of Australia in 1947? or 1971? AND IN THE INTERIM, what of your INTERNAL government?

Any syndical organization? Or just Russian mess and chaos, just Soviets run by the Warburgs?

IS there ANY American consciousness, as distinct from Fortune, and New Yorker hysteria, with fatty what's-his-name Woollcott weeping into the megaphones? Or the lowest common denominator Mr. Swing whining into the atmosphere that the Americans are humiliated. There must, damn it, there must be traces of the American RACE left somewhere on the American continent. The race that set up the United States government.

Have they lost all sense of coherence? Is American lucidity dead?

#13 (March 2, 1942) U.S.(B18)
NAPOLEON, ETC.

Monsieur Bonaparte. Napoleon I, made several mistakes, but it is generally conceded that he possessed military ability. Several of his discoveries lie outside the range of my subject but I shall probably be permitted to remind you of one of his dicta, namely, You can't conquer a map.

Not only do the main geographic features of our planet remain fairly stationary, but the nature of the soil and of the climate can not be altered suddenly even by the greediest politician, or most ignorant man hater and Knudson/Stakhalevite.

The AIM in all the more important human endeavors must count for SOMEthing. And you can not get to San Francisco by going to Boston. Granted? Or NOT granted.

No one has examined the genesis of the "muddle thru theory in old England." No one so far as I know has taken the faintest interest in my citation of the Jew prosecuting attorney, for one of America's largest, oldest historic cities.

"All I'm interested in is BUNK," he said to me. Meaning that BUNK, falsification, was his sole interest. Seeing what you can put over. This is one thing from the late P.T. Barnum, from a music hail artist, a circus owner. It is the prestidigitator's job to illude. That's what he is paid for.

It may take another 40 or 80 years to get any of you calm enough, ever again, to ask yourselves whether this is the desirable legal attitude, whether this is the beau ideal, the *ne plus ultra*, the *summum desiderium* for a public official, engaged regularly in great municipal law courts. It is open to doubt whether there are six men listening now to this broadcast who are capable of facing this question. If there are, let'em find six others. Some day you will all have to face it, and face all of its implications, not merely one of'em.

Some day the remnants of the American people will begin to wonder WHICH side was right. They will wonder whether the choice was wise. They will even begin to wonder which side of WHAT. Which side stood for which PRINCIPLE, not merely stood for which interest.

Hank Wallace has shown up the INTEREST. Gold. Nothing else uniting the three governments, England, Russia, United States of America. THAT

IS the interest—gold, usury, debt, monopoly, class interest, and possibly gross indifference and contempt for humanity.

Now if you know anything whatsoever of modern Europe and Asia, you know that HITLER stands for putting men over machines. If you don't know that, you know NOTHING. And beyond that you either know or do not know that Stalin's regime considers humanity as NOTHING save raw material. Deliver so many carloads of human MATERIAL at the consumption point.

That is the LOGICAL result of materialism If you assert that men are dirt, that humanity is MERELY material, that is where you come out. And the old Georgian train robber is perfectly logical If all things are merely MATERIAL man is material and the system of ANTI-man treats man as matter.

Now your President exceeds his powers in demanding that you adhere to his politics As Commander in Chief of the Army he can command you to assail enemy forces but even Congress in its most ABJECT and servile moments has not conceded this blood-thirsty maniac the control of your OPINIONS.

In fact as long as ANY law is left whatsoever in the United States of America which no Jew and no Roosevelt will LIKE having left there, but as long as it is left there, powers do NOT inhere in officials unless delegated TO them by law. Thus when a lying Dutchman tells you that you have GOT to prefer Bolshevism to Fascism, you can ask: WHY? Who says so? AND if you are more than cattle? If you rate yourselves above cows and sheep, you will in defense of that rating have to ask YOURSELVES whether men are more important than mere machinery.

Whether you intend to be slaves, lifelong slaves, hereditary slaves to machinery and whether you propose to sell your children and your grand children into long lasting slavery to usurers *and* to machinery.

I mean you will have to make up your MINDS. YOU can not live on cold iron, you can not live on airplane spare parts, YOU can not live well without LAWS which even the officials obey.

And for however long your answer to me is Jim's answer "No boss, no body here in America is INTERESTED in taking things as seriously as you do," there will nevertheless and finally come a time when at least a few of you will have to face things or DIE; you will have to THINK or die. Hard choice for the daisy pickers, but a real choice.

Roosevelt's gang have got you hitched up with Russia. Not a very good bet. Russians attack general Winter. Mightn't it be that Joe Bloodsucker KNOWS his army will starve in three or four months ANYHOW unless they break the Germans before that? Why suppose that winter attack means STRENGTH on the part of the Russians?

Not my job to speculate on military conditions, but might be. My job, as I see it, is to save what's left of America, and keep up some sort of civilization somewhere or other. I decline to abet the destroyers. I decline, so far as the light is conceded me, I decline to climb trees to catch fish. That's an old one, 24 hundred years old.

Mencius referred t, the folly of starting a war for something you couldn't GET; something the war could not bring to the monarch Mencius was talking to. So he said, climb trees to catch fish.

In the present juncture I refer to the POSSIBILITY that even the swiping and squashing of South America and of Canada may not catch even South America and Canada. Suckers, of course, you will get hold of some of'em. Am I fanciful?

Look at least at the possibility that this mere distention of U.S. borders MAY not be the way to get what you are battling for. It WON'T be unless you pay some attention to what happens INSIDE America.

It won't be if you lose ALL internal structure. When the turnpike depends upon Congress, local control is lost. Well, that was said a long time ago. The central government must in modern life have some powers. But as human beings it might be well to ask how many powers, and which powers?

And IGNORANCE and feeding on lies won't help you to make a lucid decision. You go yellin' hurray for Litvinov. Do you believe in the ABOLITION of all private ownership?

I'll say you do not. You have colluded in the OLD British habit of employing the savage to wipe out the civilized rival. Your school has been hooded. You have had a SLOW one put over you. For 80 years, moving imperceptibly, an inch here and an inch there, you have been euchred out of your history, out of knowledge of history, both American and world history. It can not be done, said Henry Adams to Santayana. Oh, you wish to teach at Harvard. It can not be DONE. Henry Adams said he had tried it. Yes, I came LATE, but I am still a bit ahead of the band wagon. Beard, Bowers, D.R. Dewey (not Tommie) been gittin' down TOWARD but not TO the real bedrock. Get on and PUSH. Get into the diggin' and LEARN the face of American history. ADAMS, John Adams, Jefferson, Van Buren, also Brooks Adams. It's 40 years late for Brooks Adams, but you can't do it sooner. And in watching contemporary flim-flam, do at least TRY to sort things OUT.

DO you believe in the Homestead or in communal ownership? If you believe in the Homestead, WHY fight FOR the abolition of ALL private ownership?

In taking sides in a quarrel do at least try to find out what's fighting WHICH. Do you stand for the obliteration of Finland? If not, why fight against Finland. Do you stand, those of you who are above goose gangster level, for the obliteration of all occidental civilization? If NOT, why join the Anglo-Jewish clique which has been and still is out professedly and openly for the obliteration of Europe? Western Civilization, all of it that you have still got.

Our forebears made a DISTINCT contribution. The Jesuits in Paraguay made a distinct contribution, but they were wiped out for discovering things. We were wiped out largely in the old 1860's.

A man who ain't got any foresight gets kicked in the tail. Man fed on lies and lackin' in foresight got kicked in the Guam.

DO you think that is an ISOLATED instance of the hind effects of lackin' foresight? The starve-the-enemy theme has been sung for a long time on your Victrolas.

Go back and examine it. The cornered weasel will fight. And your MIS-leaders have been out for some years annoying several things larger than weasels. Was it an error? ARE you going to start NOW trying to evaluate their misdemeanors, or are you all of you going to go plum 100% haywire and stay so?

DO you believe in the homestead or in communal ownership? If you do NOT believe in the abolition of ALL private ownership, and the abolition of ALL private initiative, watch your Nelson. He has already got a half-Nelson on you. And if you got to please pore ole Hank Wallace and go on buying all the world's gold from now till the terminus of eternity, you got a day's work comin', with 24 hours labor. And no trade union organization, legally recognized, to put up a tombstone: here lies the 8-hour day.

#14 (March 6, 1942) U.S.(B19)
WHY PICK ON THE JEW?

Well, why pick on the Jew? I have heard the term "Jewish impertinence," in fact Gaudier-Brzeska used to use it. But I think it was a fellow named Brooks, along in January, had got'em beat, and the name ain't Hebrew and I don't reckon he is even a crypto. At any rate some murking broadcaster tellin' the world or the Italian residents in the United States that America loves Italy and only got a grudge against the regime.

Waaal, as Franklin Delano was recently cursing out the Italian for what they did in 1911, before the word fascist existed, he certainly has got NO alibi, no alibi whatsoever. Now all the United States did to show how it loved Italy was to lie like billyOh for 20 years, and try to starve Italy into submission: tariff wall, refusal of Italian goods, refusal of emigrants. What way is that to show love?

DOUBTless somebody who wants 30 years sweat show now wants Italian workin' men in the United States to go work—OVERTIME. Well Charlie Marx had a word for it. That part of Marx is sound, and if bygones are gone by, and IF the Americans love the Eyetalians, there is a way to show it. Why not have a little open communication? Why not print the Charter of Labor? Why not study how far the Italian law code, the new law code, being published under Mussolini's regime IMPROVES on the old ones? How many of you have heard of the Charter of Labor? How many of you have stopped to think whether trade unions ought to have legal status? And the RESPONSIBILITY that goes with such status? If you are going [toward] fascism or nazism why not do it with open EYE, why not learn what these systems of government are? Why not ask and learn how far they are compatible with American habits, [what] is good in'em, and wherein their strength consists, INSTEAD of merely lying and cussing and trying to kill'em on the assumption (if you can call it by so mild a term) that they are something they ain't?

Conditions in German factories? How do they compare? I have seen some dirty lying in my time. I can't hold an inquest on every separate lie, but I have seen something, I have heard something, and then I have seen the American reports of'em.

I have noticed DIScrepancies. I have heard the statement, I mean I HEARD it while it was being said.

I heard Mussolini say "WE need years of peace to get on with our internal affairs." And I have seen it reported next day as a war speech. Twenty years of that sort of thing do not show LOVE of Italy. Not on the part of the reporters or news owners. In fact Mr. Brooks, if it was Brooks, is showing a new love, store label not yet taken off.

Also Mussolini talking about the fight to grow enough wheat to feed Italy as being the kind of fight he prefers. Well, that was the effort that brought out American hostility all right enough.

Will you lay off it? And if so, when so? And while you are thinking, if so, on laying off, there is something else to lay off of? Namely, a system of lending money to foreign nations in order to have a war every 19 years.

That system I suggest you look into. Your British Allies were scared that a few rackets were bustin'.

They started a war to uphold a state of things that just were NOT UPHOLDABLE. Instead of admitting that they would have to change it, they started a war singing the International and running up the cross, sickle, and hammer. Do your Allies BELIEVE in communal ownership? They do not. Do the Chinamen believe in dud cars sent over to Singapore, on not very favorable conditions, and on not very explicit statements as to who gets commissions (several commissions)? I doubt it.

Very nice to hear, I mean you are mebbe comforted to HEAR that you got 100 million Chinese soldiers all ready to die for democracy. I mean if you are a democracy. But you ain't got'em. Well, why lean on what ain't thaar?

There are plenty of people right here in Europe whose views on many subjects do not coincide with my own, but we have, most of us, some points of agreement. Nan King, Manchu Kuo, both of them on the map of old Asia and on the map of New Asia. And TWO points that I would, mebbe three points, like to get into your binnacles. ONE that America COULD have stayed out of this war. Two, that IF America had stayed neutral the war would now be over and America might have had a hand in composing the differences; might not have so many hush hush agreements to buy; purchase, absorb such a lot of South American stuff we don't need and can't use, cornering the market as usual, but mebbe not on stuff other folks want to buy. Well, exchange is said to be a fountain of wealth.

Europe is fighting for something that is not merely material, But even so, a sane and natural exchange of products between them that have'em, places that grow'em, and places where they don't grow or don't grow so easy is certainly a factor in a plan for permanent ease and peace. Of course if you are going to work 18 or 20 hours a day from now till the day after doomsday to buy all the world's gold and silver, to content Uncle Henry A. Wallace, that may be a question of taste (mighty queer taste) on your part.

Mebbe Henry has erred (not the first time), mebbe he was kite flying to see how much hook, line, and sinker the American people would swallow.'Tain't going to do Brazil any good if the whole of Europe goes back to drinking java and mocha coffee. And that ain't half of the story.

Cutting your nose off to spite your face is a very old saying.

Black lists are nothing new in world history. [FCC transcript: Hitherto there have been signs of weakness and waning— —, not signs of rising power. I mean— —and following the regime had imposed them. Not strong, confident powers.

And then, the— —of some of your allies. In fact, why did you take up with those gangs? Two gangs.

Jews' gang in London, and Jew murderous gang over in Moscow? Do you like Mr. Litvinov? Is that face— —of our Colonial architecture? Do the people from Delaware and Virginia and Connecticut and Massachusetts? Do the people who live in painted, neat white houses, with their little sign for the delivery box, erected in 1790, built in 1815, and do these folks really approve that Mr. Litvinov and his gang, and all that he stands for? Is he the implication of something that Mr. Jefferson liked best? Or— —the— —of Boston and that the first white settlers of Massachusetts belong to a race now extinct?

Well, I hope before the Lord we ain't going to be replaced by a race of Litvinovs. The South got— —and desolated in the Civil War, or— —to the city of New York, to bankers in New York City and in London, (debts) conducive of slaughter, slaughter conducive to debt, as intended, and some day you may start asking, I hope so, I hope to God you will start asking some day.]

#15 (March 8, 1942) U.K. (B15)
GOLD: ENGLAND

The ENEMY is Das Leihkapital. They're working day and night, pickin' your pockets. Every day and all day and all night pickin' your pockets AND pickin' the Russian workin' man's pockets. They call it international loan kapital. It is not international, it is not hypernational. It is subnational. A quicksand UNDER the nations, destroying all nations, destroying all law and government, destroying the nations, one at a time, Russian empire and Austria, 20 years past, France yesterday, England today.

Gold is a coward. Gold is not the backbone of nations. It is their ruin. A coward, at the first breath of danger gold flows AWAY, gold flows OUT of the country.

England don't GROW it. There is no gold sproutin' up in England next morning to replace what is gone. Taking usury rotteth the heart. I know you don't believe it. It has been going on for some time. Art Golding a few years ago writin' the life of his famous ancestor, or perhaps I shouldn't say famous, one of the best Shakespearean poets, Arthur Golding, translator of Ovid's Metamorphoses, about the best book of poetry in our language. Shakespeare learned from it.

Well, his namesake and 84th generation or whatever, descendant points out that even in the time of Queen Elisabeth the Earl of Oxford was falling. He was handing over his rents to some shyster in return for a fixed income. Ten thousand, or whatever it was, a year and then the shyster had leave to squeeze what he could out of the peasants and yeomen, out of the men working the land.

Decline of the feudal system. Ole F.M. Ford used to talk about that. Liberty is not a right but a duty.

[To] own property, not a right but a duty. I wonder how long it is going to take you to learn that. Rot and laziness cutting in under, too lazy to FUNCTION as lords and proprietors, the nobility sold out to the shysters.

In my 12 years in London, how many people did I meet (meeting as you might say the flower of the writing class in your island), how many people did I meet who had read their own history, how many who had read Anthony Trollope? It was said as extenuation of Professor Saintsbury, "at any rate he recognized the merit of Trollope." Owning property not a right but a duty. That statement is rather emphatic. Even Robespierre defined ownership of property, putting a limit on what the owner has right to. That being so, you play round with Bolshevism, thinking you will get OUT of a duty? Is that it? Or is it just chickenheaded on your part? This pinkness at afternoon tea parties.

People from East Europe, who have been over NEXT to Bolshevised countries, see different.

People that have been up against Red Bolshevism financed by Schiff in New York and Rothschild in London, see different.

If you wait too long, you may see. So far I have never met any English who believed in the abolition of personal ownership.

I see you have lost the habit of witan, the witenagemot and the town meeting. If you don't grow or find a leader, you may have to wait for some kindhearted Bavarian, or Hungarian to come free you from the Jews of New York.

Do I exaggerate?

DO YOU think that there is any basic, essential difference between a committee of kikes in LONDON betraying the United States of America and a gang of kikes in New York selling up England, and putting mortgages all over your island? Do you think that freedom and the roast beef of old England, or roast beef of old Argentine, consists in taking orders from a gang of Jews in New York? Potatoes and point [?] for yours, if potatoes, and point to where the roast beef had been or might have been.

I know it hasn't been stylish to read U.S.A. history in England. Lord Bryce and a few exceptions looked at American history. However, along in 1863 the United States was sold up the river. Ikleheimer handed it over to Rothschild. Can't let'em print national money, all American money must be controlled by the DEBT. And the debt controlled by the Rothschilds and their associated fellow Episcopalians.

I know, it was clever to send Willie over to New York City to look after your interests and get information as to how Washington was conducting the United States' business. A nice little TUBE instituted. And now the first thing you know, all your island strength has slipped down it.

Your bankers profiting by the decline of England. The hat trick? Yes, the hat trick. The banker gets on a boat, his company is registered elsewhere. He casts down the mighty. I hear even Morgan has lost his seat. Gold is a coward. At the first breath of danger gold flows out of the country.

Now Mr. Eden has declined to cooperate with the nations of Europe, oh most emphatically. He wouldn't shake hands with Neville. He left the House in disgust.

And Winston? He toppled over Japan RIGHT on top of you. Sitting out side, I mean to anybody sitting outside looking in, it would seem that this FLOP of Japan right on top of some of your select naval bases has occurred at an inconvenient juncture.

BUT you are accustomed to your parliamentary leaders. No number of errors on their part induces you to wonder whether your leaders are or are not the KIND of men who MAKE errors. Create'em, you might almost say, out of nothing.

DO YOU grow gold IN England? Do the froggies grow gold IN France? DO the Nigerian farmers get anything but trouble out of having their government run from London, by the pimps, narks, and lackey of the Jewish owners of gold mines? Did the ex-service men after the last war who went out to Africa, etc., etc. and etc. Is gold the CEMENT of empire? It is not.

Yes, you can gum on [to] the Arabs. You are allied to a few millionaires. Your Allies in India are the bunyah. You do nothing in your colonies to compare with the COLONIZATION, real colonization as Italians under stand it.

Well, I won't say you do nothing, but your main line is squeeze, squeeze, ruin the natives, exploit'em.

With exceptions, a man here and there, I suppose still doing his job, along the line of Mr. Kipling's romances. Jews all over the top of Australia. War on your dominions.

You are tired of the name of Alberta. You did everything but march troops into Alberta to keep it under. So the orientation of Canadian trade is now southward.

England is to be a Jew-owned deer park with tearooms. UNLESS of course you lift a tired and tardy eyelid. YOU have NO gold mines in England. And Hank Wallace, the American Vice President, yellin'

bloody murder that there will be, and shall be, NO peace till the whole world sells its birthright for the gold now in Fort Knox.

Gold bought from your Jewish merchants at a rigged price. That has RUINED half the American people. Gold that is totally useless, save for false teeth and spectacle frames. Not even in fashion for goggles, replaced by porcelain in swell dentistry. Mr. Wallace says you got to go on blood and tears-ing till mankind bows down to the calf. How did you get there?

I lose my thread some times. So much that I can't count on anyone's knowing. Thread, as they call it, of discourse. A nation that pays two rents can't compete with a nation that pays only one. How many rents and rates are you paying? How many were you paying before this new war was started? How many of you meet to discuss things? Toynbee Hall and the rest of it nigh a hundred years ago, say 80 years ago, there were "movements in England," amateur discussions of guilds.

Twenty-five, 26, 27 years ago night life, or night dance clubs started in London. Looked diverting, nobody wondered WHY? Ole Frida started the cave of the calf, nobody thought any evil. Possibly a little espionage, probably not even that. Wake up one morning and find the spirit of England, immortal spirit of England's May Day, chained in a brothel. Just another hat trick, undermining, cutting away. Where did she get the money to do it'?

In France things were much more professional. Marvelous fiber, England. Two hundred and 50 years usury, cutting away. Hobhouse, Cobbett, Trollope, men coming back from the colonies, TELLING YOU and being told to shut up. Montagu Webb, trying to tell you something. When they didn't shut up, they were givin' jobs, sometimes quite nice jobs, OUT of London. They were promoted to colonial posts, or as Kipling once wrote, "Jack Barret went to Quatta." But that was another story, that was for a personal reason..

Are you going to select a leader'? You haven't followed, and won't follow any leader yet offered'?

Have you a selfless leader'? Have you the sphincter strength to revive the old custom of meeting, or are all town meetings for bidden by now in England'?

Was the war what you wanted'? Were you TOLD in 1939 what Vice President Wallace has now at last told you, namely NO peace without the gold standard'?

After Winston's visit to Washington, have you mental coherence enough to recall what happened in England when the fat boy brought back the gold standard'? Must have been YEARS ago, did someone say 1925'? I have plumb forgot when it happened. America is allus behindhand, gets round to a dead British idea about 20 years after England is thru with it.

NO peace without the gold standard. Why weren't you TOLD that before you set out to keep Danzig Polish and to defend Finland against Russian menace'?

No peace without the gold standard. Is that the voice of "We the people of England, we have not spoken yet'?"

Pound speaking from Italy. *Parlando da Roma.* Pound speaking. Am I expected to wait for the people of England to speak'? Of course you'll have to find your OWN leaders, I can't pick and choose'em for you.

#16 (March 15, 1942) U.K.(B16)
ENGLAND

The enemy is Das Leihkapital. Your Enemy is Das Leihkapital, international, wandering Loan Capital. Your enemy is not Germany, your enemy is money on loan. And it would be better for you to be infected with typhus, and dysentery, and Bright's disease, than to be infected with this blindness which prevents you from understanding HOW you are under mined, how you are ruined.

The big Jew is so bound up with this Leihkapital that no one is able to unscramble that omelet. It would be better for you to retire to Darbyshire and defy New Jerusalem, better for you to retire to Gloucester and find one spot that is England than to go on fighting for Jewry and ignoring the process.

It is an outrage that any clean lad from the country—I suppose there are STILL a few ENGLISH lads from the country—it is an outrage that any nice young man from the suburbs should be expected to die for Victor Sassoon, it is an outrage that any drunken footman's byblow should be asked to die for Sassoon.

As to your Empire, it was not all of it won by clean fighting. But however you got it, you did for a time more or less justify keeping it, on the ground that you exported good government or better government than the natives would have had without England.

You let in the Jew and the Jew rotted your empire, and you yourselves out-Jewed the Jew. Your allies in your victimized holdings are the bunyah, you stand for NOTHING but usury.

And above metal usury; you have built up bank usury, 60% against 30 and 40%, and by that you WILL NOT be saved. Corrupting the whole earth, you have lost yourselves to yourselves.

And the big Jew has rotted EVERY nation he has wormed into. A mill stone. Well, an exceptionally good swimmer MIGHT conceivably be cast into the sea with a stone tied round his neck. He might perhaps untie it. If he were a Scotchman, he would remember his jackknife, before being thrown overboard.

You seem to remember NOTHING. It were better you were infected with typhus. As to federal union, or JEW/nion. There is NO question of race in

Streit's proposition. It is as proposed a union of slaves, under Jewry. Offered by liars and abettors of thieves.

You have stolen land from your late Allies, and land slips from your control. The ONLY conquests of Britain and Rosenfeld are conquests FROM their alleged allies.

All right, say that Franklin Delany swipes ALL South America—to what end? And ruin the United States of America while he is doing it. What's that to you? It is not England's salvation. Will you ever LOOK at the story of empire? You are NOT even in the mercantile system, you are in a fake mercantile system, not even mercantile. It was for a time called mercantile or the mercantilist system and defined as considering the happiness of a nation to consist in the amount of MONEY it owned, and its process to consist in STEALING, welching, pouching the greatest possible amount of same (i.e., of money) from other nations.

That defines the USURY system, the ONLY system Anglo Saxons have known or used in our time. And it will not save you. NOR will Judaized Russia. Nor will the Kahal, the Jew's central committee of bleeders. WI-IAT is their system? Unvarying, cheap goods, sweated out of cheap labor, dung dust hurled on the world, the WORLD conceived as sweat shop, to hell with the 8-hour day, down with abundance. DUMPING sweated goods, dumped against any and every nation that pays a just price for labor. That is your ALLY.

And in your past a trail of blood and of infamy. You bought Hessians to kill your own blood in America. You bought'em from a stinking feudal overlord, who was in the hands of the ROTHSCHILD; that is HISTORY. You stirred up the American savages against your own kin IN America. But now Eden and Cripps have called in the Muscovite, to burn and destroy all Eastern Europe, and kill Finland, for the sake of the stinking Jews nickel mines.

Your infamy is bound up with Judaea. You can not touch a sore or a shame in your empire but you find a Mond, a Sassoon, or a Goldsmid. YOU HAVE NO RACE left in your government. God knows if it can be found still scattered in England.

IT must be found scattered in England. The white remnants of England, the white remnant of the races of England must be FOUND and find means to cohere; otherwise, you might as well lie down in your grave yards.

You have for years had cheap goods DUMPED in from Russia. Your alliance with Moscow will bring no relief to that wound. Your Jews have ruined your home manufactures. Loans from the city of London, loans to the Orient, interest paid in cheap cotton goods, loans to the South American countries, interest paid in beef from the Argentine, and ruin of English grazing. The laws of durable government have been known from the days of King Wen. When empires go to ROT, they go to rot for known reasons.

The *Times, Telegraph, Manchester Guardian,* are there to conceal these reasons. Your press is an infamy, has been throughout our time.

The laws of durable government have been known from the days of King Wen, and when the Roman Empire perished it perished from the same follies that your kikes, your Rothschilds, Beits, Sieffs, Schiffs, and Goldsmids have squirted into your veins. Cheap grain dumped from Egypt, ruin of the Italian farming, usury, and more usury, THAT is the answer.

For two centuries, ever since the brute Cromwell brought'em back into England, the kikes have sucked out your vitals. A mild penetration, for a hundred years they have bootlicked your nobility and now where is your nobility? You had at least the semblance of control; you had, let us say, some influence with the Lords of Judaea as long as they WANTED your titles, as long as Levy Levinstein Lawson WANTED to be addressed as Lord Burnham. You could turn the worst edge of their avarice, or rather you could turn it OFF, the upper or huppar clawses; and turn it ONTO the peer. As you did without mercy.

But when the same scroungers have moved over to New York City, how will you manage'em? The same bloody minded extortioners, or their descendents. The same FINANCIAL HOUSES. The same Rothschilds who plotted with Sherman, and Vandergould to KILL the American nation, who betrayed the United States in the "sixties". Head office in London, agents in the U.S. of America.

Now the address is altered. Main office in Wall Street and Cohen in London. You send Willie over to spy on us. You send 5000 usurers' pimps over to Washington and give special passports, diplomatic, to inveigle the United States into your plans to get cannon fodder from Idaho and from Iowa to weld your slaves cellar on Europe. And this time you get dumped into the ash can.

You have even forgotten your Kipling. Pig Baldwin has forgotten his cousin; if his obscene and treacherous mind ever grasped the meaning of Rudyard's stories. Let me recall one passage to the sow face:

"The Americans," wrote Rudyard, "obligingly slaughtered each other in order that the Czechoslovaks might inherit Boston Common." *Cras tibi,* tomorrow is your turn. Damn it all, you slaughtered the flower of England in the Boer War. Then in 1914 in the first three months, the best of you went out and got slaughtered.

[TEXT MISSING IN ORIGINAL] been seen only too clearly. And your foul papers, the filth of your news print has been subsidized to keep your minds off it.

A dirty bit of meat by the name of Gollancz has used your book trade to conceal it. You have almost NO means of communication.

When a Brooks Adams writes five volumes that would help you to see it, six copies reach England. You have LOST the health of the mind. God knows how the scattered handful of Englishmen still in England can still speak one with another.

I see NO remedy in your parliament. I don't mean as parliament. I mean in the personnel. It is your problem. You do not NOW even elect your own parliament. Whether WITH an election you could get anything save old dead meat, I do not know. During the last war a few men had a glimmer of instinct. On whatever formula, they called it pacifism. Was it? All of'em I ever met were pugnacious. Was it an instinct to save the butt end of the RACE by not fighting? Is it a mistake to combat Germans by force?

Is there a RACE left in England? Has it ANY will left to survive? You can carry slaughter to Ireland. Will that save you? I doubt it. Nothing can save you, save a purge. Nothing can save you, save an affirmation that you are English.

Whore Belisha is NOT. Isaccs is not. No Sassoon is an Englishman, racially. No Rothschild is English, no Strakosch is English, no Roosevelt is English, no Baruch, Morgenthau, Cohen, Lehman, Warburg, Kuhn, Khan, Baruch, Schiff, Sieff, or Solomon was ever yet born Anglo-Saxon.

And it is for this filth that you fight. It is for this filth that you have murdered your empire, and it is this filth that elects your politicians.

You have lost your tradition. You have not even learned what Lord Byron told you. You are, as even that foul rag the Times tells you, a little late in making a start.

In the year 1942 Anno Domini, there is only one start you can make. And that is a start toward being England. A refusal to be a province of Israel, or an outpost of Yankee-Judaea.

Quando tutti saremo forti.

#17 (March 19, 1942) U.K. (B21) AND THE TIME LAG

Speakin' of Fan mail. I got a funny lookin' card the other day headed Kriegs Statlag XXI A. with the prisoners number runnin' up into the thousands.

Dear Mr. Pound. If this card reaches you and you can manage it, I would be very grateful if you will send me one or two of your recent works on economics. Reading matter from England rather scarce at present and not very enlightening.

Signed. So and so.

Well, mebbe this is all very flattering. But the point is the TIME LAG. If a man has to be made a prisoner of war before he will read my works on economics—what good does it do him? Or let us say what IMMEDIATE good. Of course he may be gittin' ready to make a home fit for a hero; in a new order England when he GITS out of Gefangenenlager.

But wouldn't it have been a sight easier if he and his 12000 fellow recliners in the Genfangenenlager had STARTED readin' my economics just a bit SOONER?

I ask particularly my American hearers, whether the START on the new economics, which would have PREVENTED the war and let the now so mangy ole worm eaten Trafalgar lion go on lying down with the French Rooster, and the assorted eagles of Europe; and left the old Killyloo bird screechin' away on the 4th of July every summer, and no bone broken, and a lot fewer oil ships sunk, and more cars on the American roads, and more rubber for tires. And abundance, no longer potential: but real. Wouldn't it have been bit nicer?

Mr. Brown, known as Buffalo Bill, tellin' you I am in propaganda. Waal, damn it all, I was runnin' this SAME propaganda, back before Hitler became Chancellor of the Reich.

I don't mean I dug down into it, not down to the bottom, I was leadin' the pleasant life, and to men like Hitler and Mussolini, if they had ever got wind of my bein' here, they would have thought me a possibly harmless eccentric. HOWever, in my perlite and refined manner, I did try to do a spot of work educatin', here or there, puttin' in a drop of enlightenment.

I didn't go in hell for leather, economics EXCLUSIVE, straight at once. I had to find out how the old show was runnin'. Runnin' DOWN.

I say it was runnin' DOWN. I began to say that in my poetry. "This land turns evil slowly."

Treatin' it by way of *young* man's intuition, I said something about getting the SENSE of a city, like the savage hunter has the sense of the forest. Somethin' was running DOWN.

There is a poem, not by me, back in *Blast*, about a mud hydro. That was healthy mud, by comparison.

Then after I saw it was BAD, I began to wonder how you could fix it. After ten year askin' questions, askin''em of Bank Lawyers, askin''em of Max Pam or any other wise guy I could git near to. After ten years, I say, I began to get top sides with the subject. Usury, profits, monopolization of money. Then I began diggin' into American history, and other history. All there plain as a biscuit. But the means of TELLIN you people? That was the question. Oh Hamlet. Oh village hamlets. Big papers did NOT want open discussion—it had to be bootlegged.

Then there was "education" beginning with the top shelves of the colleges. I am goin' to quote from a paper with an equine title printed out in Wisconsin. A little magazine, the kind that comes up alive and dies down usually rather sudden, inside a couple of years. Along in the Spring of 1935 I came up with this answer to those young editors in their quarterly as follows: The best I can do in reply to yours is to offer programs recalling a few FACTS. For 30 years I have been trying to reorganize the study of literature so that it would be of some use to the student, and for 15 I have been trying to reorganize education, in general, to the same end.

The best I can tell you to date, is contained in my *ABC of Reading* and in my *ABC of Economics* with the volumes following it, *Social Credit, an Impact*; *Jefferson and/or Mussolini*.

Why aren't they used as YOUR textbooks? For advanced students, there is my *Make it New*, which must be correlated with my *ABC of Reading* if you are clearly to see what it is driving at.

If American students will recognize that Universities are there to prepare students for life in a given country and in a given TIME, and insist on finding out what will help them to LIVE in that place and time, they can get their four years' worth. No body can do this for the students. They have got to do it for themselves.

"Mark Hopkins on one end of the log, and the student on the other."

When Abelard was kicked out of the University of Paris 5,000 students followed him into the country, [where] there were no dormitories and million dollar gymnasia. That is the sort of thing that spells "revival of learning" or "intellectual rebirth."

My generation was brought up ham ignorant of economics. History was taught with OMISSIONS of the most vital facts. Every page our generation read was over shadowed by usury. Not only was the press false, but every current idea had been warped by generations of antecedent perversion.

The ACID TEST of public men today is plain and simple. MISTRUST any man, no matter how high in office who tries to get you AWAY from the questions: WHAT is money?

Who makes it?

How is it issued?

Why can't the WHOLE people buy what the WHOLE people produces?

Start on that at once, and throw out any man who won't give you a straight answer. You can not cure Wisconsin in Pekin. I mean, start where you *are*. Don't let anyone wriggle out of LOCAL honesty, by talking internationally. Investigate the Carnegie Peace Foundation. When you find out why they avoid the study of the *economic* causes of war, you'll be part way toward preventing another.

Printed in Wisconsin in the spring of 1935, LONG before Hitler was so influential in world affairs.

You can lead a Rocking Horse to water, but you can't make him drink it.

And young America's problem is what was young England's problem. And the answers were KNOWN; the answers COULD have been broadcast, the answers could have been printed in daily papers, they could have been taught in the schools, they could have been used as the basis for action. I mean political action. And WHAT prevented it?

Waaal, go ask yourselves what prevented it? Ask yourselves why these things were NOT widely printed? Why the real thought of the American founders was hidden, stuffed into corners? Why every man in England who foresaw disaster, and who saw HOW England could have avoided it IF ... Why these men were NOT heeded. Why they were hugger-muggered out of the way, or reduced, shall we say often by FEAR, into silence.

Not all were afraid, some were prudent. Where are they? Some of'em got out in front. Now where are they? Where are the back seaters, the men who knew, but saw no way to ACT on their knowledge? The men who assembled tiny minorities? Waaal, where are they? And when will the people learn wisdom?

OZeus.

O Chan Ti, how long is the time lag?

#18 (March 22, 1942) U.K. (B20)
BUT HOW?

I unhooked my radio the other night and the word REVOLUTION came floatin' over the ambient air. Very English voice, usin' the word RE VO LU TION.

And I thought, yaaas, very nice but HOW'? How CAN they revolute.

Conjure up to my mind the pale grey light in Kensington Gardens, and the gulls floatin' over the round pond, and the so very quiet demeanor of the nicely dressed females that used to float up the broadwalk, along about 1910. How CAN THEY revolute?

Yaas, I hear Bela Kun was over in England, he was a revolution, bloody murder and all the trimmings.

But does Kensington revolute?

I am so old I can remember the end of the nineteenth century, that is the century before this one that is gettin' on to be nigh half gone. How impressed the American visitors were by the beef-eaters in the Tower, and the teacups at Windsor and Stratford-on-Avon, with the coats of arms glazed into the chimney, and the quiet lawn in the park, and a time when the Route du Roi wasn't so rotten. The Row, not of course that I knew the riders, save occasionally Mr. Cunninghame Graham, a fine figure on horse back, and ole Colonel Jackson, suggestin' I should dine at his club, he wantin' to see the expressions on the faces of his contemporaries when faced with the vorticist movement. Well, all that must be fairly well bygone.

The question is how do folks revolute? The Rooshians do it with fire and sword, and very unpleasant tortures. Very unEnglish, as England used to be in my memory. How DO you revolute?

Can you revolute without contacts, without collaboration, without COMMUNICATION? I think not.

Yaas, there is Cripps. He didn't use to be there so much. In fact my sole memory of Stafford is secondhand, old Nelly Weaver saying "A DREADFUL man!" Seems like she had a cousin, that was manager, or editor, or managing editor of a paper called Pig and Piffle, I mean by its own staff in private.

And it sold for a lot less than it cost, I mean it cost, let us say, ten pence a copy to print, and sold retail for a six pence, and turned over ten or twenty thousand a year in net profits.

Anyhow, Nelly's cousin died, and left his sons in Cripps' charge, Cripps being trustee or guardian, so my memory of Stafford boils down to Miss Nelly a sayin' "A DREADFUL man! Heaven KNOWS what he is teaching the boys!"

Waaal, if heaven didn't know then, mebbe heaven will find out during the next few week's course of hostilities.

I mean internal hostilities. I don't know that England learns from abroad. I dunno that the fall of Madras, or Calcutta will teach you folks anything, cause Hong Kong, Singapore and the Island Indies don't seem to have started you. But mebbe a few INTERNAL hostilities? Heaven knows!

Back in Queen Elizabeth's time, farmin' out their estates to some usurer, gettin' out of their feudal duties, Cobbett and Hobhouse—all sorts of velleities toward reform; confined to a few special segments.

Lord, can you call'em segments. They were mostly kind hearted fellows, thought to be CRANKS by the public.

Can you have ANY collaboration if you don't MEET? How can you meet in a CITY, unless you are financed?

Yaas, you can, or COULD meet on a street corner, or in by Mubble Arch, so long as you didn't do anything SERIOUS.

Ole Kun, Cohen, Béla was serious. People in Budapest found out he was serious. Mebbe Sir Stafford is SERIOUS. The bolo agents in England were serious, when I was last there, the top numbers in the Communist Party were all paid by Moscow, which as you know is sometimes paid by New York or London.

It WAS known to your intelligence service, all their numbers were listed, all of'em engaged in industrial espionage. I am not tellin' anything to you that some of your own rulers don't KNOW.

And now we hear of the SCORCHED EARTH policy. Git ready for an invasion. Cit ready to destroy all that is left you. Bum down your houses.

Waaal, WHO is a going to live in those ruins?

An invading army, if it ever gits into London, would, one would suppose, pick its own quarters; and a man that had burnt down his own bedroom would be left to sleep in the ashes.

Margey Daw, see saw, and the rest of it.

Do you think the people who tell you to burn down your houses and get ready for bombing raids for North Ireland, droppin' leaflets saying they only do it to help you? Do you think that these people LOVE you?

Have you got any data about the Ukraine? I am movin' toward this proposition. I assume that some of you did NOT want Mr. Churchill. He was not a pig in a poke. He may have been a Baldwin piglet, but he certainly was not CONcealed from the purchaser.

Take Carolyn Bellairs, for example, Carolyn Bellairs did NOT want Mr. Churchill. I dunno whether he, Bellairs, has yet joined Domvile in Jail. We do NOT git detailed news of your family squabbles. But I assume the Navy and the Army did contain at least a nucleus of men, with enough sense NOT to want Churchill.

I assume that there was a tiny, and languid minority who did NOT acquiesce DEElightedly in a war, which was KNOWN to be going to have such consequences as the whole world now sees it havin'.

Revolution di PALAIS? Is that it? Do you think you can *balayer* the palais? Do you think you can have a nice little revolution, in the colors of Mr. Watt's Hope Soap and Charity?

AH yes, but the MONEY. I am castin' about in my mind for some way you could CLEAN your own sewers.

Oh, but you say, we don't WANT to clean the sewers, we just want to dust out the draaaawin' room.

I comprehend you. But is that just what you can do?

I was for years all for a nice sensible bit of reform but Mr. Rothschild, and Mr. Sieff, and the rest of the British powers, Mond, Kataan, Sas soon, and the rest of'em weren't very keen to nice reforms discussed in their papers.

They put in such blokes as Eden. They put OUT anybody who said anything sensible. Nice old gentlemen, who would edge up to the truth, talkin' about remonitization of silver, or some VERY mild infraction of the gold-bugs monopoly. They, the nice old members of the respectable knighthood, or elderly colonels, who remembered the end of the other war, they would get sent out to Karachi, to keep'em from impeding the traffic (traffic in gold, and in loans at high interest) or at low interest, sometimes not more than 30 or 40% on the real money handled.

CAN YOU MEET one another? Your air isn't free. Open organizations have been "put inside." No chance of marching'round swinging green banners; presenting petitions to the King, about Coventry.

Nothing but SECRET organization. Ever hear of the Fenians?

Or revolution in the PALACE? Well, where do we go from here? Art revolution? Need three or four men even to make an ART movement function.

Can't do it in politics without at least some sort of COMMON ground, common agreement.

You do NOT believe in the total abolition of property—meaning of private ownership of your homes, and fir fields. Lord, who has any FIELDS left? I dunno. Say your house and suburban garden. What about homesteads? The air is NOT yours. The press is NOT yours. Communications by private automobile are said to be gettin' scarcer. In London you do not MEET, no man knows any other, at least not to any extent.

How can you defend your homesteads from Cripps? Homesteads? Your bed chamber, your kitchenette, and your telephone, all of'em rented. God help you. You better start SOMETIME.

Ezra Pound speakin'.

Yaaas, SOME time, while Sir Stafford is goin' big out in India, agreein' on the TOTAL abolution of private property, him and the Aga Kahn, and the gaekwar of Baroda. Pardon me, the Tovarish of Baroda.

#19 (March 23, 1942) U.S. & U.K.(B22) BUT HOW? SECOND ITEM

It was not the present speaker, but an Englishman, I believe an absolutely loyal Englishman, a sort of Royalist, not Mr. Eliot, but at any rate a King's man, and so far as I recall a man who had no Fascist or Nazi sympathies, who on May 11th, 1939 uttered the statement I am about to repeat to you. Get the date, May eleventh, 1939.

There is NO mystery whatsoever about the disappearance of Mr. Litvinov from the political scene.

The Soviet Foreign Minister vacated his office because he failed to deliver "the goods" demanded by the masters of Wall Street and Moscow. New methods to secure these "goods" will now assuredly be given a trial.

What are these "goods?" Nothing other than Great Britain, captive and in chains. Great Britain stripped of her empire, above all Great Britain, ruined financially by the collapse of the Pound Sterling and the system called "barter trading" which is based upon that money.

There, gentle Briton, you have it. Your own heroes have told you. And your own true men you have heard NOT. You have not heard your own true speakers. You have lain down and died in the gutter because you would not hear your OWN friends; your own loyal speakers.

Now as I keep on tellin' you, my friends and/or acquaintances in England, were not of any one group.

There were a few of'em Fascists; but the most of'em were IDIOTICALLY anti-fascist. They were most of'em plum stupid about the Italian regime. I am not offerin' you the ideas of a sect, I am as the strength is vouchsafed to me trying to remind you or tell you of a few home truths, that you COULD have learned not only from me, but from dozens of Englishmen.

Seems like it must have been more like HUNDREDS of Englishmen, trying to tell you for the past twenty-two years.

Now WHY did you not listen? Well, if that implies retrospect, bring it down to the true British question: W'ere do we g'ae frm ERE? I ask you.

I ask you still more HOW do you [go] from here. I can't see that any other white race in Europe is going to be very anxious about Anglo Saxon survival belong to what is usually regarded as a branch of that race.

Racially, English went to America along sometime after 1600, 1632–38, along up till 1700.

I think you lose by not thinking about this problem as RACIAL.

Yes, I know I went at it from the economic part of the picture. Brought up on American principles; no prejudice against any man for race, creed, or color.

Waaal, the chemist is not supposed to have prejudice against any particular chemical; in the laboratory some stink and some do not. Some explode and some do not—chemist's business—chemist in American sense, not the man in the drug store; say the chemical experimenter or chemical engineer is supposed to look at different chemical elements with a fair eye and mind.

So I don't reckon to go along my road as with prejudice. I have tried to see the thing straight.

Birth control, bad national health, neoMalthusian preachin', scarcity economics, all workin' Britain's downfall. Question is: Ain't you fallen down about FAR ENOUGH?

Can't you stop somewhere at least near the TOP of the dung heap, with out having the whole midden flop over on top of ye?

And HOW are you going to do it? That is what I ask: HOW are you going to do it?

You certainly are NOT going to do it by abolition of all ARYAN ownership, and the mortgaging of all England to a half hundred Kikes in New York. That is NOT going to give you a new British order.

CAN you understand, can any of you understand, that a few of you must club together, and at least try to find out what you BELIEVE?

You do NOT believe in the abolition of ownership? You do NOT believe that you should be ruled from abroad by Kuhn, Loeb, and Warburg, of the dregs of the ex-ghettoes of Europe, now planted on the neck of the American people.

Have you any hold on the country? Let us say on the Land?

I see it is increasingly difficult for any two men to meet outside London. Who meets INSIDE London?

Do they still disagree about EVERYTHING? Do three social credit parties instantly arise wherever two social creditors gather together?

Is there ANY common bond, apart from hysteria induced by your jewspapers? Or the common interests of men who hire their "seats."

I mean SEATS in the Commons. Difference between those seats and a seat on the New York Stock Exchange is that in New York the men BUY their seats, and in Westminster the members rent'em. The New York Stock Exchange system has an advantage; it may even be more democratic. I never heard democracy discussed in this connection.

But a man BUYS his seat on Change, openly and the price is known, I believe in most cases.

Whereas a member of Parliament is a renter, he is said to pay in an in definite sum per year, to DEFRAY.

Defray is, I think, the word used, defray party expenses. Contribute to the funds of the party.

That is democracy. Is it? It has never been the American IDEAL of representative government.

I have murmured on the ambient air, now and then a few soft words about my own splay footed country. Real representation when the place was more or less agricultural. Method of geographic division O.K. when many people were engaged in growing the crops of one sort or another, and the seaboard in tradin', and fishin'.

Rough sections still kept in the United States but no one havin' any say now, but the banks and the Warburgs. People who FEED the lot always voted down by the RULERS. Naive blokes, populist, subject to caricature. All lead up to GUILD organization.

Which does NOT appeal to abject NON-producers. Does not appeal to exploiters, that is the rub. Early socialists were boneheaded; didn't dig down into problem of money.

I dunno how far you now KNOW what the same men took twenty years tellin' you, and that your press took those same twenty years keepin' from you.

Even supposin' you do NOW begin to see something, how are you going to GIT OUT of your present trilemma? If SOME Englishmen could see where England's course was leading back before this war started more of them ought by now to be seeing it, seeing that Singapore is no longer called by that name.

What was the Sassoonery is now Shonanko. How do you save your homes? Revolution behind the scenes in the palace? A group of officers of the Army? Or guild formation? Movement coming up from the mines or the land?

You can NOT eat minerals, and then HEROES? The reformers all used to take it so easy. The new bright world was to be arranged over the tea cups.

Why DIDN'T you settle it over the tea cups? DID any one care for England enough to rattle the teaspoons, or risk cracking a saucer? AND now your politicians talk of CONDUCT of the war. Don't you realize that the only men with brains enough to conduct a war are the men who foresaw what the war would be; the men who tried to keep you OUT of it, and who would now try to CONDUCT you out if it? You have NOT made it a war of honor. You could have made a hopeless stand, a forlorn despair of an expedition into Poland, and been defeated with honor. Of course it would not have been right at bottom, because the guarantee to Poland was faked. It was not to or FOR

Poland. But even so, you could have made a gesture and been defeated with honor.

Can you not see that the outrage of the bombardment of Paris is but one of a series of attempts to make real peace impossible, and to prepare for the war after this one? Needless hate—sewing the SEEDS of hate for to morrow. Does it mean nothing to you that in this war you have inflicted more and worse wounds on your Allies than on the people you said were your enemies? Can these things go on forever without some glimmer of light reaching the British mind, to show the real causes of the conflict—the real forces IN conflict? Usury against peasantry, usury against farmland, usury against every man who does a day's work, physical or with his mind.

Ah, against consciousless exploitation, against monopoly, against bank deals and swindles. Against EVERY race in Europe that takes the responsibility for being a nation and administering openly, as a government in the eyes of the people.

Against the crawling slime of a secret rule, a secret and IRRESPONSIBLE rule, that takes NO responsibility for the welfare of races, and nations, but eats like a cancer into the heart and soul of all nations. Even that where of its central staff is composed.

#20 (March 26, 1942) U.S.(B23) McARTHUR

It is a privilege to fight against gentlemen. And the European radio station seems to me to have been as ready to show respect to General McArthur, as they are, and RIGHTLY are, to show absolute and utter contempt and loathing for the war profiteers, and the gang of unmitigated newts, and vermin who have thrown the world into war in the hope of establishing a gold and money lending monopoly, and blotting out the good life in five continents. They have done this from their lust for secret and irresponsible power.

And the place to fight these syphilis bugs is NOT on the frontiers, but in the centre of your own nations.

This more than bubonic plague passes over all frontiers as Dante already perceived. It rots the heart, and the soul of the nations. It is silent, ceaseless in its action. And the PLACE to resist it is for every man LOCALLY—the means to resist it are LOCAL.

And by that fact they are hard to bring into coherence. The embezzler, working behind false laws, can mobilize quickly; the farmer, worker and peasant can not.

The embezzler sets up his papers, dailies and weeklies. That curse of God Willkie was puffed up by the Weeklies. The plague does not stop with the dailies. It sets up publishing houses, it grinds down all private liberty— economic—I mean, fewer and fewer men or groups have the MONEY to run a paper.

Every cranny is infested. Every college campus has a book store. LOOK to these bookstores. Look to the LAST vestiges of approximate freedom of the press, even the scholastic press, that gets out small editions.

Communicate, Communicate, and CO MUN ICATE.

A plot was outlined years ago to blot out classical scholarship, to blot out the historic sense. It went about on soft paws, making no noise, it was DEADLY.

It worked while the nations slept. A contempt for the Latin authors. The idea *Greek* was useless. The concentration on innocuous authors. Erotic poems and NOT the state of life as shown in the Athenian law courts.

The aesthetic angle, that the whole of my generation grew up in, all LOOKING harmless, so HARMLESS.

America was killed by the kid-glove generation, looked simple. Henry James describes these innocuous flops: on the beach at Newport, none of'em meant any harm, after the Civil War the American people was tired. I'll say they were tired.

With reason. Killed each other off to make room for the vermin.

After Cato's death there was no Republic, says some old Roman historian. Perhaps after Lincoln's death there was no United States Republic. Bowers, the TRAGIC ERA, go read it. Johnson couldn't hold out against the infection. Civil War dragged on. WITH INTENTION. Halleck, why was he general? Or at least why in command? Waaal, that is old scandal. Can't fight Antietam now. Can't go back before Gettysburg, the very names are forgotten now. Names we, the men of my time, grew up on, but we WERE being taught to forget. Or rather the WHOLE of the history was aimed at FORGETTING. It was top dressing, a monotony of military encounters, done with music and banners, to KEEP the nation's mind OFF the causes—off the REAL causes. Debts of the Southern states, to the bankers of New York City.

My ole great uncle had a wooden leg,
went stumpin''round after Gettysburg.
Ole uncle dot and carry one,
and every gun was a golden egg, for the Bankers in New York.
For the bankers in New York, OHoooooo.

No wonder old uncle Hiram wrote poems about P [J. Pierpont] Morgan, that as a kid of nine I didn't understand. NO wonder the profit of 15 thousand on a lot of condemned rifles, looked like pretty poor stuff to men who had lost legs and eyes for the union.

After them came the kid glovers. Too refined to touch politics. THAT was an error. But you can't very much blame'em. Tired of five years war, of bad food, and army blankets. Also the weak'uns left, Henry James, Henry Adams, John, John Quincy, then Charles Francis in London. That part of Henry Adams "Education" is still EDUCATORY. Read it. Charles Francis Adams workin' against Lord Russell, as cold a son of a fish as ever got into Parliament.

Then he came home, Charles Francis, and didn't make a fight for the presidency. Possibly it would have been useless and then Brooks Adams trying to set down the real reasons.

Where is BOSTON? Damn it, is the Kike and Kahal radio station all that is left of Boston?

Is New England a midden? The war you ought to be fightin' is NOT five thousand miles OUTSIDE Boston. Or five thousand miles outside New York, or even outside San Francisco. It is INTERNAL.

And if you let'em bilk you with the idea. that they will PROGRESS AFTER the war is over, and a few million of you under the daisies, you will be being worse FOOLS than the Hindoos.

This war, internal war, can go on QUITE as well, SIMULTANEOUS with General McArthur gettin' killed in a hopeless fight against Aguinaldo's successors, as it can after the war is over: if it ever is over.

BEING at peace for twenty years AFTER Versailles did NOT conduce to a victory of the American people over the shysters. WHY should the twenty years after THIS war be any more favorable to setting up an honest government and killing off the Morgenthau and Warburg Satrapy: and having a United States of America State or REPUBLIC? What earthly argument is there against cleaning up and cleaning out the embezzlers DURING the present conflict? How can you DO it? Damn it, you can start by cleaning up your own minds. You can clear out the crap that you JOURNALISTS KNOW is crap: when they write it.

You can then clear out the crap that journalists BELIEVE along with their fake news, along what the advertisers LET the OWNERS (so called), let the editors PUBLISH. There is a second layer of crap that newspapermen believe to be real. BUT it is not grounded on a real knowledge of ANYTHING.

They have NOT gone into the documents. They have not read the real history. They chase one butterfly after another.

NOW the facts are NOT wholly hidden. There are fifty authors whom you could read, Brooks Adams, among'em. You could read the works of the men who fought for the making of the Republic, John Adams, Jefferson, Van Buren, hidden or kept in shadow by punk propaganda.

You could get down to the usury swindles, lit up by Demosthenes. Will you wake up to the fact that the gradual elimination of the classics had a purpose, a damn dirty purpose? Get boiled down to a few harmless authors, say to Tibullus and Virgil, taste for the unreal in poetry, and the student's eye got off the reality.

Look at John Adams' paideuma. Look at what a man in those days, with no million dollar library, could learn while living on American farm land. Boston having about 15 thousand inhabitants.

No, it is the habit of "not being interested in takin' things as seriously as"— —That refers to a young American college graduate tellin' me his friends and acquaintances weren't interested in taking things as seriously as I do.

Waal, it would have been just a bit better for'em and, as Mr. Patchen remarks in the headin' of one of his poems "I don't want to alarm you, but we are most of us going to be shot." Also a fellow named Caidwell, I think it was, went to the Spanish red war. These fellows got around to taking it serious.

What are you fighting for? Fighting for the starvation of Europe? Fighting to spread famine in Asia?

Fighting for vain boast proved false? Fighting for the Sassoonery? Are you fighting for the National Heritage? For the heritage of wisdom, the heritage of Washington, and of Monroe, of John Adams and Lincoln?

I'll say you *are not.*

You are fighting AGAINST what all these men stood for. And it will take more brains than I got, to get you out of it prettily.

Ezra Pound speakin' from Europe for the American heritage.

#21 (March 30, 1942) U.S. & U.K.(B24)
THE PATTERN

When are the American and English people going to take note of the pattern, the pattern in which wars are made, not one war, but wars, in the plural?

Whether you go back to the start of THIS war in 1696. 1696, when the virus of death, the invisible silent virus, more deadly than syphilis, was shot into the English people. Bank of England, makin' money from VACUUM, and levying interest tax in respect to it.

Waaal, you can't all be students of history. Look to what you can remember, if you are over 40.

How was the last war started? Murder at Sarajevo. Look back at the assassinations that have served as a spark for wars. And at those that were intended to start wars, but something went wet in the fuse.

Connect'em up. THINK what might have been back of'em. To use a people, to send a people into war UNPREPARED is called destroying the people.

Ideogram of the knife and the sliver. USE people in war UNPREPARED. That is called destroying the people. ALL right, do you see anyone still blotting God's sunlight with their swollen bodies? Roosevelt and Churchill, for instance, who have pushed the American and English into the war. That is the first phase. Hurl people into wars they CAN'T WIN. KNOWN in England in 1938 that England would LOSE.

Damn it, I was told in London in November 1938 that England would lose. Military expert sez to me (a furriner): "WE will lose India, we will lose all our eastern possessions."

WELL, why weren't men like that LISTENED TO? Why didn't the British people listen to THEM, and not to the dirt off the hog's hind leg, like they did listen to? What causes that? Astor, Times, Manchester Guardian, and the rest of'em. Chief Usurer's usurious brother at the head of the B.B.C. before that stable was cleaned that much, and an equally mendacious traitor to the people of England, put there to replace him, to be followed by another S.P.O.B. and Mr. Churchill's last by-blow. Yaaas, and what is the SECOND phase, or second link of the poison offensive—London OR Washington?

Cries for prosecution of the war (not of the bastids that caused it).

Bevin and company in the HIRED fake labor pseudo-opposition crying for more energetic, etc.

Get the nation's neck against the buzz saw, and then PUSH. Russians in the last war and in this war.

Something pushing'em. Someone HAD BLUNDERED.

DAMN it all, every man that dies in McArthur's army is sacrificed to Frankfurter's friends. But NOT to WIN. To destroy himself, to destroy any nation, one after another. Not that the Russian empire should survive, that the Austrians should survive, that England or the British Empire should survive, but to pull down the mighty.

Will you OBSERVE what these forces are, that shove nations from one disaster to another? France hurled against the unbeatable Germans, England pushed unprepared, and the climax of unpreparedness, the Lehman, Frankfurter, Morgenthau SUCCESS, of SUC/Cess in hurling America into the conflict, and now yelling for MORE disasters.

I did NOT stand with Lindbergh. I am not a pacifist of the prize-taking variety. There are times when a nation should fight, even without what appears a chance, as Finland against Russia.

When threatened with extinction. SUCH was NOT the case in 1939 with the United States, NO one for the past hundred years had dreamed of threatening the United States of America with extinction.

A damned fool, or a half hypnotized vacuum in our White House threatened Japan with starvation, sent silly school girl notes to Mussolini and Hitler, threatened to starve the world, talked TOSH to the Axis powers and to Japan. The world has seen that propaganda and smelt the stink.

I did not, however, take Lindbergh's line, wrong line as I see it. The Nordic race seemed to be wholly ignorant of the nature of England's owners, expressed sympathy with England, NOT distinguishing between the nice Englishmen that one meets, and the gang of thieves and murderer's pimps who have been in control of the London government.

Out-in-front-men, for the in-behind-men, Beits, Goldsmid, Sassoon's, and Sieffs and Rothschild. I said the cause was rotten, it was ROTTEN, and it was KNOWN to be rotten, and it was known that MOST of the gold in the world is in the United States, in the British Empire and in Russia. And as I was told in our National Capital, any attempt to diminish the power of them that held it will meet with fairly serious resistance.

Waaal, it was NOT honest resistance, witness dirty Donovan, in Yugoslavia, witness the betrayal of one after another by the nations who are CONTROLLED by the gold VERMIN. William J. Bryan must have been unhealthy. His family is so gone to rot that they can let Hank Wallace say, "NO PEACE without restoration of the gold standard," and NOT shove Hank's head into a milk pudding, and treat him for progressive infantilism.

WHERE are the men of the sons of the men who had the sense to hear of the CROSS OF GOLD, are they all dead?

Anyhow, that dirty alley cat is out of the BAG. Whoever died at Dunkirk died for gold. Whoever was shot at Dakar died for gold.

AND the bombardment of PARIS? As I have told you, NOT military, done to PREVENT the cessation of wars, done to so embitter French feeling that there can be NO peace between France and England. Oh yes, pullin' in more nations, hope of stealing Martinique, and Madagascar.

But for God's sake look at the POLICY, look at the pattern, how is it done? Who now is drawing pay for demanding vigorous prosecution of war?

Vigorous prosecution of Frankfurter and that golliwog glove that covers his fingers.

Frankfurter down inside the Punch and Judy show booth, and that curse of God, Franklin D. Roosevelt, gesticulating and shrieking up there in front to distract the children, to get the boys into the trenches. And the papers, the hired press, howling that the interventionists musn't be allowed to take advantage of the abysmal mess made by Roosevelt, that the war must be PUSHED.

The place to defend the American heritage is ON the American continent. AND no man who had any part in helping Delano Roosevelt get the United States into it has enough sense to WIN ANYTHING.

If Roosevelt were not BELOW the biological level at which the concept of honor ENTERS the mind, below the biological level at which human beings can CONCEIVE the existence of such a thing as HONOR, that liar would go out on to the steps of the American Capitol and commit hara-kiri to atone for the evils he has wrought on the American people.

And I say it. Here's my John Hancock.

Ezra Pound speaking from Rome, speaking as an American citizen, and hoping to God there are still some Americans left as distinguished from IMPORTATIONS.

#22 (April 6, 1942) U.S.(B27)
DESTRUCTION

Ezra Pound speaking in the name of a little sanity and human intelligence. The mere distruction of vast amount of goods, tools, ships, etc. solves NO problem, save the temporary, artificial and man-made problem of: GLUT on the market.

It does NOT solve the market problem as a whole. The mere absence of GLUT does NO good either to marketer, maker or would-be buyer if the absence of GLUT is accompanied by the absence of everything else, or even of nearly everything else.

Sumner Welles and company have, I admit, opened up a market for tankers. Anybody who can make tankers can now sell them. IF he is con tent to receive Morgenthau dollars as recompense, regardless of what the Kike dollar will buy. The continuance of destruction does NOT remedy the effects of destruction.

You have lent some more "Money" as you call it to Chile, a country notoriously in default. *The confessions of a bond-salesman*, an informative work, written by an author who had learned very little from his own tribulations, might be reprinted. The author was pretty much of an ass, but an intelligent reader might derive benefit from his revelations. The Loeb Chart of Plenty, the Chart of United States potential production has just been reprinted here. That shows the opportunity that the United States once HAD. Shows the abundance that might have been if Lehman's damn son-in-law had never been born, or if the American people had had sense enough to keep him and his likes OUT of the American Treasury, and if our lunacy commissions were more effective. NOW the American money system is cuckoo. It is dishonest. It is unethical, it is blitheringly idiotic, and every man fit to be called human knows it.

There are simple means of remedying it. Had they been applied, you would not now be at war.

Applying them now will not mend all the harm already done by Kuhn, Cohen, and Company to the American people, but the LONGER you put off starting, the worse rotted the whole country will be by the financial syphilis, whose out-in-front chief protractor is Franklin Delano.

And NO war promises have ever been kept by usurers' governments, not since Cain took a pot shot at Abel. IF the monetary reformers IN the United States of America don't get busy NOW, the opportunities offered 'em at the end of the war will be NIL.

If you can't learn from England's experience in homes for heroes, and war veterans trying to sell matches in the gutters of the Strand, after the last war, then God help you.

A system wherein the public is MILKED and bilked of TWO dollars for every dollar spent by the government is not the way to win either a war or a peace.

And the usury (now the Warburg) system is as old as the gold brick wheeze. The money system practiced by Monty Norman, and by Baruch's fireside cronies is the system of claiming MORE than there is.

The CLAIMS are printed on paper (in the old days they were printed on metal), they are also partly printed on paper, and those forms filled in with ink.

Twenty dollars printed on a gold piece will NOT buy eggs on a desert raft, where no eggs are. It is as impotent to get tungsten out of grass in your back yard, as is a claim for 20 bucks printed on a Treasury note.

The value of money, as Aristotle observed, is determined by what it will BUY.

Hence, the howls about INFLATION. I'll say inflation. Baruch will NOT want inflation until he has got out money and put it into something else, or until he is two jumps ahead of the public in unloading a dying currency like the British STERLING, and getting into Pesos or [some thing able to rise if anything in the western hemisphere] can be considered as rising or promising.

OVER a hundred years of stealing and cheating the South Americans is NOT [the] basis for lasting delight. Morgenthau's government can pump money OUT of the AMERICAN people and spend it on Brazilian Ambassadors, it can LEND it to insolvent countries, who have neither the intention nor the capacity to REPAY it.

The banks can UNLOAD some of the bonds onto suckers, of whom the United States seems to possess a super-Loeb-chart supply. CHEAP agricultural products can be BOUGHT in South America and dumped into North America to the ruin of North American farmers so long as the ships will carry the stuff. BUT you can not get tungsten or even petroleum out of the carcasses of Brazilian ambassadors.

In fact your chief purchases in South America seem to be GOVERNMENTS, and you have yourself got more government than you can use.

You are tied up to Moscow and you have not yet the faintest conception of what that union means.

You are tied up to England in a somewhat de pressing hour. BUT the knot either may or may not prove a slip knot or noose. When the strangulation becomes excessively painful, Winston's name may be spelled PAUL REYNAUD.

You should keep an open eye on these possibilities. I know Franklin has his EYE on Australia and on Madagascar and on the African gold coast the Belgian Congo, Liberia, and the whatnots.

BUT the dawg in the fable also had his eye on the meat, reflected meat in the water. The aqueous metaphor may be invidious.

If I start on all the whatnots and the might have beens, this talk may start gettin' depressin'.

God Almighty, you go get out your readin' books. They say no man knows more than his grandad. If you can't learn about money from Jackson, Adams (I mean John Adams) and Van Buren, I dunno when you are I going to start learning to read. Of course, very few people HAVE read any history and it will become increasingly difficult for you to get the real books. Henry Adams' *Life of Gallatin* cost 35 dollars last time I heard: and was out of print, nacterly, at that time. So I don't even know what is in it. But you MUST someday either DIE or learn the nature of money.

I told you about that chap in a prison camp, writin' to ME for some of my books on economics.

Seemed to me a bit late. But anyhow, he is still livin'. You CAN read about money in a Gefangenenlager, but you can't read about it in Davy Jones s locker. You can NOT. When are you startin?

INTEREST on money. When does it become a title to what don't exist? When can you divide the fruits of nature and Labor?

You can divide 'em AFTER the harvest. England, by REFUSIN' to put that into law, is now losing India. Hong Kong, Singapore, Rangoon, Bombay tomorrow. CAUSE she would collect taxes before the harvest. Farmer hadn't got any money. Even TITHES can not be paid before harvest, so Hindoo had to borrow MONEY from the bunyah, the kike, to PAY taxes, and got more and more into debt.

DEBT. Debt, or the white man's burden. The people of the United States may be fairly low in the scale. I doubt if they are much lower than others, but your Washington government still HOPES that South American Indians are and WILL STAY sufficiently ignorant of how bank swindles are swoggled, to keep a gang of thieves above water, for the next twenty years.

The last hope of [the] North American war party is a victory in South America.

#23 (April 9, 1942) U.S.(B28)
INDECISION

That yaller hound Dawg Franklin Roosevelt was complainin' the other day about "indecision" or people favorin' indecision. I trust there is nothin' Undecided about my position.

I think Roosevelt ought to be jailed, if a committee of doctors thinks him responsible for his actions, and I think he ought to be in a high walled gook house, or insane asylum if he is NOT.

And I do not belong to that romantic school of writers who think lunatics are interestin' or that their characters are necessarily more admirable than those of plain low down crooks.

I trust this statement is perfectly DECIDED, and that Lord Halifax will not get any more free feeds with Finkelstein. To have conspired to bring down the United States to a level where Finkelstein can get by the Ellis Island or other port authorities on ANY excuse whatever is to deserve ILL of the American people.

And I think Mr. Morgenthau is outside Sing Sing, through an IMPERFECTION, or indecision or lack of foresight on the part of our national legislators. I trust there is nothin' undecided about that statement EITHER.

I do like to be CLEAR. SOVEREIGNTY inheres in the right to issue money, and the American sovereignty belongs by LAW to the people, and their representatives in CONGRESS have the right to issue money and determine the value thereof. And one hundred and twenty MILLION suckers have lamentably failed to insist on the observation of this "DECIDED law," and have been DIDDLED since along about the time Abe Lincoln was getting himself bumped off. Since then the people OUTSIDE Nebrasky and Dakota have been signally slack about demanding a legal GOVERNMENT of our country. AND there is NO time like the present to STOP being such asses as the American people have been for the past 80 years, or 79 years or whatever.

THAT is the first point.

The point at which embezzlement of the nation's funds on the part of high officers becomes treason can probably be decided only by jurists, and not by a hand picked set of JUDGES hired to support illegality. BUT the swindles performed by the present administration should be ANALYZED carefully while there is still some faint memory left among us as to what the United States Constitution once was.

The American nation will never win a war or a peace or anything more than the support of a few BRIBED

South American ambassadors and bought governments, as long as the Frankfurter, Lehman, Morgenthau, Roosevelt amalgamation is settin' on , the top of our government, not if the war goes on FORTY years; you won't win it with that set of Kikettes running the nation, and the treasury acting like one huge running sore. And I haven't the latest items, I have only some old reports signed by the mute in the treasury. I use the term mute in its technical, its highly technical, significance.

I trust I am bein' clear and decided. I objected to having the United States governed by British espionage service. I object to having it governed by secret committees who have NO responsibility for the government and NONE by law to the people. I trust I am being DECIDED.

AND I do NOT want the United States to lose Hawaii. I do not much hanker to have us become a race of cheats and thieves makin' war (de facto) on the South American people for the sake of a job lot of loan sharks, but that may be beside the immediate question. A government worthy of the name from 1932 onward WOULD have made sure of the Caribbean defenses, instead of dragging Japan into war.

That is the sort of thing that I incline to regard with disfavor. I mean the neglect of what is near, for the sake of attempting to starve out some far distant nation in the interest of a kike-like Sassoon, or some other hook-nosed exotic. I am not flattering some of the so-called old timers. The stock broker is NOT my ideal.

He is NOT a sport. A poker player plays with his own money; if he loses, he loses. A man who buys a lottery ticket takes his chance with the other purchasers of lottery tickets, neither gambles with the bread of the people.

Hence the old disparagement or contempt for stock jobbers, long away back when there still was some perception of ethics, and men were supposed to LOOK at the consequences of their acts, before thinking they were being both honest and clever. This remark will make me exceedingly unpopular among the American rich, if any of'em become aware of my saying it. There are various devious and twisty ways of arguing about the uses of short selling, etc., none of'em, NONE of'em would cut any ice with a jury of IMPARTIAL and disinterested men sufficiently intelligent to understand the question. NONE of'em have any ethical weight. A century ago a congressman could rise to the creation of such a phrase as "a very undigested system of ethics."

That is what the stockbrokers have mostly got wrong with'em.

Except those who say frankly that they are predatory ANIMALS, and want to rob and predate. Well, that predatory spirit is NOT inspirin' Europe at this present moment. Certain primitive types go out of fashion, one might almost believe in social progress, the cave man, the robber baron, etc. are not in the front line. They are relegated to history. And anyone interested in the theory of historic PHASE might by now lay a conjecture as to whether the old Wall Street ideal of robbin' the widdys and orphans by means of stock deals, and rigged markets etc., may not be driftin' OUT of the picture.

EUROPE is on. Europe is distinctly ON to the speculation racket. On to what it does to a country, how it injures the plain common people.

Hence of course Mr. Eden's war. Mr. Churchill's war, Mr. Roosevelt's WAR, and the support or pursuit [or at least the tail end] CHASE of that war by six hundred renters of bench room in the British Westminster Parliament. An assorted set of skin games; sort of palm' out in the bright lexicon of European Youth, in this the year XX of the Fascist Era. ALL in favor of the men who want to do an honest day's work either physical or mental, or by using skill that combines both the labor of hand and brain, and git for it a wage that will support at least a man, his wife and two children. I said two children MINIMUM, cause if two people don't reproduce two people, the race DIMINISHES and you get invaded: as the United States has been invaded by VERMIN, among whom the Rothschild, and Sassoon, and Warburg, are more deadly than syphilis.

The danger to the United States as a system of government is NOT from Japan, but from Jewry, and whether that invasion has been absolutely SUCCESSFUL, having been gradual since 1863, but accelerated since Taft was eased out of the White House.

Waaal, that remains to be seen. But if the remains of the AMERICAN settlers population, if the remains of the races that got there and made the country don't git into action shortly, then the United States of America will register one K.O. or Knock Out. And it will be pretty right as decisive as any executive can desire. Possibly the LAST chance for the American SYSTEM of government will occur in the oncoming Autumn.

Ezra Pound trying to tell you. The danger is not that you WILL BE invaded, it is that you HAVE BEEN invaded.

#24 (April 12, 1942) U.K.(B26)
COMIC RELIEF

I came alongside a COMIC paper the other day, English of course. It was ten or twelve days old, that is, the DATE antedated the day I read it by 10 or 12 days, via Lisbon. But in another sense it was "Old"; it might have been the TIMES for March 1912, so far as the naked eye could perceive. And I first groaned "how LONG can they keep on saying it?" Then I hit an article about Italy, "Voices of Fascist ITALY."

And my face was wreathed in smiles, I declined to hand over the paper to a friend, I wanted the cream for myself, precisely for this broadcast, which will be delayed into April or mebbe MAY, 'cause I have more serious communications to make to you. But some day or other I shall read out my notes on the "Old Thunder er," old thunderer still mousin' along.

I'll probably read those notes some day when there is a lull, some day when you ain't losin' a Hong Kong, or a Singapore, or Rangoon, or Bombay or Calcutty. That will be after I have remitted the museum piece, the evidence copy from Printing House, repaired square to its owner, who is a collector of such things. Of course the nature of the object bein' the same, I shan't have to say anything much new. I mean anything I hadn't already said 30 years ago in 1912 about the venomous nature and dangerousness to the people of that frowsy old paper.

Ellerrnan Jew influence didn't cure it. AND of course like all prestidigitators the Times takes the eye OFF the immediate, geographically, spatially, *raumlich*, visible object.

The Times does NOT tell you about the conditions in the collieries [and] potteries, what were distressed areas before this war was got goin', nothing about the people who petitioned from Coventry for example. NO the Times don't bring us much news of England, except insofar as it shows us a state of mind.

No, no, the Times tells us about Italy. That is an accident, 'cause of course the Times was printed to tell you about ITALY, and you are such mugs you believe it. The special correspondent, NO *raumlich*, or spatial or geographic address given, not his lodge number or his kahal cabala indication. I think he is a subjected Aryan, from the writin'. I have met Englanders of his mental calibre.

Wall, he starts off, and somewhere in the .very first sentence he sez "the maintainance of war sentiment in Italy becomes an increasingly hard problem."

Oh, is THAT so? sez the aristocrat, wrinklin' up his nose with amusement.

So I continue readin' the tidbits:

"A SINISTER image HAUNTS the rulers of Italy. It portrays (I'spose in some kind of language an image can portray, but I ain't yet seen an IMAGE portrayin'; if the word portray means to paint a portrait.

But let us pass the Times writer choice of words.) It PORTRAYS Britain emerging from the present struggle impoverished but still sound and strong. It portrays America turning her mighty industry ... and SO forth.

Waaal, now really. If some of the Sassoon's last opium cargoes got toted up from what is now Shonanko, into the Printing House Square or Holland Park West, or wherever, there may be an IMAGE portrayin'. But the only reaction to America having an industry I have read was one about the multiplication of bed bugs; that was considered beneath the dignity of Rome radio, but might in time be found to be the only adequate reply to such nonsense.

As to Britain's FUTURE might, you git "420," *quattro cento venti*; the Italian penny comic and you will find what Italy is FEELING and thinking; during the 1914 unpleasantness "420" used to bring weekly pleasure to thousands with its "IMAGES" of Franz Josef. That is now what Italy THINKS about Roosevelt and England. And as for being strong but impoverished, there are still tender hearts, NO longer anglophile in general; but having traces of friendship for personal friends IN England and they have been known to wonder whether people who had 1000 sterling per annum will after this war have 100, and those that had 100, whether they will have 20 left'em or the purchasing power of 20 pounds per annum left to their credit.

And IMPOVERISHMENT is not strength. Neither is the loss of your eastern possessions and the British Broadcasting Company view that Malta is a (textually) "LONELY OUTPOST of empire," used to be umbelicus in my time; in the days of my heady youth.

After the comic prelude of the anonymous "special correspondent" not even alleged to be over in Lisbon, probably in Kensington West or South West, after the comic prelude he gets a bit dirty: usual mean streak of a man with a weak case. Then he talks about Apuleius and so forth. Dis liking Italian broadcasts.

Why don't he stand up to the broadcasts from Rome transmitted in English? Why is he such an abject moral and intellectual coward that he DARE not face the arguments about money that go over this air from me, as an independent speaker, and from the REGULAR staff speakers, whenever they touch on the problem of making money by FOUNTAIN pen scribblin' instead of doing an honest day s work?

Why do ALL the British papers and ALL the British Broadcasting Company bunkosteers keep so gingerly OFF all the ground where there is ideological COMBAT? Worse funk-holers [than] the Whore Behsha WHERE are the Coventry marchers? Where are the Green Shirts? Suppressed of course [This] visible image EMBODYING thought on the hoof was prohibited before the Jews got you to fighting In the whole of your rotten parasitic ranks the whole of the British Broadcasting Company hireling company NO ONE dares and no one wants and no one would be there if they did want or dare to TOUCH the real issues.

Monopoly of gold components of your gold exchange, nature of money, how it is issued, how the people are bled, state of health in Your ISLAND.

Now to get down to brass tacks, to answer that ass in the Times. No ONE here expects you to do ANYTHING in this war save to LOSE it. From Dunkirk to Dakar, with at most a few successes over your onetime ALLIES. No one expects you to do anything with or IN this war save to LOSE it. BOTH to Germany *and* to Roosevelt.

Roosevelt portrayin' (if you like the word) JEWRY No one expects you to do anything in or with this war but to lose it. If that expectation is an illusion it nevertheless EXISTS so that when the gent in the Fly Fisher s dub writes his next article, let him say that ENGLAND expects to emerge impoverished but fierce as [the] stone Trafalgar Square fountain lion of Briton, not as a stuffed lion skin, used as a bed mat.

But fer Gawd's sake let him lay off saying this is what ITALY looks to. Italy just ain't got that kind of jimjams. NO ONE here is surprised one atom at your fighting the war badly, from Dunkirk to Dakar, from Hong Kong to Calcutty. One is mildly set to wonder WHY you are fighting Europe instead of fighting Marx and P. Spencer, and Karl Marx and Lyons, and the one hundred enemies that had got you by the short hairs: and got you hog-tied BEFORE the war started. Over DANZIG, allegedly.

Over a year ago a man of the former social age, an international tennis ace, unsuspectible of political passions, the kind that jokes about these things, said his wife said to him, "WHY ever do they (meaning the English) FIGHT the Germans? Don't they know that is all the Germans CAN do? Why do they go to WAR?"

Now firstly, the lady was inexact, as anyone who has read enough German philosophy, or heard Johnnie Bach's music, or seen Albrecht Durer's painting, or knows the work of the Frobenius Forschung's Institute KNOWS. The Germans have quite a lot of assorted abilities.

But the question SUBSISTS? WHY did the people of England LET them selves get catched by the short hairs and HOG-tied, and led into losing the eastern parts of their empire, and getting allied to red Russia?

Let the TIMES go into THESE things—TELL PAPA! WHY did the Times, which LOST YOU Hong Kong, and Singapore, and Rangoon KEEP the REAL news and the real thought of the past 50 years (yaaas, not 20 but 50) years OUT of its columns. What causes that?

Well my time at this microphone is drawin' to a close for this evening and I haven't leisure to go into the other columns of that issue of the Old Thunderer. But when you are sad and downhearted, git out your back issues of the Times Newspaper of London, if they haven't been confis cated by the dog-catcher to make biscuit for miner's children, and lull yourself with Tennysonian legends, such as "Dutch leadership in the Indies," rivaling that of Luzon, resistance, all merry and bright.

I do hate to return that stray copy of the Old Thunderer to its owner. Lord knows when I shall see yet another one, and having my head chuck full of things I want to emit to you, it will be a long time before I again animadvert to the paleozoic habits of your island crustaceans.

#25 (April 13, 1942) U.S.(B20)
QUESTION OF MOTIVE

I do not expect perfect and COMplete comprehension of these discourses on the part of all of my audience.

I should be content if I get over even a small part of what I am driving at, and WHY I am drivin'. For over 30 years I have been driving at some of the same objective objectives.

I thought in 1908 and before then that a nation's literature IS important. State of a nation's literature, is important. Words, means of communication, literature, the most condensed form of communication, communication of the most basic and essential facts, ideas necessary for leading the good life, registered in the best books.

And man's duty, as soon as he is fully a man, is to keep those books, to keep that tradition available.

Keep it handy. And the public: American and English, but for the moment let me stick to the United States of America. [The] American public [is] rather like that lunatic in Pea's novel *Moscardino,* chap in gook house who just wouldn't believe that there could be enough microbes on the back of a postage stamp to knock a man cold. Thought it was doctors' fables, in fact thought the doctors had heard it from other gooks in the asylum.

Waal, the Americans and the English just couldn't believe that it made any difference what a man or a nation put inside its head via its reading.

Hence I was supposed to exaggerate when I bust out against such dung heaps of perfumed pus as the Atlantic Monthly, and Harper's and Scribner's, as they were in the year 1900 and ceased not essentially to be as long as they lasted. The stink of stale perfume contains the deadly gasses which finally poison. No language could quite cover the loathing I feel for a Sedgewick, but it doubtless seems exaggerated. Later in London I did a *sottisier,* trying to make a few people see why the printed matter on sale in that city would finally kill off the inhabitants; witness Dunkirk.

The XIX stinking century saw what is called an advance in science. People learned that bacilli can kill.

Prophylaxis entered the general mind, but an older concept got knocked OUT of the popular mind. It had been possibly once a good concept, but it had decayed. It was what is or was called a theological concept.

The age, called the age of faith, thought a wrong idea could bring evil.

In the Middle Ages they got a bit fantastic, got their eyes off the here and now, and thought the bad idea would land a man in perdition, eternal flames, purgatory, or whatever.

Then something got tangled, and the people got fanatic, and heretics were burned and so forth. And M. Voltaire tried to get that untangled, worked all his life against the cruelties of fanaticism, was called an atheist; which he was NOT. I strongly suspect that almost no heretics were burnt, at least not at the beginning, except those who interfered with the usury racket, those whose ideas were seen as inimical to the usury racket, leaving out the question. But so far as I know no research has ever been done along these lines. I am speaking of heretics proper, ideology, not people who went into witch persecutions.

The idea that a WRONG idea could damage people here and now was perhaps not fully developed.

The British theory was that free speech was a blow hole. Let'em TALK and they will DO nothing. Hyde Park corner, etc.

Gus Flaubert and I myself, and diverse others, includin' if you must go so far back, Mencius and Confucius, saw something worse than just one BAD idea, and that was the corruption of the whole and TOTAL means of communication of all ideas whatsoever. The corruption of language, the destruction of all precision in terminology, which takes man back and down to the status of beasts, or what beasts are SUPPOSED to be; namely, unable to communicate with one another.

Yet even animals, packs of wolves, and wild dogs do seem to under stand each other, and to collaborate. Very well, I set up and gradually got some ideas as to combat tin' this universal gonorrhea of language and this rotting of ALL Printed means of communication, monthlies, dailies, weeklies, mercantilist publishing system.

All of which has bloody well dished and ditched the pore old British iniquitous empire. Too late to save that now. And anyhow, I am speaking to the United States of America. Forty years ago Brooks Adams made a quite good study of England, foreseein' she would bust up, and part go to the United States of America and part go to Germany with, if I remember it right, Japan gettin' a look in. Nacherly VERY few people read Mr. Adams. I only know of ONE Englishman who has quoted him.

And I am not enamoured of retrospect. I ought to have been given Brooks Adams when I was havin' a shot at American history in the University of Pennsylvania—that's 40 years ago. Might have accelerated me in giving him a little publicity. In fact ALL history teachin' in American universities ought to have got hold of Brooks Adams THEN, 1897–1900, 1903 his best volumes.

His weak an' pindlin' young brother Henry was not the man that his elder brother Brooks was. Brooks seeing what had happened in history, seem' it pretty clearly, foreseeing what would happen in HIS time, but not seeing beyond that. Knowing that an age of faith, or ages of faith had existed, but did not see the next one. Livin', you may say, in his own phase. Foreseein' the down flop of England, that is, of the Empire, noting symptoms of England's decline, which the English remained deaf to, and blind to.

BUT not foreseeing the Italian rise, not foreseeing the change of phase: from material to volitional.

Reactin' against John Quincy Adams' judized form of religion. I forget where he notes that, maybe in the preface to his book on New England.

ANYhow trying to figure out where John Quincy Adams, whom he greatly admired, had gone off the rails, not gittin' back to his great grandad John Adams, the father of his country and inventor to some extent of General Washington.

Waaal, can't get it all into one discourse. But if there is still some campus not yet invaded by the hosts of Belial and Jewry not wholly squashed under the dung-flow from Wall Street and Washington, I suggest you start taking notes and figures. Figure out this affair of the ruin of language, the falsification of all reports in the well paid magazines, the falsification of newsprint. And ALSO the attack on historic knowledge. The rise of TALMUDIC schools, quite UNNOTICED by the high class periodicals. Note when America began to be filled with talmudic schools, not listed and having big sign boards. Note when American history went out of fashion. When the kids in the lower grades heard of Lenin and Marx and Trotsky, and not so much of Lincoln and Washington. Watch the gradual creep up of obscurantism, the neglect, *ab initio*, from the start, of John Adams, Van Buren, and Johnson.

There ought to be 700 STUDENTS, and 30 professors, digging into this question, these questions.

SOME DAY you will need to KNOW, need to know more than you do at present.

Lord knows what will come to you first.

#26 (April 16, 1942) U.S.(B33)
CLARIFICATION

For the United States to be makin' war on Italy AND on Europe is just plain damn nonsense and every native born American of American stock KNOWS that it is plain downright damn nonsense.

And for this state of things Franklin Roosevelt is more than any other one man responsible. Of course he was puffed up, and put thaar, or kept thaar, and that dirty Kike Lippmann has declared that Roosevelt is MOVED by others; and does not act *proprio motu*.

All of which whatnesses do NOT adulterate the fact that WAR between the United States and Europe is nonsense. And its makers ought to be smacked.

How long it is going to take the American people to make at least a partial return toward their senses, I know not, I do not know.

I suggest yet again that you look at the way the WAR, this war, has been wangled. And HOW it has been conducted. FIRST, the American people were SANE enough to see that the war was phony.

DANZIG, Poland, and all the rest of it, COOKED and the American people KNEW it was cooked. Second, England's offensives effective against neutrals and Allies. Third, the United States offensives effective against England, Iceland, and Venezuela, at the cost of losin' the Philippines. Well, damn the Philippines.

We promised'em independence, and the dirt in our national makeup prevented our keepin' the promise.

Our conduct as a nation to various is lands, let alone to South American republics, is NOT our title to glory. And Aguinaldo has as good a right to the Philippines as any God damn Jew in Roosevelt's family caballa. I do hate to see Hawaii endangered. We got the Sandwich Islands more or less decently, and they could have been held as a defensive position.

The Philippines WERE NOT, they were an offensive position, and the conduct of Roosevelt's government was plain downright silly, not to say nasty, not to say mean, not to say stinkin', it was all of these things put together.

Anyhow, one of the LIES of this war is the LIE about the anti-Axis alliances. Russia is NOT Britain's ally but her enemy, America is NOT Britain's ally but her enemy.

Chiang Kike Chek is the prize buyer of gold bricks, and where did Soong git his money? Mrs. Chiang Kike is always flittin' and floatin' in Semite entourages. If Charlie Soong warn't staked out by kikedom, you come here and tell papa. I can't prove this assertion, but I await any disproof, and I don't expect it to be forthcomin'.

The phrase, cut off the NOSE to spite the face, may seem invidious and SUGgestive. "Wasn't she a silly slut, to sell her bed and lie in dirt?" Yaas, SHE was, Margery Daw or Columbia, Solomon's jewel.

You have cut your nose off to the extent of three summer vacations in Europe. You have cut your nose off to the extent of what you haven't had in those three years in the way of cultural contacts and the amenities.

Whatever is happening in the way of BASHING abundance INSIDE the United State of America you know better than I do, and I am not going to tell you about Cincinnati. I have heard British fools talk about Italy which they had not visited. I have seen men get het up about what happens in other countries, meaning what is SAID to happen in other countries. And what they have read in the noozwypers, and I am not going to participate in that form of foolery.

YOU TELL ME about what is going on in the United States of America and I'll tell you what I see here in Italy. That will be fair exchange and no kikery.

I do NOT admire your making war on Finland, Iceland and Venezuela, on the pretense that you don't like Hitler's municipal government.

Or that you steal from other countries because they are incapable of governing themselves, or because their governors are incapable of stealing from them. Neither, I think, do you.

EIGHTY years peace for England would have been useful to England. Thirty years peace for the United State of America would have been useful to YOU. It would have meant a whole generation.

I don't know how long the Pacific would have maintained its status quo, but I am right, downright certain that I could have done BETTER in dealin' with Japan than any of Mr. Roosevelt's lowbrow assistants, among whom I know of none who was fit for the Japanese mission.

England was bilked, and that was NOT done without United States assistance. Well, I don't admire the men who assisted. And neither, I think, do YOU.

As to what you can do to get out of it, that is another story. Haven't you got any folks at home who can tell you? After all my mission in life had been rather special. Maybe that was my error, but one can't be in ten places at once. I believe, like bed rock, I believe, that if the American people had been consulted in 1938–39 and 40 and 41 NINETY percent of the American people would have been content to have the American government stick to its best traditions, to stay OUT of international shindies, and to USE the United States prestige. (We HAD some prestige in those days.) And the American people would have wanted used to get a SANE, peaceful arrangement of the problems of Europe. And a clean government in Washington would have aimed at that target. When, before Gawd, are we going to get a clean government?

It is time for the American people to start gettin' ready to think about that.

Whether Frankie is a gook or a kike, I don't think the American people LIKE him. I don't think they wanted him back in the White House. And the election figures don't prove it. They may possibly prove the DEFECTS of the American electoral system and the power of bribery and corruption. And then again they may not. The only excuse of most voters was "you don't vote against Santa Claus." Look what Santa has brought you now. Waaal ole Franklin Kris Kingle, Sant Nicalaus, ain't got any live children back out of the pork barrel. If that is too mixed a metaphor, let me remind you of the old French chanson, about St. Nicholas. Frankie looks to me more like gettin' the live young INTO the salt pork barrel than rescuing the little dears out of it.

As for the English, nine of'em out of ten do NOT believe they ought to be fighting the Germans. And that goes a long way to explain why a lot of them don't seem anxious to do it. They don't like their empire being ruined. They don't want their island invaded.

But nine of'em out of TEN do NOT believe they ought to be fighting the Germans. That is, down there under their skulls, down under their thick bully hides they DO NOT think they ought to be fightin' the Germans. They DO not believe in Bolshevik methods, or in the Bolshevik propaganda. None of it is spontaneous in England, and a lot of British KNOW the Bolos are HIRED.

Some of'em, not the nicest among'em, think, oh yes, they OUGHT to fight Italy cause Italy is small on the map, and the small ought to be jumped on. That is British tradition. But they do NOT think they ought to be fighting the Germans, and they do NOT want to see geography books with England's empire reduced to probable figures: but they do NOT think they ought to be fighting the Germans.

Well, think it over.

#27 (April 19, 1942) U.K.(B29)
TO SOCIAL CREDITORS

Last Sunday I came on some typed pages signed "W.A. Nyland," Secretary *pro tem*. That seems all a long way back in faded lavender. A time like this gives one time to go thru quite a lot [of] postal matter that one hadn't time to look at very thoroughly when it arrived.

A time like this, when the postal service with the Western Hemisphere is somewhat reduced. Result, so far as my private life is concerned, is that not bein' able to continue private correspondence by letter with the more lively American youth, gentry and professoriate, I had to stir round and git onto the air, only line [left] me.

Now I ask Social Creditors if anyone of'em except Major Douglas gave in the old days—the dim and distant 20s or the almost as dim 1830 and 35s—ANY thought as to the sort of paralysis that allus seemed to creep into the Social Credit movement, about as soon as it got near action.

I have told you of Senator Cutting's hope, and his disappointment. Aberhart may for all I know still rule in Calgarry, like Brian Duff in— — still. The jewbrew and rabbinical stations do NOT stress either present or past of Alberta province.

Mebbe no one has told'em you OUGHT, you really ought NOT to ask the pliant public to put a stamp on its stamp scrip once a WEEK. Lord knows I have tried in my time to stop a fairly wide set of foolishnesses on [the] part of people who LACK historic perspective, or who failed to grasp the inner workin's of economic mechanisms, and the relations between one expression of monetary honesty and another.

I am not concerned with the merits of particular bills, I am not concerned with the injected paralysis that has stopped any and all bills having economic basis in honesty since 1873, or say since 1863, gettin' back to the start of the present phase of the unending swindle. Is that paralysis due to the Talmud? Or to the spieir [?] whereof the Talmud is the most complete (and dirty) and thorough verbal manifestation extant?

There is no doubt that C.H. Douglas began to notice some years ago that certain elements, call'em elements, seemed to penetrate into the works of the Social Creditors' movement just about the time it seemed to be about to be real. In fact his writin's during the three years precedin' Mr.

Churchill's new war were largely spent in lookin' for the source of these penetrations, these injections of paralysis. He left off his a plus b, or left it in the background and got right out with Henry Ford in IDENTIFYIN' the Hebrews as a possible source of infection. And the circulatability of his publications got lower and lower.

Now what do you think causes that? And what do you think you can or could do to UNcause it, not necessarily re the a plus b theorem but in the case of ANY and every economic reform or basic reorganization that you chose to believe in?

You say: change in direction of will. All right, say you had wild imagination. Say you had guts enough to IMAGINE a man you really would like to see in the White House: I mean would REALLY think ought to be in the White House.

What would you DO? Would you communicate your thought to your neighbor? What would he do?

What effect would it have on the oncomin' elections, 1942, 1944? Has anybody but the present speaker had any such flight of poetic fancy dunn' the past 20 years? You can't tell me that Harding or Coolidge or any of'em were chosen, nominated because anybody really felt: well now, that is what we need in the White House.

Wouldn't that fellow just add to the American tradition?

Well what about it? What would happen IF every American over the age of 21 suddenly voted for what he wanted? I don't mean, for just what he felt to be the lesser evil, the less rotten apple? Now just think a minute; supposin' you went down to Washington and walked up the front path to the White House.

What would you like to find sittin' in a rockin' chair on the lawn, or find inside in a drawin' room, to greet you as the American President?

Just what qualifications ought the fellow to have whom you would like to find in there? Who would make you feel that his presence added, yes, I say, added to the joy of bein' alive?

Yes, I know it is a vision. I never had it but once. Nobody ever told me I was wrong; in fact nobody ever said while I was in America three years ago, nobody said I was foolish, they just thought it impractical. They didn't think he could get there. Or mebbe that was the trouble; mebbe they DID think he could get there.

Of course the nomination has sometimes been quite within reach of almost impecunious people. I have been given extremely low figures as to the bottom price for the ante, which depends of course on the year, and the state of the political market. But mebbe those low figures only apply to duds, whom the wise guys just KNOW won't be elected.

Such I suppose is democracy. Or perhaps such is the modesty of political parties.

Well, up in BREMEN they seem to have decided that you folks can't keep your minds on any one thing more'n about three minutes. I used to listen to their Mirror, now I hear their magazine. Three minutes talk, then a gigue tune. Mebbe Rome would give me with music included if I put up a howl. Not every topic NEEDS 12 and 2½ minutes. Sometime I feel just like askin' a string of questions; as fer example: WHY do you Yanks fall for the FOREIGN or exotic wheeze? I mean Jews from all over Europe come to America, and you think they are Frenchmen and Dutchmen. Now why is that?

And then this appointin' ambassadors to imaginary unlanded governments? Ought I to get ambassadors appointed every time one of my Italian friends wants to ask me what time is it or whether Faulkner is better'n Caldwell, and WHICH Caidwell or whether Josh Bathos writes better'n Bromfield, or what's become of that refined almost writer Mr. Thornton Wilder? Do you dare fall for it? I mean this elevated from rank of minister to that of dambastador, in order to treat with the government of Ruthenia, at 29 Wardour Street, third floor back, W.C. in London?

I should like to see that subject treated in Puck or Judge, if those monuments of the ash-barrel era still flourish. Puck used to be Democrat and Judge Republican, back in 1892. Have they conserved their old sense of coarse humor, coarse but robust and healthy, or are they all peter'd out? I mean Arno'ed.

Lookin' back and rememberin' my far distant childhood on the corner of 47th and Madison Avenue where there is now such [a?] sumptuous Hotel Accommodation Thinkin', thinkin of my Great Aunt's family furniture, moved a few blocks up the street. I wonder if the ole grand piano is still workin' for the folks that took over, foreclosed the mortgage, or something, anyhow, sold the old lady up.

And Mr. Fouquet, and pop Quackenbush, all that generation that remembered the Civil War. All gone with the ash barrels. Think of swell ballroom, right where my Great Uncle used to keep his bunch of bananas, and I used to play chequers with him; my old Great Aunt's black man of general all work, or rather any work, some work, that he used to dodge to play chequers on top of the apple barrel, before the days of the Windsor Fire, Two Hotels, Windsor and Buckingham, ornament of Fifth Avenue, back before you kids remember.

An' yaller Martha. She used to take snuff. That's a long time before the great night life of Harlem.

Back when Owen Wister, it may have been, wrote "Philosophy 4"—now why do I think of that? And why did that darkie porter in Grand Central Station look at the E. initial before my name on my suitcase in 1939 and say: Now how do I come to know that, that E. stands for Ezra? Sort of nearly undersized porter.

My mind goes back to before the invasion. I mean I suppose that is what is occurrin' in my psychology leadin' me up to the question: Have you GAINED by the interval? WHAT have you gained by the interval, from 4 to 8 million invaders, all part of a widely distributed RACE, that has a radio out by San Diego or somewhere, known as the universal world Jewry station, or some similar title, and does a HIGHLY organized 7 to 7 to 7 [for] 6 or 8 million people of a decidedly OTHER race; in the midst of 100 million or so assorted descendents of people racially European, MEAN anything for the welfare or illfare of the UNorganized 100 million? And if so, how so? And sailors don't care? Whalers don't care, landlubbers seem fairly indifferent.

Ernest Poole might write a book on the subject. Another bloke whose name I forget might write a book on the subject. Wrote a novel I rather liked, about a New England family goin' to seed on a farm that was like a white elephant. I mentioned it and was promptly reproved by a highbrow friend (not a professor) who assured me that that novelist would never write a somethin' or other. Marquand, that's the fellow's name, Marquand the novelist.

Well, I don't take such high ground. I think all those American novelists who try to set down a slice of history ought to get credit for it. Even if they go a bit heavy, or leave in 40 pages in 3 or 4 hundred that just aren't quite book-writin'. But still you get a bit of Van Buren, or a bit of some epoch that young America OUGHT to know more of; 1830 or 1930, but at least tryin' to peg down some part of our white man's heritage and tradition. Not bein' cute and cunnin', but trying to tell the next generation at least part of what ought to be known.

That's why I keep on hammerin' on the disgrace to the nation implicit in not printin' Joe Gould. I mean that is one why. And Mr. McAlmon always printed in Paris. Two sets of men, tryin' to put down American history, one doin' it in meritorious novels, that the highbrows niff at snobistically, one set or a few scattered fragments doing impractical stuff, lack of national discipline, lack of civic responsibility.

Workin' in BOTH these branches of United States incompetence. Oh, little things, here and there, just a straw shows how the wind blows. And then the United States gets bumped OFF, like the frogs did. After more 50 years warnin'. And the frogs sellin' 15 thousand copies, a whole series of editions (Flammarion editions) where American author wouldn't sell 1500.

Mebbe that is part of the national trouble, part of the great American bellyache, part of the American IMMATURITY; to call it by no more harsh name.

And then the omissions, the things Mr. Dewey, Professor Davis Rich Dewey leaves OUT of his Financial History.

Well that's all for this spasm.

Ezra Pound at the microphone.

Why not have a real President?

#28 (April 20, 1942) U.S.(B34) ABERRATION

The Daily Mail of London got round a few weeks ago to reprinting one of those libelous photographs that were shot on board the REX last time I came into New York harbor.

Well, that did not harm, unless it cast a little indirect discredit on the capacity of American press photographers. The Daily Mail seemed to be followin' in the wake of the Sunday Times. The Mail contented itself to saying my admiration for fascism was notorious.

The "Special Correspondent" (address not given) of the Sunday Times, apart from an erroneous statement as to my views of the American President, used a qualifying statement saying that "Among Pound's many eccentricities and aberrations, his admiration of the Fascist regime in Italy has long been notorious." Both papers neglected to tell their British readers that I broadcast to ENGLAND now and again. That is not the point either.

What I am a lookm' at is this word ABERRATION. They call it an aberration for me to admire or whatever the present Italian system of government. Has a fascist government itself ABerrated, or has it aberred? Firstly, if it aberred, it aberred into drainin' a powerful lot of swamp land which OTHER Italian governments had been lookin' at since the time of Tiberius Caesar and signally failed to get DRY. Those swamps had been lying thaaar breedin' malaria for over two thousand years, sometimes a bright boy would take a smack at'em and dry up a bit or a corner. But the FASCIST regime lit in and got quite a lot of [it] dried, and under healthy cultivation.

Secondly, if I aberr, it [is] in the aberration of admirin' the increase of grain yielded in Italy.

Thirdly, fourthly, and etceterarialy, there is the question of national health, bein' improved, there is the question of the increase in living quarters for the NOT-rich sectors of the nation's community, there is the question of water supply.

Sixthly, etc. there is the question of electric power. So as they don't have [to] waste their substance buying dirty old smoke coal from England. Petrified frogs, Frenchies, biologically fixed, had been yapping about la hOOOOOOuille blanche for decades. Well, the Fascist REGIME got the

Italian railway runnin' by electricity. That is by lettin' water flow down wards, OVER some selected turbines. All of which is notorious, if it an't just a little bit more than I!

But it is merely material and my respect for the Fascist Regime, for FASCISM in fact, goes a bit further. Along about the time Tony tin-toes Eden was tellin' Italy where to get off at, and she did NOT GIT. There came a day when Italy sat up sassy and defied fifty-two so-called nations, England among'em.

That required something more than mere itch toward luxury economics. And the idea of having an airplane crash onto a battle ship did not START in Japan. About the time Tony's England was trying to bully NEW Italy, there was something here in this peninsula.

Do I aberr in admiring it?

I think I do not.

And at England's present condition, I wonder if the Sunday Timesers and their parishioners aren't mebby ready to wish some of their bosses had aberrated in similar manner. The aberration of an alliance with Japan, now wouldn't England have done better to aberr into an alliance with Japan, rather than being hoffed out of Shonanko, Hong Kong, and Rangoon? An alliance with Germany, rather than with a paralytic Jewed France?

Let us say the British Foreign office had committed a few aberrations along my line, would England be today a brighter and happier country? Instead of droppin' so many old naval bases and stations into Frank Roosenstein's pocket? I don't say Washington would have welcomed these moves, but I am opening up a line of Enquiry, about the word ABERRATION.

Perhaps I should also open up a line about representation. An Italian said to me yesterday, "But so many people in England have NO representation, you could have a party of a million people in England, and it might not have even ONE member in Parliament?" Here EVERY man of what ever trade or profession has the OPTION of joining up with his *sindacato*; he don't have to, but if he wants to be represented directly, that is the method. If he don't join up, his interests are nevertheless looked after, cause if he is a carpenter, or a rice grower, or a field worker, or a fellow that trims olive trees, there is the UNION, the *sindacato*, working up to the confederazione. It's thaaar to represent the interest of peasant, or carpenter, or dentist, or whatsoever. All of which may be notorious, at least plenty of people here know it, and nothing has been concealed. No secret back of the curtain conspiracies. No trade union leader can sell out to the employers, nor blackmail employees.

I, for example, would come under the confederation of artists and professional men, painters, doctors, writers, dentists, etc. WHAT Congressional representation or parliamentary representation have the professional classes had in the United States or England since the beginning of their government system?

Aberration? If this be an aberration, let me aberr. What bloody chance has the stray man, the individual in old style so-called democratic organization, in comparison to what he has in a corporate system, EMBODIED system?

Every peasant in Italy knows where to go and KICK if something ain't done to suit'em. And my Gawd they DO kick. Sometimes in the most silly manner. Like as I said in Rapallo, when they wouldn't have tubercle bugs taken out of their milk. The Italians are the greatest kickers on earth. Started back in the Quattrocento. Eyetalian individualism, development of the personality, raised to point of exaggeration, but enlightened the world.

Nothing less than the Fascist system would keep these people together. Some of the kickin' is aimless, but the mass of it keeps things movin' for ward. If I got a kick, I know where to take it. I take it to my confederazione. If I were part of a more numerous category, I would take it to the local agricultural centre; if I had any land whaar I could grow seed, I would go to the local *agrario* something or other, known to me as the florist's shop on the road to the station.

Who would [have] (and has, when I got inquisitive) gone up to the *cattedra ambulante* (which don't mean ambulatin' cathedral) but the traveling or mobile means of agricultural and horticultural education?

Yes, we HAVE in the United States state legislatures, etc. DO they cut any ice?

The American system was GOOD for 80 years, after which it was betrayed and defiled AT THE CENTRE, and the outlying parts grew steadily less efficient, and still less efficient.

I would like to see a little blood, or oxygen infused back into'em. Any how, whatever kind of a MESS you are in in America, with your farms mortgaged to milk trusts, England is in a worse mess. I'll say a worse mess. And I reckon even the Sunday Times is about ready to wish some of the stuffed British shirts had aberrated more in my fashion. Or to see that England would have been happier had she puked out the stuffed shirts and put in some fellows capable of similar ABERRATIONS. Similar I mean to what they call my aberrations.

#29 (April 23, 1942) U.S.(B35) MacLEISH

American news items, and the utterances of prominent Americans reach me, often with lamentable delays, and often I have to grope for the possible or probable original text, through an Italian translation.

Nevertheless the drift of Mr. MacLeish's remarks toward the end of March seems fairly clear. He has been given a gangster's brief; that is, he has been entrusted with the defense of a gang of criminals, and he is doin' his damndest.

I object, and have objected to the CRIME, regardless of who may be related to the men who have committed it. And I accept the conditions of the debate, namely that the Morgenthau-Lehman gang control 99% of ALL means of communication inside the U.S.A. and that they can drown out and buy out nearly all opposition. On top of which Roosevelt has, characteristically, resorted to blackmail. ANY man who does not accept the gigantic frauds perpetrated by the Morgenthau-Roosevelt treasury is to be held up as a traitor to the U.S.A.

The reply is, that any man who submits to Roosevelt's treason to the Republic commits breech of citizen's duty. There is NO connection between submitting to the Morgenthau-Roosevelt and winning this war or any other. There is NO patriotism in submitting to the prolonged and multiple frauds of the Roosevelt administration. And to try to make the present support of these frauds figure as LOYALTY to the American union, to the American Constitution, to the American heritage is just so much dirt, or buncomb. Doubtless the tactics of EVASION will be used to the utmost. Blackmail will be used to the utmost. But if the American people submit to either or both of these wheezes, the American people will be MUGS.

There are several historic facts which the opponents of the Morgenthau Lehmans would do well to dig up. Mr. MacLeish has not gone all out for the printing of the key facts of American history, in handy and available volumes. There are several historic facts which the opponents of the Morgenthau swindles would be well advised to extract and USE. Of course for you to look for my points, points of my biweekly talks in the maze of Jew covered American radio transmissions, is like lookin' fer one needle in a whole flock of hay stacks. And your press is NOT very open. However, if some lone watcher, or *ascoltator* or listener on Back Bay, or the top of the Blue Ridge DOES hear me, I suggest he make note and ask advocate Archibald whether it helps win ANYTHING to have the people pay two dollars for every dollar spent by the government. I ask whether the spirit of 76 is helped by flooding the lower ranks of the navy with street sweepings, whether war is won by mercantilist ethics, and in any case whether men like Knox, and Stimson, and Morgenthau can be expected to fill the heart of youth with martial ardor and the spirit of sacrifice. I ask Archie to say OPENLY why handing out four billion in excess profits on the gold wheeze, between 1932 and'40, handing it to a dirty gang of kike and hyper kikes on the London gold exchange, six firms, is expected to HELP Americanism, or why it should be regarded as a model of devotion to the American spirit. Or why ANY honest American should vote for the continuance of that swindle, or for keepin' in office the men and kikes who were responsible for puttin' it over the people.

And that of course is NOT the whole story of the Roosevelt, Lehman, Baruch, Morgenthau dippings. Dippings into the country's resources.

The break with our traditions exemplified by Donovan's intrigues in Yugoslavia is no Cornelia's jewel. In fact the MacLeish, Roosevelt yawp about patriotism is nothing but the gilding on the outside of the brick of base metal. Keeping Roosevelt in the White House is not essential to winning the war. The two things can be considered QUITE apart one from the other. Had you had the sense to ELIMINATE Roosevelt and his Jews, or the Jews and THEIR Mr. Roosevelt at the last elections you would not now be at war. That is one point. BUT to suppose that you will win the war by GOING ON being mugs in any and EVERY internal conflict, to suppose that you will strengthen the U.S. abroad by submitting to continued internal bleeding and swindling, is just so much nonsense or hoakum.

The first step toward a bright new world, so far as the rising American generation is concerned, is to get ONTO Roosevelt and all his works, and the second is to ELIMINATE him and all his damn gang from public life in America. The alternative is annihilation for the youth of America, and the END of everything decent the U.S. ever stood for. If you allow yourselves to be dazzled, if you are persuaded to identify the Morgenthau Baruch control of the U.S. by secret committees, or the Warburg bank wheeze with VICTORY, you are mugs. If you confuse these things and the profits on Army contracts even with national defense, you are plain downright suckers. I shall be highly interested to see whether Archibald takes up any of the points of this discourse. If he don't, some bright lad ought to help him. Someone ought to pick up a point here and there, over some faint lonely wave-length, and apply it right in the home, right in the home town or village. Your employers are said to be going over to Russia, to git red points on the sweat shop system. That don't mean liberty in the home village EITHER. Mess, fraud, and the destruction of national well-being INSIDE the nation are no proofs of fitness to extend the nation's power abroad, nor indicate [the] likelihood of so doing. Of course if the billions of dollars diddled out of the people by Roosevelt's faction are used in an election, they may win yet ANOTHER election. But that will not be equivalent to winning the war. NOR of course will it be equivalent to maintaining or rather restoring the American system of government, which is the last thing Roosevelt has ever appeared to desire, or the Jew's Mr. Wilson before him.

If Stalin's Russia is the ideal Trotsky and F. Delano version of paradise, then that is what they are headin' for. Archie among'em. But if the American people lie down yet again and take it, it will be a long time before plenty blooms on the American mountains. The bright new world will be a long, long time reachin' the Blue Ridge. Ask Archibald why he AVOIDS so many topics of interest.

Keep Roosevelt's gang in office and you will not ONLY lose the war abroad in both oceans but you will LOSE everything worth having at home. Ask Archie why don't he use his prestige and position in the cause of ENlightenment?

#30 (April 26, 1942)U.K.(B31)
BLAST

It is gettin' on to be nigh thirty years since Mr. Wyndham Lewis, the vorticist painter, began rootin' round and prospectin' the publication of an art magazine called BLAST, the word meaning commonly explosion of dynamite, etc., but connected in the arcane recesses of Mr. Lewis's mind with blastoderms and sources of life. And this magazine or manifesto was in its way a harbinger (I am never quite sure about that word harbinger), but it does seem to be generally accepted as meaning a sign of something about to come. Well, the other war came and prevented its being a periodical or annual publication, got out a second number in 1915 and that ended it, Gaudier-Brzeska the sculptor havin' been killed in the interim.

And that manifesto was the best we could then do toward assertin' what has now become known to the world, or at least to the European continent as the crisis OF the system. Crisis OF, not IN the system; not a crisis in side the system. But of the SYSTEM, crisis OF the system, DEL *sistema*, not merely *nel sistema*.

Now the particulars about the art movement, insofar as they affect merely painting and sculpture may not much matter in themselves, you will say. But the point is these things ONLY occur, changes like that in art and writin' ONLY occur when something moves deeper down, some thing gets going, something is workin' inside, and the LIVE artists, as distinct from exploiters and deadheads, get the itch to DO something about it, itch to do something LIKEWISE.

Anyhow, Blast appeared, and somewhere inside it or in some contemporary explosion of Wyndham's there was the statement: "MATTER when there is not certain amount of intelligence INSIDE it, decays and rots." It would have been a happier day for all England, if all England had looked at that sentence. Which marks the end of an era, marks the end of the Marxist era (if there was a Marxist era), marks the end of the XIXth century usurocracy and mercantilism. Matter in which there is not a certain amount of intelligence decays and ROTS.

Waal, Blast made a bit of a stir, mebbe on the surface. It penetrated into society circles, etc., New Zealand attacked it. The stinking old Manchester Guardian took six months to discover that Blast was satiric.

BLAST could have been RECONSTITUTIVE, if the body of England hadn't been too far gone, too far descended into a state of flaccidity to be able to react to the medicine.

A copy of Blast penetrated into the lofty purlieuws of the Beerbohm Tree family.

Yes, Blast was out for publicity, it was not hidin' its head like a violet. It was made to be seen; it was said to be two foot square; which it wasn't but it was as large, and its typographic display was as impressive as Mr. Leveridge, the printer, could be induced to give credit for. And the STAGE in those days, as I suppose it still is in England, was esteemed far more than mere art, or mere intellect; so for an ART paper to penetrate into the upper reaches, as it were, of SIR Herbert's ambience, was already a proof of something or other, I won't say vitality, but at least visibility. Cause Herb, SIR Herb, was not only IN the limelight, but OF it, he was as you might say, built out of limelight, constructed of limelight, made out of limelight, as stuff and substance.

Waaal, the Tree[s] and their circle were havin' tea on the lawn; as one did in the upper reaches, with due paraphernalia, large silver tea urns, etc. and up come a storm, thunder and lightenin', and the family naturally plunged indoors, and one of Sir Herbert's nieces described to me the scene, possibly prophetic scene that resulted.

Blast had been left solitary there on the lawn, and the niece and Sir Herbert gazed elegiacally from the drawingroom window on the scene of grass and wet dampness. A FLASH of lightening lit up the lawn.

There in its solitude, huge on the flaring magenta cover, the black letters vivid, the word BLAST was written. Possibly someone ventured out to rescue the treasure, now valued of second hand book sellers, but more probably no one did. It was in many ways a languid era, so few DID.

I take it in retrospect that my tendency to action had effects, people who were bored with stagnation, and were relieved at the sight of ANY vitality, this must have been a TINY minority, and the vast majority of the small minority into contact with which I came, was uneasy, disturbed, horrified in fact: for that sign of action was also some sort of a harbinger.

SOMETHING was going on, or if not actually going ON, something might occur somewhere.

And DID.

Not only one war, but another, and the END of the materialist Era. The end of that particularly dirty *Anschauung*. Not merely the change of an IDEA, not the change of ONE idea, or notion, but the change of a WHOLE disposition toward life. Sloth, laziness, snobbishness, greed or whatever prevented the English from seeing what the change was to be, or what it was when it hit'em. Also ignorance, also that part of the constructed snobishness which had helped to blot out historic sense. (Not by accident. *That* was intended.) However, the dichotomy, the division was an age-old division. When Mencius went to see King Huei of Liang, the King said, have you got some thing that will bring PROFIT? Profit motive, already known, two thousand five hundred years before Blast; 2,400 years before Marx half swallowed Hegel. And Mencius said: why use that word, what I got is my sense of EQUITY. If you can't use that in your Kingdom, good morning, I have mistaken the address.

Well, now the sense of EQUITY, sense of justice, was what England had lost or mislaid. *Ben dell' intelletto* Dante called it, or something not very far from it. Homely English would get that down to "use of your wits," but I reckon Dante meant something nearer to Mencius's meaning. However BOTH the use of the wits, and the sense of justice or equity had gone out of fashion in England by 1914. And this is no subject for merriment. When a nation loses its sense of justice, sense of fair play to ALL corners and loses the use of its wits, it is the end of an era, or the end of the nation, or BOTH.

We have seen the Russian Empire come to an end. Grand Dukes sellin' the country, and thought not encouraged by the class that was then in power. We have seen the end of the Hapsburgs. You would think old W. Steed would have learned something from his study of the dealin's of the Hapsburgs, and that he would have applied it into his observation of England, but evidently he has not.

I dunno where you folks will come out, but I know you won't start toward coming out till you recognize the use of straight thinking. Till you stop bilking yourselves, till you get rid of the people who have encouraged you in the worst of your vices—opium of one sort or another, dumping one sort onto China, and using another sort for home consumption. Landor, Trollope, Hobhouse, Major Douglas, even ole William Yeats, plenty of your own wise men have told you.

And the Ta hsüeh, the Great Learning, First book of confucian philosophy ends: Profits do not profit a nation. Lucre does not profit a nation. The sense of equity, sense of justice is that wherefrom a nation hath benefit.

The whole of your rulin' class has run plumb haywire on profits; [FCC transcript: run haywire on lucre; despised the use of the— —, despised the good of the intellect; falsified everything.

I'm hep to your B.B.C, to your— —advocate in India. India has already given way, that is,— —and false promises. Now the B.B.C. comics arid falsification of everything. Now the only point I've heard on the London

Radio was what one Royal Canadian, who had swallowed all the— —, swallowed all the lies you had told him. Still dreaming along in the years of Victorian (jubilee). Lucre does not profit a nation.

Sense of justice is that where from a nation can benefit.

Ezra Pound speaking— —or perhaps only an admonition. That is— —is your only way out.]

#31 (April 27, 1942) U.S.(B36)
OPPORTUNITY RECOGNIZED

Over 150 years ago our ancestors, that is the ancestors of some of us, had an OPPORTUNITY—and they TOOK it. They had the opportunity of setting up a government, without being absolutely hog-tied. They made a conscious and CONSCIENTIOUS effort to set up a better FORM of government than was then extant in boosy old bribe-run England. That fact was important. After about 80 years, the American form of government was DONE in, and it took us nigh 80 years to find out how, when, and WHY we had been diddled.

Several columns of infamy, monuments to the crimes of Ikieheimer, Sherman, and probably Stanton ought to be set up in front of the Lincoln Memorial in Washington explainin' why Lincoln was shot, why Booth got out of Washington by the only road on which there were no police guards after he put the lead into Abe Lincoln, that being the ONE road, he would be likely to TAKE and the shortest cut into the south country.

Well all that needs explainin', like the hoods on the prisoners, which certainly KEPT'em from seem' folks in the courtroom when Doc Mudd and the rest were tried. Whatever other explanation ever was given or can be invented to explain this form of illegal torture?

Waaal, it is all very mysterious. And it definitely marked a DECLINE (to put it mildly) of legal sense in America. Decline of our sense of fair play, decline of American decency.

Then came the kid glove era. Then came disparagement of the system. "Decline of democratic DOGMA," wrote Henry Adams shiftin' his words about hither and yon. The decline as I see it waren't in the DOGMA, it lay in absolutely leaving the dogma high and dry. Stranded, paying NO attention either to the text of the vital affirmations of DOGMA, such as liberty NOT to harm others. Paying no attention to the vital points of the Constitution. Letting the WHOLE real power and sovereignty be swiped from the people and the LEGITIMATE representatives of the people, and from the responsible executive officers and handed over to VERMIN. And not even American lice in all cases.

"We can not permit the circulation of greenbacks," can not permit the circulation of NATIONAL money, said the kahalists, because we can not control'em. AND the American MUGS let it go at that, took seventy years to get wise to it. CALHOUN had known better. He had seen through the northern loan sharks. Waal, Calhoun was dead by that time. Well, being KILLED at the root, the ONLY effective means of ruining the Amen can system, having been extracted, filched, pilfered, TAKEN OUT of the system. The system naturally turned weak and pindlin'.

And AS the ideas inside the American Revolution had been grown in Europe a bit before we took to actin' on'em, the American soil hadn't got ready to produce much original thinking. Even Ole Walt Whitman got a shot in the arm, Hindoo ways of thinking, which he sprouted as a means of bustin' the tea-table manners of writin' imported from England.

Well, let me keep to stability, let me keep to POLITICAL ethics, and not deviate into literary SYMPTOMS of a disease. Whatever the causes, fertility, fecundity of American nature, it remains in the record that apart from some seceding colonies with what were called FUNNY ideas, little groups of people buying a bit of land and trying social experiments, in New York, Utah, and in Connecticut, there warn't much reorganizing effort in the United States of America Representation of the DIFFERENT kinds of people was BUST, not its crust was busted, its crust was all that was NOT busted. Its hoistin' balloon was pricked, it was knocked endways, and the vitality deflated out of it. Even the lawyers, who as a class or professional group, had had a good deal to say at the startin' of the American system, were eased into butler's and footmen's positions. The trades, the artisans, the farmers, the farm hands, the land owners who didn't own vast tracts of land, all of'em steadily LESS AND LESS represented; their interests, their power to LIVE, their power to USE the statal mechanism as a means to the good life, were eased OUT of their grip. Worse or better in Europe, where some stinking old systems, old stinking traditions, of the Hapsburgs of England, of the Hapsburgs and Romanovs, went along creatin' more and more hate inside their own borders.

England just never DID catch up with the AMERICAN states system, was crusteder, was nearer to the ROTTEN borough confederation, not ONLY as fact but as DOGMA. Nothing in Europe before 1920 got in reachin' range of the American system as it was from 1798 to 1860 or'65.

As it was you might say from the start of the Revolutionary War of 177b, till Andy JOHNSON got pushed out of the White House. We Americans, we UNITED STATESERS have STILL got legal rights ON PAPER which Europe spent over a hundred years regardin' with ENVY. And WE Americans are such go! darn MUGS that we do nothing with'em.

We make no use what bloody ever of the rights we BY LAW possess. We let a mean bunch of sheenies elect, that is, pick out, and choose our unsightly presidents.

We let'em put in the codf ace; we let'em KEEP in Franklin D. Roosenvelt, and RUN him conscious or unconscious, helping them do us dirt, or being kept in the dirty groove RUINING the American heritage. And the American people gets dumber and dumber each year, and shows less and less desire to git at the facts. They take NO warning by what happens to countries, like France and England, who let the kike get into the saddle and run'em, rackrun'em to ruin.

Hence my attention to the NEXT social construction. Next in point of time, next SYSTEM of government set up in the AIM that ours was, namely of providing a BETTER system of government than had BEEN BEFORE put in motion anywhere on earth in the occident.

Got to go to the great exceptional reigns [of] Hong Vou or some Emperor whose administration is mostly unknown to everyone in the United States or Europe to get anything in [the] human record better than in Germany and in Italy [in order] to make EFFECTIVE what had been INTENDED in the United States by Adams and Jackson. [Well, after 130 years, along comes another] revolution and tries to set up a better KIND of government than was anywhere extant in Europe OR America in 1920, that being the only place you CAN correlate. If you weren't headless jitterbugs, or some other acephalous variety of the species, you would at least want the FACTS about fascist and national socialist organization. You would want to know why and HOW Italy and Germany riz out of their ashes and smashes. You would want to KNOW what means are used to make EFFECTIVE the will of the people in Germany and in ITALY.

Taking the MAIN wishes first, getting FIRST what the people want FIRST, and second what they want second. GUILD organization, coordinated at the top, that being the only place you CAN correlate, defects of other proposed systems wiped out, incapacities of economic sects wiped out, incapacities replaced by CAPACITIES. First essential of life is to keep livin', to keep on living, not DIE. Every man represented IN the system, embodied IN the system with someone responsible TO him and to the centre.

There is an Italian motto— *spectamur agendo*—meaning that things get judged by their action, by their effects. YOUR first wakin' or conscious act will be to find out WHY Europe does it.

I dunno HOW to start helpin' you if you WON'T think about the American Constitution, if you won't, just damn all WON'T try to see why it does NOT function. Who can avail this? If you won't then take steps to put it back into working ORDER and damn well see that it FUNCTIONS. When your will gits turned to that TARGET, mebbe I can offer you a little enlightenment.

But so long as you are plumb determined to lie down and be walked on by the President, it will be difficult to keep you upstanding and perpendicular. Or in fact to produce anything better than a state of chordee.

#32 (April 30, 1942) U.S.(B37) NON-JEW

I naturally mistrust newspaper news from America. I grope in the mass of lies, knowing most of the sources are wholly UNtrustworthy.

It nevertheless seems to transpire, or expire that there is a difference of opinion between quite a fair sized number of Americans, and an equally large number of Jews, Jews-playfellows, and the bedfellows of Jews and of Jewesses, from Eve Curie to Lehman, and Lippmann.

The terms "interventionist" and "isolationist" do not seem to define the fronts clearly. Senator Johnson, I s'pose that is Hiram of Californy, be came warlike when Japan started in. Naturally, considering what state he represents.

BUT clarity has not come and will not come till an accurate census of the ORIGINAL bellifiyers is made and until every pro-war Jew has his name listed. I think the NON-war Jews (at least those who were non-war before the WAR started) will be found to be very, very, verrrreeee small.

In fact, apart from the thefts and extractions of the gang back of the Treasury music hail, it becomes increasingly difficult to discuss American affairs EXCEPT on a racial basis.

Whether America will awake to this now or in 20 years, will depend on Yankee enterprise, I suppose.

Whatever you read in America, we read here that the Americans, U.S.A.'ers, are irritated at finding'emselves in war UNPREPARED. Disappointed in British FLOP.

SOMETIME the Anglo Saxon may AWAKE to the fact that the Jewish kahal and secret forces concentrated or brought to focus in the unappetizin' carcass of Franklin D. Roosevelt do NOT shove Aryan or non-yittlsch nations into WARS in order that those said nations may WIN wars. The non-Jew nations are shoved into wars in order to destroy themselves, to break up their structure, to destroy their social order, to destroy their populations. And no more flaming and flagrant case appears in history than our own American Civil War, said to be an occidental record for size of armies employed and only surpassed by the more recent triumphs of Warburgs, the wars of 1914 and the present one.

AGAIN, whatever your own press has been able to tell you, it is, or ought to be news, that Europe is interested in the question of Masonry. Nothin' will come as a greater shock to America in general, but in particular to honest men who compose the greater part, numerically, of American Masonry, than the view held concernin' that order in Europe.

An American said to me a short while back, "I'm a Mason, my wife is a Catholic, the kids goin' to Catholic school, and a man would have to be pretty SMALL to let it (meaning his Masonry) interfere with his politics." That, I believe, to be the attitude of 95% of American Masons.

No one in the United States will be more surprised at the talk of hook up between Masonry, its central control, Jewry, Anglo-Israel, and the British Intelligence Service [than will the rank and file of American Masons.] This is all NEW[S] to the rural American. Giraffe!! There ain't no such animal.

Well now these scissions, these cuttings off of a NATION are damaging. I have told my select readers for years that England dropped behind, way behind France in all sorts of intelligent activity, book-writin', etc., during the XIX century because she was CUT OFF from the continent of Europe for YEARS. During the Napoleonic shindies, Germany was sent into exile, or they tried to exile her after Versailles. I myself forgot what I knew of German language, not till I got het up and wanted to read Leo Frobenius, did I git my German dictionary out of mothballs. And I ain't the worst case.

Now, isolations of this kind are BAD for a nation. George Santayana can't send his manuscript to Scribner's because of the war. That is one item, only one item. You'll find out, brother. Interference with communications' service. Rothschild, the stink of hell gittin' hold of Austrian postal service and censorship in time of Napoleon. Hundred years after Austria is the dumbest, and LEAST mentally awake country in Europe, and FLOPS. France was awake, Rothschilds git into bank or stank of France in, I think, 1843.

Inside a hundred years, France walks down her pirate Reynaud, and flops into the discard.

You'll find out, brother, before or after the belly-flop. England is on the teeter. The central stink betrayed the United States in 1863. Keeping up the hostilities, keepin' the rebels at it, *divide et impera*.

Now the same bunch of Kikes is doing [it] in England. NOT for the benefit of the American people.

Sassoons baboons, Rothschilds, etc. migrating to the United States and stinking up the whole country, in the wake of Zukor and the other fine flowers of Semite culture.

Look at Litvinov's face. The SOUL shining in beauty. Greek philosophy jettisoned, Justinian, jettisoned, the sense of LAW that built up all Europe, puked into the discard.

Sense of ENGLISH law, that was built up out of the Roman, puked into the discard. You will find out, brother, later or soon, and I should prefer it sooner, so as I should be able to meet some survivors.

Interested ONLY in Bunk, says the sheeny lawyer, seem' what you can put over. Immoral geometry, Freud, Bergson, crawlin' in through all the Crevices. HONESTY of [thought] in all and every department filched away, undermined, dry rotted, wet rotted. And simple hearted elegiac poets like Archie put out in front as top dressin'. No, brother, the American people will have to start askin' questions.

WHAT ARE THE MASONS? Where do they git their money? And WHO controls'em? Who is the big SILENT noise at their center?

WHAT is the British Intelligence Service? Secret Service? Fighting the British people? How did Willie Wiseman git there? Why don't the OPPOSITON papers, papers that say they opposed Frankie Finklestein Roosevelt, why don't they LOOK into these matters?

What is the KAHA[L]? Why don't you examine the Talmud? Talmud, said to have corrupted the Jews. Some Jews disparage it. What is really said in the Talmud about creatin' disorder? Why did the firm, publishing firm that printed the Protocols, go out of business?

Waaal, mebbe they went out of business cause they hadn't enough sense GO ON printin' me. But look into it. Don't git excited until you have got some real evidence. There is a buildin' outside of Washington, and so forth, go look at it.

Don't start a pogrom. That is, not an old style killing of small Jews. That system is no good whatsoever. Of course if some man had a stroke of genius and could start pogrom UP AT THE top, there might be something to say for it.

But on the whole legal measures are preferable. The sixty Kikes who started this war might be sent to St. Helena as a measure of world prophylaxis. And some hyper-kike, or non-Jewish kikes along with'em. I shall be content if I contribute my buffalo nickel to arouse a little sane CURIOSITY, a little healthy inquiry as to what causes the whichness.

Goethe was gittin' at something when he wrote his play "Faust." I can't do ALL the researchin' but thaaar, as I see it or feel it, is a field for proficuous research.

The error of philology in the XIX century was to split everything up into slivers, get a man concentrated on a small enough microscopic area, and mebbe you can prevent him seeing what it has to do with the next field, or with the national income, or with the health of the nation.

USEFUL, I am an authority on Arnaut Daniel, for example, any post graduate student can become an authority, very good exercise too, if he don't get loco'd and buffaloed. If he don't lose all capacity to incorporate what he knows, if he don't see that it has or may have connections—may IMPLY something or other.

Just as the LOSS, the absolute loss of craftsmanship, the CEASING of the fanlights, the carving of the wood in the fanlights over the London house doors, IMPLIED something or other. Why did our colonial architecture, what is called our colonial architecture, go to pot? Wood carving, colonial cabinet makin', I mean furniture making, not pickin Hulls and Knoxs, go to pot, American silversmith technique, why did it peter out? When do such things synchronize with other phenomena such as usury tolerance? There is WORK for all sorts and kinds of humans so long as the musician or glass blower carries his IDEA deep enough into it; the picture painter, if he carries his mind deep enough into it, will find that he is not alone, not isolated, solitary, has something to do; some revelation, VITAL relation with the rest of humanity.

Enough for this evening.

#33 (May 4, 1942) U.S.(B38)
UNIVERSALITY

The Bolshevik anti-morale comes out of the Talmud, which is the dirtiest teaching that any race ever codified. The Talmud is the one and only be getter of the Bolshevik system.

And if there ARE any Christians in the United State of America, they would do well to consider Renan's warning. They would do well to consider the difference between the Greek and the Hebrew parts of the Bible.

They would do well to look objectively at the record of Hebrew barbarism, and at the nature of Christ's revolt, as recorded in the Gospels. I do not propose to enter [into] questions of paleography and archaeology. Theologians or students of religion have said this, that, and the other about the dates of composition, sources, etc. of the Old Testament.

I do not propose to go into these questions, they can be left to professional archaeologists. Having read the Bible daily in childhood, I have come to have perhaps a more objective view of it than, let us say, Bishop Temple.

I propose to consider the statements in the King James version, taking them at their F ace value. I ask you to note what you are told in your Bibles. For the moment let us confine ourselves to the two sections, namely the Old Testament and the Gospels, leaving aside the questions concerning St. Paul.

Now the Old Testament is a collection of heteroclite work, chronicles, psalms, prophecies, and ecciesiastes. And the Chronicles record the doings of a thoroughly disgusting race of barbarians.

The prophets ceased not to object to the conduct of the coreligionaries. You will perhaps say that all dirty barbarians were at that time much of a muchness.

However, there was a fellow named Pericles, there was a fellow named Aristotle, there were various writers, such as Homer and Hesiod. And they built up a European Code. In fact, European civilization, and as much of it as has infiltrated into the outlying Islands, islands lying off the North West corner of Europe, such of it as has been trapsed over the North American continent. People taking grand pianos, and little plaster busts of Mozart and Haydn across the Mississippi River and into the Michigan pine woods.

This CIVILIZATION sprouted in the Mediterranean basin. And this civilization had ENEMIES external and internal. Barbarian tribes beat against its margins, and corruptors infiltrated into it, just as they have in filtrated into the United States of America for the past hundred or 160 years.

ALL right, now what does your Bible tell you about SOCIAL organization? It tells you the Jews went into captivity, that is, into a state wherein they had NO CIVIC responsibility, in great part a slave condition. As to their own organization it consisted in what still survives in the kahal sys tem. There was a LAW, NOT an ethical system. This law was a set of finnikin prohibitions, and there was little distinction between the transgressions; what there was, was related mostly to the MAIN purpose of law; namely to provide FINES, payable to a gang or tribe of allegedly religious superiors, who seem to have had no particular ethical status.

IRRESPONSIBLE taxation, taxation to and for the benefit of a gang of exploiters.

Just like the Bank of England or the Morgenthau, Warburg system in the United States. Taxing the people TWO dollars for every dollar spent by the government.

That is BASIC; all particular grafts and swindles over Army contracts, or contracts in peace time are EXTRA, over and above the main wheeze. I leave out all questions of detail, questions as to what Moses learned in Egypt, what the kikes picked up in Babylon. I ask you WHY WAS CHRIST crucified? He was crucified for trying to BUST a racket. There had been mystic sects in Palestine before the ZERO year of the Christian era. Some say they had been there for 200 years.

I am not considerin' the religious and mystic question. I am asking WHY the Sanhedrim and the Priests and Levites were so dead set on Crucifixion. Pontius Pilate couldn't make it out. He wasn't interested in having a revolt on his hands. So he washed'em. BUT what stirred up the big men in the kikery?

Will you note that there is in the Christian Gospels NO provision for TAXING the public? There is NO institution of a central governing authority authorized to TAX the people for infringements of understandable in fractions of a finnikin code of laws.

That hit old Caiaphas RIGHT where he lived. Right where the kikified Englishman still lives; namely, RIGHT on the pocket. As to the Talmud, that is something much lower. That is the code of vengeance, of secret means unto vengeance. AIMED specifically at the destruction of all non kike order. It is a dirty book, and reading of it might well be reserved to mature and responsible students of psychosis and of pathology.

OUT of it came the Bolsheviki. Out of it came the determination to ruin Europe, to break down Christianity, to set up no-Godism. And it is either irony or tragedy that English and American Christians should find'emselves hog tied into a collaboration with bloody Russia. I am personally highly skeptical as to the depth of English and American Christianity. My Great Uncle Albert said he preferred the Episcopal Church, because it interfered neither with a man's politics nor with his religion.

I suppose there ARE American Christians. I have never found'em as Christian as Germans and Italians who happen to be religious. It is not my job to sort out the sheep from the goats. I see the Padri Emiliani in Rapallo working hard, day in and day out, to bring up a bunch of orphans and make'em into good artisans.

I see out of my bedroom window a chapel built on a sane economic system. Namely, the peasants up that side of the mountain had the stone under foot and wanted a chapel, so they got the stone out of the mountain side and put up the chapel. I suppose they believe in something. And it is quite certain that the FASCIST regime approves of this sort of activity. I have my own sort of religion, and nobody here bashes me on the head for believing it. I don't say it is adapted to all sort and conditions of humans.

It suits me and I got it. Nobody, not even the Archbishop with whom I occasionally converse animatedly and upbraidedly has asked me to chuck out on the dung heap. He occasionally gets in a word about the Gospel's containing good gospel. He is older than I am, and not quite so explosive.

I see and approve the folks in Rapallo coming down to the sea on Easter morning, not so many as used to. I see the peasant women bringing their silk worm cocoons into church about Easter time to get'em blessed, hiding them under their aprons. All this shows respect for divinity. Nobody taxes'em for doing it, or for NOT doing it. They bring out their grass that has been sprouted up prematurely by puttin' the seed on wet flannel and put little rows in front of the altars. All that is very pretty, it may or may not be part of a theory. I think it conduces to the amenities; ANYHOW, it is part of the good life, part of the art of living.

ANY Chinese gentleman, on Wang Chin-Wei's side of the line at least would respect it, and Japanese Samurai would respect it.

I also respect it. I consider it part of civilization against which you have a horde of bloody barbarians financed by a bunch of skunks. Meet a few Mongoloid or Tar Tar communists. Meet a few of Baruch's importation, of Warburg's importation, meet the lower strata, not merely the Willie Wiseman's who have been given directorates. Meet a few of these dirty swine, out to destroy Bach's music.

Bach? OUT.

Shakespeare? OUT.

Destroy everything conducive to civilization Damn civilization. The Kike is out for all power. The Kike and the unmitigated evil that has been centered in LONDON since the British government set the Red Indians on to murder the American frontier settlers. Has hurled the Slav, the Mongol the Tartar OPENLY against Germany, AND POLAND, and THE DURATION Finland, and Romania. And SECURELY against all that is decent in America. Against the total American heritage. This is my war all right, I have been in it for 20 years. My Grandad was in it before me.

#34 (May 9, 1942) U.S. (B39)
THE DURATION

I said last time that my grandad had been in it before me. Said this was MY war, and that my granddad had been in it before me. And we were and ARE BOTH on the same side. Last time I saw the old man, I must have been about 12 years of age. I can still see him settin' in our so called library in Wyncote in a big spring rockin' chair, facin' a funny patent iron coal grate that was under my greatgrandma's picture. Other side of the family that rather thought their side was superior.

Yaas, been socially etc. though I doubt it. Whaler's great great grandson studyin' Greek, while the other side was goin' to college. Waaal, so happened I went abroad, and knew very little of him, till my dad come on along over and by chance brought a few scrap books. And there were cuttings about old political shindies 1878 Grover Cleveland etc The swindle over demonitization of silver.

I could write a whole American history by implication stickin' to unknown folks, in four or five families. But the WAR has been the same war. John Adams, Jefferson, Van Buren, and Jackson, and finally Abe Lincoln, V.P. Johnson, my Grand Dad. All fighting the kikified usurers, all trying to git an honest day's pay for a day's real work BY the people. All trying to have the government money run honest. I haven't had Henry Adam's life of Gallatin, whether that kike was honest, or merely clever, I leave to men who can get hold of Henry's Life of Albert Gallatin and ulterior documents. If Jefferson had stuck by John Adams, instead of making it up when they were both on the retired list, things would have been different. But no might-of-beens count much in history. Jefferson at least stood out against Alex Hamilton.

Two great friendships, at the base of American history. John Adams and Jefferson, Van Buren and Andy Jack son. You can pass the time readin' that history. It will make the boys better citizens. Make any young man more American if he sticks to seein' American history FIRST before swallowin' exotic perversions.

How did we get where we are? WHY was Signor Zobi in 1850 holdin' up the U S for the admiration of Europe? Tellin his readers about George Washington. Why was Lartdor, known to most of you for Greek culture, why was he turning from Pericles and Aspasia to write a poem to General

Jackson? That was America. It was promises. I'll say it was promises, and a DAMN SIGHT MORE. You look at that, Archie, America wasn't only promises. America was colonial architecture, good food, even in my young times, the black cook could make a brown stew. No second-rate cookin' ever entered my face till I got to eatin' in restaurants when goin' to college. And then, God Damn it, an oyster stew was an oyster stew. I mean as cookin' we were second to no man, even to no woman of any nation.

French chefs were mere fancy. But the ice cream made of CREAM, all cream and peaches, solid peaches, was NOT surpassed by Sindar, it was not distinctive of Europe.

American silversmiths, American colonial furniture, even the carvin' on American tombstones, if there were no sculpture to speak of. Jefferson's house, for the house of a rich man, or a man who lived like a rich man and went bankrupt. Monroe's house, I should say a man lived inside his means. Adams's house, the two houses, house of poor man and son of poor man. All those houses could teach you something, something of POLITICS, in the high sense that ole Harry Stotle held up, held up for man's admiration.

Something in a way higher than ethics, the further extension of ethics got to grow out of sound ethics. Then something bust, 1867 it BUST or was BUSTED. And the documents are available. Hazard circular, correspondence of Sherman, Ikleheimer, and Rothschild. When will you folks start thinking? Then ten years later a bill slid thru, knocking out silver. And there waren't never again enough honest force in our Congress to get thru an HONEST bill about money. Some flyers, some attempted amendments trying to save what was saveable. Trying to keep "IN CIRC. as currency" some of NON-INTEREST payin' part of the debt. Calhoun would have understood it, would have understood that phrase about NON-INTEREST payin' part of the debt. Of course no need for it to be issued as DEBT whatsoever. Calhoun would have understood the bearin' of that phrase about, AT LEAST PART of, the debt that did NOT bear interest. Did not TAX the plain man, every man in America, wakin' or sleeping. John Adams would have understood it, Lincoln would have understood it. AND HOW.

Page Mr. Sandburg, I say, Carl, do TELL Archie, ask Archie about that NON-INTEREST bearin' part of the debt. What does the eminent Congressional Librarian have to say about that word NON-interest bearin'? And if not, why not? After all Archie waren't in on that fly-by-night company of the President's, floated to take it off the people of Europe, during the German inflation. Archie is fairly late comer to the kike's table. I hope you ain't eatin' shoe-bread.

But you would do better to innoculate your children with typhus and syphillis than to let in the Sassoons, Rothschilds, and Warburgs.

Then of course there's this silver business. Silver never quite OPEN. Wanted to break gold MONOPOLY but not by real honesty. Wanted to prevent the gold racket from being exclusive, but by means of another RACKET. Good men feeling they needed backin', like Sir Montagu Webb, gettin' the silver boys back of'em, but not tellin' ALL of the story. Very hard case of conscience. A man gets into Congress BY silver, has silver backing. Has a RIGHT to want as much rights for SILVER as the gold lice have for their gold. BUT: wants his rights to be raised into a racket. Don't give a cuss for the rights of the sheep men and wheat men. Waaal, that has been silver's weakness. No commodity has a JUST right over any other commodity and you can't eat these METALS.

Commodity dollar, old pop Warren was right on that line. BUT who is to ISSUE the dollar? Back to the old Constitution, old betrayed Constitution. What has the gol darn Baltimore Sun, or New York Sun to say about the U.S. Constitution? What has Col. McCormick got to say about the U.S. Constitution? Put me out, or his weak-kneed half masted editors put me out of his Paris paper too soon. Don't matter a hoot. But what has he got NOW to say about the U.S. Constitution? Mebbe he has waited about 20 years, mebbe longer, that are JUST 20 years too much.

I'll be seem' you. What have the silver Johnnies got to say about national money? No, I am not a social creditor. I passed by that alley away. I am a national money man.

And there ought to be more AMERICANS WITH ME.

#35 (May 10, 1942) U.K.(B40)
THE PRECARIOUS

Mr. Vernon Bartlett, whom I shall define later this evening if my time holds out, and I haven't used it all up on more important items, Mr. Vernon Bartlett has nearly crowned his long and not wholly ambiguous life by writing an intelligent sentence.

He says that England's position at the peace conference will be PRE CARIOUS. I'll say it will be precarious. I haven't an etymological dictionary handy in my hotel bedroom so I don't know whether "precarious" really springs from a couple of Latin words meaning the state a thing gits into before it goes rotten. The English word is usually used to mean in peril, uncertain. I'll leave it at that, not go battin' round for a word like POST CARIUS.

Precarious, in the common sense, I'll say it will be risky. Just as RISKY as Germany's was at Versailles. With this difference—that the next peace won't be made by a pair of kikes, one at each side of the table, or standing behind the stuffed shirts who represent'em in front of the public.

And the basic aim of the peace will not be Versailles' basic aim. Namely, to prepare the next war.

That's what Versailles was aimed at, with its daggers and cross lines, its Skodas, its synthetic states. Its gun factories run with Jew money, run on loans, based on money sweated out of the Aryan peoples, sweated out of the farm laborers and industrial workin' men. Stuck in positions of danger. The next peace will not be based on international lending. Get that for one. And England will certainly have nothing what bloody ever to say about what its terms are. Neither I think will simple hearted Joe Stalin, NOT wholly trusted by the kikery which is his master.

WHY have you got where you are, and where are you? YOU are down under the filth and dung of humanity. You are down under Maisky and Litvinoff, and if human degradation can show anything lower, go fetch it.

LOOK at your masters' faces! How did you get there, and why is Bartlett in a position to say so?

Bartlett is one of the noises, as you will say, not a bad fellow, has many pleasant intentions.

CAN HE AFFECT'em? He can not. He is a journalist, under the rump of the usury system. Under the rump of the usury system, certain pimps rise into prominence. I noted it first in the economic brothel.

Pigou, every time Asquith government wanted a swindle put over, Pigou was expected to fix up the SCIENCE of economics to suit it. A few figures, a few statistical tables. He waren't quite lively enough, so a confidence man named Keynes was invented.

One of my grave diggers of England, one of the boys that got paid for puttin' brass knobs on your coffin. Let me stick to three diseases of the Anglo-French-American system. The syphilis, typhus, and tuberculosis of the mercantilist? No, not even mercantilist, the USURY system, with trimmings, not even the medieval, or metal money usury system, now dying out even in India, and giving way to the galloping CARIES of the Anglo-English bank system, that stakes out the old fashioned usurers, and devours even the parasites. Fake economists are one form of the journalist bacillus. Put out in front to lie, and rising on the wings or tin toes of ambition, permitted (on the leash and chain system) to get out in front and holler.

Quoted from one press to another, NOT because they ever print anything useful, or tell the truth, or approach it. They are either men who KNOW NOT, or men who say not, and who put up a word screen, or esCHEW certain issues; who do NOT make revelations. And whose interest even when quoted internationally is NOT due to the INTRINSIC meaning of what they actually say. Their blather IS symptomatic, and is studied and quoted as a symptom of the diseases. And what the Times says indicates one of two things. The Times says what its controllers want said that is basic. Either what its controllers WANT fools to believe, or what a given group of knaves feel they have to admit to keep up credibility.

The poor bastids who write it never enjoy what de Gourmont called writer's sole pleasure. They most of'em never even get to a mental world in which Gourmont's concept exists or can enter.

Remy de Gourmont wrote to me in a letter "frankly to write what one thinks, that is the writer's pleasure." These duds or prominent journalists, some infamous, some well intentioned, are of two sorts. The absolute simpletons who believe what they are told by their masters and the absolute knaves, who are usually part simpleton.

In Keynes' case, we can take it, I suppose, that he is mostly knave and part simpleton. At any rate he is now at your rudder or near it. Bright spirit, etc. The second microbe of the disease is the son-in-law who is sometimes made by the third sort of pest. Such let us say as M/G A/Q. Shall I name her? Probably not even a whore. In days past William Watson protested, he came very near naming her. Watson protested against the infamies of the Boer war, now forgotten. Already an antique when I got to London. The old boy once taken out of mothballs and roared a few sonnets at us, uncomprehended, what was it all about? Decimation of England was part of it. Three decimations of England. The aristos, the English of English stock, who were killed in the Boer war.

B. Adams, noting England's decline, AT THAT TIME and her proximate and probably further enfeeblement. Decimation of 1914, the KIND of Englishman, 100% of ENGLAND, that was mowed off in the first three months. Kill'em off at the top, pogroms start at the bottom and are NEVER so very effective.

Third shot at Dunkirk, with a few nuts and raisins for Maisky. The second disease works on the Queen Esther or Salome method. SONS and nephews rebel. Baldwin's son stands up to his father. Winston's nephew gets Winston's number, and shows himself to be at least a different sort of an ass. Men of the same RACE rebel at a certain moment. Some dirt they refuse to eat. Some kind of dirt they won't eat even if their own fathers tell'em to eat it.

Hence son-in-laws are required. And females are needed to get'em. Marry a little below'em when a RISING man appears on the horizon, over the tea table. All right take the bitch in question, probably not even a whore. Marries a RISER, and runs him, but does NOT help him. Absolute failure to cooperate, or to MAINTAIN a governing class, to function as one of it. *Dévergondage de la guerre*, etc., may not even go to bed with the Jews, but plays round, in serious moments. Oh well, let us lay OFF the ladies.

Now for the sons-in-law. That pink haired snot Alex Hamilton was the perfect example. Study his story, half Jew, spritely, a whole box of tricks and a great man with the ladies.

Now how do these sonnie boys RISE? They most certainly are SE LECTED for lack of principle and for pliability and ambition, often for their credulity. But always because they have a certain pliable mechanism, their boosters know HOW they work, know how to work'em. After a point they can be turned loose, as adjusted wreckers, their own passions will run'em and run the nation to ruin.

Yes, yes, Mr. Bartlett, the position of England at the Peace, did you say CONFERENCE? The position of England at peace time will be PREcarious if it ain't rotted already. England has chosen birth control INSTEAD of Eugenics.

You could see that 30 years ago, and then they went to breeding fool-blooded grey hounds and *whippets*, not even farm edible farm stock, IN STEAD of trying to make human thoroughbreds.

The so-called example of the race course, horsebreedin' would have served the English race as a paradigm, but they didn't use it.

Contraception, killin' the native stock before it was hatched, instead of BREEDING a population.

Good evening.

#36 (May 11, 1942) U.S.(B41)
A FRENCH ACCENT

One of the jobs I took on way back before half my listeners were off milk diet or out of their diapers was the education of the rising American literature generation as to the contemporary (and anterior) production of French high class writin'. I held, even in my young days, that a nation's literature has a certain importance.

I also had patriotic motives. I also felt for the stranded young inside America. I clomb out, by fingernails. I only had half a toe hold, but I at least clomb up to whaar one could see what was what on at least the writer's horizon. American boys wantin' to write started with 20 or more years as a handicap.

Most of'em have it still, Gauss down at Princeton for example, doing quite a serious book, careful study, thoughtful but 20 years late in startin'. When I got along to be 40 or 45, I thought I could hand over the job to someone younger.

I think Sam Putnam was ready to take it over, but pore Sam hit an unlikely moment, 1924–25, French writing was pindlin'.

I had already said that after de Gourmont's death there was no froggie whom I could trust to send in a monthly letter about French contemporary authors: for the Little Review or the DIAL. The French were biologically fixed and they were losin' the sense of RESPONSIBILITY, intellectual responsibility, only a few elderly blokes like A. Mockel and Valette still it. I mean they didn't have to think. For them a good book was a good book; and you didn't argue, you didn't even have to think that it was your duty to the state to boost a REAL book, and leave the fakes in the discard. And Valette was tired, so tired. Offered me the American rubric, at a time when I had not time to read 40 American dud books and make little notes on'em. Printed the first criticism of Ulysses (mine) in the Mercure that was published in France. Remy de Gourmont lived in a world in which it was inconceivable that a man would CHANGE his thought or withdraw a line of his writing for ulterior motives.

That was the vanishing world, that was old France. One of Gourmont's friends, La Marquise de Pierre, had never before seen an American. She looked on me as the representative of Benjamin Franklin. The United States was still the land that Lafayette went to. I went up her stairs and was received as if I had been a flamingo or sortie other rare exotic. That old France is NO longer with us.

Now after my study of the real poets, from Gautier onward, I dropped into Paris in, I think, 1919 and I asked what was doing. And they told me a lot, some of it hooey, but nobody mentioned Cocteau. Only after six weeks did someone say, after I had refused a lot of dog biscuit writing, as NOT what I was lookin' for, oh, well, there is Cocteau. Just as some years before a Harvard man entered my hail bedroom, if you could call it HALL, and told me about American writing and, when I declined to eat it, he added, oh, well, there is Eliot. I thought the isolation of Jean Cocteau indicated some nastiness on the part of his colleagues, but didn't notice their stud book.

Jean had his own particular line. Not everyone could be expected to like it, but he was way and by far the BEST poet and best prose writer then livin' in Paris. Only real criticism of his limits came from Picabia, who had on his own part limits. Curiously enough (details extraneous to my present subject) ten years later the best new writer in Paris was René Crevel. *Les Pieds dans le Plat.* Have you read it? When he died, I expected to see his contemporaries make a fuss, and lament him. They did NOT.

I had thought by then I could draw back and do my own stuff and leave funeral services and criticism of the young to the new generation. Not a bit of it. After hemmin' and hawing, and waitin' I had to lay a wreathe on Crevel. Nigh coincided with the demise of Possum's *Criterion*. Well now what was CAUSIN' this, what was causin' this state of affairs? YOU tell papa.

I am not, as you might think, indulgin' merely in retrospect. I am recallin' these things because I have been readin' YET AGAIN a French author. Way out above other French authors. Say Cocteau was 1919, and Crevel 1926, and the new man been now writing for just a decade. I hear he is a doctor, been working in Paris suburbs. Seen a bit of reality. Writes without fuzz on his tongue. Prose writer who bursts in[to] poetry, into verse writing. Next time, next time, be the last ONE. Gnrr, gnrr, gnrr, gnrra. Suicide of the Nation.

No fuzz on the blighter's tongue. Voice of France, as when France was young. Only Sam Putnam I think today will be able to find out a way to say in United States talk what the frog has been tellin''em.

This frog has been telling'em back in'32 of the war to come. It is not only that the FRENCH of Rabelais has come to life again. It is not only that spoken French, the French of the mechanics is at last put down on the page. It is that it takes hold of the page; it is alive on the page.

The dirty old siren mermaid sticking up out of the mud of the Seine, blowsly, boosy, unappetizing, starts tellin' the author where to git off at, she tells him, he tells her, there is no wasted politeness. There is none of the heaviness that sometimes creeps into Ulysses. None of the aimless search for exaggeration that makes Finnigan's Wake unimportant. Joyce hit his high in Ulysses. There was still exuberance. In Finnigan he is hunting, he is experimenting with a technique, bourgeois diversion. I haven't patience to wade through it. Thank God I am not employed to estimate the exact percentage of real metal in low grade ores (no pun intended).

France HAS an author who in 1938 could write, FRANCE HAS NO ALLIES.

That one sentence is enough to establish an author.

Oh yes, the rising American writers, the writers of 1940 to'50 will STILL have to read a FRENCH author. I mean ANOTHER French author; one not yet in the school books, one no Amy Lowell will bring home in a sachet case.

France stank, and the stink is recorded. It is recorded with a COPIA: whereof probably no frog since Rabelais has been capable. But the copia, the supply of words is an accessory. It is the clear view that makes CÉLINE important.

Yaaas, I am talkin' of CÉLINE. Last book suppressed I hear in Ole Brother Pétain's France. Don't like the SUBJECT. Some folks don't like the SUB JECT. Now WHY don't they like the subject? Céline was all out to save France. I reckon he is still out to pick up the pieces.

Forty million population in France in 1938; 25 million Frenchmen, soon to be a minority. CELINE was tellin''em, and they did NOT listen to Céline. Nacherly Mr. Chamberlain's friends, and Mr. Eden's playmates did NOT encourage the publication of Céline. Naturally his work was not welcome in certain quarters. Nevertheless the *École des Cadavres* had gone into 51 editions by the time the copy before me was printed. His best KNOWN works are *Voyage au bout de la Nuit, Mort à Credit, Bagatelles pour un Massacre.*

Bonjour, Ferdinand. I don't hold it my duty any more to run a chronicle of French publications, but I still know a real book when I see one, what ever the contents.

Ferdinand has GOT down to reality, Ferdinand is a writer. Next one will be the last one. Gnrr, gnrrn, gnrrn, gnrr. Suicide of the Nation.

La prochaine sera la derniere. Gniéres! Gn, gn. ça sera le suicide de la Nation.

Au pays n'en riviendra guére.

Not only for his copia, his abundance of language. Not only for the force of his prosody, but for the content. You will have to read Céline sometime. The active members of the community will have to BUY their own copies of *L'École des Cadavres*, not enough to hear me 5 minutes over the air, or dip into a copy at a friend's house.

#37 (May 14, 1942) U.S.(B42)
TO BE LATE (ESSERE IN RITARDO)

I hear one of my ex-editors has been saying, oh, yes, Pound's talks are all right but they are, what was it, belated. No, he said something different, tardy, was it OUT OF DATE, OUT OF DATE, that was it.

Well damn it, two things. One, if you hadn't been such mutts you would have heard me (and Céline for that matter) long before now.

Some of you would have THOUGHT about what Ferdinand, L.F. Céline, and the present speaker started saying a long time ago.

I started long before Céline. So far as I can make out, I s'pose he is 15 or 20 years younger than I am.

Unless of course he took up his young days doctorin' in the Paris suburbs and only got round to writin after he had got through with his patients.

He says in one place folks don't understand him. That is they understand him all wrong. Does this remind you of some of the best Jersey writin'? I translate it from the original, One constructs little illusions, one thinks one is understood, and then, not a bit of it.... One writes out thousands of prescriptions ... one will never know the good that they do.... You have been understood all WRONG, always. If you have written it out in your largest and clearest script and then sung it:

Half a teaspoon full in a cup of tilleul, WARM, at the moment of getting into bed.... The patient, the client, will do it his own way, he will take thirty teaspoons full in a cup of bouillon when he gets OUT of bed and that will cause a horrible scandal and he will come around and blame you ... and there will be complications, no end of them.

In all humility, I am telling you these things, that is sure. But I do not pretend to TEACH you anything whatsoever.

About ten years after I left Paris, M. Céline discovered why he left France; being a Frenchman he doesn't put it that way. But he has, quite amply, noted the biological fixity of the French. He is quite eloquent about the ten years during which Pasteur was kept from reachin' maximum utility, logic, cartesianism, etc. The difference between boiling instruments 20 minutes and boiling 'em 3 [minutes]. He also notes that he has never found a poor Jew of no importance who speaks evil either of Rothschild OR of the

Soviets. The United States may take 20 years more to get to where Céline was ten years ago.

Belated I am belated I am not an alarm clock expected to tell unhearing America, of every first book by a new European author. Especially when I have said things analogous before said author had broken into print. Céline writes with the clarity of R. de Gourmont: he is a great writer. The search for reality leads men of different races to similar quite private discoveries. In fact, that is the basis of science, which relativity tries to destroy. Céline denies that there is ANY fundamental and irremediable hate between the French and the Germans. It was my own conclusion after four years in Paris. Hence of course Mr. Roosevelt's determination to starve the French in unoccupied France Hence the opposition to Herbert Hoover sending Horlick's milk or whatever to babies in Europe.

Céline noted that his compatriots are biologically fixed, or static and tend to disappear en masse. Well, Kokka, the ex-Russian General Staff officer agreed with me on that point years ago Biological fixes In 1938 he was writing and printing: the DEMOCRATS want the WAR. The democ will finally get it.

I came back to America the spring after that date to say that there was a force INSIDE the United States that was not only trying to bust up the Monroe Doctrine, not only trying to betray our tradition of keeping out of the European mess, but trying to start a war IN ORDER to get America into it. Ferdinand, the Céline, not the Bull, yaas, you said a mouthful. And France did not hear you.

I am no prophet of doom. The democracies WANTED the war. That is, the satraps were hell bent on startin' it, and their slaves GOT it. Right on the old cervix, right on the cervical column, when the hen got it.

One by one; Czechoslovakia, born says M. Céline in Paris. M. Céline is quite good on Benes [?].Why laugh, you got Litvinov in Washington, and Maisky is over in London. Why think you have anything on the Frenchmen. Certain of your own writers have told you. Told you the melting pot theory is EXPLODED. Mr. Zangwill invented the term; he was gauche, he was pathetic. But the word had a career.

The idea was tempting. So was the old Yankee idea of trying a woman of every nation, or of as many as possible.

What's wrong with halfbreeds7 Do you know one of'em who don't suffer sometimes from cleverness, that don't quite come solid, sometimes from a peculiar sort of stoppage INSIDE the head, leadin' to a kind of sense of frustration?

For 60 years mankind has been experimentin' on guinea pigs. All sorts of experiments. Seems fairly clear that you fix a breed by LIMITING the amount of alien infiltration. You make a race by homogeneity and by avoiding INbreeding. The wisdom of China long ago ruled out inbreedin'. The hundred names, no man to marry a woman of his own name, that was a barrier on the one side.

Céline has got down to the other. The next move, the next world movement is a move toward the production of thoroughbreds. Think it over. That idea is a risin'. Means no hardship to anyone. It is eugenic. No argument has ever been sprouted against it. You like it in dogs and horses. One would think the human race was worth as much attention as the British fanciers give to whiffets.

Albert Londres had a hunch that the French ought to try it on blacks in their Africa. He hated to see the Africans going rotten, covered with scabs in French colonies. Céline thinks it would be useful to use that much sense on Frenchmen. So I suppose Admiral Leahy, or whatever Layafettist [?], is over there at Vichy trying to blackmail Pétain, will be trying to git ALL Céline's books forbidden or pinched in the UNOCCUPIED parts of French territory.

Oh, it's a lovely world, as Candide has told us, all that is, is the best possible.

Mebbe in time the American college boys will gil'round to reading me or Céline or some of the Livin' authors. BUT don't git to thinking that, just because the Clipper ships carry so little NEWS, that there is NOTHING being written in Europe. Ole Europe is still here on the continent. Josh Twostep, Josher Dos Passos hasn't succeeded in persuadin' Europe that times like these are times in which the writer should lay off writin'.

Times like these are times when a writer should git down to bedrock and talk without fuzz on his tongue. Céline does that all right enough. Time to read Céline for the simple truths that stand there in his writing, expressed with perfect lucidity—and simplicity. You may be a bit late in startin'.

A great writer is one whose straight simple phrases stick in the memory.

L'âme n'est pas venue sur la terre pour se faire émerger.

#38 (May 17, 1942) U.K.(B45)
FREE SPEECH IN ALBION (ALIAS ENGLAND)

The propaganda for free speech in Britain (listlessly elegiac, retrospective) r sounds as follows: "The murderer stole my watch but his wife told him not to. We have free speech in this family." That is how it sounds HERE. No one denies that free speech is a fine old British tradition. One complains that it is a moth-eaten tradition: a shadow with small present substance. The series of outrages committed by British governments in the past. Chesapeaken Leopard, etc. are in history. That Bright protested, etc. during the United States Civil War, is in history.

What the B.B.C. does NOT care to admit is the profound resemblance between England's *divide et impera* during our United States Civil War, and her policy on the continent of Europe.

All of which is most keenly analyzed in *Mein Kampf*, a book as slandered in England and as much obscured by press mud as any other.

It is the points to WHICH British free speech does not APPLY that we want to hear about. Free speech has been cornered. We complain that the British press was rotten, and had been for over a century. My memory goes back considerably further than Mr. Bridson's, whatever Winnie said in 1936: I can match it. I remember the pavements of London "WE WANT EIGHT" back before the other war started.

Winston was allus shoutin' for gun sales, high pressure salesmanship of blood, cannon, and slaughter.

BUT at the same time upholdin' a usury system which made it impossible to deliver the cannon. Hence bringing slaughter on Europe.

It is not the question of British chauvinism, but the mixture of chauvinism and absolute utter dishonesty, and a refusal to look at the economic causes of war that disgusts the foreign observer. That some Englishmen dislike being betrayed needs no argument. That the English people did NOT desire the war needs no argument. The point is they kept on having governments that insisted on having a war. The British people are NOT represent ed. The B.B.C. may run a very good (up to a point) retrospect about Free Speech in England. BUT to couple that with the unholy alliance with

Russia does not convince the opponent of England's bona fide, rather of idiocy and dishonesty.

Kumrad Maisky's FACE, like the hindend of a pig, for example. WHY does England suppose that Kumrad Maisky will hesitate any longer about bumping off George VI and Elizabeth, than his pals did about killin' the Czar, with Temple of Canterbury sayin' the blessin'? No, Temple is a prize comic, possibly Lang WOULD have pronounced an Episcopal benediction? Temple don't, I think, mean any harm, just fat headed.

Rhetoric about "our representatives in Parliament" is NOT the point. The point is your Parliament does NOT represent you. That is the syndicalist complaint against Parliaments in the old rotten borough or disguised rotten bank-borough form.

Every CONstructive measure proposed to camouflage the iniquity of your usuries is a slavish copy of the corporate state.

BUT without the corporate structure, just patchin', and NOT hitting for the main evil. Money is admitted by at least one B.B.C. yapper to be a financial label. But interest? When does that occur properly?

And WHO fixes the label, and in whose interests? And IS there a Jewish problem?

Perhaps, along with Carlyle's love for his wife, and the fine old husky sailor voices telling of the Chesapeake and the Leopard, there might be a historic sketch of the Jews and Noll Crummwell, and a FEW probes into the WHY of the present struggle, and the REFUSALS to cooperate with the civilized world, and the hook-up with Russia.

Does the Bolshevic government stand for the best English traditions: free speech, and no taxation without representation?

Fat lot of representation your tax payers have had in this budget. Though I dare say they have been by now so hog swoggled by propaganda, appeals to their finest feeling, that they are ready to murder their children and grandmas in the cause of 60% on real deposits. And a perfect fury of abuse and hysteria when some Frenchman opens a book of geography and discovers what was long since known to Theophile Gautier, namely that France is a part of Europe. ON THE MAP, geographically, France is a PART of Europe, and her sanity and welfare would consist IN functioning as PART of Europe.

Preferably a Frenchman, not a half nigger, half Jew bridged head of Anglo-Judaea. Some idea, that is the GEOGRAPHIC idea, may someday enter England. But no signs of British desire to collaborate in a new order have yet emerged from the British Bleat Corps halls of transmission.

Divide et impera. I dunno who translated *Mein Kampf* into English. Here Bompiani or someone had an idea, and stroke of genius, and printed the second half first, so Italian readers, some of'em, came straight on the program, constructive program, health, responsibility, personal, and a study of history. Elsewhere in the book, you can see Hitler (if you have YET begun to develop an interest in that opponent of your infamies: you can see Hitler thinking about the evils of having Innthal, valley of the Inn, cut off from the rest of the German Volk. You can see him, figgerin' out for Germany, what a few Americans figured out for the United States of America. *Divide et impera.*

Of course, you are gittin' divided for the same old Sassoon [who is] wantin' U.S. farm boys to squeeze interest out of the Hindoos, now that T. Atkins is getting scarcer.

The rest of the world is tired, bloody well TIRED of having Chesapeakes and RESULTS: accompanied by Mrs. Burglar Bill tellin' Bill not to do it. Yes, some British protested against chattel slavery. The wheeze, the BANK wheeze, now KNOWN, and recorded in history, being that wage slavery was CHEAPER, that LESS responsibility devolved on the OWNERS (alias employers) of wage slaves than on the owners of black slaves, who had to feed'em to keep up their workin' potential. ALL that is HISTORY.

The world, especially Europe, is tired, tired, and the English stock, the part of the English RACE in the colonies was tired from 1750 onward of being sanctioned, of having their OWN money censored.

Sanctioned, forbidden—their AUTARCHY, such as it was, sabotaged, their prosperity sabotaged by a kike gang or a sub-kike or super-gang of grafters and monopolists, headquarters in London.

And YOU will, I'spose, get your karma, your *contrapasso* when the head office shifts from Last Cheape, and Thredbobbin Alley over to Wall, Street with Wailing included. Shama Yssrael, the one true fatherland is the pawn shop.

Why take that INTO your so very [valued] tradition. Beatin' your breasts. Give us a nut to crack and God can crack it. As for the people, one of your own living poets has beaten his hairy breast as follows: We can think as we are told to think

We are the echo of the loudest bark.

We are the arses kicked by better men.

There is this very uncurious mixture in British propaganda. The wailing wall, AND the reminiscence, the old lavender, the Spanish Armada, etc. The TRADITIONS, the better of which 20 years of British politics have done so little to maintain.

You can't expect me to stenograph all your noises. [I'd] go out of my head when I wake up the next morning in a country that asks RESULTS and about which YOU apparently know very little.

Why, for example, should Hitler and Mussolini who have been through a great deal more than I have, who have been thru a great deal I have not, endured hardships I have not, why should they be scared by Mr. Hull, Mr. C. Hull or Eden, when these stiffed effigies can't even scare ME?

Why all this talk of the German Staff regardin' with fear and trembling the arrival of a few motor boats at Le Portel, or wherever, the 33 or what ever out of the 50 or whatever remained with their ammunition; pore devils? TO take England's MIND OFF England's business, the business she OUGHT to have been minding and HOW, since 1919, since Versailles defrauded Italy.

#39 (May 18, 1942) U.S.(B43)
WITH PHANTOMS

Two topics that I have rarely touched in these conversations—Germany and Lord Tennyson.

And of Tennyson I now quote but a verse and a fragment.

"Shall come to fight with phantoms and to fall" (maybe it was fail). I haven't been readin' Tennyson lately, but that much sticks in my head from the Idyls.

"Shall come to fight with phantoms and to fall." I guess it was fall. Take it as prophecy. And the phantom that the Anglo-Jew world is fighting, or that the Anglo-American is fighting, a Jew usurer instigation, is the German PHANTOM, NOT the reality. And that phantom has been built out of lies, till the pious and kindly American, and simple hearted British boob BY the million believe it, see it, hear it.

And FAIL to grasp or to face the reality.

Now I almost never talk of Germany because I have seen very little of Germany. Ole Ford toted me'round about Hessen Darmstadt in 1911, tellin' me what a fine country was Germany. Then he wrote *When Blood is their Argument*. Since then I have been to Vienna and to Frankfurt for Antheil's opry, and passed thru Munich and from Wien I went up to Wörgl. And as the young can't be expected to know my past history I'spose I got to preface it.

That I was interested in CIVILIZATION from the age of 12 when I first saw Venice. Venice looked good to me. Anyhow, I came to Europe to git kulchur all right, and to a great extent got it. Started in U. Penn. at 15 to FIND out what had been written, and what was the BEST of it, in as many languages as I could gil under my occiput; to KNOW what the real thing was. And thence to HISTORY and economics.

To SEE what was going on in the world TODAY, as I needed it in my business, my business being WRITIN', and an Epic being a container of HISTORY.

Of course you need music to understand real versification. But comin' from a duck-board country, I was interested in LATIN order. Order in stone work, in paintin', *Adamo me fecit*. S. Zeno Verona, architect had cut that column by HAND, by his own hand, want INTEGRAL, totalitarian interest in the job of buildin' S. Zeno. Church of S. Zeno. I liked Quattro cento paintin'. P. Uccello. First freshman theme, I wrote was on Paulo Uccello, picture in Louvre I reckon.

Anyhow, apart from Von der Vogelweide, old Schnitz Brandt lettin' me jump the prose and come to the osses, the poetry, medieval German poetry, in 1904 or 5. I didn't much cotton to German literature, in cf. with the Mediterranean. Dante, Villon, provençal Canzoni writers; anyhow, I didn't cotton to German literature. And then philology, ERROR of old German university system got my goat. And I laid off readin' German till I hit Leo Frobenius.

Also being in England 12 years, I certainly saw the last war from the Lon don angle. Lump in my throat when I heard even in this one, that Vimy Ridge had been taken. I could take all the rest of it but, when I heard Vimy was taken, that was a tough one. BUT JUSTICE IS JUSTICE. And lies are a poor Ersatz for justice. And as to LYING I reckon Hitler has been lied about more than any man livin' except Mussolini.

Now re Mussolini. I KNOW they are lyin'. I['v] been here 17 years and I have known for 17 years they were lyin'. Lies and threats against Italy, after the Versailles cheatin'. That offense to humanity, Robert Mond, threatenin' Mussolini. Waal, it used to be said in London that Alfred looked like one end of a pig, and that Robert Mond looked like the other. And the FORM certainly did show the spirit inside'em.

I believe the younger generation felt it, and has had a lurch over toward honesty. But he sure has heredity workin' against him. And a Jew who wants to run honest certainly ain't chosen a bed of roses. Sure, some Jews aspire to honesty, kindly impulses, gestures of opulence. But gawd help'em. And God save humanity FROM them.

Well, very few real reports about Germany have got into English or American circulation. I doubt if many of'em have got into second editions. So when I contradict lies about Germany, my ground is limited. I have one or two fragmentary first hand reports. I have PRINTED data. Now when I was doing my job on Sig. Malatesta I came to the conclusion that DOCUMENTS, personal letters and what not, PROVED ONE THING:

A letter PROVES what the bloke who wrote it wanted the receiver to believe ON the day he wrote it.

The rest of history has to be derived from computation. IF documents DISAPPEAR with remarkable coincidence, say reports of an event in February in 1424, there was something someone was trying to KEEP from the public.'Specially if the despatches for a particular day disappear from six archives simultaneously, and *so weiter*.

Well I know the Times, Telegraph, N.Y. Post and all the damn kikery also kiker Archibishopery of England, LIED about Italy. And I know f rpm first hand that facts about Germany did NOT git much anglo-yanko publicity. And I keep off guess work when writin' my history. That is, I separate guess work from SOLIDS. And a solid is, for example, that a certain idea was PRINTED on a given day. And I do NOT assert things to be so from readin' translations till I have seen the originals. That is, I treat translations as translations. And not having read the English version of Mein Kampf I will not discuss it.

That book was translated into Italian and printed in 1933 (yaas, a delay, not an immediate publication) and Bompiani had [a] *coup de genie*, published the second half first, so the Italian public had chance to GET the program clear and at the start. And I affirm that there has for years been the most God damned ignorance and misapprehension of that program in England and America.

I myself had only a vague idea. I wasn't intent on Germany. I had my job with my writin', and my recordin' of ITALY. Trying to git things straight. I could see it was GOOD here in Italy. I said it was the ONE inch of solid ground. That's why I came here. ONE inch of solid earth where a man could see straight and write it; could buck the international money swine and NOT disappear altogether. And I reckoned in a general way that Germany etc. etc. NOT till the time of Sanctions did I begin to consider Germany from a new angle. Up till then I had drifted on, pretty much in the old 1914 view that Germany ought to be etc., etc.

APART, that is, from my view of *Drang nach Osten*. Germany, natural civilizer of Russia, ought to keep western edge of Europe at level of civilization and amenity already reached, at least that. And let Germany go East leaving the old balance of power. Not till I was settin' by the bandstand, or standin' and I heard "*forse con mciggiorgiustizia*," voice on the radio, givin' a survey of Europe, did I begin to wonder: Well, maybe. I was behindhand in readin' *Mein Kampf*, but do you YET know what is IN it? Have you a clear idea of the PROGRAM? Hitler in 1924 saying that Germany ought to lay off the Tyrol, ought to SEE Italy. See Italy Fascist as the ONE ray of light in a world that was going to sunset, sinking. Just as I saw it as the ONE inch of SOLID basis. Well, Brother Adolf did do something about it, while I was lookin' and listenin'. An' I hand it to him that he is more efficient than lam.

Now what were, and are the THREE planks of the Hitler program as set forth in the opening of *La Mia Battaglia*, Italian translation of second half of *Mein Kampf*?

First, HEALTH, health of the race. Now every American (or Englander of my generation or of that before or after my generation) knew and knows that we were up against the problem of "be a SLAVE or not breeding." Any man not born rich in our time KNEW he had to mate late. Breed LATE, and breed few, or else go into slavery. Mr. Curtis Moffit said to me that he saw what would happen if he was a good boy, so he decided on badness. Said he would be a BAD boy, and float on the TOP of the current. Waal, I landed in Europe, as my incipient biographers have stated, with justice, with 80 bucks, American dollars (pre-Morgenthau) in my clothin' and that led me to a practical view of some problems. As to the Hitler program, it was (what we ALL knew, and did nothing about, namely) that the breedin' of human beings deserves MORE care and attention than the breedin' of horses and wiffetts, or even the breedin' of sheep, goat, and the larger livestock. That is point ONE of the NAZI program. Breed GOOD, and preserve the race. Breed thorough, that is for thoroughbreds, conserve the BEST of the race. Conserve the best elements. That means EUGENICS: as opposed to race suicide. And it did not and does NOT please the Talmudic Jews who want to kill off ALL the other races whom they can not subjugate; and drive down what he thinks [is doin', his USF to his race or nation consists in seeing the OBJECT and writin' down what he sees, and not falsifying his record.

SECONDLY, what is the second point of the Hitler program? Personal responsibility. A political system in which you can't pass the buck. Very unpleasant for hired M.P.'s DEBTORS (Jews, butter-and-egg-men fakers like Wendell Willkie, and M.P. congressmen, etc.). Financed by Jews and put in the legislatures to defraud the people in usurer's interests and kept there by bank money who can be on committees, and always, always avoid ALL responsibility for swindling laws. Such as was the demonetization of silver [in] 1873, the sale of the country in 1863. The Federal Reserve System, and its infamous workings, making the people pay two dollars for every one dollar spent by the government.

Hitler, having seen the Jew puke in the German democracy, was out for responsibility, government officials etc. to be RESPONSIBLE for their acts. MOST unpleasant for Monds, War burgs, invisible de facto Jew governments.

And the THIRD point was a STUDY of history. To look at the history. Waaal, now WHAT program does this CONTRADICT? I ask you, if you are such low down and gol darn suckers, or such British blockheads, or such unfathomable and irredeemable IGNORAMI, as NOT to know what program this contradicts, there is not a great deal of hope for your posterity. I may tell you someday where the opposing program is found, if you are too weak-kneed and puny to trace it. And when you, or if you do trace it, you may see why the stick screen was erected, and why people began to speak evil of Hitler. As to who spake and speaks evil of Hitler, we will someday go into that also.

#40 (May 21, 1942) U.S.(B49)
E. E. CUMMINGS EXAMINED

I have to go on tryin' to tell you. And I now tell you that your Mr. Cummings is a very great writer, I tell you he follows H. James, and Thoreau, and Whitman. I tell you he is the most intelligent man in America.

If that is an earful, TAKE it. I don't know what is to become of our educated intelligentsia, or whatever. An American, fullblooded American, writes a book in every way as BIG as the Apes of God or Ulysses. It gets some attention, it does not get nearly enough. You make a contribution to the world literature of tomorrow, and you pay very little attention to what happens right thaar under your noses.

I told you once before that this book [Cummings' inspection of Russia makes a trilogy of big books, along with those of Joyce and of Wyndham Lewis, with *Ulysses* and Lewis's APES, *Apes of God* by ole Wyndham Lewis, also like Mr. Cummings a painter. That fact has its bearin'.

Both of'em used to USING their eyes. Use of the eye assists human beings in making direct observations. I am not up to comparin' their painting, I know very little of Mr. Cumming's painting, save I saw one bit that had UGH! I am talkin' now of his writing. And in comparin' EIMI, or AMI or however your different Greek professors tell you to pronounce it, with the other two volumes, I say, or mebbe repeat that Joyce was writin' in retrospect. Ulysses dishes up the capitalist situation, the HELL made in great cities by the usury system. That is a limit. Not a very new point of view about anything.

Well I dunno as Ole Wyndham's *Apes* had a very new point of view either. Rowlandson, Fielding, Hogarth, all might have seen that boil on old England's neck from similar standpoint. Irish, English, and America, Joyce had no philosophy. Gasps from his chapel parishioners, Joyce had some ruck end of theology and a VERY conventional outlook. Lewis had philosophic views.

I nacherly never agreed with either of''em about much of anything. I agree with my compatriot or ex-compatriot, Mr. Cummings, a very great deal. But not wholly. I back up damn near anything Mr. Cummings has said or will say. I have to think back after having reread him, I have to think back and wonder, now just what was it that I wanted to ask him, where was it I wanted him to go on a bit further.

Lewis' limit in that particular hefty volume, inhered in his subject, he was doing the carbuncle on Johnnie Bull's neck. Cummings, followin' ole Hen. James, was doing all Russia, and doing it in the Jamesian sense, that he was constantly comparing that nation, or state of existence with the American state of existence, with a peripheric view of countries adjacent.

Oh, yes, e. estlin was a carryin' on from his forebears, both James and Thoreau, and I repeat it, [from] Whitman. That just unfinish, on certain pages, that weak spot, or what seems a weak spot to the European.

Mebbe three or four paragraphs that I as professor would probably cross out of his manuscript, or would have crossed out, and said, here bo', you rewrite this, 432 or 431 pages. I should have been much more severe on Flaubert. How is the book greater than Joyce's volume, or than Lewis's *Apes*? If we must use this terminology or why do I like it better, if I do like it better. Or say why does it come easier to me, I am hoistin' up over questions of technique, Cummings' neologism, his punctuation. Well I am American. I perceive his technique, which Jefferson, Tom Jefferson, would have justified; which is justified by the measure Jefferson applied to neologism. Namely, new words justified when NECESSARY to express a new meaning. A great deal of Joyce was NOT new, and a great deal was needless, was in the do main of experiment, colors being mixed on a palette. Lewis needed his emphasis, often as EMPHASIS, not merely as meaning save insofar as emphasis is part of meaning, which is not always.

Cummings I believe needed EVERY single split word to say what he was saying. In no other way could he have registered Russia, 1931, and it was a very great registration. Also you might now take it as psychic and warnin'. *Ulysses* was not a warning. It was a certificate of demise. *The Apes of God*, was, and HOW a warning, unheeded. There is still time for the U.S.A. to read Mr. Cummings before worse things happen, I mean happen TO YOU.

Now in part Mr. Cummings teaches a doctrine which is very ably condensed (dichten, condensare; to write poetry is to CONDENSE), Mr. Cummings teaches a truth which a contemporary German author has stated quite clearly, as follows:

What we are used to call public opinion is based only in very small part on per sonal experience or indeed on the experience of particular persons or indeed on the knowledge of individual voters, but for the most part on a collective representation (collective picture) which brings about in a strangely obstinate and insistent way a so called process of clarification of the problems.

Now the USE of a great writer to his RACE is due precisely to his having PERSONAL direct perception, and puttin' in down on paper. Don't matter what he thinks [he] is doin', his USE to race or nation consists in seeing the OBJECT and writin' down what he sees, and not falsifying his record.

Mebbe by an' by afterwards that word photo, that diagram, that TRUE diagram can serve to enlighten his people. Don't forget they are HIS people as they will never be the people of any member of Congress.

And Mr. Cummings went, unbelievably, he might now say, went down into hell, alias Soviet Russia.

And you are now allied to Soviet Russia. A thing estlin cummings certainly never thought of when he was writin' his *ami* or *eimi* which, as byproduct, the American people, you American folks MIGHT now use for your OWN gettin' enlightened. I'm tellin' you. Apart from the joy of readin' a great American book, IF you read it slowly, it might be of practical use.

I once had a kike friend who had a theory about poetry, namely, that no one ever read ALL the words on a page. It didn't, that theory didn't lead him to making his poetry quite satisfactory, but as theory it may also serve to enlighten you.

Now Mr. Cummings writes PROSE, whereof every word tells its story. And I myself made an error first time I tried to read him. Tried to read him too fast, got impatient. No use approachin' him that way.

Got to read slow. More on one page than on two pages of most other authors, so you get as much in three minutes readin' him slow, as you do to readin' Josh Passos faster, or readin' Wilder at ten pages a minute.

You CAN skip in some authors, you cannot in Cummings skip one word on page ten without maybe losin' the bearin' of what he is saying elsewhere. Go at him slowly.

Second point is his parenthesis, are his parentheses. Well old Henry James worried his European readers to death by his parentheses. They are an American habit, they mean something to us and for us as Americans. They mean something more than the one track mind. But they do NOT imply deviation or lack of direction. They are a desperate attempt, no not an attempt, a DEVICE, to avoid leaving out something NEEDED, some part of the statement needed to set down, to register the direction, and meaning.

Well, Cummings said a whole mouthful; he said a bookful. Was out above the glooms of *Ulysses*, and the factor of Lewis top hole in London. There is in Cummings what the Chinese say with an ideogram.

Ideogram that I have translated as candid. I don't much hold with Mr. Legge's translation of that sign, though it means what he says in the context wherefrom he was translatin' it. He translated it: devoid of principles, passage in Confucius about lawyer making speeches in court with NO reference to rights, fairness of justice, just spoutin' their rhetoric in the hope of a decision. The ideogram is worth more than is to be said in that context. It is made up of two signs, + [and] negative; sign for heart, sign for AZURE: meanin' a man who has no open sky in his heart. [In the positive] meanin' azure hearted, or candid. Here comes in Thoreau, here comes in Silver Lake in Mr. Cummings' composition. BUT herewith stays also Mr.

Cummings' text, like that German statement about direct sight or perception. [FCC transcript: That sign heart and azure man with his sky in heart is a sign for Amencans. I hope you won't lose it. As to the direct vision, that is the painter's genius, it is the genius of Cummings. Few men could have gone into Russia and not be beaten by ideology.

Now what do you know of Russia? If you are studious, you know what you read in——and the——for example, and——you have learned from, etc., but since then what record? There is one record available in both American and English readers today, namely, that made by E.E. Cummings. It may be too late for you really to use it, but you want to live also to morrow, perhaps not. At any rate, if you want to live, even today, you better read it. You better learn what Roosevelt and Atlee and Cripps are importing into America, into England, and what has already been dumped into America, with the horse of a——shock troops, bubolic plague in the——. Whether America, whether the American heritage was an invasion, what invasions in person in the——Bolshevised immigrants. What racial invasion, what invasions of American ideology? Not only from Russia, there are Dr. Freud's imported stinks, not a Slavic invasion, or not a Slavic invasion only——. And the azure hearts of America threaten, and how, oh, yes, threaten the New England heritage (present).

I emphasized this book among other things because you have so few books available, and what you have are in part unhandy. You won't read John Adams' ten volumes, they aren't handy. You have not read Brooks Adams, you could read him.]

Some of you have a vague suspicion as to what controls your press and your radio. Few have any concept of what runs your university endow ments. Most of'em generous, most of'em honest in intention, partly from vanity, from sense of magnificence, from desire to hand some of it back. The magnanimity is in most cases unquestioned, but the OVERHEAD and the effects of overhead were not thought of.

Even the Academy of Social and Political Science circulatin' Jew propaganda: probably in utter unconsciousness of what they are up to. The ACCEPTANCE, supine, groveling, half witted, in sense of half conscious, or wholly unconscious, of the SUPPRESSIONS. The idea that the boss is dumb, that a radio company is CONTROLLED by a filthy sub-Zukor. A whole generation, or two gents accepting that sort of suppression, while listening to blah about democracy, freedom, baloney.

You don't YET know what Hitler has written, let alone what Mussolini has written. You WON'T read the works of the men who MADE the American nation. You don't read Hollis' *Two Nations*. Well damn you, read Cummings if you won't read Brooks Adams, or better read both of'em and try to find out what has been done to you. What is being done to you, conducive to material, spiritual, and intellectual RUIN.

#41 (May 24, 1942) U.K.(B47)
BRAIN TRUST

On a bright Sunday morning, recently, after listening to the London Brain Trust, I turned the button to Rome and was regaled by the statement *"Abbiamo trasmesso un programma di musica varia,"* meaning we have transmitted a program of mixed music. Than which no comment conscious or unconscious could have been more apt.

Yes, I now listen to your Brain Trust's polyphonic obligatin' abd[?] you have there your British best: and it does you good, I mean it, to some extent, redeems England's prestige and makes up for other B.B.C. trans missions as, for example, the crass imbecilities emitted about Japan by some [uninformed] unformed Pittecanthropus.

The Brain Trust indeed now skirts gingerly on the edge of several of almost my questions: BUT does not face them and CONtinues, possibly involuntary falsifications of diverse issues.

I have spoken before of Mr. Bridson's very able skit or whatever you call it, radio dialog dramedy or whatever on free speech.

Well the point for all Europe is that Free Speech is merely a concom mitant of crime, injustice, infamy, or worse, if it be used as a mere diversion, a mere camouflage and mere flapping of a cloth to GET THE auditors MIND off the FACTS; [it] is NOT a passport to the world's universal esteem.

It is a fine old, that is, it is IN ITSELF a fine thing UNDER some circum stances. It is fine to protest against wrong and injustice. BUT NOT if that protest is used merely or mainly to cover some greater evil, some greater injustice.

Now England has a guilty conscience. You may as well face THAT issue. Mr. Bridson wisely admitted a number of England's past crimes. He did NOT quite face England's present crimes and evasions.

The attempts against the American colonies, the press campaign against Lincoln, the list of England's past crimes is a long one. BUT Britain, France, Spain still fail to MENTION what was possibly the MAIN cause of the American Revolution, namely, the suppression of Pennsylvania colony paper money (and to almost a Gesellite system), in 1750.

Suppressed in 1750. Usury you keep off of; the interest problem, problem of WHEN is it just to receive annual payment on invested capital is NOT yet in the brain trust's repertoire. I think .it was a certain Ingram who pussyfooted all round it.

I am beginning to have a certain respect for the Brain Trust. At least England is still the INTELLECTUAL capital of the anti-Axis forces, even if England's power and Jewry have shifted their center. The U.S. is still being a colony mentally.

BUT England's CRIME on the intellectual plane is OPEN and flagrant. You have not admitted and do not admit, and among people presumably as EDUCATED as some of the brain trust members (despite the funny grammar used in their conversations at sudden moment) among such representatives of England, top drawer intellects, it is flagrant and shameful—such non admission is.

Now the Brain Trust ought to know that Europe has committed in the past several feats of PEDAGOGY and is STILL [teaching England. Despite all your guns, cannons and bombardment of] French civilians, England is STILL learning from Europe willy-nilly, and mostly nilly. BUT practically ALL the new measures [of which] you boast are TAKEN from Fascism. You have cursed, sworn, lied, etc.

about fascism and now in moments of trial you BOAST, and the few things you say with a clear voice and conviction are all on this line. You take over one Fascist measure after another and then pretend that your quarrel with Europe is only with regimes, not with the total population of Europe. You are intellectually dishonest in your refusal to recognize the great gifts which Rome for centuries and which Germany since the days of Holbein has given to England and you turn on the bloody Russian savagery to smash the whole of European civilization and you get out the pig-ended Maisky to boast of how much is to be included in the smashing.

Your very name Trust meaning in current terms Monopoly is an unconscious assertion of imbecility and pretentious. You probably think you have the monopoly and you most certainly haven't. You are so purse-proud and, what is worse, head-proud that you see no intellect outside the circle of your own interests. And you will pay for it. You will pay for your high horsey presumption as there is justice or as in the physical world there is a law of reaction in relation to action. You have overweaned.

Free speech, as I have said, is NO universal passport. Not if it follows free lying, and skillfully directed lying and *mean* innuendo. Your anti- German propaganda is mostly mean innuendo. Italy has had so much of that from you that this rather strengthens the Axis bonds. Too many nations have had the same treatment from England not to recognize the symptoms. Laval is getting it now and that might convert several former sufferers who otherwise would not have felt any sympathy for him.

As to the meanness of some of the Jewish voices from London, speaking in foreign tongues, I don't'spose the Brain Trust notices THAT. Who in deed are they to take note of the foreign tongues in their Babel, of the foreign sounds squirming OUT from their Babel? *Gnossi seauton*, slight con fusion, perhaps between goosing and *gnossing*. Yaas, I know, I occasionally put over a mean one. In the war of nerves I am right out on the point, I am takin' it.

You, maybe, can bust me. Keep on a tryin'. Perfect peace, down in Canterbuggy cathedral? BUT YOU are learning from Italy. I don't think you have yet started on Germany, I mean learning from Germany.

And as to Japan, that I suppose will be relegated to the School of Oriental Languages in East London, or wherever Ole Sir Dennison put it. "1 inquired of the ostrich. Why did you swallow that wrist watch," etc.?

Alleged portrait of England. A great man for foolin' was Dennison.

Your Brain Trust runs up all'round the world, even learns geographic facts about Texas, get water from mountain springs, and the rest of it. Some of'em must know that there is a place called the ORIENT.

Now apparently takin' care of itself. That's not my subject, not for the moment. Now needed is to get you English to understand that there IS, yes IS, a place called Europe, a continent, and that you OWE something to European civilization, vastly more than you owe to the Warburgs and other holders of Anglo-Israels' I.O.U.'s. And that debt you have NO present intention to recognize. In fact, you have called in the bloody baboons from the Urals to beat up, and if possible to kill off your creditor.

AND the creditor is OBJECTING and has a bloody good RIGHT to object; and no amount of freely spoken objections on your part, freely opened Into, and most skillfully and on 20 wavelengths thunderously emitted in all the known languages of five continents, are going to break down the BASIC case against England. May break up England, she may break up herself. But there remains the basic injustice, and the whole series of lies used to cover it, used to distract world attention from the basic JUST claims of your opponents.

I won't even say enemies. I have seen very little real enmity. I have seen determination toward justice.

The illusion of British gentleness was strong. The prestige of Glad stone's humanitarianism was so great that many Europeans still rub their eyes and say: can this EVIL be England? And that amazement you have tried to exploit, with your persisting lies about the feelings of Europe.

No one attacked your free speech. You set up a Jew government in Germany and the Germans HAD to get rid of it, or die. You behaved with crass injustice to Italy and the Italians woke up and reacted, until I hear from my best tempered friend on a tennis court—might have been while your ex-emperor was playin' golf on the other side of the bushes, but I reckon it was a month or so later— *gli inglesi sono porci*. Pigs: the English are porci PIGS, or the dog in the manger.

I take it the Duce has seen some rough stuff in his time, but I think ONE thing in his later life has surprised him, and that was the sheer selfishness and meanness of England.

I am not speakin' officially, I haven't had anything to go by save my own intuition, and whatever evidence is open to anyone. NOT one syllable has come out of England during the past two years or three years, to show that England has one iota of consciousness that human beings can be other than English, that there are human beings in Europe, endowed by nature with rights equal to those of sentient human beings. What has the TRUST or monopoly of your brains got to answer to that indictment? For God's sake, LOOK at the parallels.

As to Anglo Jewry, that is YOUR problem. But as to parallels, as to PERSISTENCE in the same kinds of criminal action, AFTER, for decades, almost centuries, AFTER your Wilkeses and Burkes and Bradlaws have free- speaking PROTESTED against this or that infamy, what is your Brain Trust's answer?

One man, or hero, protests, England does evil. She loosens the red savages against her own kinsmen.

She loosens Russia on Finland and Rumania. And if she proposes now, as she did in the 18th century, to crush a high civilization by an incursion of savages. The leopard stays spotty. England helped to protract the Civil War in America till the South was crushed and the U.S. NEVER recovered: except on the plane of material products.

The U.S. NEVER got back to the level of economic justice she had, kept on fighting for UP till the Civil War. The documents were mislaid or hidden. It is only recently we have begun to get at the facts, facts of the great betrayal, the sell out to London Jewry. - And if you think you are paying [for] your sin, LOOK to it, for the *contrapasso*, the kharma, is now in function. As the U.S. was sold to your Jews, you are now in the process of being auctioned, heirs of the same business houses, or of the same USURY system. Offices now in New York.

Will the Brain Trust look into this history? Will they observe that Americans will some day come to see what England has now tried on Italy and on Germany? And to UNDERSTAND it by precedents in England's treatment of them, treatment of the American colonies, and of the U.S. divided by the war of secession, and by the DEBT period that followed that brotherly slaughter?

Possibly the Brain Trust does not mean to exist ONLY in the dimension of the evasions? Mr. Bridson, being younger, possibly errs merely from lack of full information. Your out-in-front man offered you tears and blood. That's O.K. if you like it. But why expect Europe, and two thirds of Asia to think you have a brain monopoly if that is all you can offer it or in deed offer yourselves?

Free speech is NOT full compensation for government by hidden and IRRESPONSIBLE forces, interested mainly or solely in squeeze, in tip and run, WITH the profits. I know that isn't the Brain Trust's main aim. They are interested in conversation. And gettin' the cream off the surface in one way or another.

But what about JUSTICE? What about usury, interest, speculation in the breed of the people, monopoly not only of grey matter, as announced in a half serious headline?

Seems like the ONLY free speech on CERTAIN topics has been left to ME on this Radio, thanks to a civil tradition, thanks to an age old tradition; two parts, Cicero against Verres and the Renaissance. Mebbe the Brain Trust is forgettin' its Latin? Mebbe it never had enough Latin? In Burke's time M.P.s used to quote Latin. Some of the Brain Trust's members speak almost Yiddish. And when not, the substance, Judaic substance is thinly veiled. Oh, very clever your B.B.C. stage acts, with the local accents, I git that.

My typewriter, and Jim's typewriter, and few Irish and American typewriters, against VAST resources, I see that. But what about Justice: and money interest?

#42 (May 28, 1942) U.S. & U.K. (B50)
AS A BEGINNING

If there is anyone capable of serious thought anywhere in range of this broadcast, let him at least try to think what I mean by the following statements.

Let him start trying to STUDY the two revolutions, the Fascist and Nazi revolutions. God knows if Hitler is telling his people that THEY should study the Italian fascist revolution.

YOU need a thousand more times to study it, and to study the resurrection of Hitler's REICH. How can anyone worth the name of a man in England or in America face these two great movements in the half baked, or not even HALF baked ignorance into which his newspapers have led him or dumped him?

Something has OCCURRED in old Europe. Even the cloistered apes of Oxford or the inventors of stink gas in Harvard ought by now to have heard that, at least that, something has happened IN EUROPE, and you do not know what has happened.

You do not know what has HAPPENED. And the first thing to DO about it is to pull OUT of this war—a war that you never ought to have flopped into. Every hour that you go on with it is an hour lost to you and your children.

And every sane act you commit is committed in HOMAGE to Mussolini and Hitler. Every reform, every lurch toward the just price, toward the control of the market is an act of HOMAGE to Mussolini and Hitler.

THEY are your leaders, however much you are conducted by Roosevelt or sold up by Churchill. You FOLLOW Hitler and Mussolini in EVERY CONSTRUCTIVE act of your governments. Damn you, you follow Moseley, go back and read over his programs.

As to the pity, etc. of it. You insisted on having your war. You would not budge out of your constipations, you would not listen to your own savants, by which, by the word savants, I mean the Englishmen who KNEW something, AT least, about something, and who told you HOW to keep out of the slaughter, how to cure your own plague spots and diseases.

And you WOULD not, by Jheezus, you would not. England interests me far more in this moment, in this year, than America. England was further on mentally than America; is possibly still the intellectual capital of America. The sword and the purse leave the island: but the brain is still faintly pulsating in England. There are more men STILL in the island than in the United States who are capable of serious correlations.

I could name ten Englishmen for every American who knows ANYthing about anything valid in economics or history. There were at least little movements, nuclei, meetings.

America had not awakened to her dangers. She was pitifully UNAWARE of her history. Especially that of her past 80 years. Christ knows what sort of chaos the United States is in for. Christ knows how long it will take her to untangle.

And God knows when England will know her own saviours or would-be saviours. As distinct from her wreckers and provocative agents. Your jails have never before been so full of political prisoners guilty of nothing save their own beliefs and convictions. But not since the days of Noll Cromwell, and never have English voices in exile so agonized over your errors. Voices indubitable for their sincerity and conviction of the truth of their messages. They are not all of'em Irish. There has been nothing like it since Englishmen drank to the King over the water, silently passing the toast and the wine glass over their water glass. And with less valid reason.

Are you incapable of noticing anything? Do the phenomena of today's history absolutely and utterly fail to make any dent in your blubber or whatever else you have pulled over your eyes, heads, and ears?

Have you no eyes, no history and no memories? No eyes, no knowledge or memory of your own history, and no memory of events that have happened before you?

Do you know only watery pools where were the cellars of London, only the material ruins, having NO knowledge of causes, of deeper causes, of why these things have come on you, of what you have done, or in most cases omitted, and which have caused these things to come on you, and have you no wish to know WHY this has happened?

You have at least a chance of organization in England. You have at least there three native races: Welsh, Scotch, and English, not wholly rotted and on which you could build up something. You have at least a common tongue, which you could unite on.

BUT you will NEVER qualify for a part in the New Era till you, that is, some group of your leaders, are capable of comparing the TWO revolutions, fascist and nazi, and of understanding why ONE thing IS here in Italy, and a KINDRED, but not identical thing IS in North Europe.

And why you are caroming, and crabbing backwards, crabbing sideways. Time, geography, history, that is, the age old conditioning of a place and a people, affected by TRUTH, by natural forces, made by Human WILL directed on forces. These forces are not your forces: this will is not your will, but they and it are in part analogous. You can, or could learn something from events: from phenomena. But you will not learn from mere smoke screens, from mere lies, from B.B.C. and Fleet Street propaganda, that is *sgonfiato*, deflated weekly almost daily by known events and phenomena.

TWO great races have learned something you haven't, learned some'at YOU haven't yet learned.

Responsibility of the person is part of it. And part of it is a return to age old common sense concerning the homestead, concerning the HOMESTEAD.

There is no decree of heaven that the man who plants things in the earth shall forever be diddled by usurers. There is no decree that a system which puts men on the land to increase the land's product shall give way forever to a system of usury, of exploitation.

For as long as I can remember America has vaunted dollar diplomacy, she made no bones about dollar diplomacy, commercial penetration as a means of extending her domination 40 years ago. It was thought a rather bright dodge. (We Americans don't always invent our own novelties: we quite often think something is new when it isn't.) But at any rate we made no bones about dollar diplomacy at the turn of the century.

Is there any divine prohibition to all other races stating that they should not recognize such penetration as an extension of American domination? There is not.

You do NOT believe in Communism. You do at bottom believe in the homestead, at least in theory, each of you thinking up, or most of you thinking up some reason why it shouldn't apply to you in particular.

Nevertheless the world's best in both hemispheres has come out of the homestead, by whatever name it is called in whatever language. That is the basis.

There was in the United States the romance, as it was called, of the merchant princes. No one has very carefully recorded the less humane details. The so-called social question was not given modern publicity.

And possibly no one now listening is aware that anyone ever said or thought that to run one's commerce, to run a firm's or an individual's or a family's trade, shipping, etc. on borrowed money was "unmercantile." Such a statement any time in the last 80 years would have seemed at least eccentric to 99.9 percent of all possible auditors if not down right loony.

I think there was not in mens' minds much distinction between mercantile, the word mercantile, and the word mercantilist as applied to a so-called mercantilist system. Which means that the difference between TRADE and Usury was not very clear in the Western mind after the year, say, 1527. Do be patient. I know the air isn't the habitual place for bedrock, but I might get one auditor in ten thousand who was willin' to follow an argument. Even a hard one.

I assure you the problem of JUSTICE is not superficial. The problem of interest on money is NOT superficial. Europe once spent a thousand years gettin' an answer. I mean the RIGHT answer.

Namely DIVIDE your crops AFTER the harvest. *Usura* and *partaggio*. Two things, different, need to be divided inside your heads. A corrosive charge that finally undermines ANY nation. Undermines it at home, drives it into unsound foreign relations, drives it OUT of land gone to waste (needlessly left to rot, to erode), drives it into indecent incursions into less civilized countries, or smaller or weaker countries.

Always eating away at the life inside the nation.

Divide your crops after the harvest.

I know what is worrying honest men. I know what worried me when I first came up against the doctrine of the free play of forces. I haven't got a century and more of Quaker tradition in one side of my family not to be worried by ANYTHING that seems to go against peace.

BUT injustice goes against PEACE, and don't you forget it. Injustice is NOT pacific. I have told you before that the class war is a fake in America, or an imported exotic, and I have given you the illustration of the Wadsworth family at their reunion 250 years after the two brothers Wadsworth landed in Massachusetts. All sorts and conditions of folks in that family. From members of the stock exchange down to commercial salesmen, drummers, and two old ladies for whom a collection was taken. And earlier in those family annals the boy of sixteen who sold his hair for a shilling, and that was the first money he ever did see.

From that to "Remember the Maine" was some distance.

Class war is NOT an American product, not from the ROOTS of the nation. Not in our historic process. And the RACIAL solution, which is Europe's solution, which is IN Europe's process, rooted deep down, un-uprootable. What about that? You have got to, or you someday will have to study the American or United States historic process. Colonies pretty much racially homogenous: evolved. They found a solution for the problem of money, not of FIELDS against money, not of colonists, farmers FIGHTING money, but of fields AND money working together, and they found it in Pennsylvania and the world said "how marvelous." And an UNJUST usurious monopolist government shut down on the money. Money handed out to the colonists to facilitate their FIELD production. The repayment NOT going to a set of leeches and exploiters. And the unjust monopolist government, namely the British, was hoofed out [of] the colonies 30 years later.

Are you proposin' to do the same fool thing NOW that the various London bleeders and scoundrels tried on the American colonial people? Usury penetration, and trying to throttle other field workers and planters?

#43 (May 31, 1942) U.S. & U.K.(B48)
BRAIN TRUST: SECOND SPASM

One of your brain monopolizers or trustees remarked during April: if you could, breed human beings like cattle. That is perhaps a good sample, a just and fair sample of brain trustees' methods. It hides the crux or the issue. You possibly can not breed human beings "like cattle" but you can or could at least bend as much human intelligence on the problem of human breeding as you do on breeding cattle or wiffets.

And on that BASIS Hitler is also YOUR leader. TWO basic texts were enounced in EUROPE, ON the continent. Mussolini's, and it is summed up in the Consegna, or brief yearly order to the Fascist party of the year XI of the present regime or era. "Discipline the economic forces and equate them to the needs of the nation."

THAT you are learning Hitler's basic text you are still dodging. I don't of course mean to say that the economic discipline is all of fascism or even its base. It is a consequence of a greater fundamental *directio voluntatis*, basic assertion that man is OVER matter. That the human will (or spirit) is lord even over the mud of this planet, and is not to be put down by machinery, or anything man-made. And money is man-made. Comes not of nature. but is NUMISMA; from custom. NOT the master of man, but his servant.

Machinery to be humanity's servant. I am late telling you all this now. I at least SAW something about the time Hitler saw it. Along 1923/24. That, as Hitler put it in Mein Kampf, there was ONE ray of light in a world moving toward sunset, and that was Mussolini's regime in Italy.

And that being so, you with your cheatings and with your Geneva and sanctions, set out to crush it, in the SERVICE of Jewry, though you do not even yet KNOW this. And you have not digested the proposals or instructions of Jewry. And you have NOT understood fascism, or nazism for that matter. Very few of you have read the writings of either leader. It is and has been for 20 or more years, God knows, nearly impossible to print news from or to Italy or translations from Italy in your country. You have NOT read Mussolini, and I don't suppose you could now get hold of his speeches in coherent order: not many of you; or understand the points and situations that they apply or applied to.

One of your best Rome correspondents, war veteran and fervent patriot, said to me at time of Sanctions (Abyssinian war), I have to be so very careful of every word, if I put in any phrase that they can possibly (they being his London office), that they can twist and use as a headline, they do it. Meaning to falsify what he sent'em. [This?] man did damn good work FOR England all thru that period. Very severe critic of things Italian; serving his country. BUT he could not get the true story printed and when a book of his that had been welcomed and published in England and reviewed as the maximum of impartiality went out of print, and there was talk of a second edition, suddenly his publishers bunged it back at him with: we don't want Italian propaganda.

YOU have NOT faced the two revolutions, you have called in what you do NOT believe, namely Red Communist Russia, or the left hand of Judah. You have not heeded the symbols, the symbols of destruction, not only against the grain symbol, but against those of sun and fecundity. You have not seen the hammer and sickle as destructive EVEN of the mason's trowel, which is a tool for construction, or the compass of calculation. You have gulped down destruction: and the signs of destruction. The smashers and Finland shall come to judge you.

As to breeding, your Brain Trust evaded the issue the morning I heard it. It is mere evasion to say you can not breed humans like cattle. Some things you can do. You can, but DID NOT take proper measures against syphylis, tuberculosis, malnutrition NOR breeding itself, whereof RACE is a component. You have encouraged the most fatal admixtures, you have not run [wild?] as in the U.S. of A., because you had not the same opportunity. But you have bandaged your eyes. You have not squared up to the problem. It is part of England's tradition insofar as that tradition WAS good, to do what can be done by what was called "the force of public opinion" rather than by police regulations, up to the possible limit. Instead of concentrating on breeding of thoroughbreds, you went in for neo Malthus, and the dirtier portions of Freudism, with banners flying. All your wit and worldliness, bent on monopolizin', bent on avoiding the basic issues. And if Mussolini stands for social justice, for breaking the usurer's bondage, the Nazi revolution was based on the BREED. Based on sane breeding, and on that basis Germany rose from her sepulchre.

It may be that England, being far from the Mediterranean, takes even now centuries to LEARN from the CENTRE. ROMA *eterna*, Shakespeare learned singing from Italy. And don't forget it. Even Kipling, dying, fortunately for his peace of mind, before the fall of Shonanko, was of an English era that looked back to the Romans. Puck of Pooks and the rest of it. Trying in his one-eyed way to establish the true English heritage. Retired, living OUT of touch with the present, with what WAS the present during the last 30 years of his life, or DODGING the issues. Naturally dodging them LESS than Printing House Square or the great organs of obfuscation.

DIRECTIO voluntatis, direction of man's will toward justice. The Roman IMPERIUM, whereof all else in the occident is derivative, all else that raised the standard of justice. Germany was nearer the centre of that Imperium. And Charlemagne gave us proof of it; proof of that nearer-ness. But the law of true Britain was for centuries PROUD to derive her law from the Roman. When free speech was unavailing in Britain, limited to an inefficient minority, a voice rose in the American colonies, claiming justice, and hurling against injustice the statement that the unjust had Bracton, Fortescue, Coke, Foster, Rapin, and Rushworth directed against him. Voice in— —to cry: law is the subject's birthright. Meaning the Law of England, the English common. And also to remark that furs from the Hudson Bay colony sent to London were sent to Siberia. Meaning that he was a practical man, interested in good sense as well as in justice; which is of common sense a great segment. Elsewhere in that Era, England was strong, and ROMAN. In her dealings with the 13 colonies she was not strong. And her weakness lay in INJUSTICE, as it lay from 1919 onward in her dealings and attempted dealings with Italy and with North Europe. Her policy of lying was almost identical, as any even moderately well read student of American history can observe from numberless passages in the works of America's founders down to the [use of?] Russian false news. Send out these cargoes of lies. It is the way (England's way) of passing [up?] the winner, remarked Mr. J. Adams, senior. If you haven't a library, you could at least get the main points from my outrageous and obstreperous Cantos. There is enough there to show that what you do now AGAINST justice, against all of Europe you did then against justice, and against what there then was of America. No wonder your conscience is ticklish. Yes, you had then some luxuries, for example "the house of the Banker CHILD."

You had some pretty and taking habits. Taking at most times, and not always so all fired pretty. And you had enough free speech to mention the war of Jenkins' ear, wherein perished Mr. G. Washington's brother.

And Mr. Adams WON the American Revolution as a law case, before you turned your cannon against him.

Just as Europe would have won this case as a LAW case, had any court been established to try it.

You can say, figuratively, that EUROPE did win the war as a LAW case. England was OUT of justice.

Whatever pretty little ways you had left, I admit some of you have parlor manners: UNTIL something upsets you. EUROPE won this war as law case, and your Brain Trust WON'T face that. And your Brain Trust will NOT even LOOK into the crime, the nature of crime. You read Ed Wallace, a very exciting author, who writes in praise of detectives, detectives sprung from his fertile fancy, but you will NOT face the findings of the two real detectives, Duce and Führer. You have passed over their evidence, and you had, BEFORE this war started, pretty well thrown out the testimony of your OWN witnesses: Gibbs, Yeats, Brown, and the rest of'em. And it has NOT been lucky. and I don't think you will git back Shonanko. And I do not think your policy in refusing to collaborate with the continent OF Europe has been either prudent or wise, or that it has been based on any very lively thirst after justice. Whatever you are still free to SAY openly on this subject, there is plenty that is LEFT OUT of the Brain Trust's Sunday evangelical service.

But one thing I tell you, and believe you me, Europe will not go back down under the usury system, debt system. And neither will the people of England once they find out what it is and once its Jew centre shifts out of London, into the New York, New Jerusalem cellarage. And the melting pot in America may have been a noble experiment. I very much doubt it. At any rate it has flopped, it is a failure. And the idea of BREED was not always unEnglish.

The mongrel may be clever. Varietism may be very amusing, and fin de siècle, oh undoubtedly, fin de siècle. Other empires have decayed, why shouldn't we? But it says NOWT to tomorrow, absolootly, it says NOWT to tomorrow. The Brain MONOpoly will have to square up to the RACE problem or perish.

Nichevo! and the rest of it. You will have to square up to the race problem or perish. To hear'em you would think the Brain Trust was interested in producing the sort of carcass that can support the greatest number of lice, namely parasites. Subhuman or other. The Brain Trust will have to face the problem of race. You will have to face the problem of race. And you apparently DARE NOT face it. Who are the Schaschan? I ask you?

#44 (June 4, 1942) U.S.(B55)
AS TO PATHOLOGY AND PSYCHOSES

Nebulous notions, fragments of messy ideas floatin' above a pea soup of IGNORANCE, deep impenetrable ignorance. Ignorance of Europe, ignorance of Asia, ignorance of the capacities of the American Navy, ignorance of the lower deck morale.

Now what causes that? Have you not pathologists in the country? If you had read as much of the Fenollosa papers as I got into print about 1917, you would not have underestimated Japan. You would not have let the grossest and most blatent asses in public life in the United States tell you such imbecilities.

And you would not have swallowed the insulting lies of the British papers on the subject. Some of the lowest London dirt, splashing military titles, was concerned with feeding you guff on the subject of Nippon, and the utter squalor of the public mind in the Bill Billy section of Washington was a close second or first.

Absolute indifference to fact. Blind and supine adhesion to the WORST of the point in the protocols of the so-called elders of so-called Zion. Who ever wrote'em shows in this policy. The author of that filthy perverted work has given away several shows. Amongst'em the aim at obscuring all history. Of providing blather about what is not. Plot to tell plans for tomorrow so as to take the mind of the boob, and the sub-boob (called specialist or university president) OFF the known facts of history. Where from our knowledge of process is derived.

Well, you fell for it. And HOW you fell for it, and you can't blame it on any single spavined, crack brained exponent of the NATIONAL, the almost universal United States contempt for all ethics, all facts, all knowledge, contempt of fact, contempt of history, contempt of knowledge.

And the result is, for one thing, that no jape, no lark, no phantasy devised by Rome humorists has been able to keep out in front of the absolute idiocy of your owners and masters.

Take the FRONTIER, for example. A year ago I was joking, you put your frontier on the Rhine. Next it was on the Danube; that skunk Donovan was pushing it around the highlands of Yugoslavia. All to the glory of Jehovah and the Bank of England and new Jerusalem. I suggested Tibet. Did it stop at TIBET, or the Yangtze? It certainly did not. Your expanders of dollar diplomacy and purveyors of Empire shoved it on down into Burma and to the Philippines ever expanding our frontiers: now they have got to Hawaii and the coastal waters.

My COMpliments on your acumen. But whaaar is the old Yankee humor? ABSOLUTE bloody IGNORANCE of every goldarn thing on this planet except how to make noise. Well what causes that?

And your communications. For God's sake, read the Protocols if the last copy hasn't been taken out of the bookstores. They were printed 20 years ago. I never bothered to read'em till I had learned all that is in'em from other sources, thereby convalidatin' the evidence. You DID not know what was comin'. And the ineffable British, ineffable weaklies that feed your weeklies did NOT know what was comin'. Copies of those London "Alice in Wonderlands" oft remind us of the sounds of pish and tush. Little paper flowers embedded in dirty glass paperweights. The ravings of your new allies of the Gnu Statesman and un-nation, remind us of what England expected. And you were not one jot wiser. Look what your tolerated and pushed-up journalists and alleged highbrows told you. Then read the protocols. As you didn't know what WAS comin', and What HAS come, mebbe you better git primed for what is now COMING.

Reduction of interest rates, but monopoly on money maintained by the ....? by the what, by the kahal, by bless your buttons, if your buttons ain't yet been rationed.

STRANGULATION of all communications. You have no secret postal service? Papers get held out, and then starved out if they are not pro-Jew. Soon you will not be able to motor over and talk to the neighbors. And if there ain't just a faint whiff of claustrophobia somewhere, it will be ... eh ... veree pee-hen, I mean very pee-culiar.

Our forefathers had the guts to set up committees of correspondence. That was before even horse and buggy days. What chance have the rural? What chance have the scattered against the super-Zukor, sub-human transmissions of EVERY radio station in your Jew ridden country? I mean what chance of gettin' together or agreein' on any policy? You can NOT get any news from Europe save over this radio and other radios that dislike the kahal. And you are so fed to the gills by the kahal-made superstitions that you, quite naturally, do not believe what you call news from the enemy, or what when I say it, you call Axis propaganda.

Regardless of when I first said it, regardless of whether John Adams said it before Mr. Hitler's great grandad was chopping down trees in the Tyrol or serving the Austrian government. No one has been able to tell you any thing YET, that was of any advantage, I mean advantage to YOU.

The Japanese are an ancient people. The Australians are NOT; and I ask any curator of any gallery of Modern Art, or any municipal gallery east of San Francisco, WHAT is the kangaroo contribution to civilization?

An American woman married to an Italian said to me yesterday: "Yes, I am an Italian citizen, but before I got here, I knew the names of about five Italian cities and that was ALL." Well half the American Congress is full of nuts that know about half that.

While people are blaming (quite naturally) the executive and the sly-footed rump end of the brain trust, why not speak about the muckers in Congress, the unfathomable ignorance of college professors, the flee-mindedness of the popular American authors, as part of the national sorrow? My boy has the American tragedy in his lap. Multiply that by the million.

And have you no pathologist? Yes, we have no psychiatrists. The contact with reality was never strong in the White House. As a matter of fact that April speech would have qualified for several institutions.

Then of course there is the high philanthropy, not to say PROfound intelligence implied in spending half the national income on LOSING the Philippines. That was a Santy Claus. I'll say that was Santa Claus on the hoof with eight reindeer. And who said they were going to take over the Polar Ice Cap. The Squalus has risen, *Krist ist erhoben*, and therefore all them boats in Pearl Harbor will rise with healing in their springs, and the Democratic party will triumph once more over the skepticism of the clinical forces of party reaction, with Finkelstein in the proscenium box. Oh my country,'tis indeed of your land of the Cluett Collar, land of the B.D.V. or B.V.D. or whatever the label is. Oh shades of Lydia Pinkham; yes, yes, those Pink Pills are what is probably needed, with a plate of cakes for the British Imperial Staff in our Capitol.

And I would like a little news about Frankie and Johnnie. Are they still as they once were, keen on the family honor? God, how they did luvv.

Is all our educational system in the hands of inventors of pizin gas? Are all our allegedly serious *Zeitschrifts, rassegnas*, quaterlies, annual and semi annual bulletins, subsidized by the [?] Hebrews? Are ALL Americans with out distinction of church, club, or society, still convinced that nothing is serious, that when boats sink it is merely a headline, and that sailors don't care?

Or to put it another way, is there NO one who NOTICES the habit of saying "Oh the boss is a Jew, a sort of sub-Zukor, of course we couldn't put on anything HIGHbrow, we couldn't go into that subject."

The absoloot bloody cringe of the man who makes 4,000 dollars a year when faced with an organization engaged in paying him and sabotaging the nation, sabotaging fact, sabotaging communications, is a PATHOLOGICAL symptom. When are you, the Yanks, going to get fed up with that symptom? And the way you go running down the road after IRRELEVANT anecdotes, is another. Any sad tale is enough to git your mind off WHY did it happen. That is a symptom. Watch it in B.B. Kike propaganda, which means ALL the Anglo-American air for this decade.

Ezry Pound speakin'.

You ought not to be in this war. The United States ought not to be IN this war.

#45 (June 8, 1942) U.S.(B56)
THE KEYS OF HEAVEN

I suppose if I go on talking to you kids LONG enough I will get something into your heads. If I go on poundin' from day to day, every day and in every way, I will finally teach you kids why you got drug into this war (if you survive it), and when you know that you will know more than your fathers did by the end of the last one, that is, more than most of'em ever discovered.

And I got to go back, and go over and over the same little table of facts, same little table puttin' the dates on'em clearly. And this war started in 1696, or say'94, when Mr. Paterson got the idea for the Bank of England. That is a scheme for gettin' rich, scheme whereby a few men were to get rich without workin', and by defraudin' the general public.

"Bank hath interest on all the moneys which it creates out of nothin'." All right, that was just before 1700. And what did it lead to:

SUPPRESSION of the Pennsylvania colony money, sort of Gesellite money, which had brung abundance to Pennsylvania, and the dirty old skunks in London shut down on that money and on other colonial money. And THAT is NOT in the school books, and that OUGHT to have been in all the public school textbooks for the past 150 years, and that is what kids ought to be learning about American history by the time they are 12 years old.

And after that shut down, and several other mean devilments that you ARE told about, unless the like of Lenin and Company has excluded ALL American history from the kosher districts of Brooklyn and parts adjacent. Bank of England suppression of Pennsylvania colony money. Then came the Revolution.

Patrick Henry, George Washington, Samuel Adams, John Adams, with Mr. Jefferson writin' the trimmin's, and some of his best ideas bein' deleted.

When I was a kid in school, and still worse when I got to the University, we were told about Paul Revere, and General Gates, and the rest of it, but we were NOT told about the Bank of England, and the Pennsylvania colony money, and we were told very little about John Adams. Well, Cornwallis surrendered and the Americans set up a government and no sooner had they won that Revolution than muckers began to undermine it. I believe Mr.

Claude Bowers has said a word or two about "assumption." Meanin' the scandal whereby some financiers and their left fins in Congress lit out to defraud the war veterans. In fact, war veterans are the special and habitual prey of one kind of swindler, specialize in swindlin' veterans of the wars, do some kinds of swindlers.

Well maybe that ought to have led to syndical representation. Well it couldn't have, because there had just been ONE revolution, and the United States of America was a century or more ahead of any other government on this earth in its ideology, in its principles; it was by God the best government system that the occident had up till then thought of and thought out, despite its flaws and deficiencies.

And they were inside particular men, NOT in the concept of government and that WAS the American heritage. Merely some shysters, a pink-haired half-breed named Hamilton, and some natural born sons of cheats in the Congress—Page, ole pop Schuyler, and 30 of the people's so called representatives.

Representin' themselves, and the people's vices.

Well, that is in one way a parenthesis, and then Jefferson and Jim Madison compromised to git the national capitol transferred to the banks of the river Potomac. God bless'em. I thought for a while they hadn't ought to have done that. Well, they were good men, far above human average, and they were right in at least one way. In those days it meant getting the government quite a few hours off and AWAY from the Banks of New York. But Lawdy! And John Adams was lackin' in tact. Or mebbe he was just strong in a confidence that the human mind can LEARN from experience. At any rate, he lived to see little Johnnie, Mr. John Quincy Adams, elected President, and he, old John said with great foresight, if you git in you will stay just 4 years, like I did. They will NOT reelect you.

Well, John Quincy was in some ways a communist. Wanted national ownership of most of the national land. Wanted the proceeds to go to education (includin', gil drat it, astronomy). Wrote a treatise on weights and measures INSTEAD of havin' the sense of Cleopatra and occupyin' his time with the question of MONEY. That was his error, that is one of his errors. But no slouch, and could swim the Potomac until quite late in his human career. I hear he could plow a straight furrow. I don't mean metaphorical, I mean with a plowshare.

Well, that is in some ways parenthesis. But it helps to understand how we got here. How we got into this war. One hundred and more years later.

However, to keep the main line: 1700, 1750, and the American Revolution betrayed by Hamilton, as far as he could, restored by Jefferson, Madison, Monroe, upheld by the Adamses. And then came the next fight. NOT stressed in the American school boy's school books. The WAR of Biddle and his God damn bank against the American people. A war WON by the American people, duce Mr. Jackson, with Van Buren assistin', and that friendship is the second great friendship in our history. John Adams and Jefferson.

Jackson and Martin van Buren. And there had been Jefferson and his circle, and the tradition of those men WAS the American heritage.

And then come the Civil War. And the assassination of Lincoln. And that war was SAID to be about slavery. And the American school boy's school book says very little about the effects of DEBT. Debts of the Southern States to the bankers of New York City. And if Calhoun's name is still in the textbooks, his most significant words do NOT receive emphasis, not enough emphasis.

Both sides upholdin' an evil. South wantin' to keep chattel slavery. And the North wantin' something CHEAPER than slavery. Talkin' pious, but knowin', that is a great part of'em, number of the worst of'em sniggerin' that hired labor is cheaper than slave labor. And you don't really have to feed your employees.

Whereas if your stock is in slaves, you damn well got to feed'em. Rothschild, John Sherman, Ikieheimer, Morton, and Vandergould. Just put your mind on those dynasties. Just remember those family names, which WERE NOT the names of the men who freed us from the shysters of London, Ikieheimer, and Vandergould, and John Sherman and Rothschild.

That's what Bismarck was referrin' to, in his remarks about responsibility. And why did that war last SO LONg? Well, you can all of you look into that question. It is discussable, it is highly discussable. But the outcome was the shootin' of Lincoln. And the END of publicity, for Lincoln's idea, Lincoln's idea about money. Which was holy verity, and the health of the people. And gave to the people of this republic the greatest blessin' they ever had, their own paper to pay their own debts.

You boys will have to live a long time, and fight like hell and fight somethin' nearer home than the Philippines to get it. You will have to fight nearer home than kangaroo country to GET back to that blessin', and I suggest you start fightin' tomorrow mornin' if not now at once, when I get to the end of this discourse.

Greatest blessin' they ever had. Own paper to pay their own debts. When I think of the INTEREST you boys will be asked to pay, a thousand BILLION dollars of debt if you don't git busy and BUST the debt system, Jew system, Rothschild and Morgenthau ANTI-Lincoln system. Well, my heart, does it bleed for my country? I would rather have my head work for my country.

If you can't, or won't think of the cause of your misery and of this conducement to the slavery of your children for ten generations, God help you.

You are in for billions of DEBT, and you have NOT got your own paper to pay for it. You, most of you, haven't the groggiest idea what Lincoln was sayin'. You don't know what he meant by it. Sheer ignorance of coin, credit, and circulation, said John Adams 80 years before Lincoln.

Ignorance, and of course GREED. Greed is your ruin. The lust of evil means to git labor for next to nothin'. Lust of the planter to get African labor and when that showed signs of not payin' ENOUGH, the lust of the North to get in immigrants, with NO regard to the national welfare, no regard to the RACE. No regard to keepin' the human breed high. Just blind greed, blind haste to get in as much cheap labor as possible. NOT noticin', my God—how many people did NOT!—the quick one Sherman and Rothschild put over. The whole government of' the United States of America handed OVER lock, barrel and stock, to a gang of kike bankers in 1863, several sub-kikes assistin'.

'We can not permit the circulation of greenback, because we can not control them." Can not, that is, OWN the nation, BUY the public officials, bleed the whole population.

Well, there is no ambiguity about the Hazard circular and none about the correspondence between Ikleheimer and Rothschild. And until you learn it and its meaning, till you learn the bearin' and depth of every word I am tellin' you, you will be more IGNORANT than the American President, even if you do think yourselves more level-headed.

Ezra Pound at the microphone.

Why did you get into this war?

Of course I can't examine you. But you stick'round and listen, and maybe in time I will teach you some history.

You ought not to be in the war.

#46 (June 14, 1942) U.K.(B32)
THE BRITISH IMPERIUM

Savin' the British Empire is not my job. Time was when I sweat a bit thinkin' of how one could save England. I have no objection to conservin' the English race. I belong to one part of it.

That don't make me believe it ought to be an infamy or a world-nuisance. Bein' an all-fired persistent nuisance is perhaps NOT the road to self-preservation. And bookish men are proverbially led astray by analogies. Allus pickin' the wrong analogy or doin' their pickin' too late.

The way for England to have conserved quite [a] bit of her cushiness was I believed, and I still believe it, WAS by honest economic reform. By saving the people of England inside England. The baronial halls, etc. could have persisted for decades. PLENTY was possible. Plenty was CRYING to come into being.

Honest Englishmen after the last war were fed on sawdust. They wanted to work, they tried farming in Anglo-African colonies. They tried chicken raising in England. Someone of'em wanted to increase England's farm output. There was finally a book, *Famine in England,* by Lord Lymington. There was 20 year's work by five hundred honest men ALL wantin' to save old England, by 50 thousand, by more honest men. Was all of it wasted? No, damn it, all of it was not wasted, but its yield is not yet. And the ruin of most of it is due to the liars. Has ANYone in England studied England's problem as Hitler studied the German's problem before and after the last war? NOT bein' led astray by analogies, but not blind to analogies. The analogy that most hits one in the eye NOW, if one is outside the uncharmed circle of your press—that is your smoke screen—is the analogy of England and of Austria as she was in her dying years.

You have three races on one hitherto privileged Island. The Irish you never swallowed, any more than the Germans of Last mark [?] swallowed the Magyars.

Hitler's sanity shows in his perception of the difference of races inside the Austrian conglomerate. No, not conglomerate. Inside the Austrian stuck together, glued together, tied together with stray string dynastic contraption.

I don't want to waste time in retrospect. You are NOW dreaming of an Anschluss. Anschluss with America. The analogy is superficial. Your conglomerate of Scotch, Welsh, and English was and is fairly solid. It has been there for centuries. You have never crushed out the Welsh language, but the nationalism in those two races has not been political in times known to living men's memory, or their father's.

The Scotch like their own superiority: "Been to London,'ave seen few Englishmen. Waal ye see I was seem' maistly heads of deepartments." Aye, see what do you think of the English? Seen none.

The Welsh have dug out your coal and given you singularly little trouble for centuries. They make a queer noise at the Eidstedfod, and what does London care or think of them otherwise?

You were not and are not as was Austria on the eve of an internal bust up. Oh yes, there were and ARE sorrows in common, but not that particular trouble. As to Anschluss, all the sentiment toward an Anschluss was external. NO ten million Englishmen, ten million RACIALLY English sat in Rural England feeling a nostalgic longing for union with the GREAT main body of their own race, living on the other side of an immediate frontier.

Any Anglo-Saxon or English *race* nostalgia that there *ever* was, was from the descendants of American Tories, negligible in American politics, expressed in a few sketches by Kipling and Henry James [which] rather lit up, [as] Henry James did, some of the dangers of trying American, Anglo American nostalgia on the unblushing non-emigrants of the mother land.

The American colonies rebelled, they were not lost in dynastic squabbles. The United States is NOT a collection of folk of homogenous race in process of coalition, as was Germany, Bismarckian and postBismarckian Germany.

You now propose to Anschluss with the melting pot? Or do you propose merely to drop into the melting pot? Blindfold? I have met Englanders who have NO SUCH ambition. Indeed, I have known Englanders who I believe would find the very suggestion unwelcome. It is against your historic process.

But a dirty part of your process has always been calling in savages. You did it in the case of the Red Skins against the colonists. You are doing it now, and HOW, with the bloody Russians.

Your habit of using mercenary troops may be petering out. CAN you save the English race by persistin' in your worst and most disastrous habits? Do you think the Yanks are just one more set of barbarians to be hurled against the older, more cultured [peoples?]? THAT analogy will be FAR more accessible to the man in the London street, real or faked, real or entrapped by the B.B.C. microphone when he looks ready to sign on the dotted answer.

"Oh you will come in and HELP us," not merely one Englishman or women said that to me. What the ... ahem ...

Which leads me to considerin' your favorite pastime or parlor game for dark evenings. Your pastime of "after the war," or what will we do with and TO Europe, devastated by the Russian scourge?

In contrast to which lunacy, I still conserve one or two memories. I still think there must be a little sanity in England and some capacity to look ahead with greater clarity, meaning modesty, in this case: meaning modesty. Looking to a possible place in your misty climate, some place in your Constable's typical landscrapes, Devon or Darset, or Norfolk, or the English race and traditions to continue. YOU will NOT get it by usury. You will not get it either by imposing the League of Nations, alias the system of lending money at interest. Or BY accepting that system, when the boots on the other foot, i.e., when you are at the borrowing end of the swindle.

Usury never yet saved ANY race. And you have NO great solid racial block with whom you can Anschluss. Your dominions look far more like falling under the usury-yoke of a conglomerate NON-English people.

If any man among you is RACIALLY thinking, he will see that there are two problems or rather that race conservation presents TWO or more possible tactics. EITHER reconstitute the RACE, the English, or the Anglo-Scotch, Anglo-Welsh, hardly figures. Neither is the extension over all the Island of Britain. The best probable approach toward a strong solution: you can either HOPE to reconstitute the RACE in England or you can divagate into wondering what can or could be done to reconstitute the race in Canada, the United States, or elsewhere.

Hitherto the best United States thought has not been racial. The majority, 99.9%, of the serious thought in both England and America has been economic. And it has NOT brought reform into being. We may have been ALL of us wrong, except Lothrop Stoddard, and a half dozen writers: better known abroad than in either England or in America.

Let your Brain Trust (or monopoly) speak on this question.

CAN you save your own race? Which is my race, though you may not like that phase of the problem?

Or are you determined to bring that race to an end? For POLITICAL reasons? Or for reasons of finance, which have replaced the reason of STATE in so many of England's transactions? Such as futile atrocities, intended merely to stir hate, and impell the rest of the world to WANT your dire combustion. What in heaven's name IS back of your policy?

Have you got to that state where your vices are your dearest possessions? Meaning the END of your paideuma, the end not only of your imperial mandate but of your race consciousness, your race conviction.

Brutality, perfidy, and pugnacity [are] all primitive instincts, but NOT *enough* for survival. Must be something more IN a race than those three instincts. Pugnacity, great asset in war, when NOT coupled with a superlative talent for being misled, which some people think you now show in a degree quite superlative; quite, almost astonishing to the outer spectator.

I hear the Times once printed *Mein Kampf* in installments.'ow remarkable. Of course God knows HOW it was translated. But out of the mouths of your opponents you might someday learn something.

From your opponents instead of putting up with stucco busts of Nicolai Ulianov Ilitch, etc. If you would look back to the old murderer's installments, and read what Hitler thought of the DlSgermanization of Austria. It might be good for what ails you.

I don't mean you need to be "converted to Hitlerism," I mean you might one day want to know how Hitler has done what he has done. Just as for a century you have been mildly interested in Bonaparte Napoleon. A CORSICAN. And from your point of view a foreigner. No longer known to mankind as the Corsican ogre. Hitler was worried by the DlSgermanization of Austria. Have you yet found an English LEADER who is sufficiently worried by the disEnglish-ation of England? Clumsy word. If I say deanglicization, someone will misunderstand it, and think I am gettin' religious.

Will you realize that if there weren't something IN Italy a damn sight better than you have ever dreamed of existing here, or been willing to admit COULD exist here, I would be writing these things in jail on waste paper, instead of tellin''em to the world via Rome Radio? And I do not mean a spirit of compromise. There was a time, 25 years long, when Europe would have welcomed COLLABORATION.

There still is an INTEREST in the true answer, which is NOT YOUR answer, it is not an answer with England king-of-the-castle. But there are men who will not leave the English race even a place ON its own island. Those men are neither in Italy nor Germany.

I don't MIND an Anglo-American hookup if you hook up with the RIGHT kind of America. I should dislike seein' England, a mere provocative bridgehead, a Czechoslovakia financed from abroad to run Vickers gun works and bring on six or either other wars. Would it not be, in any case, GEOpolitic? After all, there is the shape of five continents to consider and the sea-space between the two hemispheres.

And one more factor: every German knows that he fights for Bismarck, for the work of Bismarck, every Italian knows that he fights for the work of Cavour, of Crispi, and Ricasoli.

But every American with a knowledge of his own history, possibly a MINORITY, but still a segment not wholly negligible, I repeat: every American with any sort of grasp of the glory of American history, knows that he is NOT in this war for the work of Adams and Jefferson, of Van Buren and Lincoln. Not yesterday that was written: ... try to drag us into their real or supposed coalitions.

For my part thought that Americans had been embroiled in European wars long enough, easy to see that France and England will be constantly at manoeuvre to work us into their real or imaginary balances.

John Adams

Ezra Pound speaking.

The Americans are unqualified for intervention, they are DISqualified by reason for their intense, abysmal, unfathomable IGNORANCE of the state and past facts of Europe. Even my colleagues in the Academy of Social and Political Science have no competent perception of the DIFFERENCE, the basic difference between the American problem and that of Europe. And most of them have not made any adequate use of even such fragmentary fragments of knowledge as they possess.

#47 (June 15, 1942) U.S.(B58)
VIOLENCE

I have been looking over a careful study of America by a careful writer, it is not an edition deluxe and the photo reproductions are not pretty. Some of them deal with gangsters, and gangsters' ends. There are also a few Negroes suspended from trees, without apparently due trial by law.

There are also photos of Mexican pyramids. The traveler was quite impartial, he recorded whatever he saw, or the parts that aroused his interest.

The book leads me to reflections on violence. American lynch law had its origins in the Jewish ruin of the American South. It is very hard to explain lynch law to Europeans.

The Ku Klux once had a reason. Today the survival of lynch law appears, at least from Europe, to be a sheer manifestation of COWARDICE. It is an expression of course of brutality. But the European sees nothing distinguished in a mob of a thousand men, chasing one man. It does not find lynch law heroic.

Neither does he find British treatment of Italian prisoners a convincing proof of British honesty or civility or of military capacity. All that will in time go into history.

What I am trying to work out in my head is WHY American violence always takes such a monotonous form. Perhaps Clemenceau found the answer in what he alleged to be the American incapacity for ideas.

You would think with all that anarchy and violence and contempt for everything, that political violence might be possible in America, yet it apparently is not.

I am asking, I don't know the answer, does anyone in the audience, in visible audience, know the answer? You lynch the Negro, you glory in the manhunt, but you are incapable of political violence. But the degraded Finkelstein, coward and accomplice of murderers, accomplice of the men responsible for the labor conditions on the Stalin canal, put such utter swine in an official position, and Americans at once become little Lord Fauntleroy.

The British poisoners have become sacred persons. The 5,000 members of a wholly corrupt secret government get diplomatic passports and all is suave and serene. Perhaps some of our college psychologists will explain it.

The American has the head, evidently of a chicken, he is incapable of political revery.

The existence of a secret and IRRESPONSIBLE government does not worry him. It has been there at least since 1863 and he takes it as a matter of course. It gets worse daily and hourly.

All the means of intercommunication pass into the hands of the secret and largely Semitic control; and the American dreams of Thoreau and says, "who am I to interfere in such muchness?"

The Stalin Canal is a matter of psychological interest. The British treatment of Italian prisoners is a matter of pathological interest. But unfortunately I arrive at these points after the fact. The historian's job is not soothing. One would rather have used preventive measures. I, quite honestly, don't see what more I could have done to prevent this unholy shindy. I have tried, I think fairly, to diminish my personal ignorance. I have only two eyes, and not very good for readin'.

No one can accuse me of not trying to communicate what I knew, what I have known, during the past 20 years, often with tactless insistency, often when I might have gained official approval by not sayin' it quite so soon. History shows us certain recurrin' phenomena. Goin' back to Philippe le Beau or before that in Europe, going back to the days of King Wen, and before that.

I have done what I could to give some of these facts—what seemed to me significant facts—some publicity, as far as was in my means.

As to Churchill betrayin' England and the people of England, I don't know how far the boosy old hog knows what he is doing. I should lay a bet, and quite heavy, that Mr. Churchill was picked and put into the place he could do the most dirtiness exactly because he is an obstinate fool. A fool possessing almost unsurpassable cleverness in appealing to what is most utterly damned rotten, brutal, and stupid in the worst type of Englander. Just as I think other idiots and pathological specimens are often picked for a set job of wreckin'. I don't want to descend into vague general statements. When I was in England in November '38 a good soldier told me: We will lose India, we will lose all our Eastern possessions. Meanin' IF England goes into war. A Naval man told me how rotten material was bein' put into British submarines, or at any rate he was tellin' it to company at a lunch table where I was present. I heard it stated, with perfect truth, that the profit system was so rotten and stupid that no matter WHAT they spent, no matter how many millions sterling was spent, the British industrial system could NOT deliver the goods. That bein' so I consider that England has suffered treason, low treason, high treason, red, green, pink, purple treason. And that Eddie may have felt it was comin', at any rate he hadn't the backbone to stick it [out]. And the traitors were afraid that he might balk at the last moment and refuse to sign on the dotted line, for mobilization.

Well, that is guesswork. I don't know that the little shrimp was much fit for his job. But as to the betrayal of England, Mr. Churchill has at least some responsibility. But knowing EXACTLY what kind of an obstinate idiot he is, the men who put him into the Premiership have MORE responsibility. Concerning which the English have as yet shown no EFFECTIVE curiosity.

Well, you are their allies, and the allies of the Stalin canalites. Now what causes that? Press lies in part are responsible. Who HIRED the press lies? Are you, NONE of you, even amateur sleuths? Are all your Ellery Queens and Van Dines on cheap fiction paper? Is there NO Yankee curiosity left? Is New England (according to birth statistics) to be populated only by bohunks at the end of the next 60 years?

Razza, race? Is the ruck end of the old colonial stock so hog stupid, so sterile, so stubborn that NONE of'em have the sense to raise the race issue? That none of'em have an even polite parlor interest in enquirin' even the ouija board or the whist table whether the American colonial race shall survive?

Kipling said it: he said the Americans obligingly slaughtered each other during the Civil War, so that the Czechoslovaks could inherit Boston Common. Well, what causes that?

Is it too late to inquire, is inquiry become impolite and unYankee? And what races coalesce or amalgamate? What races can dwell together without constantly inciting other races to start fraternal slaughter, and civil assassination?

The Welsh didn't spend 800 years trying to get English and Scotch to murder each other. The Irish refused to forget their race for hundreds of years, but they weren't continually fomenting internal warfare in England, no third race was at the bottom of even the Wars of the Roses. English, Scotch, Irish and few minorities made the American colonies. Germans, and Italians came in without causing civil slaughter. If the American intelligentzia ever THOUGHT about anything, these facts would enter the mental range.

[The] point I took up the other night might do with an emphasis. Also my curiosity; WHY does the intelligent American, the bright lad who CAN write, but doesn't, why does such a man take it as a matter of course that to earn his living he has to hide his intelligence and work for some blob-headed vulgarian SLOB?

Whence comes this superstition that the worst pays and the better doesn't and that the BEST is impossible; that America has NO place at all for the best, despite the American instinct [of] knowin' the best, and insistin' on having it, the minute they are in position to get it? No other race on earth [is] so almost fanatical on wantin' maximum, up to what they know. And then the refinement, the flair in some of these Americans who get over to Europe. Of course they may be exceptions, but I have known cases, I don't mean persons of genius, but people of moderate mental energy, and with that funny little flair for the best. How do you figure along with this, the acceptance of being bossed by pigheads, by almost inhuman objects; the equivalents of Litvinovs and Maiskys at the head of big industry, big radio corporations, the

[whores?] of the Hollywood ghetto? What is there in the ruck end of the American era that makes Americans stand it?

Have they all been bred down into halfbreed and quarterbreeds? I ask you, I don't quite make it out.

Doth avarice make cowards of them all?

As for their opposite numbers in Britain. They aren't quite opposite as against Americans working for blob headed kikes on your radio. England has naught quite similar, they have refinement. Perfect Alice in Wonderland, perfectly poisonous, but refined and unconscious. I don't suppose you take it very seriously either. I have always told you the Atlantic and Nation were festers, spoon fed from the nectar of England.

I daresay you can't see that. Well, get some of British equivalents, say by New Statesman and Nation.

ALICE in Wonderland. G.D.H. Cole. As long as a printin' press functions in London, those blokes will go on gettin' 25 dollars an article: doing IMAGINARY geometry. Imaginary futures for the land that never was and never will be. Schizophrenia. Alice in Wonderland, Little Lord Fauntleroy, private worlds, in the gook house sense of these words. Over Hell's Kitchen. It is perhaps time for young Americans to start reading the classics, Plutarch, or Cicero against Verres.

#48 (June 19, 1942) U.S.(B59)
THE FALLEN GENTLEMAN (IL SIGNOR DECADUTO)

Among my American memories is that of the fallen gent in shabby overcoat selling lead pencils in a Washington soda bar. Wishing to get something, other than Senatorial and Congressional views, on the results of the nude eel and subsequent American cataclysms in the year 1939, in fact about cherry time, I inquired of him (rather than of the wristwatch-swallowing ostrich) what HE thought of it all, and got the indubitably uncontrovertible reply: "AHG, we're all mixed UP, this gennerrrrashun!" That undoubtedly represented the real man in (or at that moment very slightly and momentarily removed from) the street, as contrasted with the B.B.C. hand-picked specimens.

And any man's clarity must start inside his own head. I therefore propose to put my own ideas in order, and to communicate that order in the hope that it assists the hearer in finding out where he or she is.

Now in the FIRST place, every sane man, including finally some British M.P.'s, KNOWS that every sane man prefers Fascism to Communism, as soon as he has any concrete factual knowledge of either.

The labour conditions, the mode of treating human beings, known in Russia as human MATERIAL on the Stalin canal, deserve study. The auditor knows nothing of Russia until he has heard or read the reported facts of that horror, inciting eagles and the rest of the details. Until he has considered the number of lives crushed out by Stalin's system BEFORE the massing of Russia's gigantic armies in the threat to all Europe's heritage. And enough of those facts are printed to enlighten any sane man.

As to the Bolshie system of persuading people to build or pay for the building of apartments, and then taking chunks of said apartments from them, that I have on first-hand information, from a victim. Neither farmer (peasant) nor business man has anything to hope from the Communist system. Bolshevism, yes, Hank, the belief that non-Jews ought not to own property.

As to Bolshevism two things are established everywhere save possibly in the dim mind of a Gunther or Thompson. First, that Bolshevism pretended to be an attack on capital, that it was financed by New York Jew millionaires, and that it, in effect, attacked private ownership of land and of living space (which would be YOUR kitchen and bathroom, as well as YOUR farm or workshop.) And England and the United States got OFF sides, they are caught OFF sides, alling themselves with the Red Russian horror.

I might say, in historic flashback, that the difference between the American Revolution of 1776 and the French terror following 1789 lay largely in Mr. Adams', Mr. Jefferson's and General Washington's race. OUR American revolution was an Anglo-Scottish Revolution and the French Revolution was not, hence the analogies between its breakdown, its massacres and what our time has seen in Russia.

England and the United States OUGHT to be on the Axis side AGAINST the Red terror. And every Englishman and American knows that. Probably even the new comic of Canterbury is aware of it and his genuflections and prayers are signs rather of episcopal flurry than of conviction. In fact the Rev. Temple has got all mixed up with his vestments, tangled so to speak in his lace, his dalmatic, his cape.

The Occident is based on the homestead. By which I mean, the civilization of the whole Western world comes up from the soil, and from the personal responsibility of the man who produces things from it.

All mixed up? NO, as long as men face the responsibility of feeding themselves and their families from what they can get from the earth, by planting seed, reaping crops, raising cattle, there is NOT any great confusion. That responsibility includes NOT letting the cows eat all the grass in the fields when part of it should be stored as hay to feed the said cows during the winter.

All capital is NOT (in our muddled world) the result of labor. John Citizen is not only mixed [up] about money, he is mixed [up] in his views about gold.

Now GOLD is the product of labor. Apart from small beady particles, nuggets, nature offers man a natural mixture of quartz, heteroclite substances and gold in a crystaline or at least hard hotchpotch bouillabaisse, or in the sands "of the Indies."

And that gold chemistry is studied by students of INorganic chemistry, it is not rams and ewes, it is not amoebas, as Shakespeare definitely indicates. He points out that gold is NOT fecund, it does not increase and multiply as the sheep and goats of a herd. Plant it, and it does not come up in the spring, yielding 20 fold, or 30 fold or one hundred.

MONEY does not become interesting until it means something more than that sterility. Money is not interesting until it CAN represent something fecund, such, namely AS rams and ewes.

This difference between money and metal, puzzled mankind for millennia. It goes back into prehistory.

The idea of interest existed before the invention of metal coin.

And there is MUCH more justification for collecting interest on a loan of seed, on a loan of she-goats and buck-goats, than on a loan of non-breeding, non-breedable metal. It only remained for the philosopher or the expert in ethics to figure out HOW much interest. For a thousand years from St. Ambrose to St. Antonino some of the best and most candid minds in Europe worked on that problem.

And Europe in the interim built her cathedrals during an age when usury was classed with the vices.

COIN being used as counters, and the work of makin' those counters considered as work. I don't mean that the public had a clear view of this process. There is a considerable amount of Latin writing about the question of intrinsic and token value of money. Totin' round the counters, etc., havin' the money ready and handy required a lot of technique. A lot of technique was developed. Then somebody found out they could do without metal counters. Just like Loomis found out you could send an electric signal without using wire.

Found out electricity would travel thru air. Nothin' practical came of it, till Sig. Marconi got it into a system.

Credit HAD existed, just like lightnin' existed. Men had known about credit long before Ben Franklin sent up his kite. Difference being that Ben was a scientist. When he hitched his latch key on the kite-string, he was in search of knowledge. Paterson was lookin' for profits when he sent up HIS kite: Bank hath profit of the interest on all the money that it creates out of nothing.

Moral for good little boys: Mr. Franklin died honored, and I believe fairly well off. Paterson died unhonored, and almost undiscovered; I forget if it [his profit?] was cast away on a desert island, anyhow he went bust. Yet Paterson got Europe pretty well muddled. You have THREE phases in what might be called the increase of muddlement.

FIRST, mankind's natural allurgicity, his natural rebellion against belief that metal breeds, that silver or copper or gold will grow if you plant it or shut it up in a box.

SECONDLY, the perception that MONEY which represents something alive, vegetable or animal, may up to a point have the right to a periodical profit or interest if used in a way that helps to produce something useful, something enjoyable.

THIRDLY, you have the lowdown Scotch trick of trying to collect that interest on money that represents nothing at all, money that is just FLIGHT of an airy fancy, or that banks on human credulity, or on the known trustfulness and laziness of mankind. And THAT'S what the shootin's about, brother Henry, that's what the shootin's about TO-day.

Do you follow me? Do you follow me? Or am I to be once more accused of speakin' in a rambling manner.

Faith, said the Irishman, NO man could be in two places at once ... uh ... uh, not unless he were a bird. I am NOT trying to be in two places at once. I am trying to get you to DISSOCIATE a few economic ideas, trying to get your mind to conceive the nature of motion, to conceive the difference between money and credit. Some other time I will try to get you to understand that credit is a social phenomenon.

Money (I am now quotin' Aristotle), money comes not of nature but from custom. Money is something man-made, it does not exist by itself in nature. Money is a social phenomenon.

Credit is a social phenomenon. I am not going into that now. I may have already said too much for one talk. I dunno whether the United States listens to B.B.C. nonsense. I should like to put my compatriots in condition to DEBUNK British B.B.C. nonsense as fast as they hear it, and this talk of mine is aimed at gittin' over to you one point and one point only, or say one dissociation of ideas, or dissociations about one point. That is the question of INTEREST. The difference between the interest on metal and the interest on money, and the interest on credit (that is the interest on money that isn't THERE).

Dearly beeloved brevrem, this is ole Ezry speaking. You probably do not doubt it. You probably have derived that belief from the intrinsic nature of the discourse even if you tuned [in] after the announcement of what was comin'.

#49 (June 25, 1942) U.S.(B62)
THAT INTERVAL OF TIME

People are allus tellin' me to be PATIENT. Even now when you would think a state of emergency had not only been declared but become almost apparent, people tell me to be patient about one thing or another.

Well, I have said before, said it in poetry and said it in prose. I was twenty years late in startin' and as my friend Carlo DeVoto sez to me on the tennis court: "Twenty years at 5%! What do they care, if it runs 20 years, they double their capital. And most of the dirt in this world is put over by people who have NOT twenty years to run. After them, then hell-bust and they should worry!"

It is that 50 year interval, that FIFTY years between the time some European finds OUT. The devil gits his work in durin' the 50 years between the time some European discovers what the hell is going on, and the time the news reaches the general public. Europeans have SEEN their countries goin' to ruin, but they didn't get the publicity. Brooks Adams saw various processes runnin' along. He even said we were in for 30 years war, and he was only 15 or 20 years after a fellow named Drumont.

Then again these people who see too much so often have their own peculiar conditionings. Some bloke with a phobia against Orleanists writes a book that no Hoosier is likely to read.

What's an untranslated European BOOK against the whole howl of Howwywood? Or the combined kosher radios of Baaastun [Boston] and Schenectedy?

The sons of the pioneers! Lord, are there any sons of the pioneers? The decline of New England. No damn it, the WHOLE of the American people, of the real United States stock isn't dead, it's just lazy, and muddled, and jitterbug, and things were so EASY, up there in the university levels. BY comparison I mean with the subcollege levels. And there is a defect with the non-family system. I mean people shiftin' around, people NOT passin' on what they know INSIDE their families. And then there is snobism. That's another great barrier against learnin'.

HOW are you goin' to know Europe if you don't KNOW the United States of America? I don't mean tourism; you can see a lot of sights at the cinema. Only you don't generally see anything but stucco and paper. I mean IF you have no clue to what is goin' on IN America, how can you know what is goin' on here in Europe? If you don't know ANY history whatever, how can you understand HOW things happen?

You don't expect a bloke who has never SEEN a game of football to rush in and play a star game.

There are moments when I git plumb discouraged. I mean I sweat for a couple of hours over some volume of history. Then I reflect on what I learned ABOUT history itself. I mean when I was doing my Sigismundo Malatesta I wanted to git at the facts, original documents, etc. and I noticed how loosely some history is written, in fact about 97% of it. Abstract statement, DUE to ignorance, bloke just don't KNOW, so he makes some generality, then when he does GIT right down to the bone he finds he can't always print it.

Or Mr. Henry Adams, pindlin' Henry, sez to his brother that he has no hankerin' after martyrdom. I mean some of these blokes git scared. Lord knows there is plenty to scare'em, in one sense.

The chronicle of human chicken-headedness is SO long, the sheer heedlessness of the majority of mankind is so persistent. Nevertheless a man must do what he can.

Boy named Mac ... no I won't give you the rest of it, he may want to pass an examination—at any rate he shows a couple of REAL questions to a professor and the professor shows blank incomprehension.

Don't shoot the pore beggar. Most of your professors were up against what you are up against. Those favored few who GOT the cushy jobs got there for a reason. They didn't annoy their precursors. And the ones that RISE were those who showed no EXCESSIVE curiosity. Don't matter whether it is literary merit, which is largely precision, or history. Well, well, HISTORY is a VERY dangerous subject.

But keep on a pluggin'. Some college libraries have a FEW books. All the public libraries haven't suffered from the habits of borrowing, that is, not fatally. Some of the real books are still on the shelves, and not represented by wooden dummies.

Dig in. Look up the ECONOMIC background of Cromwell. I keep hammering on the BASIC facts of our own American history. I don't want you to lay off that subject. But you may as well know WHAT the Pilgrim Fathers came to New England to get OUT of.

Don't think the usury process STARTED with the invention of modern banking. So-called. Most swindles have prototypes that were already known to Demosthenes. Of course the swindles get bigger and LARGER.

The technique of war loans, peace loans, has extended. Figures keep getting bigger and bigger.

And the SPEED of the operations. If it took what were called "the AFRICANS" 150 years to ruin one European nation, seems like there is an American speed record impendin'.

Entertainment in soldiers' canteens on the one hand, I mean immediate, entertainment for the United States armed forces, by the legged forces. And then comes the payment of interest. An *old*, tough country probably takes longer to bust. Peasantry has been ruined. Every country in Europe has seen repeated duels between the plow and the mortgate.

Mr. Warburg calls'em both CAPITAL—both the plow and the mortgage. I forget if he coined the phrase "capital in the form of transportation." Gettin' a lot of DIFFERENT things hugger-muggered in under one label. My boy, you BEWARE of folks who lump things under one label. You call a plow, plow, you call work, work, you call a stock certificate a stock certificate. And try to learn the difference between a bond and a share.

Naturally a lot of fancy language has been used to conceal that difference. Get any company prospectus, about common, preferred, etc. and the need of three lawyers and an expert to know what the difference is between the common, preferred, pink tipped, etc. before and after the 3rd, 5th, and 14th conversions. You'll be needing them and they'll be needing a consultant. Beware of folks who lump DIFFERENT kinds of things under one label. Such as a plow and a mortgage and call BOTH of'em capital. Keep lands and hands QUITE separate in your mind. And remember that all capital does NOT come from labor, and that the reason WHY the JEW has been able to wreck one European country after another is that the ploots, the nobility, the better classes, the NICE people in those countries were always ready to borrow money. And that the whole of life in our time has been run by people who were collectin' interest on money. Kings, dukes, merchants, all in a row fallin' for that "false help" in time of emergency.

War loans, peace loans, that is how necks get into nooses.

I am still waitin' for indication or confirmation that any appreciable body or ganglia of men in the United States have any real perception of what has been PUMPED *out* the country, by the treasuries. Eh ... policy ... the bastids call it a POLICY. As to assumption, Mr. Bowers might like a list of precedents, just showing that the CLEVER financiers, the Gouverneur Morris's, etc. didn't INVENT anything—all the jokes are so much older than Harpo.

And apparently when it is a matter of finance or a legislative assembly cheatin' the people, NO wheeze, no dirty swindle EVER wears out. The

Hoosier NEVER learns, no nice college boy ever fails to fall under the spell of a plateglass partition, and a few holes and [a] fine marble floor.

Here lies America, she died of the romance of luxury. The wreck of a country, the wreck of a nation starts when the ruling class starts being bribed. Same old story, Grand Dukes betraying Russia, French nobles selling up France, British nobility utterly worm-eaten by greed. And now the old United States of America dying off, 80 years after the sellout to Rothschild. Eighty years of usury taking, 80 years of grovelling before wealth, being ready to accept pay without ever thinkin' what causes it. Damn [it] all, I seem to be gittin' moral. Well, what about it? Be scientific, HOW much pizin' can the national body stand?

That question can be put scientifically, just as well as puttin' it in a hortatory form, or asking what is nice, or what ought a decent man do. No man will *do* anything WORTH doin' till some sense of "OUGHT" enters his system. Profit motive is silly, in the sense that it ultimately kills the good life; makes the mare go, yass, makes the mare go, money makes the mare go. And then somebody wakes up crazy.

And that takes JUST long enough, so nobody notices what is going on. Suddenly wake up and find American abundance has been chucked out of the window. Ten billion here, ten billion there, and then ease has departed, and sailors don't care.

Saxony under the Kings of Poland had emitted bonds, Slauer that had fallen to 35%, reimburse'em at par. The Congressmen who voted for assumption invented nothing, they were just being dirty. And all of'em ought to have been shot. It's a long list. Tunis bonds. These particular kinds of swindle weren't invented in the new United States of America during the times of the early Congressional sessions. Just small town stuff, provincial villainy. Should we keep on after 160 years? Does it show political development?

What the United States lacks under the Morgenthau infamy is any sense that dirty swindles bring misery to thousands of people, hundreds of thousands, that we have risked something more than mere comfort.

My time is about up for this session.

Ezra Pound speakin'.

And of course, you ought NOT to be in this war. Even to cover up the gross failure of the Administration to govern the United States of America, let alone fixing up the affairs of Europe and Asia.

#50 (June 28, 1942) U.K.(B64)
THE GIFTIE

It was Bobbie Burns, and no Englishman, who sent up his prayer: O wad some Pow'r the giftie gie us

And the emotion behind the lines is probably more unEnglish than anyone who hasn't lived amongst it for over a decade can ever imagine.

I am having another go at it. And if wandering about Mayfair in 1916 the life of your ruling caste appeared to me perched on a very thin crust of painted cardboard, what must it seem now when looked at from OUTSIDE the circle of your tight little private world of illusion?

In those days I felt it, as I said, perched on a fragile crust, and my own brief role or my own feelin' rather that of John Baptist's poking up a scrawny head from the cellarage. Through the grill of some grating.

Some of you I do not name, because it would be too much like a family squabble. No malice on my part, but too much intimacy to be suitable to an international discussion of anything.

One cannot attack public figures when one has saved family photos from wreck and destruction. Or can you, or should you? That may be a case of conscience. Jezabel in her pram, and the rest of it.

I tell you once again, and I try to make myself, even with my peregrine accent, intelligible at least to some of you.

The wave of disgust that sweeps over the outer world at hearing some of your propaganda—after all, radio is the only free speech left—the wave of disgust is due to the absoLOOT falsity of your statements and of the assumptions underlying them. Even those of you who have been accustomed to the forgeries of your own high-hatted synagogue [must] shudder at some of the transmissions sent out by the cheap kikes of Schenectedy, New York, and Baastun.

The grease is laid on so thick by Mr. Churchill's [English] Hebrews and Mr. Roosevelt's American Hebrews. Can any of you, would any of you, as an exercise, as a mental setting-up exercise, be persuaded to look at some of your more piffling and prominent SERIOUS weeklies three or four months after the fact, just to gauge what IS fed you by your alleged intelligentzia?

You are NOT going to win this war. None of your best minds EVER thought you could win it.

Nevertheless, your Alices still mince around on the other sides of their mirrors.

Mr. Cole, for example, known as Goddamhell Cole, Alice in person, the world after an Anglo-kike victory. Is it friendly to the people of England, is it friendly to ANYone to put up this false horizon? Are you all Zukor's employees?

You have never had a chance in this war. You had a chance possibly, at least from here it might at some time have appeared, did in fact appear that you had a chance for a *beau geste*, for a vindication of national honor by going thru a set of belicose motions, and sacrificing a reasonable number of men.

Immolation of victims, as atonement not for the crimes of your empire, but for the imbecilities of the ruling gang and the bad, nay the wholly atrocious taste shown in putting up Eden.

An elderly colonel of my acquaintance volunteered to participate in a defense of Poland by air, for example. But that was NOT in the plans of your owners. Nothing but a protracted war and the maximum of profits on debt and gun sales suited your rulers. I don't mean your acknowledged rulers, I mean the creditors of your bullies and popinjays. The men back of the puppet show.

And nothing HAS contented them save the most ignominious deliquescence of a great empire that history throws up on the screen of my memory. There may have been more ignominious ends. My studies have not been sufficiently extensive to enable me to recall them. Never have so many allies been let down by ANY one empire. Never have attacks on late allies been so notorious.

Never have the reasons for alliance been so base as those in your alliance with the Red butchers of wherever Stalin is resident at this moment. And never has the folly of a half wit been more flagrant than in the acts of your ostensible government.

As sheer imbecility, FIRST the policy against Italy, then that in entering a war on Japan. Truly the mind and intelligence are in small esteem among Britons.

By May 15 I was ready to mention your loss of Australia. I don't assert you have lost it, I merely wish to date the day on which I was ready to believe you were losing it. In fact after the Australian bombing of an American what was it, torpedo boat or something, I heard the murmur; *hanno individuato il nemico.*

They, meaning the Aussies, have identified the enemy.

That was an exaggeration. You and the American people HAVE indeed an enemy, but the enemy wasn't on board that torpedo boat. The enemy is greed, avarice, usury, falsification incarnate in a group of unpleasant persons WHOM your intelligentzia, or your bloomsbury, or your professoriate, seems curiously unwilling to look at in the open light. ALLergic to all symptoms and indications. Allergic to justice whatever the other party *in lite* has interests opposed to what you have been taught were your own, but which sometimes WERE not.

FOR 25 years it has been apparent, and I dare say plenty of Europeans saw it before then, it has been apparent that the world could only be saved by a conspiracy of intelligent men, and that they would have to conspire AGAINST the Normans, the Sieffs and the Goldsmids, together with the minor lice over in Paris, the Iazards, Mandels and the rest of'em.

AND your tolerated writers, your half witted socialists, your publicists, your Garvins, Beaverbunks, and the rest of'em did NOT join such a conspiracy. You are barkin' up the wrong tree, and your bite has not proved very toothy, not if measured by Axis and Tripartite standards. Your smell, as caricatured in the Japanese papers, a couple of young ladies holding their noses. You are almost qualifying for ostracism.

You can not, oh hell, you can't believe THAT.

You are such nice mannered people (when eh ... nothing annoys you). Or as Charles Ricketts said:

"No, people who are doing something for the world have NOT nice manners" (His own were a bit slinky).

He continued: "The people who have these nice manners are the people the world is doing something FOR."

Well how far off that seems, Ricketts and Shannon, the Haken [?] press printing the works of Laforgue in the'90s. Alice in Wonderland, Mr. Cole, the denizens of the New Statesman and Nation. Don't believe me get the old copies, back from the lost era of January or February 1942, that is the year current.

Pomp of power, and so forth. When, gol drat it, WHEN you are wrong, when your chief ape has been wrong time and time over, does IT never enter your noddles, or noodles, to look for the source of error?

Does it never begin to strike you that Margot Asquith is being unconsciously humorous when she writes— —. If you hadn't been bred out of all thoroughness, if your thoroughbreds hadn't been decimated in three wars one after another, ALL [for the] power of Jewry, all piling up debt and debt interest. Repudiations, repudiations of debt, enormous burdens of tax needed according to your LYING and treacherous lackeys and professors and so called economists for service, or interest payment on DEBT, public, national, municipal and the rest of it.

COULD have been drug to the present pass. Would none of you have had the civic guts, the intellectual sphincter strength to organize SOMEthing, anything against Churchill's creditors? And the owners of BOTH your out-in-front parties? Morrison is a pup no cleaner than Winston, and just as fanciful and Mr. G.D. Hell Cole.

And as for your relations with the Arabian, Persian, and Mohammedan peoples? I trust none of my dearer friends are in service on those torrid frontiers.

For one drop of sincerity, for one voice on your air to say that the Emperor is NOT wearing clothes!

Yes, you will be left with the land of your island. Lymington and a few others may start a new hive.

But you will have a very large population [and] no land space, unless you make some arrangement to ship a good deal of it out to Rhodesia. The question remains whether you will take measure to SELECT the stock that is to remain in old England. To see to it that the ENGLISH remain and the Yiddish go forth to Bolivia or wherever. And you will NOT do it on usury, you will not do it in contempt of all ethics, or of all fair knowledge of the nature of money, numisma.

A small state, a fascist state unless you like Stalin. That last phrase is not serious. England will NOT build tomorrow on the work system of the Stalin canal, but that will be thru no fault of Sieff, Goldsmid,— —You will have to lay off your trappings, you will have to study new hygiene, you will have to give back their naturalization papers to the sweepings of Europe.

Let the Jews BUY a national home somewhere in your ruins. They have sold a good deal of Africa into serfdom; and NOT been nice to the ENGLISH who ventured on WORKING there, who went there to raise crops of food stuff. The usury system is unpleasant. The world is almightily ONTO that system. The Bürgermaster of Worgl, or in other words, common honesty, is of more use to Tomorrow's England than all the gold of the Indies or all the opium of the Sassoon, and the consequent revenues, concerning which Bobble Cecil can or should by now be able to supply ample details.

The effect of the B.B.C. transmissions is that, in the whole pack of their transmitters, there is no one who dares mention the Jewish problem, Brain

Trust included. Probably lose their jobs if they tried, and what can be expected from a profession with Shaw and Wells at the top who think 24 hours a day of their incomes and of the truth at spare moments? Only England dare not mention the expulsion of Jews by Maria Theresa, nor England's blackmail of Maria Theresa, nor the Jews' relations with Cromwell. American radio is silent, partly from ignorance, the poor hicks just don't know any history, though a gang of foolish youngmen had the exuberance to get jailed for plotting to bump off all the Jew members of Congress. Had they succeeded, such is the American gangster and anarchist psychology that the only comment inside the United States would have been "and a damn good thing too." (With echos in unspeaking England.) The only place where anyone would have been shocked is in Italy, where there is a millennial conservatism and a prejudice against— —.

#51 (July 2, 1942) U.S.(B65)
DISBURSEMENT OF WISDOM

My friend F. Whiteside never tired of a very well known story of Chase and Whistler. For those of you to whom Chase's name is unfamiliar one may as well say that Whistler was a painter of very great talent. He had limitations, his drawing bothered him, some of his paint has now sunk into the canvas and the nuances he so labored may not last forever, but he was certainly one of the ornaments of his time, and with Henry James the two Americans who lit up the horizon of American youth at the turn of the century, and certainly some of his work will give joy to the elite as long as the canvas or paper remains.

Whereas Chase was, in painting, the equivalent of Harper's monthly magazine, Chase returned to the American like Howells, but on one occasion he disagreed with Jimmy, and on being kidded, he broke off:

"I won't argue with you any longer." To which Mr. Whistler with weary patience: "But, Chase, I am NOT arguing with you. I am just telling you."

The Chinese have a more monumental exposition of the same theme: In evil time the sage can enjoy his own wisdom; when the land is well governed, the people benefit from his instructions.

Now apart from any national talents that I may or may not possess I have, first in poesy, and then in economics, which is one of the components of history, spent considerable more time and thought, and I do enjoy or suffer a thirst for knowledge which is, to put it mildly, above the common.

You are in a bloody mess. Bloody in more senses than that word has in British jargon. You are in a bloody MESS. Who got you there? Why did he do it? Does he know why he did it? Does he know HOW he dit it?

You have all of you been chicken-headed, frivolous, etc. You don't even know whether your various races of European origin will or CAN survive on a continent that has seen the fade-out of Mayas and Aztecs. And you have an ORGANIZED minority of a different race amongst you. A race that never tires, a race possessed of subcrocodilian vitality. And the lively lizard is "on this earth very antient" as huddy (W.H. Hudson) remarks of the condor and other predatory foul of the Andes.

AXIOM. Against an organized force of four or more, probably EIGHT million, a hundred individuals can NOT prevail until ORGANIZED. The sporadic efforts of a few excited young men are no use. The dilettante velleities of a few theorists are NO use. And the rest of the inhabitants of the United States can organize on ONE basis only, namely, that on which Europe has finally been constrained to organize its rebellion against the pervasive the ubiquitous Yidd. Pacts may be signed between the Pennsylvania Deitsch and the scrawny New Englander of British or Anglo-Scotch origin, but on no basis save that of race, and of allied more or less consanguineous races can you cohere.

You have, as opposed to any such projected order not merely the 4 or 8 million kikes in New York and points penetrated already. [From] New York to San Diego or wherever the pan hebe, the world Jewry, has set up a radio. Which is bloody well more than the rebellious British reformers were able to do in England during the four years before the betrayal of the British race by Churchill and Eden.

That being the vital point in the German program and the press being in the hands of kikery (high kike) and the subjugated servants of Jewry, some possibly only 1/2 or 1/3 conscious of what they were up to.

Religious base, no use; has been exploited. History of massacres re theology points [to the] downfall of Byzantium, as LONG as it was possible to stir up war on religious basis; that label was used to stir up strife.

Tacitus: Jews back, of persecution of early Christians. Fights in church between iconoclasts and the religious part of the church, down to the Germanic wars of religion. With the quite simple advice of the opponents, i.e. Jews, to THEIR component members; to GET into the church; get into the church, get into the prebends; to take holy orders and corrupt the church from inside (documented). Till you get the almost perfect instrument, Luther, both religious fanatic (on the question of the trinity, etc.) and a very good politician, rebelling against being taxed by an ecciesiast central; already corrupted, and fallen into the hands of a banking family.

Religious base, no USE, that is written and proved over and over in European history which you do ill to ignore. Church split into fragments on one hand; and then any diplomatic representative of a foreign race can SO easily go thru the motions of getting converted. Nothing new about that and the thin veil of observance, torn off in a jiffy whenever it seemed opportune even after centuries of pretending. No, no great hoax, that of combatting on religious base. Simple-minded European tribesmen fell for it, were weakened during about 1600 years, continual attrition. Wonder we're here at all. Must be something tough in European and Mediterranean fibre.

As to effects on, let us take a test tube specimen, France. According to some reckoning France had 38% of the population of the great powers in Louis

XIV's time, 27% in 1789 and has 13% at present. I don't know just what powers are included in those figures, but on whatever calculation it has been made, it indicates a DECLINE.

Anyhow, religious basis NO use. What CAN you organize on?

Can't move'em with a cold thing like economics. Marx advised fighting on economic basis. I still meet people who fall for that bit of eminently semitic strategy. For ONE HUNDRED years, simpletons and inexperienced young men have tried AS, damn it, my friends, of a dozen sects, economic sects; I tried ever since my kitten of mind got its eyes half open. And what came of it? Five thousand in prison, Wörgl, Alberta.

Yes, yes, we lily-livered humanitarians fussed'round wantin' to cure the evil by honest accountancy; and we did NOT prevent this war.

I think my most obtuse opponent, or my most enthusiastic opponent, or Frankies' most faithful UNhappy warrior Archie MacLeish will admit that the reformers, the monetary reformers, the men who wanted honest functioning of the treasuries and of finance in England and America, did NOT prevent this war. (And damn lucky if they stave off the next one.) Oh yes, the kahal makes'em in series. SERIES technocracy, why waste the plant on ONE world calamity? The last one was nearly a world war.

The Talmud announced destruction of 75% of the goy. Yes, brother you have an OPPONENT. And what CAN you rely on? Dan Boone out shootin' squirrels. Hit'em in the eye every time, but the Boone era, Daniel Boone era, has gone forever. The Boone era seems to have got mislaid for the moment.

Prosperity has went, it has vamoosed. We wipp, nichishin, chippewa language has vanished with the pure injun dialects. Even the mixed idiom such as *"que voulex you buju, nicichin"* is no longer current on the Canadian frontier. And Henry James already noticed a change in New York phonetics.

On the seventh day gawd rested. I noted THAT even in [the] days of the Little Review. Either the European stock now resident in North America ORGANIZES or it sinks still deeper into the morass of high kikery. Its ideals and ideas have WENT. The structure of the Anglo-American landwidg is kufuzzled.

About 20 lost men in the United States DID notice the race problem, if not in time, at least in time to be read by Europeans who were really thinking about the WAY OUT. Undoubtedly it is pleasant to think that IF you get rid of capital system the Jew becomes harmless. That was oily Marx's bait, and what happens is the Stalin canal.

A FAKE elimination of capitalism, an attack of ALL civilization, even as much as had leaked into Russia. An attack on property, that is on private ownership of LAND, plows and bathtubs, but the USURER left in command. Not only have the nice and polite amongst us who TRIED to reform the hell of the stinking capitalist, i.e., usury world, by honest accountancy, monetary and economic reform been shown up as ABSolootly incapable of gathering a mass of adherents powerful enough to DO anything, let alone resist a barbarian avalanche. BUT when capitalism has been dethroned etc. *Slobody, Slobody* for the fishes, open the fish breedin' tanks, in Slavic enthusiasm. That elimination of so called "capitalism" is merely used as a flail, a steamroller to crush out the rest of the non-chewish world, that is as much of it as it could ever run, in collusion with the decrepit, syphilitic, Sassonic, beCecil's sewage and mould of the British plutocracy.

The rot eating in since Cromwell, since the Constantinopolitan kikes were so INTerested in that damn hypocrite that they sent over an embassy to see if Cromwell was their Messiah. Much more in their line than the young fellow from Nazareth. I am not arguing, I am just telling you. One of these days you will have to start thinking about the problem of race, BREED, preservation.

I do NOT like to think of my race as going toward total extinction, NOR into absolute bondage.

The Cincinnati etc. erred from snobbery. They did not in George Washington's time organize on racial basis. No one thought of it, no one could have then thought of it. There WAS a racially homogeneous population in the newly freed colonies. Certain privileges were dear to the privileged. Snobbism is NOT conservative. Fashion is not conservative. *La Mode,* etc. is a ramp. Cf. with Hungarian and Roumanian peasant linen, one shirt or blouse lasts a life time, indestructable as real Chinese silk, "no can tear."

That is what the advertising trade diddles you out of and you will have to think about Race.

#52 (July 6, 1942) U.S.(B66)
CONTINUITY

Had I the tongue of men and angels I should be unable to make sure that even the most faithful listeners would be able to hear and grasp the whole of a series of my talks.

That is the disadvantage of the radio form, and heaven knows when I shall be able to print these texts in book or books available to the American and English public. Book implying that [the] reader CAN, when he wishes, look back, take up the statement of the preface, see where Chapter X hitches onto Chapter I. Nevertheless you may as well make the effort to grasp at least the fact that there IS a sequence in what I am saying, and that the conversation of February coheres with that of April. And if you, you in Iowa, Wyoming, Connecticut, DON'T make that effort, if you don't listen and TRY to get [the] main threads and cables of what I am telling you, you will lose time.

Just as the writers who did NOT read the Little Review lost time. Many never made it up. There is no one of any literary size, or even pretenions among you who hasn't by now read the Little Review authors, or authors formed by the Little Review authors. Authors indebted to the Little Review and to its authors for their force, their take off, the initial jab that set'em off.

Pity is that many got only a fragmentary view. Joyce and not Eliot, Eliot not W. Lewis. I hear a million Americans have taken advantage of Mr. Hemmingway's last production, and so they ought to. TWO million ought to read it (probably ... I haven't yet seen a copy but that is due to conditions of Atlantic transport).

PITY is that there is so much else, so much essential else that they are unblissfully UNaware of. And I honestly do not know where they can get essential parts of that else, except from my broadcasts. And out of them, out of these talks, the young men in England and America will have to build their souls, or at least their minds for tomorrow, or LOSE time, never get into life at all.

They will not be tomorrow's Hemingways, or even today's Clark Gables. They will be just shelved, left on the cupboard floor, this way inglorious and ungloried, back numbers before they are dated. Like neo-Georgians who read Mr. Eliot 15 or 26 years late, and tried to cut little nitches in his umbrageous cathedral, mouse holes in his choir stall.

And after a hundred broadcasts it is STILL hard to know where to begin. There is so MUCH that the United States does not know. This war is [the] fruit of such vast incomprehensions, such tangled ignorance, so many strains of unknowing.

I am held up, enraged, by the delay needed to change a typing ribbon, so much is there that OUGHT to be put into the young American head. Don't know which, what to put down, can't write two scripts at once. NECESSARY facts, ideas, come in pell-mell. I try to get too much into ten minutes. Condensed form O.K. in book, saves eyesight, reader can turn back, can look at a summary. Mebbe if I had more sense of form, legal training, God knows what, could get the matter across the Atlantic, or the bally old channel.

Art, economics, pathology. You need to know MORE about all of'em. Need to GIT out of this war, need to stay out of, or prevent the next one, need to change the stinkin' old system.

ROT in art, art as pathology, university delays. How come class war? What is it the professors don't know? Got to choose between two or four subjects or I will git nothing over in any one talk. Very well. I will start on: How come. Two bits of ignorance that have recently been rubbed into me by a mob or congress of professorial persons. NO ... let's start on something that HAS been discussed IN America for twenty years, 30 years, Doctor looks at literature. All this quite silly talk about the diseased mind back of modern painting.

It bored me like hell. It was mostly poor stuff. BUT the fault lay in its limitation AS criticism, not in the main worry that caused half educated medicos to go into it. What was wrong with the criticism was lack of proportion.

HEALTH is MORE interesting than disease. Health is TOTAL. Beauty is MORE interesting than distortion.

We have most of us been buffaloed, or at any rate the intelligentsia is mostly an ass. NOT from having no brains, but simply from partialism in the original sense of that word. Intelligentsia is mostly a nuisance because it runs on snobisms and fragments.

At [the] age of 15 a consumptive gave me a copy of Salomé with Beardsley's illustrations. I cut'em out, they were so ugly. But for more than ten years of my life I considered this an act of genuine fanaticism. I came to see the ... damn it all, call'em merits of Beardsley's distortions.

GROANS from the effete, elite and superior sophomores.

Later a distorted but amiable female presented me coyly with an inferior Beardsley, that is, a volume of distortions by a pink nailed esthete. The significance of THAT act was apparent even to me. I don't think it was conscious on her part. The book probably gave her relief or comfort that she could not have derived from Praxiteles or Botticelli. At any rate I was older, and the drawings weren't even good Beardsley. AND I wasn't interested in pathology. So I have never mentioned the incident before.

The medicos who started worrying about the disease behind modern art were right. That is, they were RIGHT to worry. They were mostly silly in their statements of detail, and this was due to ignorance, lack of cultural heritage. But they were on the right line.

I affirm that future art criticism will be able to tell the component of usury tolerance. How far the TOLERANCE of usury prevailed, or did not prevail when a given picture was painted. Sense of design, precision of LINE, will give way to interest in detail. Suggestion of luxury will augment as people lose an ethical basis of life, as they lose passion for justice, love of real distinction between one idea and another.

Diagnosis will replace love, analysis will give way to squalor. There are steps and slopes downward toward Avernus, falsification will enter. Honest men, when a dogma or style has been falsified, will turn analytic.

They will be partial, the first ones emphatic and vigorous. They will aim, that is, the best ones will aim at health.

For example, Manet, fed up with falsification of color in painting, Manet reduced to analysis of light and color. Both making distinct contributions to world art. Manet one of the world's greatest.

But what is temperament in a sound man becomes by excess, disease in a weak man. Unbalance, hard to divide at certain point, and if one drifts with the current, one grows tolerant first of weakness, and then accustomed to weakness, and then plops into squalor.

Mediterranean sanity and beauty, order. TO KALON, the world was saner when the cult of ugliness did NOT engage the attentions of anyone.

I know all about chocolate box, pseudo beauty, etc. BUT a deflection of the AIM is a decadence. It is a false ripening, it is green fruit going rotten. Beardsley was a sick man, knew he had to make a name quick if he wanted to make it. Personal wish, NOT belief in what art is or ought to be. Knew he hadn't time to learn to PAINT. HIS sane youthful impulse was to pre-Raphealite beauty. Early drawings, Burne-Jones, that's what he WANTED.

Yeats asked him why he hadn't stuck to it. Beardsley was no slouch, he was a courageous invalid. He was a heroic invalid, up to the point of his force. He didn't lie to himself nor to his friends in private. He answered:

Beauty is so DIFFICULT.

We have all seen the cult of beauty turn to slop. Esthete: an artist who won't take pains, who will NOT face the work needed to paint a good picture, or write a good novel or poem. All fragmentary, nothing total. And the GREAT perversion, the great decadence, when the painting is made to sell, when the artist stops wanting to live. Worth his hire, MUST eat, but EAT secondary AS desire, to will to paint, or to make. Then to git rich, that is the END, the absoloot end of a painter. Few men can resist the lure, we all like comfort. That is my weakness and I have seen men who can do without it. I know no American will much believe that, and some of the men who can do without it are lunatics and fanatics. And snobbism doth make coneys of them all. So far as I know, nobody else had the courage to point out that the German pavilions at the Binennale di Venezia four years ago was the best. All the little daubers in the shops, doing Monet and Renoir 60 years late were shocked by the hardness of outline. It was almost the only pavilion not rotted with slobber, some more, some less.

The futurist rooms are always an affirmation of propaganda that could get along by itself without any painting whatever. I mean the main line of futurist propaganda is an idea, the painting an adjunct. An adjunct that proves the idea has other dimensions than the merely ideologic. It is a good idea, it is NOT a WHOLE idea. But it needs plastic expression: it has imperfect plastic expression, which is a sign of its force. But it does NOT arise from a plastic need.

Health is CRUEL, or rather health is often accompanied by what seems cruelty to the baccillus. The man who is totally healthy don't worry about baccillae. He isn't perpetually surrounded by patent medicines, bottles of disinfectant.

For God's sake LOOK at your art. When art is subordinate to the picture dealer, the museum in the United States gets what is LEFT after the European connoisseur has taken the pick of the billing.

Ezra Pound speaking.

I know I haven't got very far in this talk, so wait for the next one. HEALTH, damn it, think about HEALTH in the interim.

#53 (July 10, 1942) U.S.(B67)
HOW COME

HEALTH! I said health, last time. Don't you let anyone kid you out of it. Don't let'em kid you out of looking for health in art. I am now goin' on to: How come.

CAPITAL does NOT come exclusively from labor. Not one man in a hundred EVEN in Europe has digested that truth and its implications. But what happens when a man who is living on the part of capital that does NOT come from labor first finds out what he is doin'? He gets scared as hell. He starts trying to conceal the cause of his privilege. HE starts the class war; class war does NOT come from the bottom. The man who is doing an honest day's work feels his strength. He feels the justice of drawin' his pay. And until he's nearly starved, until he is worried to death by fear of losin' his job, you cannot get him to DO anything at all about what is taken off him. Nothing is rarer than a peasant revolt. Save in the most atrocious circles. The peasant never does more than grumble a bit, he never bothered about his overlord gettin' something. So long as he ate he was happy. And LONG after he ceased to get a just portion of the returns from his own labor, he was certainly wholly innocuous.

What happens on the other side? MAN finds he hasn't justice on his side, and gets a panic. He sets up university chairs in economics to bamboozle the public. And this he does from sheer lack of culture. The concept of the cultural heritage took a long time to crystallize. The phrase is fairly new. I don't recall a CLEAR formulation of it in pre-Douglasite writing. It is latent in medieval terminology, but that terminology was invalidated when the so-called aristocracy came to include such a vast mess of what was anything but the best. Aristocracies ROT, they fall under usurocracy. That is their pathology, their slop-down, their decadence. Now in spite of lean years, and how, I have always enjoyed a large share of privilege. Got stocked up with University advantages. [Great?] deal of mental pleasure. Always could bask in the best of what had been written and thought. That was nice for me, and it delayed my public utility for a decade. I had a nice time, but I contributed singularly little to curin' the world's diseases. I don't'spose I worsened'em any. Let me keep to the rich man's panic, the bourgeois panic. This panic starts when he begins not to KNOW. Lord it don't start as a clear perception. He begins to smell that CAPITAL comes from something that isn't an honest day's work. And he is scared out of his pantelettes at the idea of what it would mean to him if he had ONLY what he could earn doing a workman's work. Knowing he couldn't do it anyhow.

It takes a Whistler to reply to old Eden's lawyers, "NO, not for an half hour's work, for the knowledge of a lifetime." But the cultural heritage is NOT merely the piled up skill of a master craftsman. You can't think clearly or see clearly till you get WORK into THREE brackets. The work a man does today. The anterior work that piles up into SKILL (material skill, handcraft, hand sleight, knowledge, discrimination.) And the WORK done by men, now dead. Work done by the family, by the race, before you started workin' or loafin'. An instinct for the justice of the claims of ANTERIOR work leads to the craftsman's pride. It leads to family pride, and that ROTS when the man or family loses the passion for justice.

Man with passion for justice, or even a sense of justice, or an uneasiness about the existence of justice, starts rootin' round, starts trying to delimit the claims of the three orders of WORK: 1) work today, 2) work yesterday by the folk who are still livin', 3) work by the departed. And ONLY on that basis can you have sane law and society. But I have sat in on a professorial conference of several hundred persons, and not three of'em had any glimmer of this simple tripartite division.

ALL purchasing power does NOT come from labor. All real wealth comes from natural resources PLUS labor. The shyster wants to hog natural resources, and sweat the hide of labor. That is the cause of unpleasantness. There is no wangle or dirty wheeze that the shyster won't think up and use to get a monopoly, to violate the just price, to keep labor sweatin'. And the shyster is pizin'. He is the sworn blasphemer, false swearin' and cheatin' FOE to all labor, past, present, and labor to come. And you better discover this. You better kick him out of your hemisphere. You better invent some bug poison that will eliminate him from your system.

That's what non-shyster Europe is drivin' at. The shyster got hold of Russia. He sweat the hide off of labor, he built the Stalin canal, and I advise all readers of the N.Y. Herald to GET the official reports of the treatment of human MATERIAL, carloads of "human material" dumped into the making of the Stalin canal.

One kind of shyster succeeds another: shyster penetrates ANY organization, church or state for the sake of livin' on the Purchasing Power that DON't come from labor. Shyster joins EVERY new movement so as to be there when it gets big and to be at the exploitin' position. Gangster shysters, medieval orders of chivalry rose to combat the gangster, to combat universal brutality and injustice in range of the individual knight. Or the body of chivalry rose to an idea. With these two forces, i.e., gangsterism AND chivalry, the feudal system developed. As law it was a RESPONSIBLE system. The DUTIES of the overlord were enormous.

They required DISTRIBUTION of wealth. Naturally this annoyed greedy overlords, and weak overlords, and the shyster entered the system. Ready to sweat out taxes, to sweat the hide off of labor, and to collect money interest. In fact the shyster is always a rent collector. And the worm ate into the fruit.

Reniou, provençal word meanin' interest on lent money. Gangster barons kept and lent all right whenever they could so wangle it. Greed, violence, nothing new about vices. When the two had rotted the world long enough, there came an explosion. The difference between OUR American Revolution and the French was enormous. OURS rose with the perception that dead men do not EAT. That is, with a perception that there is a just limit to the rights of work done by men [who] have ceased to breath. Jefferson said it: the earth belongs to the living. As He did not say: the earth belongs to idiots. But on the other hand, he did not clearly assert that the management of the earth requires the intelligence of men who are prepared, and FITTED to govern. An assault on mortal man, an assault on the exaggerated privileges accorded to the whims and greeds of the dead was NEEDED. It came.

Naturally the Revolution was betrayed. BUT it lasted sixty years. Or rather the government set up on that basis lasted 60 years. Count it longer dependin' on when you count the start of our revolution as from 1776 or 1750? Or 60? The French revolution flopped in a hurry. The Napoleonic dream was not merely a dream of conquest. To witness the CODE, code Napoleon, Napoleon's law code. Desire for justice, Mediterranean sense of justice. But a lot of good sense got lost. The guilds, the anti-trade organizations, with their grades of apprenticage, got chucked into the discard. They were NOT 100% innocent. Against the feudal greed, trade greed developed. Nevertheless the guilds left a dream. Left THEIR code of sanity, code of sense, necessity of order and preparation.

There is now a new code in Italy. STUDY it. Is it better than Napoleon's anti-feudal, anti-privilege demonstration? It is a matter of interest, something you ought to know You ought NOT to be in this war and that CODE is a proof of it. Proof of what you are fightin', but that you DO NOT know you are fightin'. All the hopes of Ruskin and William Morris, work being done, work done by men still livin', work done by the departed. includin' in the latter two brackets ALL the masterwork, all the cathedrals in Romanesque style, and in Gothic. (The first lot the more satisfactory.) Henry Adams got to Chartres. Ought to have seen San Zeno, and Cathedral of Modena. All the best work of the great authors, all the best painting. All that has place and right, has its rights in corporate order.

And the shyster is out against it. Against all order, all beauty. Against all work? And you ought NOT to be on the side of the shyster.

#54 (July 12, 1942) U.K. (B72)
FREEDUMB FORUM

Prof. Laski out of the Talmud by the beast of a thousand legs, usura, pulling the legs of a couple of simple hearted blokes named White and T. Young. Such was the Freedom Forum of the B.B.C.: White and Young for the classics, etc. apparently NOT knowing the protocols and not seeing Laski ONE hundred percent Talmud, wanting to annihilate all history, substitute programs of the future precisely to PREVENT the masses or any one else learning LIFE as recorded in Demosthenes.

I.e. the effect of kikery, the Talmud, the perpetual forgeries in bamboozling simple-minded Saxons.

The classicist NOT realizing that Latin went on being written after the demise of the Roman Age and that Salmasius wrote it.

The London School of Economics does not want to teach history but conceal it as the Whig endowments concealed it, wants to prevent a knowledge of PRECISE problems, such as interest on money, the way it is made. All specific issues to be shelved in generalities such as the forum ran on about May 29th.

Then when White, I think it was, came back about the labor leaders trying to get a culture to equal or at least *ersatz* the classics, what does he trot out but the Bible, meaning the Protestant Old Testament, choked to the eyes with Jew mentality; and Milton, another already poisoned from the same source.

The really super naiveté of the poor old gents, dealing with the cockatrice, and NOT recognizing that ALL Laski's program IS the Protocols, whoever wrote them, i.e., whoever garbled that particular form of Talmudism in order to claim later that it was a forgery, and the kike is slandered.

Why don't the gents, still let on the British air, listen to some of the poison that accompanies their song and dance in foreign tongues, exhortations to assassinate in three languages; while tender messages to the kiddies in Canada float on the ambient, in the most chocolate box accents: oh quaite Engliash, while the yittisch female, claiming to pee vrfence entuneth in her nose-full tunefully about Hun consfiscations of Rothschild's embezzled tapestries and bibelots in the occupied territories, with no reference [to] the French background, as say available in Drumont du Camp, or the Goncourt.

By May 30, we say that England's only hope was in a few Yiddish assassins. Not only the last youpine whom the mild English accept as French, not only the ghetto sweepings, but right up to Westmonster itself, the dirty voice of Walter Elliot, like a bit of yesterday, day before yesterday's salad dressing left on a plate, unsound but still creamy.

Westminster, the tocsin, for a few attentats— —. No proposal of military action. ELLIOT encouraging the duped workers in the belief that a Paris riot will save England. Well, what about the Rothschild money in Skoda? Did THAT save Europe OR England? Disgust and tragedy. YOUR tragedy is that your able bodied men were killed in the last war. PUSHED into war by the financier whose race is not uniformly 100% British. The men who ought to KICK out your Walt Elliots, your Priestlies, were killed in the first three months of 1914. Noticed it in Paris literary life, in another way. No elders the young could respect.

That is the way the alien race wormed into the system. Kills off not only a government system but the race itself. It has taken my generation the whole of its time, 1910 to 1940, to discover the meaning, I mean down to [the] bottom of the word corruption, social corruption, corruption of a race and of national order.

The continent is a few decades ahead, France is in decay, the French have been studying the effect of Jews on France for over 50 years. Germans found out what it meant, reacted, serious STUDY of the Jew AS problem.

No longer haphazard programs. Serious study of what Dr. Laski means, I don't mean what Laski tells you, but of the phenomena, PENETRATION by Talmudic tendencies, bacilliae carried by a particular hostile, but whining race, humiliation doctrine, doctrines of humiliation, doctrines of shame, none of your Aquinas, *santo atleta*, as Dante called him. None of your Christianity conceived as intense luminous thought. The tensity that built the romanesque cathedrals, none in what is called romanesque style: duomo di Modena to St. Hillaire of Poiters, Mr. BowWowWow Steed in his dotage, saying that it will be a WIND, really!! For 25 years Steed has resisted abundance economy, derided, refused to read economics; and now he hears it from Perkins, that AFTER the War, after the Jews get control again, Geneva at 60% usury; interest on real deposits, then the old bleeders will all be Christ child, and Santy Claus.

Really ENGland needs something younger, something that WILL answer straight questions, re economic control. The slavery that Europe will NOT reaccept is slavery to the money monopolists, with no race, or no avowable race. Mouse nose or hwousse hnosse Hwood: or was it Falls telling us the Kharkov battle wasn't sufficiently serious, and the Germans forced to bulge out their line at both ends, eventually incurring the risk of encircling the Hroosians, a tactic or strategy which he deplored, hephlored, and so on.

As to the really good historical, reconstructions. NO one despises your Wilberforces, BUT they have been dead for some time. Their modern equivalents are NOT on the BBC. NOR are they respected in England to the point of giving them any power. Sierra Leone does not excuse Smuts, nor the DEBeers, nor the exploitation of English colonists IN Africa, by a government, local, colonial entirely in the hands of the kikes.

The example of France, the example of Poland, apparently taught England nothing. The weekly "Truth" nibbles at an edge, corruption of France, a by-word, but *meant* nothing. *La vie de Bohème*, romanticized. You make normal conditions, family, etc., impossible BY economic pressure, and THEN preach, is no use.

The ROMANCE of *La Bohème* was that a few individuals of high sensibility are forced into poverty.

IN those impossible conditions, the fineness still persists, or the consumptive simulacrum of refinement, not from desire toward eccentricity but they wear picturesque clothes, because these are the only clothes they can get, or what chance has thrown them. Then all that is falsified, vide W. Lewis' continual harping on the APing of la Bohème by the rich. Also the artists "dare" wear'em, those clothes, because no clerk in an office, no office boy (remaining office boy till age of 40 or 60) would be allowed to wear'em.

The CONtrast of the refinement with the need gives the romantic formula but does NOT make the accidents of la Bohème a NORM of life, as which the false romanticism set it up.

Naturally, if there were no bait, fish wouldn't bite. Drugs, advertised alcohol, spirits where there is no nutritive wine. Plenty of preaching but no potentialization. Ridicule of the middle class as bourgeoisie, etc.

all fits in, boredom exploited. Attitude that [it is] "all part of the game" whenever one gets to bedrock re the vice of usury, snarl from the London School of Economics products. Really bad, not to say vicious temper of these brutes when their private beef or bone is menaced.

The insurance RACKET, yet when an insurance man with a sense of humor really says something to a banker, the banker has but one word; and that word is HUSH. First silence, then babel to drown out the reality, then daily papers of 80 pages an issue, to HIDE what can't be excluded absolutely.

Arthur Meyer said to the Compte de Paris, vot uou needt iss an agenzy, hence there was Havas. Havoc of France.

Now, say I am incoherent, say I have not given you a formal discourse. Let us be CLEAR. YOU COMPARE Laski's total program with the total program of the Protocols of the Elders of Zion (without going into the sources of that document). COMPARE the two programs, and then come back and tell papa.

Oh, you want to know what I am talking about, well it is this. You get a couple of nice cultured old gentlemen, and they have lived in Oxford, and dined, and breakfasted in the shades, and they have read the so-called CLASSICS, without much curiosity, and they have not burrowed into the dirt of history, apart possibly from a few pawky bits of Latin pornography. And they are innocent as babes just born of the bearing of certain phenomena. Such, for example, as the getting rid of Latin studies, or the lowering of interest RATE, while increasing the total burden of interest to be paid.

The TOTAL going mainly to a very few, and strictly NON-patriot, non-national centres, whereas the lower rate of interest merely lowers the political potential of what is left of the responsible class that used to govern England nationally, instead of as a HED [?] company for high Jewry. These points escape you, and you and the nice old gents, neither of'em having read the Protocols, DO NOT recognize the symptoms of Laski. You fail to see what he is up to, and HOW exactly it fits into the program of high kikery.

That is your sorrow, or somnolence. You have heard that they are a forgery or a plagiarism, and you haven't stopped to ask what they are a forgery or plagiarism OF.

God know they are not pleasant reading. They are heavy, no style, very dull, but do you know what is in'em? Have you looked at Lord Sydenham's preface? Naturally not, that is, very few of you have, and so when Laski starts being clever you DO NOT see what he is aiming at you fail to detect the point of his aim, which of course he will deny; I mean he will swear blue, green, and pink that his aim is other.

But watch him.

#55 (July 13, 1942) U.S.(B68)
DARKNESS

You are in black darkness and confusion. You have been hugger-muggared, and carom-shotted into a war, and you know NOTHING about it. You know NOTHING about the forces that caused it, or you know next to nothing.

I am in the agonized position of an observer who had worked 25 years to prevent it. And I am not the only observer who had so striven.

Apparently NO man could prevent it, that is up to the point that it was not prevented. A belief in destiny does NOT necessarily imply a belief that we have NO duty, that we should NOT attempt to learn, that we should sit supine before age-old evil.

Given a little more knowledge, given the elimination of a small number of shysters, the war need not have happened.

Well, Europeans who ought to have known more than American farm boys got toppled into it BECAUSE they were ignorant. Books may sell 15 editions in 40 years without penetrating the mind of a nation. Some things that I say are NOT new, but I believe they are all necessary to knowin' which way the wind blows. You have got to learn some things or die, got to learn some things or perish.

All purchasing power does NOT come from labor, shysters try to live on the part of purchasing power that does not, that does NOT come from labor.

There is enough of purchasing power based on labor, and on labor only, to RUN all the culture, to keep up all studies, arts, all the amenities, the good life in toto. The extra purchasing power does NOT create these things, it corrodes them. It does NOT create what makes life fit to live, it attacks it. It spoils it.

It rots it.

A thousand years of European thought went to makin' what is best in life as we know it, or as we HAD known it before the last two outbreaks of bellicosity.

As outbreaks they were NEEDED, needed to bust the fog, the stink, the fugg, the chains of monopoly.

There was NO intellectual need of the liberation being conducted by cannon, tanks and machine guns. That is to say, human stupidity and chickenheadedness were so dense and so wafty that without the explosive publicity humanity evidently would not understand, and would not even turn its attention to the roots of the evil. Europe is fightin' for the good life, the shysters are fighting to prevent it. Even British minorities are muddleheadedly gettin' obstinate over some phases of the amenities. The decent English fight or urge others to fight in the name of a few amenities. I admit that the public voice in Britain pretty well keeps off of this topic. But there is a squashy, soft, vague underlyin' feelin' in England that something would get lost if the Axis licks'em.

That view is an error. There is MORE sense of the good life in Italy than in England. England don't know it. England does NOT know the good life in Italy. Italians are different. They even criticize one another.

Talk of organization, I mean to talk of organization. BUT there is no use organizin' till you know what you organize FOR. You ought to organize against world-wide sabotage, sabotage of everything that makes life fit for human being and for a sense of justice. Sense of justice corroded for decades. Corrosion gets in its work LARGELY because people don't know, and fear is begotten of IGNORANCE. WHAT *are* you fightin' for? Fightin' for the congressional system? Fightin' for parliamentary system? I doubt it.

Democracy? What *do* you mean by democracy?

A man might fight for justice. Many men fight from greed ... not their own greed. Fight from instinct.

That's O.K. up to a point. Fight for survival, that's health. Man ought to fight for survival, and for RACIAL survival. But are you fightin' for racial survival? I doubt it. I doubt if you have got to thinkin' of racial survival. I suggest you start thinkin'.

British instinct had paled, lot of'em so worn down they are ready to prefer suicide. I mean consciously. De facto, as a matter of fact, they've been suicidin' their race for some time. Even openly gloryin' in the small family, gloryin' in not breedin'. That is NOT aimed at survival. My fight from bad temper and natural kussedness, that also is understandable, but not admirable.

The English and the Americans, IF they ever fight to survive will, I think, have to come to the European state of enlightenment. They will have to fight on a basis of race. Other bases have failed'em.

Got to organize on basis of race, thereAFTER you might arrange an agreement of races, of racial strains, but be careful. One bad apple stinks up the whole barrel. Congressional votin' systems are all superficial, well not wholly superficial, BUT there has got to be something down under, got to be conviction, a reality, can't be all hoakum and shysters.

Of course you COULD put Congress on the air. Then you would know more of what your representatives are puttin' ON you. You could AGAIN learn from Europe. Remember our system was set up after careful study of anterior institutions, study of the British old system, with hopes to improve it.

You could keep the Constitution, and under that Constitution every state in the Union could reorganize its system of representation. Any or every state could elect its Congressmen on trade basis. Pennsylvania, or New Jersey, or Delaware (it might be rather difficult in the barony) but any or every state could organize its congressional representation on a corporate basis. Carpenters, artisans, mechanics, could have one representative; writers, doctors, and lawyers could have one representative. You could perfectly legally and constitutionally divide up the representatives of any or every state on the basis of trades and professions and the life of that state, every man in it, would gain REPRESENTATION in Congress; and Congress would take on an honesty and reality that no American in our time has dreamed of.

Present Congressmen are mostly so ignorant that some people have thought it might be useful to have a bit of congressional education. Insist on Congressmen being able to pass an exam in at least SOME of the subject matters they are expected to vote on. That would be like Chinese Mandarin system. Well no, that glorious exam system in China had merits. It also presents possibilities for not workin' perfectly. It might, I don't say it mightn't be well for Congressmen to pass an exam, before they become *eligible* for NOMINATION. That I would tend to be all for. BUT I see difficulties. I think the representation by trades and profession would be a better way out, with, if you like, DIFFERENT exams for the different trades and professions. That could do no harm whatsoever. Man to represent steel workers, to be able to show he knows the workin' of steel; miner to know the workin' of mines; professional to REPRESENT his profession, really to represent his profession, the best qualities, most acute knowledge of his profession.

That would certainly lead to efficiency, health regulations would be decided by someone who knew something about sanitation. Rules for minin' coal, rates per day, decided by someone who knows coal don't just crawl out of a mine, while somebody sits round playin' pinochle.

On that memorable occasion when I penetrated the dim and useless halls of the British Parliament, TWO men said somethin' sensible. Of course no attention was paid to'em. Lloyd George got up and barked, and Cecil emitted some dribble. But one man had been down in a mine, he explained how coal lies in the rock; one man had been in an engine room. Of course no attention was paid to'em. BUT if they had been talkin' to representatives of their own trades and professions, what they said would have been effective.

When the interest and knowledge of a trade has been concentrated in a proposal, that proposal should go to the kindred trades, and when there is a clash of THEIR interests, that should work up and be decided according to the national interest. As practically DOES not occur in the present English and American parliamentary systems, in which the people merely get buffaloed. Where decisions are bought, or huggermuggered thru by what is called "pressure," alias bribes and boycott. All these devilments would be much harder to put over in a chamber organized on trade and professional basis. I am tellin' you. I am just tellin' you. As Jimmy Whistler said to the painter, Chase, I say I am not arguin', I am just tellin' you.

You can keep the ole Constitution. Mostly sailors and landlubbers no longer care, but as a technicality (if no more than that) I am tellin' you. Lots of folks want to bust it, so as to fish in the troubled waters, lots of folks want to keep it rusty and inefficient, so'z it won't interfere with their various rackets.

I am tellin' you how to oil up the machine, and change a few gadgets so that it would work as the founders intended.

#56 (July 17, 1942) U.S.(B69)
PERFECT PHRASING

As a writer, oh a quite persistent writer (if I am not patient, thank God I am persistent) as a writer I object to the misuse of words. No man will ever be a great writer, not even a good writer, a useful craftsman of letters if he persists in misusin' words. Such for example as writin' or sayin' DEMocracy when he means judeaocracy, or when nothin' but his bone ignorance of the facts, past and present, prevents him from knowin' that he is talkin' about judaeocracy. I suggest that with 8 or 10 million hebes in America, it is time you at least devoted as much attention to the problem (Oh it's a problem O.K.) as has been devoted to Pueblos, the Spanish convents in N. Mexico and S. California.

Cause you haven't yet done so, and time presses, oh yes, time presses, and politics became pressure politics, and Jews became very precious or at least very dear to some circles, dear AND expensive. All them Morgenthau dollars for example: your dollars pumped into London, buyin' NO food for the Anglo-Saxon inhabitants of that metropolis.

Take it back to the Talmud, dirty, greasy old Talmud, all flesh is grass for the Hebrew pasture, human material, just browsin'' round, innocent as lambkins at Easter, cute an' amusin', no shame. Appeal to pity, and— — more so, appeal to greed; if you got it, appeal to vanity, that is, give you publicity, advertise everything you don't need or want until you think you want it. And then, brother, you are hooked. You want a new automobile violet tinted, you want a Tudor mansion, a trailer, a penthouse, all in the fashion paper, keep up with the Jones's. And lose the colonial ease, lose that homemade product of thick cream by the quart solid with peaches, that ice cream like used to be made in American kitchens. Mortgage your farm to the milk companies.

Why don't you study the phenomenon, the mode of being of your invaders? Don't get excited. The subject is full of interest for the psychologist ... and sociologist. "The fewer the higher." Lord, how that phrase puzzled us sophomores back in 1900 and one or two. The fewer, the higher. How ANY bit of absolute nonsense catches on in America. How the substitution of the ridiculous for the fine order is popular. Billikins, and the rest of it, ain't he cute!

Now in proportion to a nation's ignorance, or its chickenheadedness (its habit of INattention), it is easy to victimize. [The] Roman empire got a bit lazy and sleepy, back in the old Roman imperial days' great upheavals, upheavals, persecutin's of Christians. Factions within the church, crusades (vide Brooks Adams). Economic factors, all very interestin' if you have a serious turn of mind! Then the wars of religion. What caused'em? Then the turn about, one nation after another decided to turn out the Jews.

France turned'em out under some Louis or other. Been makin' laws since time of Philippe le Bel and Philippe Auguste. Anyhow, when France got rid of'em, France rose up and became *La Grande Nation*. I don't fancy Louis XIV but in his day France was important. Had, in fact according to some sort of reckonin' 38% of the population of the great powers. I don't know just what they figured to be great powers on that statistical table, but by 1789 France had 27%, and now has 13%.

And nobody with ANY historical knowledge says that the French revolution occurred without Jewish assistance. Nor that since that somewhat bloody upset and series of subsequent upsets the Jew warnt cockawhoop in the French capital. A knowledge of the French commune would have helped us to understand the Russian November revolution IF we had had it. But handy and useful knowledge has a teasy way of gettin' mislaid. Now what causes that?

Napoleon wanted to be real nice to the Hebrews, and they ditched him. Oh yes, they ditched him. Italy was bein' humane to the Jews, and they started gittin' rambunctious. Partly because of Italian clarity.

Italian perception that Kuhn Loeb had a hand in Russia. Wasn't that funny? And now you got Soviets right in the home. Or at least in old English cloisters almost adjacent. [The] Archbishop prayin' for no-godiler Russia. The British are funny people. Character, England the home of what was called character, crusted, crusted characters, crusted pert. Why don't you meet your allies? Now Mr. Browder is out to be President, with ten million Jewish votes. For democracy.

Do you admire what the Jews have done for England? I mean, is that what you want done to YOU? Or the work in the Stalin canal zone? Is that your ideal for the future? And the substitution of the Talmud for Tacitus in our most refined university circles?

Lady I know met her dusky ex-kitchen maid goin' to, is it George Washington University, the dark one in Washington, takin' elective subjects, in her case, black lady's case, it was Hebrew. How quaint.

As the damsel of color said to Mr. Sitwell: "are you high class?" Mr. S. allowed he was class, and she continued: "I don't hold with race prejudice, but I think the classes should be kept separate."

I don't believe in race prejudice, but I do believe in the study of history. So far as is known the dark Africans have done no harm to civilization for over two thousand years. S. Zeno was an African, St. Augustine had an African style, as they tell me, and it warn't good for the writin' of Latin, or at least some writers objected. But that is about the extent, debatable extent, of the damage. But all races are perhaps not useful to the concert or concord of nations.

Undoubtedly the simpler the race, the easier it is to bamboozle it. Look at the Mujiks, perfect happy huntin' ground for the Hebrews. And the slow witted Britons, well they hold up being slow. Their wreck took at least from Cromwell to 1939. A tough and pugnacious people, but your fibre is thinner. I don't mean your granddad's personal fiber wasn't as tough as or more so than any Britons, but your social order is looser, more gangly. Organized political action has NOT been an American talent, no CONstructive political organization for the past 80 years. And your ignorance has been a spreadin'. [The] contents of the American mind been gittin' more and more flimsy every day of the week since Andrew Johnson got pushed out of the White House.

Even Henry James noted the strength of the executive, but bein' a kid glover did not dwell much on the topic. Notice the habit of JOININ, Mr. Gallatin joined Mr. Jefferson. It is said they do not want to form any opinion IN PARTICULAR, they just want to be in a position to form opinion. Look at that lousy KEN [?] assembled a committee to decide which policy would PAY best, then started on those lines. Always on BOTH side of a question, some of'em here, some there. Always have conservative papers and left-wing papers, both of which avoid severe topics, such as the problem of interest.

Man said to me, "[Why] his manager spent 30 thousand dollars gettin' the nomination! He was goof, he could have had it for SIX, six thousand dollars." Otherwise to be classified: devise on temporary debility of a so-called great party.

Why confuse judaeocracy with DEMocracy? And why not DO somethin' about it, if you wish to survive. I personally am all for survival. I should like some AMERICAN life to survive. I should like to see some 100 million Americans represented in Washington, I mean in the government, gettin' the things they want.

I can't believe the sons or descendents of the Massachusetts colony, the Connecticut colony, or even the sons of Rhode Island really want to PAY two dollars for every dollar spent by the government. I feel sure Alabama doesn't. Nor does Nebraska, nor Kansas, nor Idaho, nor Wyoming.

I am sorry this question of industrial silver has come up so soon after the arrival of Sassoon in America. I wonder if you have mortgaged any of your silver mines to him. I wonder if you have, or had, swapped a few of 'em to him for some of his hop joints, opium smokeries in Singapore and Shanghai, just a bit before the Japanese got so active.

Of course industrial use is the future of silver. As for gold it is a bit heavy to use copper-bottomin' in boats with, and said to be a soft metal. I s'pose they'll find some kind of alloy that will harden it up into sothing useful ... some day ... and plenty of people still wearin' it inside their faces. But porcelain is more in fashion for high class dentist's work in most countries.

EZRA Pound speaking. Why did you get into this war?

#57 (July 19, 1942) U. K. (B73)
JULY 16TH, AN ANNIVERSARY

Several thousands of people in England may recall where they spent the evening of July 16th in the far off and happy year of 1939. In fact only three years ago, the British world bore a different aspect. And of the thousands [who] remember that evening, a few may be fortunate enough to be able to hear the reminder. A British patriot was offering them in the midst of the world's most prosperous empire, a patriot was offering them FOUR points of sanity. And the text was "A Million Britons shall not die in a Jew's quarrel." To defend Britain it was not necessary to intervene in every Balkan problem. Britain could be strong enough to defend herself WITHOUT entangling alliances in Eastern Europe, I might add in the interests of the Sassoon. Britain had her own man power. Live and let live.

FOUR POINTS: 1. Disinterest in Eastern Europe. 2. Disarmament in Western Europe. 3. Return of the German colonies, which England did not need, as [she] already held a quarter of the world. 4. Concentration on their shamefully neglected British Empire itself.

Might of Japan as the more imminent threat to British Empire. The speaker at Earls Court also pointed out that Japan constituted a far more effective menace to the Empire than did Germany. That Europe was divided by a financier's vendetta. He even mentioned kicking [out] of [the] British at Tientsin. Three years have passed. I think Germany will get back her colonies. Japan has already demonstrated her capacity. The British Press was then, and still is controlled by Jew financiers. Money then could not be found for New Zealand and Newfoundland, but industries in China, India, and Japan were being financed with British capital in order to depress the industries of Lancashire and Yorkshire. There was no such thing as free press in England. The Union of the British people was urged. The old parties do NOT seem to have served you up to the "optimum" if I may be permitted to use that new bit of slang.

My scrapbooks may be unsystematic, my plan doesn't run. I don't run to a filing system, but the oddments are fairly rich. Next to that Earl's Court program I find a cuttin' of August 3 of the same fatal year, 1939. And the olive blossoms were rich in that year. LOANS from England to friendly nations in Europe then totaled, according to the Times, thirty-one million sterling plus: Turkey, 16; Poland, a bit over 8; Rumania, 5 and a half; Greece, 2 million 40 thousand. Poles had not accepted conditions for another 5 million. The 8 million plus said to be repayable during 16 years, beginning 1941. Loan to the Orient, interest paid in cheap cotton goods, ruin of Manchester. Loans to South America, interest in beef and ruin of British cattle grazing. British people will never apparently understand the effects of international usury.

Nor of course that of usury in the home, municipal rates, proportion of taxes that go to interest payment, in short strangle hold of high kikers, its servants and its affiliates. Death by exhaustion of England, unless the RACE revives, and stands as a race, and until you stop accepting foreign Jews setting up every kike refugee as a provisional government of some country that IS NOT the land of his fathers.

The only kike country is probably Samaria, and you have not yet appointed an ambassador to Tel Aviv. Or have you, or would that imply welching a bit on your promises to the Arabs?

Masochistic yidds shrieking, howling for the destruction of Paris (along with dear Winnie). Eve Curie howling that America shall not feed French children. YOU will have to look into the question of race. You will have to remember the tradition of thoroughbreds if you want to make ANY sort of comeback. An alternative? Laski's protocols. Well: COMPARE Laski's aims WITH the protocols. Dear old Snow White, and tender, or Young or whatever his name is ought to meet Laski right in the home, right in ZION, right in the Talmud, which is his spiritual habitat. It is the touching and surprising ignorance of that more than wasteland, oh— —don't suppose it IS surprising. You have read the Times and the Telegraph for so long.

And I still have somewhere in my files the correspondence with the old Morning Post received here when I suggested they print a line from the Raffalovitch correspondence concerning a little douceurs to the Times and Telegraph.

Well, I wonder where the old honest Englishmen are in this hour?— —still mildly elegiaic, I suppose.

Still thinking there is some other reading of Genesis. The Gods made heaven and earth. Then came Jehoveh and the Jew boy. I made it, get the hell out of here.

That is your story, oh England! Wilberforce may be regretted, men who remember a DIFFERENT England haven't all died yet. Normalization of chewisch relations, Jew promises the rump of England world dominion, no, not even that promise. In partnership mit dh yitts. The distinguished French, Dutch, Polish, etc. Yitts, and of course the Yitt are to hold, well let us say 51% of the stock, or that isss too little if Rothschildt puts up 75% of the money, by chewisch consortium. Call it Geneva or what not, so the chews should have 87% of the control. But the lords will all have dummy directorates, at from 5 to 40 thousand per year. Lord Beit, Lord Melchett, Lord Goldsmid, the flower of Chivalry und Lord Burnham. And Lord Laski, and then the commune. Laski's program IS the program of the Protocols? Have you yet heard of the Protocols? The intrinsic matter OF the protocols, whoever wrote'em. Compare IT. Compare it with what you are offered.

And then the so-called racial hatreds, what chance the Frenchman you dislike ISN'T a Frenchman AT ALL? That the European you dislike, the continental you dislike, isn't a European AT all? That needs looking into. Yes, you all have a few Jews that you like? Think it over? Is it quite satisfactory? They are everywhere save in one or two small organizations. I know of a third which applied the proportional quota.

Horrors of antisemitism. What about the horrors of NOT having a sane bit of discretion, as France under Blum, and Reynaud?

When I started walkin''round the South and Center of France in 1912 I found a VERY different race and spirit from that of Paris Montmartre and putridity——and the rest of it. As late as 1922 there were still some French left in the onzième arrondissement.

I saw Blum at a press lunch sometime after 1927. I am not sure of the date. The impression was unfavorable. I don't think he fooled Sparrow Robertson either. There was a certain lack of frankness in Blum's exposition. Certain phases he seemed rather to wish to avoid. And you in England seem to me rather to fall short in that swift perception of relations, which Aristotle so admired. I mean if YOU fail and PERSIST in failing to perceive a relation between Blum, Laski and Reynaud, *verbum sapienti verbum*.

Well, a word to the sap-head is quite ineffective, it leaves the sap-head unsatisfied.

#58 (July 20, 1942) U.K.(B71)
SUPERSTITION

You ought not to be at war against Italy. You ought not to be giving or ever to have given the slightest or most picayune aid to any man or nation engaged in makin' war against Italy. You are doin' it for a false accountancy system. You ought to go down on your knees and thank God for Italy, thank God an Italian, possessed of Mediterranean sanity, showed the first ray of light in the general darkness, showed a way to git you out of the hell made by a false accountancy system. Or I don't care if you go down on your knees you can set with your head in your hands or you can go out muskelunge fishin', but you ought to be thankful.

All purchasin' power does NOT come from labor, not in the world as you have known it. And NOTHING good in that world NEEDED to have come from false accountancy. You were buffaloed into thinking that false accountancy helped some of you to play golf and own automobiles. And that was just BUNCOMB. The Loeb chart showed it was buncomb. But you didn't read or didn't understand the Loeb chart. All purchasing power does NOT come from labor. But you were so ignorant of the timing of labor that you thought you needed to be scared to death of Gottfried Feder You are at war to conceal the fact that a lot of purchasing power, a lot of capital comes from a hoax.

Damn the hoax. But don't go out and die for just bein' idiots. Or for your tolerance of being run and ruled over by dumheads who are pushed on by shysters.

Feder's sentence was simple and clear. It contains about all mankind needs to know about economics.

But only the very intelligent know enough that it is the root fact. Hence the need for more explanation.

Feder got it into one sentence and Germany rose from her ashes, ran from her miseries and her chaos.

Douglas (C.H.) found it out. But he said it with more wrappings and trappin's; and England went further and FURTHER into the discard. However, that sentence of Feder's gives about all you need as a basis for Social Credit, by the light of which truth Alberta at least had a Prime

Minister. At least declined to lie passive and sign on the dotted line, and SAY all glory to the Soviet's owners.

Douglas was a worryin' about so much, his first volume is very moral. He made a mistake (or not) as the case may be, but mebbe he made a mistake in not being more moral. He was gunnin' for practicality.

He knew the kind of S.O.B. who was runnin' the rackets. The rackets INC. The high courtly, pompous high hatted rackets, the British Empire and its succursales. The slave works on which the sun never rose.

Page Judge Colahan about the Kingdom of England's interests. And Douglas tried to argue. Thought avarice was the human motive, thought comfort was *the* human motive.

England doesn't much like ideas. We have been buffaloed. English so worn down they glorified muddle. Glory of the intellect was represented as spiritual pride, by such low grade intellects as the Episcopal British bumbishops. Oh Lord! grovelin' humility is an old wheeze. Every time a Christian wanted to get anything done he was told to be humble. Veritable grovel of humility was set up as an idol as an ideal norm of conduct, also muddle. Brits were told muddle was kindness, and proof of a superior civilization. Gloried in muddle, abhorred anything lucid. You can put the blame on the climate. Well the U.S. hasn't the fog-bound excuse, there is clear air. Arizona and Nebraska. Why muddle, why muddle any longer, why grovel before your bond-holders? And why, on the other hand, be buffaloed by the half-baked idiot who says there ought to be NO stock that pays interest on productive investment, by which I mean share holding, sharing in [a] proper sense, SHARIN' in the fruits of labor and design combined into industry. Why be bolshevised, that is, hoaxed, into thinking every man ought to be a lavatory attendant?

There are resources of American production, or at least there WERE, before Roosevelt canned'em.

Before ALL useful effort, or half the national income, or whatever you hoaxers call it, should be turned into making tank for Chiang Kai-Shek that he can't get because your air force ain't strong enough to tote them over the N. Pole BY AIR.

Naturally IF all or most the American production effort is turned into making munitions to be sunk on the high seas, there will be LESS production of American comfort. Mince pies will have less proper ingredients, short cake will run short, and strawberries rise in price on the internal market. You will be told: yes, we have no bananas, sweet potatoes, or even cabbage.

Mebbe the Americans of European origin and of African origin for that matter ought to leave N.Y., leave Manhattan Island, retire to the American mainland, and make the cloak and suit trade pay for its eggs and spinach.

But the world's thought goes marchin' on. No Lenin's body, no cubic mausoleum, all that is old stuff.

You ought to wake up and listen. I mean listen to something BETTER, and can the shysters; turn out the pikers and shysters, and at least put a dent in your ignorance. I am willing to believe in the existence of Christians. I have met very few. I know one obstinate Christian, obstinate from sheer ignorance, but with rather less élan, less enthusiasm than one associates with feelings about a Yale-Princeton game.

I have known men go into the church from policy. I can recall one serious Christian, the head of Fordham University. When I talk into [the] microphone, I have to think of at least one or more people who might conceivably understand what I am saying. I should like someone to notify Father Miller or any other serious Christian that I propose to speak on the topic: what is wrong with Christianity? And the answer is: it is completely DEmoralized. I mean that in [the] strict sense, ALL morality has been carefully and gradually and over a period of centuries [been] removed from it. All coherent ethics, or all ethical system has been extracted from it. Trickled out, got mislaid. The lllovely hymns sung in Equador by the strawberry tenor, no, not a whisky tenor, a real strawberry ice-cream-soda tenor, down in Equador singing sentimental church hymns, or singing Christian hymns in a moonlight manner. ALL for the sake of diddling the S. Americans and maintainin' a ROTTEN false accountancy system. That is one phase.

Temple prayin' for the no-godites in Cuntyburry Cathedrau. That's another. Identification of Christianity with greed. The American Catholic bishop's economic manifesto, that is a sign the other way. I will allude to that some time.

Christian ethics. I'spose there must be a chair or settee of Christian ethics in some American theological college, must be courses in ethics in at least four or five universities. How does ethics match up with Christianity, I mean Christianity on the hoof, as preached and as practiced? Perhaps ought to say: as muddled.

Restoration of slavery in Abyssinia, or looking back a bit, policy of maintaining a powder keg "in the Balkans." POLICY, British policy, your Ally's policy of deliberately maintaining impoverished, disordered areas hither an' yon. Abyssinia, Balkans (proverbial powder keg), Skoda gun works. NOT for any honest avowable aim. Simply for [the] sake of having something into which war torch can be thrown. All blessed by the churches.

Or all tolerated BY the Christian churches during the incubation period. And except a few manifestos, rare, my God: HOW rare, NO Christian effort toward ETHICS in economics whatsoever.

Now how did the Christian religion get that way? Have you thought of the matter at all? How many parsons have EVER thought of it? I have heard Brit and Yit propaganda so foul in these weeks that it has given me nausea. Irrelevant flimflam.

Little Johnnie threw the kitten out of the window, and when his ma went to smack him he ran away and fell up the stairs, and his nose got all bloody, and it bled all over his pinafore; isn't that CREWEL?

Ain't Hitler just awful?

THAT covers 80% of the cringe from London, and the boo-hoo from Schenectady, from the General Bowery Electric and the Columbia Rachel's jewel. Boo-hoo all over England, but what had England done before she was smacked?

Prayers for civil disorder. That is their other line. While the Axis propaganda TELLS you about order, the financial gang that brought Civil war into Spain, the money lenders that financed the Spanish left go on trying to start civil war. And to that end I call Claude Bowers, or anyone else who has been near [a] civil war, to say WHAT civil war is. And I quote la Signorina Pilar and Conchita, "When a foreign army invades and kills, they go away after the war is ended. But after [a] civil war, the people who have murdered their neighbors, are still there next door to the neighbor's family." That is what the British Society for Prevention of Cruelty to Animals is preaching, and the Jew American radio is preaching night and day. England that does not fight with an army howls to the CHILDREN of France and Holland, to shoot the forces of occupation. What England could not do at Dunkirk, she openly prays to have done for her by five young men who got away in a canoe, and by the women and children.

And England is your Ally and you have not yet started thinking.

#59 (July 26, 1942) U.K.(B76)
AXIS PROPAGANDA

A Yiddish refugee who has been a publisher of pornography in Berlin, collaborator in the corruption of Germany that followed the judaization of the German government after the last war has been indulging in some impertinence in one of your weeklies, one of those lax productions that the Jew seems to find it so easy to bring forth, when good literature fails to PAY the publishers in money.

There is nothing surprising in a Goy nation falling under the domination of the Jewish print. However as this unwanted adjunct to your Sieffery, your Sassoonery, your Beitery, Isakery and so on, has used the term "Axis propaganda," I propose to give you a few quotations that canNOT, I think, by any stretch of imagination, in fact, cannot by any stretch of anything, save the infinite impertinence of the Yid, be considered Axis propaganda. In fact, I propose to quote an ANTI-Fascist paper printed in England on October 14th, 1939. And then await the SILENCE which greets all unanswerable data in your unhappy land. The passages I'm about to read were gathered together by L.D. Byrne on the date indicated, 1939.

QUOTE:

Just as I told them in Ottawa in 1923, exactly what was going to happen in 1928, so I tell you now in 1934, that before 1940 if you have not changed your financial system, it will change and probably eliminate you.

That was Major C.H. Douglas in the Alberta legislature, April, 1934. Next quote.

As I came here tonight I bought an evening paper, on the front page of which were the words "Germans in the Rhineland." We are back in 1914 where the financiers said they would get us.

Douglas in Westminster, March 1936. Next quote:

For 20 years the Social Credit movement ... has persistently warned people that in the absence of effective and timely reform of the financial system, that system would precipitate war and revolution on a scale which might destroy the fabric of civilized society That is from Byrne himself, who next quotes Thomas Jefferson: I believe that banking institutions are more dangerous to our liberties than standing armies.

And:

If the American People ever allow private banks to control the issuance of their currency, first by inflation and then by deflation the corporation that will grow up around them will deprive the people of all their property, until their children wake up homeless on the continent their fathers conquered.

End of quote from Thomas Jefferson. Again quote:

I have two great enemies, the Southern army in front of me and the financial institutions in the rear. Of the two the one in the rear is my greatest foe.

That was Abraham Lincoln. Quote, that is again quote:

The money power preys upon the nation in times of peace and conspires against it in times of adversity. It is more despotic than monarchy, more insolent than autocracy, more selfish than bureaucracy.

It denounces as public enemies all who question its methods, or throw light upon its crimes.

That was William J. Bryan, and I trust Mr. Ullstein or Isaac Schmollensnout or his makeup editor or his printer devil is served.

As to whether Jefferson, Lincoln, Bryan and L.D. Byrne were engaged in offering Axis propaganda, I leave it to the remaining British denizens of Britain and the United States to decide.

It is time; it has been time for the past 30 or 80 years for the people of England and America to understand the war process. To understand that they have been edged into war NOT *pro patria*, not for their father's land or their nation, BUT for the profit of a few scoundrels and for an ENEMY, an enemy that desires to cast down from their seats all the mighty, and all the orderly, to cast down every nation that exists openly, every government that exists OPENLY *pro bono publico*, for the people.

And the program of this ENEMY is known, and the action of governments in the hands of the ENEMY SHOW the nature of the AIM of the enemy. Their aim is not to win war, but to make peace impossible. These bombings of towns are NOT military, they are done to rouse hate, to be causes of hate.

What does a Belisha or a Sassoon care for Canterbury? Nothing. It is not his Canterbury, it is NOT his cathedral. The destroyed monuments are not monuments to the glory of Judah. They show NOTHING that the Jew can be proud of. IF medieval, they were built in open defiance of the Jew slime, and of the Talmud. They are an offense in the eye of the Jew; they are what his oily race has NOT accomplished.

Insofar as there are monuments to OTHER races he is against them. And from the moment they are classified as national monuments he cannot TRAFFIC in them, and they are therefore useless to him until they are reduced to fragments that can be sold in antique shops.

HENCE his alliance with the bishops of England, and the stockbrokers and the lenders of money, who first lend for war and then lend for reparation.

The words for Englishmen and Americans is "Know thyself and thine enemy." These outrage raids are NOT made to win war, they are made to stave off a possible or a durable peace, to sow hate, as of course are the constant exhortations to riot and assassination which are the stock and trade of the BBC radio in foreign transmissions, which contrast with the soft soap and chocolate of their "love us all" howls in English.

That is my comment. Let me return to Byrne's article. Quote: The issue which has swept down the centuries and which will have to be fought sooner or later, is the people versus the Banks.

That was the Lord Chief Justice of England in 1875. And a further item from Byrne's compendium:

"During the 20-year period prior to 1938 some twenty million persons perished in Russia.... Wholesale execution, periodic liquidation." That refers to YOUR ally. Perhaps Ullstein, Churchill, and Eden will offer an emendment to these Russian figures?

By way of contrast, (and the Social Crediter assures us its facts are mainly from Jewish sources, the Jewish encyclopedia, etc.) correct me if I err, Edward I, determined to solve the Jewish question as it existed in England and in the Statutum de Judaismo, forbade the Jews to lend on interest, and granted them permission to engage in commerce and handicrafts and even to take farms for a period. Some resorted to highway robbery and a considerable number appear to have resorted to clipping the coin, as a means of securing a precarious existence.

As a consequence in 1278 the whole of English Jewry was imprisoned and in 1290 finally expelled.

Many settled in the ghetto of Paris. As to whether Edward the 1st was interested in the welfare of England, we must leave Mr. Ullstein to decide for you, as you seem averse [to] making clear cut decisions. And as Steed and Priestley are unlikely to say anything offensive to so influential a new Hebrew amongst you, or in fact, to oppose themselves in any way to kahalism in your tight little island.

All this is from an anti-Fascist and anti-Axis paper printed in England before I had begun to speak on Rome Radio. Let us hope Mr. Ullstein is served.

Spending so much of my time in Rapallo and being lazy I don't always see the latest novelties, but I finally got round to seeing the war film, Italy's documentation "Two Years of War." Of course, you can't see it. It helps one to think of the difference between a nation BASED on its farm population, its agricultural population and GOVERNED by men of the same race, of the difference between them and a nation EXPLOITED by usurers, who are NOT racially identified with the people they govern.

#60 (February 18, 1943) U.S.(C8)
MORE HOMELY

Don't shoot him. Don't shoot him. Don't shoot the President. I dare say he deserves worse, but don't shoot him. Assassination only makes more mess, as fer example in the case of Darlan. And Hank Wallace....?

Frankfurter can feed hot air to Wallace just as fast as he feeds it to Frankie, probably faster.

What you can do is to understand just how the President is an imbecile. I mean that, learn JUST how, in what way he is a dumb cluck, a goof, a two fisted double-time liar (oh well, you know THAT already, and lyin' is NOT a sign of intelligence) but don't shoot him. Di/ ag/nose him. Diagnose him. It is not only your out, but it is your bounden duty as an American citizen. DUTY begins at home.

If you can't do it yourself, no one can do it for you. I may have been on the wrong line quoting Brooks Adams, I mean about Sennacherib, and the Shalmanaser, and the decline, that is flop, of the Babylonian empire? May have been talkin' over your heads. Possibly I ought to have come nearer with a more familiar or homely example.

Say the Cumberland Turnpike, P. 344 in Bill Woodward's *A New American History*, published by Farrar and Rinehart. Or say The Erie Canal, something you may have heard of. Well look it up in your copy of Woodward, and meditate on his paragraphs; and then call the President by his address.

Bloomingdale's gook house, or some establishment of similar nature. The National Road, known as the Cumberland Turnpike, funds raised by sale of lands in Ohio, broad highway was built from the head of navigation on the Potomac to Wheeling Ohio. Officially called National Road, popularly known as Cumberland Turnpike.

Baltimore and Philadelphia were the chief beneficiaries. Why? Cause a trade route brings benefit to the trade centers. N.Y. slippin' behind in 1817,'cause OF the new trade route. Twelve thousand wagons arrivin' in Philadelphia in 1817. And not to N.Y.

So what was done as an answer? The Erie Canal was the answer. 365 miles from Buffalo to the kapital of N.Y. state, Albany on the Hudson River. Supposed to be longest canal in the world of that era. Mr. Adams who is considered a more highbrow historian than the more cheerful and inconsequent Woodward would have put down his foot and EXPLAINED the passage, or correlated it to a general principle. As indeed Woodward had done in his own mind before he selected those items. Though he don't make a splurge on the page, and assert a general principle about trade routes: vortices of trade, vortices of civilization. And ANY state department or executive that wasn't fit for the gook house, or an institution for the care of the feeble minded would have done likewise. Hence I say diagnose him.

B. Adams' bright and enthusiastic view of America's NEW EMPIRE was based on America's geographic position plus the invention (British invention, let's give'em credit) of railways; and the oncoming canal thru the Panama isthmus. The U.S. was to be the focus: the vortex of trade movin' economically from Asia to Europe.

England, as Brooks Adams saw, was declinin' after 1897. Triumph of Pittsburgh steel, exhaustion of British tin mines, etc. England, because of her mental torpor and material circumstances, AND greater activity of other nations in makin' use of mechanic invention, England was on the down, and the center of trade was a hurryin' westward, to roost in Manhattan.

BUT it was movin' westward. The Japanese were a very brave people. They were an active people.

The British record in the Boer war was an indication of whaar England was floppin' to. The Japanese heroism at Peony Mt. and at the Gemmu Gate had told the world the meaning of Bushido. And the U.S. at the summit of her diplomacy had collaborated with Tokyo in keeping the European powers out of the Chinese bonanza.

So what, In the days of your squalor. So what. America on the brink of abundance. Loeb chart to show it. Prosperity round the corner. Land flowin' with milk and butter, no need for any American family to have less than 4 or 5 thousand a year. Not with a sane money system, and so on. What does your prize pig of a President do ON you? He cuts off the trade with the Orient. He cuts off the trade with Europe. What is the answer?

France in 1900 was already eccentric, commercially that is, eccentric; off the central line of the main traffic. England is off there like a postage stamp. An island, Denmark, OFF the main short line of traffic.

And the U.S. is NOT in the center. Geographically the position is unchanged, BUT the trade is NOT passin' thru the great American landways and waterways. The U.S. faces the bumsides of both continents.

Back to Europe and Back to Asia. And the trade gettin' set to move by the other channels. Already circulatin' like billyo INSIDE the main bulk of Europe. But certainly NOT layin' for the return and enrich Jew York City. Or San Francisco. Hence the Jew croak about Universal domination. Universal police force. Page Mr. Wallace to prevent all people who aren't kike-owned from trading with each other without a gang of Anglo-Saxon gangsters owned by Judea, buttin' in and bustin' their tradin'.

That is what Franklin D. Frankfurter Jewsfeld has done to the American people. He has busted the bright hopes of being the center of world exchanges. Out of sheer ignorance, greed, and stupidity. And that is the grounds whereon you ought to diagnose him; his kikes and his politics.

Need I go back and UNDERLINE it? The American diplomacy of the Mark Hanna, McKinley, Root (Elihu) era. The high of American acumen. All the material base: AND the intellectual mercantile base of the then belief in American imperialism. The state of mind that could see and understand the significance of the mineral wealth of Shansi, and prospect a trade system. An economic system, a trade route. The acumen that euchred the European powers, prevented the dismemberment of China, IN HARMONY with Japan. As contrasted with the squalor of the Frankfurter era, the stuffed senilities, Knoxes, Stimsons, Leahy—probably his father spelled the name LeVY. The INCAPACITY to look at a map, to SEE that the islands of Japan lie smack across the patch of the route to Pekin.

Beaten, licked to a frazzle before Pearl Harbor. Beaten by their own pimping idiocy. I know I say sometimes iggurunce. The political idiot is the politician who does NOT look at his own ignorance, and try to chart it, to diminish it. Knox, Stimson, Roosevelt, put'em in a glass case and charge the public ten cents to look at'em. America WAS promises. The possibility of forming a new trade route in collaboration with Japan, thence centering the world trade in America, running the Asian trade to Europe and the European trade to Asia via the U.S.A.

That was what the American acumen had charted in 1900, after the victory of Pittsburgh Steel. That was the material base of America's chance for preeminence. NO monopoly, I said preeminence, in a world system. Not the fool cluck idea of forcing the world into paying an unjust price, of starving the earth in the interest of a few slobs of upper Judea, but a collaboration in a world system wherein trade would follow the easy courses. BECAUSE those trade routes could have undersold other routes, because different goods lay at different termini. And the U.S. lay in the middle. SO long as she collaborated with Tokyo. That is what Frankie D. Roosevelt has foozied. He has cut off the trade with Europe. He has cut off the trade with Asia.

America recedes into something like where she was in the days of T. Jefferson. Larger, yes, larger: but not more powerful in proportion to the world powers.

Three generations from shirt sleeves to shirt sleeves. Mebbe you folks will learn something BY it.

Perforce constrained into thinking of autarchy, into isolation. That Anglo kikes have failed to force upon Europe. BUT which Europe had the foresight to provide for, and is increasingly attaining.

A little decency would have kept the U.S. from error. An amount of horse sense comparable to that reigning in the U.S. when Tom Edison was a young man, when H. Ford was making his first automobiles.

Waaal, who would have thought that men of my age would ever have thought of lookin' back to the days of Wm. McKinley as a great and brilliant American era? Days of American engineering preeminence and of dollar diplomacy.

#61 (February 19, 1943) U.S.(C9)
THAT ILLUSION

Met an American lady on the seafront tother day. Married to an Italian, so she is still thaar on the seafront.

Says to me: "That WALLACE, hasn't sense to come in out of the rain."

I seem to recall a report of a Delphian convention about six years ago, when Henry W. was trying to tell'em something about American agriculture; how you eat more if you grow less, or some such ingenious piece of Jew brow kikosophy.

Hank of course is appealin'. I mean, gives the effect of bein' a nice kind hearted feller, with infinite capacity for believin' what the wrong people tell him. He don't see that a world would be just as warless under an efficient Japanese or European police domination as under a kike monopoly—probably more so. I hear that in occupied Russia they get a Jew to supervise Jewish labor. In fact the lack of sequence. and coherence in H.W.'s kite flying would be remarkable if Hank didn't come from the corn belt. He must be gettin' his ideas from the B.B.C. latterly. He is not a sadistic slob like his leader, but still I s'pose he has no mother to guide him. Yet YOU, in fact you got your responsibility. Can't always blame it on the executive, and the pseudo-executive. Diagnose'em. Diagnose'em. IF you can't see how crazy some of their talk is, who is going to SEE for you?

Most of you never go near a political meetin'. Most of you don't know what are PRIMARIES. The young ought to start looking into the actual political system. Go round to the wigwam. You got a vote. The ward boys won't throw you out if you ask him politely what you can do for the party. It don't matter which party. Go round to the wigwam. Don't lie back on the divan and think not listenin' to my voice on the radio will bring political salvation and economic salvation to YOU and your honeybun.

No political system will run itself without human intervention. All the intervenin' you can probably do is comprised of YOUR OWN intervention. Go, find out politely which political party is worse than the other, if either is, or conceivably could be, worse than the other.

Manners will probably be politer in the Republican wigwam. The obvious percentage of kikery will be lower. There will be possibly less humanitarian flimflam. BUT in any case diagnose'em. And the first piece of quite foetid bunk to diagnose OUT of the Roosevelt-Wallace synagogue sob stuff is this bunk about FREEDOM, which does NOT include economic freedom. Take that every day and all day; and whenever an office holder, a sergeant, a chewish staff officer or a member of the cabinet or executive says FREEDOM, point out that his (if it's Wallace) HIS proposed freedom, omits freedom from debt. We fight for world freedom, says the dead cod in London, over the synagogue radio.

Wallace has the sour faced gall to get up and talk about the freedom of a world in DEBT to America.

Whenever Wallace or any other palooka pulls that by word of mouth, on the radio or in private, git a shovel, or try and see if the flush mechanism is workin'.

THAT much at least you ought to learn from this war. Ought to have learned it in 1920. Ought to be there in the school books from the 1st grade and upward.

There is NO freedom without economic freedom. Freedom that does not include freedom from debt is plain bunkumb. It is foetid and foul logomachy to call such servitude freedom. And really Mr. Wallace, with his kindly smile, and his pious palavar ought to catch up with the 20th century and realize that that line does NOT work any longer. The whole of Europe, Asia and Arabia is ONTO that hoakum. Heckle him. Whenever Hank or any one of the high Jewsfeld committee pulls that wheeze about freedom, enforced by Jewish world police, centered in Panama and in Palestine, ask: does he mean freedom from debt? Ask: what does he mean by freedom. Freedom from debt? Freedom from payin' two dollars OUT of the people's pocket for every buck spent by the government? Ask about freedom. Don't shoot the guy, diagnose him.

Good God, have you no columnists, have you no caricaturists left in America? Even little Eddie asked you what you would do with your GOLD. Christ, you are in debt. You are indebted. You have for years been pouring out America's wealth. Pouring out the purchasing power that ought to have stayed in the American people's pocket.

You have bought gold at 35 bucks per ounce. You have paid quite needlessly 75 cents for 23 cents worth of silver. All paid INTO the pockets of other people. America was promises; "TO WHOM?" says Archie. Promises to Rothschild and Rothschild's co-nationals, Archie? That was promises TO WHOM?

Paid into the pockets of people who keep the Roosevelts and Wallaces IN office for the sole purpose of having the levers held by people who will swallow that sort of bumcomb. Who will get up and talk about freedom without seein' that freedom is NOT unless it be freedom FROM debt?

Yes, freedom from all sorts of debt, INCLUDIN' debt at usurious interest. Two dollars fer one. Yet even Gallatin during the war of 1812 has sense enough to emit some purchasing power (notes under 100 bucks) that did not bear interest. You are SOLD. England is sold. France has been OBVIOUSLY put up at auction. Switzerland is still where she is because Jews weren't allowed to settle there until 1864. Wherever the Jew gets control of a nation, that nation gets into difficulty. I'll say: into difficulty.

I am taking my whole time on one point durin' this little discourse. Sometimes I try to tell you too much. I suspect I talk in a what-is-called incoherent manner:'cause I can't (and I reckon nobody could) tell where to begin. What knowledge one can consider as preexisted in the mind of the AVERAGE American listener. When I was wonderin', the American press men left Rome; I was wonderin' if anybody listened to what I said on Rome Radio and an experienced well broken journalist said: don't worry, there'll always be some fellow in a newspaper office sitten there, trying to get something for his column or something.

Debt is the prelude to slavery. And you are now, I'spose, arrived at the intermezzo. America WAS promises. America today is largely, shall we say, promissory notes that simply can NOT be honored.

Britain's debts in the last war—who paid'em? Oh, some of'em didn't get paid. England in 1935 [was] a bankrupt trying to live by the lending of money. But, brother, England in 1939 was inhabited exclusively by millionaires. In comparison to what England is today under Churchill; and still spending her treasures.

Still losing bits of her empire. No, no, your DEBTS will not be paid by England, nor by the French Jews headed by Jewsieur de Gaulle. And your debts: oh yes, you have some. One hundred billyum dollars unless some of your radio voices exaggerated. Well, has anyone offer'd to PAY those debts FOR you?

The pressure to increase hours of labor IN the U.S. of A., where prosperity was just'round the corner.

Am I to believe that you no longer have complete liberty to eat and to use automobiles? Some of the reports from the U.S.A. seem exaggerated; but in a country that swallowed Morgenthau's reports of the goings on of the American treasury: what CAN be exaggerated?

One point for this evening. One point that the most humble citizen's political responsibility can stretch to. You, I mean YOU, can doubt the intelligence, or shall we be forced to say, the sincerity, of any speaker who uses the word freedom in any context where ECONOMIC freedom is not implicit in the meaning of his whole sentence or discourse. Without freedom from DEBT, there is NO total freedom; there is no condition that can be called freedom save for the purposes of babboozling the auditor or the elector. That is the primary lesson for the Mr. Wallace, before he ruins his bright and beamish hopes for incumbency in the White House by being indellibly branded as the Jew's mouthpiece.

That might show political ineptitude by the year 1944. Say that Mr. Wallace were UNIVERSALLY recognized as the Jew's choice for American president and were opposed by a non-Jewish, candidate. Mr. Wallace being, I mean'sposin' he and his are dead set to carry him into the White House. Get him to inspect the source of his funny notions. Such as plowing under, and world freedom under Jewish police, or a Jew-owned police force. I know he thinks he thought it all out for himself, but get him to look back in his memory, and see WHO first explained it to him? Who first demonstrated over the dinner table or across the desk in his office, that you plow under for the good of the farmer, and to have better food and cheaper food for the workin' man, and that it is NECESSARY to force people to do what they would do anyhow if you didn't put a police force there over'em. And how Russia is the true guide to humanity.

Get Mr. Wallace to tell you WHICH Jewish patriot first explained these things to him.

#62 (February 21, 1943) U.K.(C5)
SERVITI

I regret the troubles of certain Englishmen, but I can't see that the blame falls outside the borders of England. I do NOT believe reports from America, because they are American reports. The American press lies. All Jewish news agencies lie. That is what they exist for. The American press, it would not be quite true to say, lies LIKE yours does. It lies differently. Yours lies from a sycophantic love of the LIE. The sycophantic love of keeping up hoary humbugs. The American, from the love of the tall tale. The technique of salesmanship implied in having a bigger headline, and a wilder imbecility.

Result: I do NOT know what is going on in the U.S., and I am not under any illusion that Roosevelt's press bureau will send out ANY reliable information. And until I can get personal reports I shall treat all U.S. reports with reserve. Just as I would treat with reserve a British official statement about anything under heaven.

BUT IF you are disliked in America, if there is a growing restiveness to the Judeocracy and a growing desire to let you down, pick your pockets, carve up the nick of your empire, you can blame yourselves!

YOU flooded the U.S. with foul propaganda, and the offsweepings of the *Economist*, the London School of Economics and hybrids of the Anglo ghetto. Instead of lining up your Sassoon before a firing squad, or dealing with your criminals INSIDE your empire, you dumped'em onto the U.S.A. So that you deserve NO good from the American people.

It would have been better to send over a plague ship. A cargo of rats innoculated with tetanus bubonic microbes; typhus and leprosy would have been a better title to American gratitude. And as you have done unto others, Judas at the helm and Einzig in the chart room, why wouldn't the new Jerusalem, the new Jew Roosevelt oosalem do unto you?

I mean all in the usury, and usual process, the usual line of biszniscz, the Ellerman, Sieff, Norman method. All very regrettable from the cultural angle, but all very much in the financial process. Silk stockings and all. I am speaking against usurocracy. I am speaking against the spread territorially, and the protraction of the war because I think the protraction and distention, in themselves, constitute gains for the usurocracy. Whether you can LEARN anything from the flop of France I can not make out. Up to now you appear to have learnt NOTHING, absobloodylootly nothing. Yet the French debacle might still teach you ONE thing. Note that two such different authors as B. Adams writing in 1909 and W. Lewis publishing in 1936 both pay their respects to the power of French finance. Looking to Paris as the centre of banking power.

The word FRENCH in this connection will raise a smile in some quarters. But so was it. Paris before the Russian revolution was, let us say, a great center of usury. The French Army in 1938 aroused professions of admiration, *cras tibi*. The eccentricity of France's material position, that is to say the way in which France lay OFF the main trade routes: her off-centerness, her not being in the center, had worried French rulers since the time of Louis XIV. You beat France and Holland. You grabbed the sea routes, and you HAD mineral under your grassy soil. Your iron mines hit high, yielded their maximum in 1882 with 18 million tons of ore. By 1900, that was down to 14 million. Copper, 1868, 9,817 tons; 1899, 637 tons.

Lead, 73,420; 1899, 2,552. Tin, 1871, 10,900; dropped to 4,013 inside a year. And apparently a good deal of your coal was, at the turn of the century, already being bought by your own ships at your coaling stations abroad, so that it couldn't all count in trade balance. You know whether these trends have continued. By 1903 B. Adams thought that your END seemed only a question of time. I don't quote Brooks Adams as divine revelation, I quote him as a prospicient author whose perceptions are worth careful consideration. I also quote him as indicative of the most active American thought of his time, though he stood high above most of it. Let us say that the mercantilist outlook never had better exponent. It was a pragmatic age. It is highly interesting to measure human knowledge today against what his was at the turn of the century. To see where he left off. Where if ever, he erred. Mr. Adams was in a privileged position to estimate your position. I mean he had perspective far above the common. His father Charles Francis Adams had been ambassador at [The] Court of St. James during the American Civil War and wrestled with Russell; his brother, Henry had been secretary to their father during that period, and possessed a far from common capacity for leaving a very clear record of events. B.A.'s grandfather had been American Ambassador to Russia during earlier and eventful years, and Charles Francis had edited HIS grandfather's papers. B.A. at turn of century was nevertheless a bit elated by the contemporary elation of the U.S., the period of great combines, of the new efficiency of combined (or trust) organization. He felt that America, by which word all U.S.'ers meant the U.S. of North America was expandin', and that the U.S. of A. was headed for imperial destinies. He saw it with mercantilist eye, shall we say, as material tendency.

He noted that in 1870 a chief source of British prosperity had been agriculture, but that already a Bagehot had been writing about how British money circulated round via Lombard Street, saving British landed gentry, almost as that used in discounting bills from British industrial areas. That Bagehot's words were hardly in print, before a shift of the world equilibrium had set in.

Mr. Adams noted the apparently meager accumulation of POPULAR SAVINGS in England and that during the Boer war you seemed to be relying on foreign bankers. I don't want to insist unduly. But let us take a date five years later than the publication of Mr. Brooks Adams' *The New Empire*, say he meant the American empire. The great American reorganization WAS complete in 1897; a decade later almost any average American arriving in London would have been full up with ideas of PROGRESS. He would, if he had met an intelligent British Tory (the two words COULD at that time be joined in at least a few cases without being ridiculous) he, the imaginary, *homme moyen sensuel*, average American, young or middle aged, would have encountered something absolutely new TO him, something unknown, and I think undreamt in America. Namely the conSERVATIVE view, the utterly surprisin' idea that things weren't gettin' better, and that you, meaning England of course, but being an Englishman, the English Tory would have applied it to the universe, on which the British eye never rests. Well that people, mankind, etc. better go slow, better not agitate, better let things stay in status quo. I believe that any and every American who heard this view for the first time was "struck all of a heap." It was unbelievable heresy.

What, not progress, not everything moving upward (not to say onwards) toward bigger and brighter bonanzas? Mr. Adams in 1907, or 1908, or 1900 would have been one of the few Americans capable of locatin' the Tory outlook, *Anschauung*, disposition, in relation to something concrete, to something real in the then status of England. I have said before that his perceptions pretty well covered the world as it remained during his life time. In 1903 he thought that England, France, Germany, Belgium, Austria, the core of Europe were "apparently doomed not only to buy their raw materials abroad but to pay the cost of transport." That view is interesting today. It may shed a bit of light on lease and lend sport. He cast his eye fairly wide over the world. He found Siberia "a narrow belt of arable land bounded by ice on the north, and by mountains and deserts on the south." Seemed to him a poor bet as against the American continent, plus [the] fact the Rhoosians were still a bit unhandy with new fangled machinery.

Those are a few items, say [a] few high lights of the world setup as seen by an American expansionist in 1903. And I'spose the pale blue Tory eye that greeted me in Kensington five years later was lookin' backward. Backward toward Her own (that is' England's own) agriculture. Down till 1845 it nearly sufficed for her wants. ENGLAND. Ole Viktoria's England. Advantage over the olde Roman empire.

Instead of bein' drained of her bullion England sold cotton to India, instead of havin' to buy grain from Sicily and from Egypt, and so on.... No such favorable conditions had perhaps ever existed. An equilibrium so stable, had not some fellow gone and invented the steam locomotive. "Given effective land transportation," wrote Mr. Adams, "the North American continent seems devised by nature to be the converging point of the cheapest routes between Asia and Europe."

Possibly not quite the present day view. But NO view of tomorrow's trade routes is a going to put England plumb in their middle. Brother: whaaar do you land?

Ezra Pound askin'.

#63 (February 23, 1943) U.S.(C10) COMPLEXITY

You have to have more than ONE idea in your head to understand anything. You have to have possibly one idea and a mass of concrete data either conducin' to your general idea, or opposin' it.

And I try occasionally to get you to think of one, the other or both. It may be confusin'. Get you to think of an economic system, or a MERCANTILE system, or a monetary system. That is, of an organization of facts. Brooks Adams wrote a good deal about a mercantile system. Called it an economic system sometimes. Anyhow, am I clear if I say he wrote about TRADE routes? Raw materials pass over a trade route TO a point where they are wanted. Sometimes to a place where they pass into manufacture, then to a place where the finished stuff is wanted for consumption. The seats of manufacturin' shift.

Obviously convenient if they are or can be shifted to the sources of the raw materials, not always handy, but whether the stuff moves raw or in finished products, the merchandise tends to seek, as they say, the most expeditious trade route.

On one turnpike four horses could draw three thousand pounds 18 miles a day. On the Erie canal four horses could draw 200 thousand pounds 24 miles in one day. Hence the prosperity of Manhattan. That is a simple and homely case out of Woodward, "A New American History." Brooks Adams took a wider sweep. Sargon, Alexander, the silver of Quedi, the Foires de Champagne, Flemish cities, working out a general law for the vortex of trade and dominion. Might call it the material base for an economic system.

Only it isn't. It is the ADMINISTRATIVE BASE, the material base is the raw stuff and the labor.

Brooks Adams was the mercantilist philosopher, or theorist, or better say ANALYST, analyzer of mercantilist materialist process. Possibly the most distinguished mind that ever tackled the subject. He saw a great chance for the U.S.A. IF the U.S.A. kept awake and observed the general laws of mercantile progress. Natural flow of goods by the easiest routes (easiest routes ought to be cheapest and ARE the cheapest save when the usurer or blackmailer intervenes).

BUT Brooks Adams observed that after Waterloo the mercantilist had got the push and that usury reigned; blackmailing the terrestrial universe.

I want to separate in your minds the mercantilist administrative basis of an economic order, and the accountancy, the tricks played with bits of paper: bank ledgers, engraved certificates. You can't understand the dirty deal that has been put over you till you can keep those two things clear in your minds.

And you have got the gold damndest ASS of a government in Washington that ever the American people was called on to suffer from. Eastern idea about money, said Bankhead of that saddistic slob in the White House. Down on his knees every morning adoring the usury system, saying his prayers to the usury system, maintaining six sorts of racket for bleedin' the American people. That had been going on for some time. Mess of bleedin' by gold. Mess of bleeding the American people by silver, and then to war. The major ineptitude, the cutting of trade with the Orient, the cutting of trade to the European continent, the blackmailing of South America, and the dry pie crust left of French Africa.

Well, the French were NOT the world's star, the cynosure, best admired model when it come to colonial empire. You are not taking on a perfectly arranged productive system, such as Italy was setting up in HER colonies, and in Abyssinia. You were being rotted by a paleozoic usury system. I'spose there are still cavemen and relics of the ice age in the Republican Party who don't yet know what was wrong with that system. It's a pity'cause the Republican Party could have built up an opposition to the infamy of the Democrats.

And of course one of the first steps toward prosperity or toward sanity would have been to bring the U.S., if not up to date, at least to shorten the time lag so as the people could have got to where Jefferson had arrived in 1816, or Gallatin in 1813 as camouflage perhaps to his bonds, which the New England Yanks were not buying'cause the privateer racket paid better, and they did not trust Mr. Gallatin's government.

I may have been late myself, but not quite as tardy as most of you. Twenty years ago I had got onto the money racket. Mebbe I have learned something since then, movin' round on the continent.

Your economics professors are driftin' behind. Lot'em were behind, oh, SOMEWHAT, when I was last in America, but it ain't enough for'em to just get to where I was in '39. EUROPE has been a movin'.

When I shifted out of London and Paris, I found a prejudice, what seemed prejudice, against what was called "money magic." European economist saying, "no money magic," meaning hocus pocus accountancy.

Europe was thinking in terms of the material basis, NOT mercantilist, but productionist, with distributionist as the corollary. And they go further than the money reformer, perhaps because they started at the rock bottom, RAW materials, WORK. After that come the trade routes, and on top of it all the accountancy. Now being discussed by German and Italian economists. Not only Funk and Riccardi, but Dr. Hans Fischboeck. And what that Italian phrase about money magic meant was simply that you can't do it with money alone, you can't do it merely by changing accountancy IF the material base isn't there. And that, as mankind apparently can NOT grasp accountancy very quickly, and has, historically been flimflammed more easily by usurers' palavar and propaganda than by any other one swindle. It was politic, it was horse-sense to insist on the productive basis.

BUT your government violated EVERYTHING. In fact, there is apparently NO department, administrative, mercantile, monetary, where the maximum of stupidity has not been attained, coupled with errors which it is difficult from this distance to attribute to anything save the maximum of rascality. I may be in error, the actions of the Roosevelt-Frankfurter government may be due to sheer imbecility and not to ingrained rascality. Or the two may be twin born and inseparable in that milieu. Go to it: diagnose'em.

Don't shoot'em; analyze their tropisms, their behavior, and tell us whether their policy is due to badheartedness or caries of the cerebellum.

NOT only did the present American regime NOT set up a monetary system which would distribute American abundance so that each American family could have enough, if not a just share, BUT they proceeded to destroy the mercantile base of a vast hunk of that prosperity.

The land was erodin'. Some sane steps were taken toward afforestation (at least so I heard); that was also before Morgenthau got into the White House. And something was done about power plants, bases of public convenience. BUT the trade with the outer world was BUSTED by the gold draddtest series of imbecile actions that are to be chronicled in ANY era of American chicken headedness, bar none.

The cutting off of the trade with the Orient; the severance of trade relations with the continent of Europe; the endeavor simultaneously to carry on war in the most diverse and widely separated areas on the planet: Iceland, the Solomon Levy Islands, Calcutta, the Sea of Azov. Well, you are out of the Sea of Azov and you are not garrisoning the hinterland of Czechoslovakia, and you are not putting up much of a show in Tibet at this moment. But Napoleon and Alex the Great would be hard put to it to determine the unity of your strategy in the lands of your alleged allies. I am not an expert in military affairs, but even the B.B.C. wishful thinkers haven't yet made out a case for the enlightenment or divine guidance of the Anglo-Jewish command. And the word COLLABORATION, world collaboration, as an alternative to tyranny by the incompetent has not yet found its place in Mr. Wallace's vocabulary. In fact, I don't think he is very clear in his own mind, on the subject, and of course if Baruch or some other American patriot hasn't explained it to Mr. Wallace, I don't suppose Franklin has troubled to go into the matter. I am not advocatin' return to the horse and buggy days of American economy, but even what they knew seems to have perished without your having joined with the present.

#64 (March 7, 1943) U.K.(C13)
TOWARD VERACITY

My talk this evening is not controversial but narrativie, in fact recounted from personal experience. I note that when I first began to listen to radio— that is, after two friends determined to break down my antipathy to radio had planted, that is, given me a small sized medium wave apparatus, and then fled the village—I began and listened sometimes to London. When I began to speak over the air, I definitely tried to listen to London but with the passage of time I listen to London less. I listen to Berlin more. This is the fruit or result of experience. It has not been done by directing or forcing my will, it has resulted from inclination; and to explain that inclination I have found nothing better than a passage from the letters of J.B. Yeats, old man who used to be rather better known as Yeats' father, a painter, who used to talk with his models, that in fact was his method of studying anthropology. His models were not exceptional people; and his conclusion about talking with them was that he listened with inter'st not to remarkable sayings, and not to displays of unusual brilliance, but that the interesting talkers were those who were simply telling the truth.

And now in the year 1943 I find it almost impossible to listen to London. I stuck along a while with your social comedy, the unconscious humor of your *Hirntrust, sogenannt*, the tortuous meanderings of Mr. Laski, etc. But now I just wearily turn the button.

The monotony of your evasions breeds infinite boredom. Berlin by contrast is placid, as against your gallic hysteria. Patient but firm German voices go on explaining *urbe et orbe* just what the war is about, just why it started. They go on EDUcating their public, fact on fact, many of the facts can be found in your own best writers, that is approximately all the facts that existed before the war started can be found in your own best writers. The injustice of the Versailles Treaty, the history of Danzig, German since, I think it is 1300, no 1200, Capital of the Duchy of Pommern.

The unqualifiable swinishness of the yittisch position at the League of Nations, against Italy. The absence of malice on the part of Europe toward the British empire; e.g., C. Del Croix marvelling at English opposition "but we don't want to do any harm to their empire."

The undeniable horror of your own slums, in contrast to slum clearance under fascism and national socialism. All that, plus details of *bonifica*, of improvements, just price, and the homestead. Exposition, calm and patient, of ideas that every decent Englishman accepts, and that are, I repeat, to be found in the minority books printed in England, by two dozen authors, by two score authors of books, and two hundred writers of articles. BUT which are opposed to the lies which you all know to be lies; the frauds which you—most of you—know to be frauds that are upheld by your Jews, your monopolists, and your internal national enemies. And against which the best men in England had been protesting for 20 years. So much for the positive facts, and secondly your repressions, or suppressions, and the omission of vital topics, such as international jewry.

You preferred Jews to news. And you've got'em. You were extremely obtuse in dying for Jewish interests. You have poisoned America, that was perhaps imprudent. You perhaps got in, or mobilized the wrong lot of cannon fodder, after centuries of success in stirring up or exploiting backward nations, hurling savages against the more civilized nations, you have perhaps mobilized the wrong set of roughnecks.

A minor point has been made recently, namely, that you have discovered that the U.S.A. is not wholly pro-English. You have discovered that the invading American troops in Ulster stem from a number of continental stocks, and are NOT all sighing romantically for the British homes of the ancestors. That much I have told you. In fact I did tell my rare and select readers several plain truths about Anglo-Yank relations.

And it is now being slowly discovered in England and her dominions that the Yanks are more interested in their own interests than in yours. Your sentimental hold on the U.S. was confined to a Tory sect, and to sentimentalists. BUT among the English stock itself you had and have always had your most strenuous opponents, those who had the American tradition, something stronger than Jew propaganda.

Ah, but, you say, look at Wallace, look at this solidarity of the kindred races. And there you are mistaken. You exported Anglo-Israel. A body of doctrine, or superstition NOT taken seriously in your governing classes; but which can be found in England among housekeepers, nursemaids, people with weak minds, but some leisure, or rather hours of enforced solitude, have to stay IN, for hours when nothing very exciting offers [itself]. And they, even in England mug up these fantasies about the Stone of Scone, and the prophet Jeremiah. But what you fail to note is that it is the ISRAEL end, not the Anglo end of the curious compound that has hooked the American Vice-President and his similars.

When Cromwell betrayed the British race, unintentionally perhaps, but at any rate, when he "had to speak to these men," the religious sectaries "in their own language," as he said by way of his excuse to his cousin Waller when he brought back the Jews, and when Bible reading became prevalent on both sides of the Atlantic, the way was prepared for curious fanaticisms, witch burnings, etc. And traces of religious mania, or vagrant fantasy are still found. Wallace's hallucinations come from Bible reading, not from being pro-English. And of course the U.S. is being had. The sanity of the 18th century is gettin' snowed under.

And it is NOT the Jew that America loves.

It is merely the dialect of that curious King James translation that has perturbed the mind of the simple hearted Americans. In fact has wormed into the American popular mind for some time, though the effect has considerably waned in the more sophisticated American circles. Post-Christianity has set in, as one of your better writers has dubbed it. Of course the minute a man says he accepts the decalog and the crucifix simultaneously, he has got into a tangle. As was shown in Engand where the crucifix went by the board, about the time Cromwell was committin' mass [muder?] in Ireland. Old Crumwell feedin' on powder an' ball as he appears in that touchin' ballad, "Blarney Castle; me darlint."

You have been singularly unconscious of that undermining and of subsequent underminings. One of your writers who died a few years ago made gallant efforts to awaken you. Her novels were not widely read. She wrote one called "The Death of Felicity Taverner" that would pay you to read, as sociological study. Dear Mary's work rather distressed one at times things came out with such a raw edge on'em, and the style was sometimes so jammed and elaborate. She presented a couple of South Afrikanders in another book, more raw than the general reader was used to. In Felicity Taverner she has gone under the surface. If your people were painted by Holbein (the Lady Butts) and if your Great Grandfather was a patron of Blake, you might conceivably want to preserve something that Lord Beaverbrook hadn't heard of, that the Daily Express wasn't all out to uphold. That is the crux of the *Felicity Taverner* novel. In England an heritage going back at least to the days of Holbein but NOT limited to that period, and inimical to that tradition, to the fine elegance of the older houses, to clarity of English air on the western seacoast. There is (in the novel and in reality), as I think you may wake [up] too late to perceive, there is another force working. Something not very open, something that you decline to take very seriously.

For 25 years to my knowledge there has been a difference of view, I mean among the serious minority, of the intelligentsia, as to how far the attack is conscious, how far it is part of a plan, premeditated. How far the evil is brought in by carriers. Unconscious agents, that bring an *Anschauung*, an attitude toward life, poisonous as the germs of bubonic plague, carried by animals who don't know they have got it.

Maiski of course KNOWS he has it. Litvinov has made no bones about having it. But it is not merely political, it is molecular or atomic. It destroys all scale and all sense of proportionate values. It calls to the basic laziness of the mind, the basic softness of human organism. It profanes. It soils, it is greasy and acid.

It revolts all men who have any desire toward cleanliness. But it entangles the clean, it entangles them because of their inconsequentiality, their inability to see the connection between one thing and another.

Facilis descensus.

The young are unheeding. Nothing is more tiresome than the moralist. Nothing more difficult for a profane author than to draw the line somewhere, or to persuade his reader that certain sloppiness of outlook can possibly have any consequence.

I make a tardy acknowledgement to Mary Butts, author of the *Death of Felicity Taverner*. I did not advertise the book during her lifetime. It may have arrived while I was busy, and I was not a reviewer; not specifically. I was concerned with very rare books that conformed to a certain canon.

Your own press and your own native critics might have done more for it. They might start doing so now. Add it to the list of books and add its authoress to the list of writers who did something for England.

Tried to maintain something English, in the face of something unclean. Who knew that there had been values, in England, values based on tradition. Values that no nation can root out from itself, or allow to be lost, without losing its place among nations.

There again, under the slightly too jeweled style, the interest of the narrator, rises from the narrator's veracity.

#65 (March 9, 1943) U.S.(C17)
POTS TO FRACTURE

By the time 1836 had come round the debt was liquidated. The government did not owe a cent and there was a surplus of 36 million dollars.

This refers to the U.S. National Treasury. But for havin' a Jew at the head of the U.S. Treasury in the present unfortunate century and a man of unsound mind, to say nothing of his personal character, at the head and stomach of the American government, the American people might today see their treasury in a similar happy condition. The adjectival term crackpot is sometimes applied to economics by persons of imperfect education, and ill furnished with historic background.

A measure for distributin' the national surplus of 37 million among the states was introduced by Henry Clay, for once being in agreement with Andy Jackson. And 28 million were so distributed, before the long and dirty hand of international finance working from some bank failures in London, brought on a panic, such as the usurers have always brought on whenever a government ANYwhere shows signs of NOT allowing itself and a nation to be bled by people like Roosevelt, Morgenthau and his British accomplices.

But the New Yorker is often provincial; I mean when provincial a Parisian is the most limited of Frenchmen and the New Yorker the worst hecker in Uncke Sam's once happy dominions. There is NO sense; that is, there is no patriotism, no devotion to the welfare of the whole people, in fact there is nothing but downright devilment, or bone ignorance, in allowing a national debt to increase in normal times, or to be made a permanent yoke on the necks of the people.

Naturally if a nation is governed by swine whose sole, or main aim is to enslave the people, [it] will occur. In fact that is WHY such people go [into politics or are put] into office by kikes and the lenders [of money]. Nothing but unsoundness of the national mind as a whole could have led the American people to elect the present government. Nothing but bone ignorance and mental squalor would keep'em dazzled by international complications, and steadily more and more unmindful of the havoc being wrought on'em in the home, by the Kikefurter, Morgenberg, Cohen, and company administration.

And nothing but mud in the head would permit American college presidents to hold down their jobs with one buttock and prevent the study of American history with the other. Yes, they occupy chairs, that is the official designation of a professor's position, he HOLDS a chair. The French used to have chairs made in a pattern no longer needed in the houses equipped with modern convenience (ref. M. le Docteur Cabannes, for details of French domestic life in the earlier centuries). Quote: A universal economic crisis whereby we shall throw upon the streets the whole mobs of workers simultaneously in all countries of Europe. These mobs will rush delightedly to shed the blood of those whom, in the simplicity of their ignorance, they have envied from their cradles, and whose property they will then be able to loot. OURS they will not touch.

Do you recognize the source of the quotation? If not, why not?'We gave," I am quoting again, quote:

"We gave the name great to the French Revolution, the secrets of its preparation are well known to us, for it was wholly the work of our hands." Unquote. I am quoting from a brochure published some years ago; more American college students ought to read it.

Quote: When we have accomplished our coup d'etat we shall say then to the various people: Everything has gone terribly badly, all have been worn out with sufferings. We are destroying the causes of your torment, nationalities, frontiers, differences of coinage.

Considering that this program was printed, in its English version, some 20 years ago, and that Small Maynard brought out an American edition (and quite naturally went broke after doing so) but considering the date of the publication, MORE of you nice clean-limbed young college boys OUGHT by now, 20 years later, to take an interest in the nature of the program, so slickly carried out by Mr. Roosevelt, YOUR president, with the so able collaboration of the kikery whereby he is almost completely peninsula'd.

I continue quoting: "On the one hand to reduce the number of magazines, which are the worst form of printed poison, and on the other hand, in order that this measure may force writers into such lengthy [productions] that they will be little read, especially as they will be costly." Yes, someone had thought it out with some detail.

Taxation will be covered by a progressive tax on property. When the comedy is played out, there emerges the fact that a debit and an exceedingly burdensome debit has been created. For the payment of the interest it becomes necessary to have recourse to new loans which do not swallow up but only add to the capital debt.

Unquote and so on. But doesn't it strike you, doesn't it strike one per cent of the possible auditors under 20 or over 20, under 30 or over 30 that it would be useful for more of you to take a look at the full text of the quite interesting little brochure from which I am quoting and quote: "all these peoples were stage managed by us, according to program." Well, now can it happen to you? Does this curious and fantastic brochure apply only to PAST and European actions? Quote again: In the third rank we shall set up what will in appearances be an opposition to us, and which in at least one of its organs will appear to be our very antipodes. Our REAL opponents at heart will accept this opposition as their own, and will show us their cards.

How VERY fantastic. "The Great Power, the press which with a few exceptions that may be disregarded is already in our hand." Unquote, that was printed in 1922. Do you think things are now less so, or more so?

All of this being printed, in 1922, less than a century after General Jackson had extinguished the American national debt. Well, now wouldn't it be more intelligent of the American people, or at least the American intellengentsia, to realize what was implied by Jackson and Van Buren in extinguishing the national debt as well as showin' a more active interest in political and/or economic programs, published during our present life times?

I am not saying the U.S. could or should return to the rusticity of the Jacksonian era. I am saying, and repeatin' that it is a shameful, and ALSO dangerous thing to be bone ignorant, ham ignorant, ignorant to the point of squalor of so much that was known to Jackson, and Taylor; to be complete acephalous asses on so many matter wherein our great grand fathers showed a most laudible horsesense. You can not get all American history from one volume. Woodward's *A New American History* is an admirable introduction. It is better reading after you have digested Brooks Adams taking the grand, but inhuman sweep, seeing ideas, and material forces. Woodward realizin' as Voltaire had realized that ideas and forces move and are moved by human beings, each with his own quirks, kinks and limitations.

I think Woodward underestimates the Adamses and Van Buren. I also think he would be a good check on anyone who, like myself, tends preponderantly to see a man's aim, his idea, and what might have been.

Seeing the reasons why certain ideas have not fully gone into action, or have not attained their completion as custom, as law, as event.

There are several points omitted by Woodward. And that fact should be borne in mind by the student.

But the professors who high hat Woodward, because he does not write on stilts and carry a pair of lemon colored gloves peeking out of his pocket, are in error. There is probably more American history in Woodward's 875 pages than in any one volume that covers a similar stretch of American history. Needing checkup, needing additions, needing reference to the actual papers of four generations of Adamses and those of Van Buren.

#66 (March 14, 1943) U.K.(C15)
ANGLOPHILIA

I have before now told you things too soon. I mean I told'em to you (the small select elect who have listened), I told you that Wilson had NOT the power to sign treaties for the American people. And so on? I told you that a line of poetry could be poetry, could be poetry even if it did not contain precisely ten syllables arranged in the order of ti tumti tum ti tum. And so ON.

And I told you, I think I told you over this radio that in the U.S. of America there is a basis of anglophobia, quite deep rooted, and having ascertainable causes. I hear that this simple perception is gainin' ground in your country.

Mr. Kipling wrote *Habitation Enforced*, Mr. H. James replied to it in a rather more realistic study. In fact he took up Kip's romantic sentimental theme, and examined it.

Kip presenting the dear American who came over and fitted in perfectly, and Henry James the American sentimentalist who came over expecting and very much annoyed the British remnant of the family, who didn't understand what the fellow was up to. Well now, suppose you quietly try to analyze the basis for the supposed anglophilia. Apart from Whore Belisha's ad hoc propaganda, Anglo-Israel and other spurious articles.

Yes, there were, in America, Tory families and rebel families. I mean in 1776. At [the] start, say 1750 or 60, almost nobody wanted to separate. But the bullheaded swinishness, greed, dishonesty, meanness of King George's government's ruling pigs of the period finally forced half the Torys into the opposition.

Remaining Tory families think very highly of themselves, but are not, and for 150 years have NOT been very highly thought of by others. The old revolution families think very, very highly of themselves, but no longer constitute a majority in America.

Alas the day, etc. they did NOT develop a lasting sense of responsibility. I know a few of'em had it once. At any rate, with them it is kifkif, 50/50 as to whether they take snob in their ancestry, and British origin, or are still fighting the Revolutionary War (as I am, at odd moments) for your own good, oh naturally. The Anglo Saxon race never fights a war except for the good of somebody or other. BUT the ruling class in America is no longer wholly of English origin. People from Thraxstead married the Rileys, for example. And that wasn't all of it. In and about 1848 there was a beneficial German migration, not merely the *oirish* ever enamoured of the Crown of owld England, and later migrations. Slaves from Africa, chattel slaves, black ones, then more or less white ones, or swarthy ones, got over, dumped in for purpose of industrial slavery, and to work for the usury system.

As you have discovered, at least some B.B.C. boko discovered in Ulster, there are Americans who do not speak English, whose native stock is not English. I say do not speak English, I mean not even in its American dialect form. Even if they are choked up to the eyes with propaganda, they have not an interior basis for adorin' you and your empire. Many of the denizens of that empire do not adore you.

Why should they fight for your empire? You might get me on sentiment. The romantic period of my life was passed in London. Blood is thicker than corn juice. But I am not a majority specimen.

It would probably never occur to you that the attitude of my compatriots was hostile to me, during the 12 years I spent in London. It turned friendly in 1920 when I shifted over to Paris. What causes that? I am not trying to prove anything, I am just telling you. A truly representative American, the well known and very widely read writer, Mr. E. Hemingway considered me in 1922, the ONLY American who ever got out of England alive.

That was a perfectly sincere opinion, given in a decade when neither Hemingway nor I were being political. Mr. Hemingway is hardly ever political. I believe his father was English. The most violent Americans I have known, at least two of'em had English grandfathers, they were NOT anglophile.

The charm of London is feminine. I suppose your colonials know that. London is romantic. That is, the three or whatever million surplus females in England open up possibilities to the traveler. BUT to balance that the young Englishman, in nine cases out of ten, strikes the young of ALL other nations as a fatuous sap head. The lack of the most intense stimulus to competition can but take effect in the course of the centuries. The exceptional man, the, as Mr. Hemingway would call him "the good guy," does NOT constitute the mass of the population. He goes out and gets shot in the first months of 1914. His mass weight in the democratic majority tends to diminish. You must take count of these things, these imponderabilia in estimating the force of the cohesion of nations.

Even to me, naturally prepared for Anglo American amity so long as it be not blatantly and palpably Jewish, and a mere wheeze of and for the usury system, even I can not pardon you for having poisoned America. Sending your WORST type of emigrant such as silk stockings Sassoon to that country, yes, Victor. The Emperor of Opium and the Orient, and your scum from the London School of Bankocracy. I try to tell you the story, your cramming of America with propagandists, culminating in Cuff Duper was NOT a motion conducing to amity. I have told you before the ONLY propaganda giving the Dies committee a headache in 1939 was YOUR propaganda. NOT German propaganda, not Russian red propaganda but YOUR propaganda. The American differs from the Englander, does not like to be humbugged. He likes to humbug someone else, but he has not your love of pageantry and your taste for maintaining a humbug.

I believe Bagehot said something rather good in that connection: "The mass of the English yield a deference rather to something else than to their rulers. They defer to what we may call the theatrical show of society." Walt Bagehot [on] the English Constitution. Cf. that with [the] American condemnation of Polk (Congressional motion) complimenting the officers in the Mexican war. If had, the American admits it, he don't try to embalm the swindle in Busbys, and Beefeater uniforms, and pretend it was holy. I am not attemptin' to be insultin', but as simple narrative; I believe the average American considers the Englishman to be both a snob and a sycophant.

And as Roosevelt loses his puffed up bought ascendency, YOU lose. 50 thousand Americans owe him death or wounds or dispersal, but the democracy trend is to pass the buck, shift the blame. You get blamed for it. YOU dragged us into the war. I know Roosevelt was hell set on gettin' in, but the public will not stop to think of that. Even supposing the general American really KNOWS it. What the public knows is your propaganda. I quote: "Too many foreigners in Washington, natives are run by them and know it."

Letter dated October 27, 1940 from the fine old American stock, south of Mason and Dixon line, roaring democrat, of the era that took party line seriously. "Japanese are our biggest headache." That from a senatorial family, six weeks before Pearl Harbor.

You might remember that during the last year of my broadcasts I was guided from inside America. I mean by personal and quite reliable notes sent me from most competent private observers, NOT in the pay of Jewry, NOT writing for Hollywood and Mr. Roosevelt's owners. It was my intention and endeavor to speak in KEY with the opinion of enlightened Americans.

At no time have I intended to use the radio to present personal idiosyncrasies, but to speak a true record. The U.S.A. will be no use to itself or to anyone else until it gets rid of the kikes AND Mr. Roosevelt. I don't mean the small kikes. I mean the LARGE kikes. Often YOUR castoffs and exports.

When I say the Americans don't like being humbugged, I give you instances; to an American a Times correspondent means a drummer for Vickers, drummer, a traveling salesman, a bagman. He, the American, don't try to wrap that up. He LIKES to debunk, to drag the sham into the open, and to mock at himself for having been a sucker the day before yesterday or half hour ago in having been humbugged. That is at variance with the British theatrical temperament, which WANTS to maintain the sham.

I state these things to illustrate one source of misunderstanding: 50 or more years ago the Americans invented the word Anglo-maniac. That meant a "dude" or a man who wore a high collar. It certainly meant the Astors and people who exported American money to England (capital, or pocket money), who married into English society. That was called "buying a duke." You probably don't consider me an Anglo-maniac.

When I lived in England, I was an "expatriate"; when I went to Paris I was white washed, I was again considered American. All this is probably very superficial. Permit me an easy evening: permit me for once to trifle with these bits of swansdown floating on the social and political stream.

#67 (March 16, 1943) U.S.(C20) TO EXPLAIN

It probably seemed very eccentric that a man, any man should suspend playin' tennis and trying to understand the Confucian anthology, and after a long period of years return to America to protest against ANYTHING, or to offer suggestions to his fellow citizens about anything whatsoever.

After four years, I should however like to have a few minutes MORE conversation' with Mr. Sam Pryor, and with young Elihu, and a few other lights of the party; and see whether they are more disposed now to believe what I then told'em. I do NOT believe that the third election of Roosevelt was necessary. I take it the U.S. now knows that the election was an error. My contention then was that people wanted something different. Wilikie was NOT something different, he was the same, worse, and more so. And the people did not elect him.

Most sane Americans now wish Roosevelt and his kikes had never been born. But none of'em seem to have any clear idea how to eliminate the nasty consequences of the untoward event. Sage Republicans in 1939 may have felt that Roosevelt had thoroughly puked on the American floor, and that his Party ought to clean up the mess.

I did NOT agree with'em. The subsequent mess shows no signs of producin' its own vacuum cleaners. Well let bygones be bygones. I am NOT blaming the Republican chiefs for lack of omniscence.

Few people have it.

Some of'em thought Mr. Gallup's Jew-aided poll was an indication of popular feeling, but failed to look at a calendar. They are still faced by a clever opponent, void of scruple, and likely to be backed in 1944 by all the billions that international Jewry has diddled out of the American people, and out of the subject races. Hope long fed on the bottle may not grow teeth at all.

As nobody is likely to believe me, I suggest that they start thinking it out for themselves. I suggest that a DUD candidate for 1944 is just as undesirable as it was two years ago. I suggest that consummate incompetence in the Cabinet is undesirable. The Republicans HAD in 1940 the makin's of a strong executive. Providin', that is, that they followed the early American system of having a President and a cabinet. Several

Republicans in Washington could have functioned, and kept America out of war, piloted her thru the stormy period, and perhaps, though I doubt it, even have prevented the war bustin' out.

I reckon Jewry had Churchill by the short hairs so close that nothing would have saved him, or England, from him. Apart from war, the British Empire would have elegantly dissolved, or inelegantly dissolved. But whichever, the U.S. by staying OUT of the war could most certainly have absorbed the fragments: without being put [to] the extreme inconvenience which a great lot of the outer world now hears the U.S. is incurrin'.

Now Vandenberg, from my point of view, lives in the year 1858 or before then. But Vandenberg with a CABINET would have made a better President than either Roosevelt alias Cohen, or Wilikie, alias the rest of the synagogue. I would NOT have selected Senator Vandenberg because I do not think we have ANY economic views in common. All I am saying is that the Republicans HAD the makings of an administration, both strong and in many ways sane, though conservative, that is, set in their ways.

I dunno that they have yet learned ANYTHING. Some of the old horse and buggy ways HAVE been jolted, by three years of conflict. But Vandenberg mayn't have heard of it. Bridges may not have heard of it. They may not yet know that Mark Hanna is dead.

My view was and IS that the cabinet should be the school for the executive. That system worked under Jefferson, the only thing I have against Jackson is that he had a theoretical notion against it which merely led Van Buren to desist from the cabinet long enough to qualify for the succession. Useless formality. An executive OUGHT to have some sort of executive training. No place like the cabinet for providin' it.

Businessmen's government, NUTS. Mercantilist or usurious mind is NO good for any problem dealin' with the whole nation. Hence use of LEGAL minds in formin' governments. At least [they] have some sense of law, as something for the whole state, the whole of society.

Only man who ever raised any real objection to Gesell in argument with me puzzled me bit. He had arguments that comptrollers and cabinet ministers had not raised. He puzzled me. I had to think it out.

Answer was, he represented a sort of shareholders union. He was looking at the whole show from point of view of a section of the community, NOT as to how it would effect the whole nation, the whole society congeries.

Man spends his whole life thinking how he can welsh a profit out of the public, produce more, regardless, I mean regardless of anything. Even thinking how to produce a good article, well, that is better.

What happens to THEM. Get confiscated. BY the profiteer's, racketeers in the government in favor of Kaiser's coffins.

Mr. Williams gave me some space in Greenwich Time, not that he is to be implicated in my present opinions. But he might take up that idea about the CABINET on his own. I believe a man fit to be President ought to SEE his way to having a CABINET, and his party ought to see his way to having a cabinet, and WHAT kind of cabinet, before the people are asked to elect him. John Adams had a bad cabinet, duds left over from Washington's misfortune. I mean after about all the MEN had left Washington's cabinet he was left with the rinds and remnants; and John Adams from democratic feelin', [having] been badgered about his authoritative tendency etc., kept on these duds out of sentiment, and about wrecked his administration. Good cabinets have made great administrations. As far as I recall there has been NO great administration without SOME cabinet talent. Even Lincoln had Seward; personality sufficiently interesting to get shot simultaneously with his chief, and NOT by an actor either. That simultaneity is NOT sufficiently stressed in the history books. Do I ramble? One can't just isolate an idea.

If it is real, it is bound to have bits of fact and sidelights clingin' to it. Dewey, a nice young man. But would make a better president AFTER four years in the cabinet, than he ever would if put in from outside, in the fair flush of his second moustaches.

I am of course glad Lehman is OUT. I wish all his friends were in Australia, and he with'em. It would conduce to the good life in the American continent. But the movement toward eliminating Morgenthau's gangs from Albany has NOT gone far enough.

I know I said something rash a moment ago. I said the Republicans would have all kikeria, all the kikes profits OUT against'em in 1944. Well, that ain't the sole possibility. Because if the Jews felt that it wuz time to leave Mr. Roosevelt, I mean if he is so loathed by 1944 that there is no chance of electing him for the fourth, fifth, sixth and seventh terms, and if Hank Wallace has got too far out on the limb, why then of course all that kike money, profits of gold sales and of usury might come RIGHT over into the Republican Party, about two or more months before the election. Like perhaps some of it did last time; bringing that Trojan Horse (with apologies to the equine race) Mr. Willkie. Only next time they would bring something worse, with the intent to elect him, and rob the people.

Your correspondent should of course note, in fact your correspondent HAD noted that most of the gold acquired by the Morgenthau Treasury was purchased AFTER it reached the U.S. and that gold sent to that country may have been owned by the government or individuals in another country. Yes, that is so, and perfectly rational. STILL it would, or SHOULD interest the American people and even the Republican National Committee to know which filthy kikes in New York acted as agents for the Rothschilds, and other branches of the candle stick of Judea. And the author of a standard and most highly respected university textbook, writes me: "I cannot recall any account of the activities of foreign banking or bank agents in the U.S. aside from the correspondence connected with President Jackson's efforts to get a settlement from France during his administration. Indeed I do not know that there is a clear account of these activities and presumably the data would have to be dug up from the correspondence of these state and treasury departments."

Well damn it all, go start diggin'. You will find it as tough as Babylonian excavations. As crabbed as the clay tablets in Nineveh, but you may as well start excavation. Not of course that your work will be immediately welcomed by publishers and universities, but still somebody ought occassionally to do an honest day's work for the nation or years' work for the nation.

How the hell [do] you expect to have any economic or financial history, or in fact any history writin' except dilletante impressions until you do have a clear and detailed account of the activities of international kikery and its agents IN the U.S. I do not know. And neither do you, and you won't, till you have put your mind to it and GOT the data. Mr. Morgenthau isn't going to just HAND it to you on a plate.

#68 (March 19, 1943) U.S.(C21)
MORE NAMES

I treat information from the U.S. and England with reserve. It is quite obvious that the only way the B.B.C. or the Lehman and Judah radio in America could deceive anyone would be by telling the truth, that perhaps the American people have really less to eat, perhaps some men are in jail. If Roosevelt's critics are muzzled BY the police, and by the incarceration method, perhaps they have taken the wrong line. Obviously no one can advocate America's losing a war. BUT floodlight on Morgenthau, Katz, and Sommerleigh can have no detrimental effect on American military and subnaval operations. The knowledge of Katz and Sommerleigh, OR of the peculiar ramifications of the Morgenthau family can not diminish the output of Kaiser's coffins, or make bad ships worse, or unskilled sailors less skillful.

When I turn over my letter files of the past decade, I don't know where to start quotin'. I have quoted a notable speech in the House of Representatives. I shall probably requote it. "Involve her," that is the U.S., "in advance in the next European war." House of Representatives, February 3, 1933. That from north of the Mason and Dixon Line. From Carolina, in 1934, I quote the following: Henry Morgenthau is related by marriage to Herbert Lehman, Jewish Governor of the State of New York (the Lehman to whom President Roosevelt has referred to as "his right arm") and is related by marriage or otherwise to the Seligmans, of the international Jewish firm of J. and W. Seligman, who were publicly shown before the Senate committee of investigation to have offered a bribe to a foreign government, and to the Lewisohns, a firm of Jewish international bankers, and to the Warburgs, whose operations through Kuhn, Loeb and Co., the international acceptance bank, and the Bank of Manhattan and other foreign and domestic institutions under their control have drained BILLIONS of dollars out of the U.S. Treasury and the bank deposits belonging to U.S. citizens. Etc., etc. This clique of international bankers or certain members of this clique before the rise of Hitler, every year sent hundreds of millions of American dollars out of the country to Berlin from whence it passed into Soviet Russia.

And that incorrigible kike Isidore ben Isaac Solomon ben Henrich Morgenthau is STILL taking dollars out of your pocket and gold out of Russia to pile debt on debt, Pelion on Ossa; to turn the U.S. into one grand

Stakhano vite hell, that is into a concentration camp of forced labor. ALL according to kikifications.

And you being suckers. As since the record in Genesis. It is a very long story, dating from the forgeries of 500 B.C. parable against usury, faked into allegory against procreation. Medieval propaganda for suppression of procreation of the intelligentsia. Iconoclast struggles: Guelfs vs. Ghibbelines, decalogue against crucifix, all that story needs reexamination.

The Japs are unlikely to fall for that line of hebe propaganda. In fact, they are being sternly New England pioneers, that is of the large family era. The office boy of the Japan Times was printin' photos of villages, where, as he said, the inhabitants just don't do nothing else BUT.

And according to Amery there are 150 thousand political prisoners in England, Mr. Churchill's and Margot's England, probably for nothing more than attemptin' to raise the race issue, and to ask for the genealogy of a few hundred chewisch peers; and the printing of the interlocking Jew directorates who control the stooges in Parliament, and Mr. Vansittart.

I take it the Americans are still backward about coming forward to examine the racial origins of the alleged French refugees now in America. Eighty per cent of them chewisch or playfellows and bedfellows of sheenies, and sheeniessesses. I don't quite know what pattern you THINK this war is fitted into. It was certainly NOT planned by the Englishmen and Americans who fought in the last one. It was certainly not huggermuggered through by the YOUNG men of England or America. The youngest pink toed advertisement for Piccadilly and Burlington Arcade collars and ties is Anthony Eden, who was dead sure NOT to be called on to face bullets. Stuck into a nice cushy job.

The rest of the war makers were senile bed bugs and usury vermin. And it was NOT unexpected. Let American youth remember that it was NOT unexpected. And NOT for the conservation of England, not for the benefit of the sailors, the brave merchant sailors, any more than the kikes had been out for the past 100 years to maintain the agricultural population of England. In fact that bright halcyon (if that is the word), that bright prospect of American domination may have been hit by Henry Adams' theorem about acceleration. You may be awaitin' the great boom that has Horace Greeleyed. Go WEST young man, go west. Well maybe it has wested RIGHT across the Pacific ocean. Calculat' THAT on Henry Adams' theorem. Yes, this time I said HENRY, not B. Adams, Henry. I said look at Henry's equation about the acceleration of historic process and ask mama or Uncle Ted whether that may not have hit the trade vortex.

The two oriental races which are not yet bekiked are the Japanese and the Chinese. And possibly Wang's millions will never more accept a KIKE cheque.

Well, all that is conjecture. What it would be useful for you and George and the rest of you to ask one another is: just WHICH of you are free from Jew influence? Just which political and business groups are free from JEW influence, or, bujayzus, from JEW control? Who holds the mortgage? Who is a dominating director? Just which Jew has asked what Jew to nominate which assemblyman who is in debt to WHOM?

And which whom is in debted to Jewry, or dependent on credits which he can not get without the connivance of Jewry?

Just which college or university will distinguish itself by adding to its history courses a course in the study of chewisch history, and the Fuggers, and the effects of Jewsury and of usury on the history of Europe during the past thousand years? Or two thousand five hundred years, ever since the so touching experiment of Cyrus the Persian, who sent'em out, but not OUT enough. With of course reference to Cromwell, and the French revolution and the role played by kikes in the French Revolution. And where all that happens to us, where it concerns us, why it is not all old lace and retrospect, embalmed and perfumed with lavendar.

What I would like to do in these talks is to arouse curiosity, even ten cents' worth or two bucks' worth of those rare virtues: intellectual awareness and curiosity. Alice James, the Great Henry's sister, complained that we Americans would not show moral indignation, that is, at times when she would get all set for having an American show moral indignation the American would just fold up and not do it.

Of course, the James family warn't exactly English or exactly American. In fact some of'em come from Ulster, which explains a lot of the mystery that has hitherto enveloped their peculiar reactions, if you can [explain] Ulster Irish.

I take it I sometimes do display some sort of indignation. But I can't get up indignation over some things. I mean, ever since I started writin', people have called me in to give opinion as to what to do for their relatives, when they got a bit queer in the head. Just like Cheever in Paris. My old concierge saying: what, Monsieur, you spend all your time locking [up] lunatics? People think, because one writes poetry, that one knows about people's heads? So that I have on occasion conferred with pathologists. And when a man comes out and says: NO American boy shall be sent out to fight outside the country. Then a few months or a year later, you hear him holler: Millyums of American soldiers are in all parts of the globe, ain't it wunnerfuuuulll! Am I expected to display moral indignation! Two hundred corpses floatin' about in the sea off the harbor of Cadiz? Whaaaa, only 200, why in a year or so there'll be thousands and thaaaaousans of corpses floatin' all over the ocean. Ain't it wunnnnnerful!

Ain't it WOnderful, watchu waitin' for? Waitin' fer him to receive Maisky and Litvinov and other high diplomats with feathers in his hair? Whatch waitin' for?

#69 (March 21, 1943) U.K.(C16) POGROM

DON'T start a pogrom (*bis*). The problem is not insoluble. Don't start a pogrom; the problem, the Chewisch problem, is not insoluble. Don't start a pogrom; SELL'em Australia. Don't go out and die in the desert for the sake of high kikery. Don't die for Tel Aviv, and Goldsmid and Jerusalem: SELL'em Australia. Don't GIVE'em a national home. SELL'em a national home; if they'll buy it. Of course at cut-rates; long term credit. Firesale terms, and the rest of it, you'll never get the full price of what you sell'em, but it would be cheaper on the whole in the end to SELL'em Australia. They aren't likely to go out and conquer a national home. Of course if they want to, you can sell'em the guns and munitions. I don't think it can be done for cash down. I don't think they will rush out to form cohorts and battalions, but try it FIRST if you don't believe me. When it has failed, sell'em Australia. And give'em Cripps for High Commissar, and Eden to be their Prime Minister; and fatty Temple, clothed in an ephod to serve in the synagogue, or to be high priest of his new synthetic religion. Cooking in Westminster to support international usury to reverse the decrees of the church, and deify usury. With Muddleton Murray, and Norman Angell, and Montagu Norman and the Montagues that are not real Montagues, and Mocatta and Rothschild.

My, your country is overpopulated. I mean, especially after the war with the loss of your tonnage space and the loss of your markets, you will have to thin out your population. Sell'em Australia. And SELECT the seed for the new penal settlement.

England, merry England, Chesterton's England. A nest of singin' boids: the England of Dowland and Purcell. THAT England. How are you going to get back to that England? HOW are you going to win back that England unless you weed out the Sassoon, and the Rothschilds, and the Lawsons, the Levy Lawsons and the Burnhams, the Lawson Levys, and Leverton Harries: and all the sequelae, with Gilbert Murray to go with them to the antipodes? And soapy Si [?] and Sam Hoare and Vansittart and all the semi-Aryan pillars of kikery. HOW are you [going to] have merry England ever again?

There is nothing so very startling in my proposition, sell'em Australia. It would at least shift the problem. Your problem, distinctly, is England, merry England, without slums, without usury, without a Jewish religion, without shoestring building. It would solve at least part of your problem, or some of your problems. Churchill hands over Venezuela and your American bases. Well, those go to the Jews who have already gone to America. Sell Australia. You won't much want it. Sell it to the Jews who have not yet left England. And then let'em go out to develop the industry. It would solve some of your problems, it would help you to pay the compensation for worn out coal mines to the ex-owners: without bankrupting the people of England. I mean if they aren't already bankrupt.

As the Marchese C says: "In all matters having to do with the Jews, the Aryans name is MUGG." Sell'em Australia.

It has taken a long time to bring up the subject. Sell'em Australia. I know you are compensatin' the mine owners and settin' up a commission to investigate the conditions of mining. Somebody even got up in or near Parliament and suggested you should humanize the living conditions of the poorer British inhabitants.

HOLY progress. The news of Europe is a-percolatin' into your island. Isn't it wonderful? The compensation idea is NOT new. There was a kike down in San Salvador GAVE his bank to the government. For a life compensation. Sell'em Australia. Will the Countess of Oxford and Asquith lift up her wail in protest? Will she rush out to tell you of the benefits you have reaped from the Rothschilds?

What of it?

She was telling us a few weeks ago, over the air, warmed to the B.B.C. temperature, that she had known eleven P.M.'s, from Gladstone—"Say your prayers, Margot"—down to the present. It is a great pity she didn't tell us what the OTHER ten thought of the present one, the present P.[M.] That would have made snappy hearing. With a few quotes from William Watson.

However, as you can't bring the Duke of Wellington to the microphone, I suppose you have to do something. Now speaking of Jews, and the problem. The Jewish problem, which The Economist does NOT elucidate, because it belongs to the Jews, that is to Rothschild, and its editors serve their owners. The Economist has discovered officially that some Americans do not see eye to eye with the Anglo-Jews. Is it a pity? I think it is not a pity. The Jews have ruin'd every country they have got hold of. The Jews have worked out a system, very neat system, for the ruin of the rest of mankind, one nation after another. Now many Americans are ignorant of this fact, and The Economist does its periodical bit to maintain that ignorance; but YOU like the ignorance. I do not think the normal American likes his ignorance. That may produce a fundamental dichotomy.

The Economist and its affiliated papers; that is nine-tenths of your press wishes to uphold the present ignorance. That is very English, I mean that is what the American means by a newspaper policy being English. A more piercing eye might consider that it is, in a certain sense, anti-English. The Countess of Oxford was once an admirer of the Rothschilds, perhaps she still is. When last at the microphone, she said nothing about it. I don't know that the American people are very much interested in her views on finance and government; but they would be more likely to see eye to eye with some of the submerged factions in England if more people said something clearer on the subject of the Rothschild, and on the subject of loan capital, and international lending, and the Hebraic or semitic or kike elements in your economics and politics.

Such, for example as the patronymics of some of your peers; I mean the names that they started life with, or that their parents started in life with. AND the relation of your M.P.'s and governing class TO various financial establishments. Which sometimes have offices both in New York and in London, or chronologically speaking with regard to chronological sequence; whose business during the course of eh-hm, the last couple of centuries has spread from London westward, as the Sassoons' has in our time.

Now we Americans, when we hear of The Economist and Mr. Crowther, and Mr. Einzig, are apt to think of Einzig as a Jew, and of Mr. Crowther as a servant of Jewry, and The Economist as a Rothschild paper, NOT as a paper owned by a clean Englishman, or by an Englishman at all. Perhaps a more definite use of terminology would help Mr. Crowther, Einzig, and the other members of The Economist staff in establishing a clearer understanding between themselves and the American public. Of course, their understanding with Morgenthau, Ben Cohen, Frankfurter, Roosevelt, Mrs. Hull's Husband, Lady Halifax's husband, Mrs. Perkins, née Rabinovitch or something equally Oriental is or WAS perfectly clear. But several Americans would regard that rather as an agreement between a set of kikes in London, and a set of sheenies on the other side of the fish pond.

Of that understanding, i.e., the understanding between various sets of international yidds, doing business simultaneously from various busnisch addresses located in different world capitals, the no longer in ALL the world capitals, there has never been any doubt. That is, not for the past 20 years, or past 40 years, save in uninformed circles. It is the increasingly well lit nature of the understanding between the Jews who run Russia and the Jews now pullulating in positions of power in London and Washington, that helps the better type of American to understand both Mr. Churchill and Mr. Roosevelt, and the forces that have raised those highly undesirable specimens of inhumanity to the prominence they now enjoy, if enjoy is still the right word. I doubt they did enjoy it till quite recently. But we doubt if their personal pleasure is being increasingly shared by the governed. In any case the Jewish proposal to make Roosevelt world emperor and to locate the New Jerusalem on the Isthmus of Panama, with NO checks and controls imposed on it, by even the angry Saxons, is an idea which ought to inspire the Countess of Oxford, and Mr. Crowther. Perhaps the B.B.C. will explain it, with a footnote or two by Mr. Shaw.

#70 (March 25, 1943) U.S.(C22)
TO RECAPITULATE

This war did not begin in 1939. It is not a unique result of the infamous Versailles treaty. It is impossible to understand it without knowing at least a few precedent historic events, which mark the cycle of combat. No man can understand it without knowing at least a few facts and their chronological sequence.

The war is PART of the age old struggle between the usurer and the rest of mankind: between the usurer and peasant, the usurer and producer, and finally between the usurer and the merchant, between usurocracy and the mercantilist system.

There are almost no absolute novelties in economics. One can, in most cases, merely say that such or such phenomena date AT LEAST from such and such dates.

The true basis of credit was known in Siena at least by A.D. 1620. This knowledge went into the founding of the Monte dei Paschi, a bank which still endures, and was the only bank in Italy that did not fail at the time of Napoleon.

The true basis of credit consists in: the abundance of nature and the responsibility of the whole people.

In that case: the whole people of Siena.

The present war dates AT LEAST from the founding of the Bank of England at the end of the XVIIth century, 1694-8. Half a century later, the London usurocracy shut down on the issue of paper money by the Pennsylvania colony. A.D. 1750.

This is not usually given prominence in the U.S. school histories. The thirteen colonies rebelled, quite successfully, twenty six years later, A.D. 1776. The first Congress of the new American Union defrauded the revolutionary veterans by a very simple device, which appears in variant forms after most modern wars.

The soldiers pay certificates issued by the states, depreciated. After they had been brought up at twenty cents to the dollar by speculators, the national government "assumed" the payment at par. That is at face value of one dollar per dollar.

This constituted the scandal of "assumption." Claude G. Bowers gives a good account of it in his *Jefferson and Hamilton*. After writing at least three good books, two on Jefferson and. Hamilton, and one of the Reconstruction era, Johnson's administration after the American Civil War, Mr. Bowers was made ambassador to Spain. So far as I know his voice is not now heard in America.

It has been customary for well over a century, at least, that currencies become inflated in war time, the value of the monetary unit declines, as more and more human effort (WORK) goes into making munitions and instruments of destruction and less and less into things people want for their personal use.

Goods are destroyed rather than exchanged against other WANTED goods, during war time. The ratio of units of currency, money, to things people want to eat and to wear is altered, i.e., there are more dollars in circulation in relation to goods, or pounds or other monetary units. Debts mount up. When they have reached hitherto unprecendented size, the manipulators of currencies "return" to what they have called "sound money."

After the Napoleonic War, after the American Civil War, the world returned to gold, thus forcing Indian farmers to pay up twice as much grain to meet their taxes and the interest on their mortgages as they had done before the "return."

Considering the vital importance, or the deadly importance of this process or swindle it would at first sight seem curious that mankind has not spent more energy in diffusing the knowledge of it.

The late Arthur Kitson spent a good deal of his life trying to educate the British and American publics along these lines. It is a pity that the press of both these ineffable countries did not more potently aid Mr. Kitson. Mr. Kitson believed that process was due to deliberate design of the usurocrats, the financiers who govern and outrage the world by financial, or in plain terms, the usury system, and various methods of monopoly and the control of the currencies of the nations.

Mr. Kitson heaped up a good deal of evidence in support of his theory. No rebuttal of Kitson has been attempted, the enemies of mankind prefer darkness.

There is a considerable library of polemical writin' and a vast mass of official documents which support Mr. Kitson's views.

The historic process operative during the past three hundred years can not [be] ascribed to the particular wickedness of men born since 1880. A knowledge of the world that we were BORN INTO is requisite for the understanding of the events subsequent to our birth. A deliberate attempt has, I believe, been made to blot out the historic record. And that attempt I propose to combat. I have, in fact, been combatting it, for some time. As did my grandfather before me.

My talks on the radio will eventually have to be judged by their content. Neither the medium of diffusion nor the merits or defects of my exposition can be the final basis of judgment. The contents will have to serve as that basis. I have taken up one point after another, one bit of evidence after another, trying to explain the facts in the simplest possible terms, trying to catch and hold the attention of individual hearers.

Wars in old time were made to get slaves. The modern implement of imposing slavery is DEBT. Usury is an instrument for increasing debt, and for keeping the debtor in debt perpetually or at least for the longest possible period.

It is foetid hypocrisy to prattle of liberty unless that liberty includes the freedom to KEEP OUT OF [DEBT]. There are ample records available from the agitation for the "new tables," *tabulas novas*, new account books, in the time of Julius Caesar down to the present. The auditor or reader who wants to understand these things, can not excuse his ignorance on the grounds that there are no sources of enlightenment at his disposition.

#71 (March 26, 1943) U.S.(C23)
FINANCIAL DEFEAT: U.S.

Quite apart from military operation, from the results of military operations, from the possible results of any military operations that may occur, the American people appear to have suffered crashing defeat, at the hands of the financiers.

There is no understanding of history without some understanding of finance. And nine people, at least nine people out of ten are ready to tell you proudly that they understand nothing about finance, and that they do not understand economics. It has become the hallmark of the end of the bourgeois era to proclaim ignorance of economics.

Yet you can not allocate the responsibility for an event, for a crime, for an accident, until you know what has happened.

Supposing that people DID want to know what has happened during the past three decades, during the past ten decades, or twenty, it might be helpful to stop using such cloudy and mysterious terms as finance, the social problem, economics.

It might be clearer to say: production, exchange, mortgages and the lending of money. People would then know what one meant. Or would they? Would any three of them or any two of them understand the lending of money? Not, until the term money were correctly defined, and the definition made so clear that everyone could understand it.

I took a banker's opinion about money, the other day. He replied: money is the statement of the government's debt to the bearer. Meaning it says how much the government owes to the bearer. I should have preferred to say the "state" or the community owes to the bearer.

I am perfectly aware that I might as well be writing Greek or talking Chinese with a foreign accent, so far as making this statement clear to the hearer or reader is concerned. And the public can most certainly not be blamed for this, as you could read a hundred books, by no means despicable books, on economics, without finding any hint that such an idea about money is possible.

The only statement in even an approximately similar form that I can recall at this moment was made by a Congressman, back in 1878. He said that an amendment offered by him to a bill about silver coinage had been: "an attempt to keep some of the NON-INTEREST bearing national debt in circulation as currency."

I repeat in quoting these statements that I might as well be talking Chinese or Tibetan so far as the average reader or bearer [*hearer?*] is concerned. Money is a means of exchange, an implement by which exchanges are effected, it is a measure of exchange, it is called "a title to goods," a measured claim. It is both a title and a measure.

The use of measured quantities of metal should be considered as barter. Powdered gold was still being used in India when Kipling wrote "Kim." He describes the gold broker dipping a wet fly in the gold dust, and popping it into a box, the adherent dust being his commission on the exchange.

For thousands of years men have been used to using metal discs, stamped with an alleged value, and intended to be of uniform weight and fineness. By the year 649 A.D. the T'ang emperors had found something more convenient than lugging about bags of metal. Their metal was what has been metaphorically called earmarked, or held in deposit, and bits of paper marked with designs, and seals, remarkably beautiful designs, were put into circulation. Marco Polo found the Kublai Kahn using this system some centuries later. He thought it a clever wheeze. The idea is so practical that in— —Sir Basil Zaharoff wrote to the Times about it; or rather about extending it so that gold wouldn't have to be shipped from the vaults of one bank to those of another, across national frontiers.

The Times referred to Zaharoff as a philanthropist. He shared other great munitioneers' floral tastes.

He was, I believe, a grower, or at least a connoisseur of roses. Whatever you think money is, or whatever Zaharoff thought about gold, Arthur Kitson quite conclusively pointed out in his report to the Cunliffe Commission that something had happened to money not once but several times over. His report was printed under the title "The Banker's Conspiracy."

METATHEMENON TE TON KRUMENON, as I think Aristotle remarked. The Voluntary variation of the value or purchasing power, or the metalic content, or the amount of metal, referred to by a given piece of money has attracted the attention of a great and élite set of people: Demosthenes, Dante, Cleopatra have all found the subject interesting, quite interesting.

It is curious that no snobism has yet been openly erected by monetary economists, Bacon, Hume, Bishop Berkeley a most respectable set of men have all thought it worth their attention. John Adams, Lincoln, Jefferson, Gallatin, Justice Taney, naturally men in official position HAVE glanced at the problem, ever since Phillippe le Bel caused such distress to his subjects, both since then and before then.

Monetary crime is divisible into perhaps two major sections: the usury wangle, and the wangles in variation of value, both of which are sometimes forced by monopoly, by cornering the control of the currency. The sovereign power over the issue of money CAN of course be used for maintaining justice.

Kitson's study related to flagrant injustice. He found that men who had become indebted in cheap or depreciated currencies had been forced on more than one occasion to pay those debts in money worth twice or much more than the money wherein the debts had been contracted. In Kitson's opinion this was not by accident. He thought it was the fruit of design. He cited a good deal of conclusive evidence in support of his view.

Now supposing that Kitson's view was correct, would it not be interesting to pursue the subject further? Would it not be of interest to know whether the SAME banking firms had indulged in this little practice or wheeze, several times over? Let us say after the wars of Napoleon, after the great and terrible Civil War in America of the 1860's and after the "diktat" of Versailles?

#72 (March 30, 1943) U.S.(C24)
USUROCRACY

Brooks Adams observed that after Waterloo no power had withstood the power of the usurers.

We will try to maintain a distinction in our own minds between the production system, the system of exchange of actual goods, and the wangles or corruptions of accountancy or the money wangles that corrode both the system of production and the processes of exchange.

The page of the usury system which we are trying to analyze dates more or less from Paterson's perception that the "Bank" (of England) would have benefit of the interest on all the money that it creates out of nothing.

According to Lord Overstone, everything rolled on merrily as long as the Bank actually discounted all bills rising from legitimate transactions. Overstone is now considered an idealist among usurers. The Bank according to him was there to "satisfy the true needs of commerce."

But Sam Loyd thought up another one. He saw, as Brooks Adams puts it, the possibilities of the single standard. He understood that as business and exchanges increase, the value of the monetary unit IN AN INELASTIC money system, will increase.

That is to say, with the same amount of money and increasing goods, the goods get cheaper in relation to money, and money more valuable in relation to goods.

He saw that a class or gang possessed of sufficient means could wangle a rise almost at pleasure, and could doubtless run it to almost any length. Also maneuver a contraction of the fiduciary circulation. As for example had been done in 1935, debtors could be made to accept almost ANY conditions dictated by the creditors.

The wangling of foreign exchange, that is, foreign money exchanges, were used for this purpose.

There is no item in this present talk that I have not mentioned in preceding communications, but the historic importance of every one of these items is so tremendous, and the difficulty of getting them [in] their sequence, their cumulative significance into the public head is so difficult that I should be justified [in] repeating them ten times over. Kitson's *Bankers Conspiracy* was written to show that extortioner Loyd's little perception had become the base of a system. A regular practice among Rothschild's and the rest of the bleeders.

The world was to be enslaved according to plan. Slavery consists in having to do uninteresting work, at another's bidding. The modern means of getting a man to work are lack of money, his lack of money, and debt. Mr. Kitson quoted Mr. Lindbergh's quotation of the now famous Hazard circular of 1862: It will not do to allow the Greenback, as it is called, to circulate as money for any length of time, as we cannot control that. But we can control the bonds and through them the bank issues.

The "we" naturally refers to the financiers.

The great debt, capitalists will see to it, is made out of the war, must be used as a mean to control the volume of money. To accomplish this the bonds must be used as a banking basis.

They were. Lincoln said "and gave to the people of this republic (the U.S.A.) the greatest blessing they ever had, their own paper to pay their own debts." Lincoln was shot. The bankers triumphed. It was all very simple. Some 30 years later another letter was sent to the AM. nat. (as they are called), the American *national* bankers.

Dear Sir, etc. The interest of national bankers requires immediate financial legislation by Congress.

Silver, silver certificates, and Treasury notes, must be (note that imperative) must be retired and national-bank notes upon a gold basis made the only money. This requires the authorization of some five hundred million to one billion dollars of new bonds, as a basis of circulation. You will at once call in one half your loans. Be careful to make a money stringency felt among your patrons, especially among influential businessmen. Advocate an extra session of Congress for the repeal of the purchase clauses of the Sherman Law, and act with other banks of your city in securing a large petition to Congress for its unconditional repeal *as per accompanying form*.

I.e., sign on the dotted line. Quote continues:

Use personal influence with Congressmen and particularly let your wishes be known to your Senators.

The future life of national banks as fixed and safe investments, depends upon immediate action, as there is an increasing sentiment in favor of governmental legal tender notes and silver coinage.

One takes an example from Cleveland's time rather than from Van Buren's in the hope that some aged survivors of the 1890's may still dimly remember the actions referred to.

Mr. Churchill as Chancellor of the British Exchequer, the Cunliffe Committee, quite naturally paid no attention to Kitson's recommendations. And a few years, merrily, after the Indian farmers were paying up twice as much grain to meet their interest payments and taxes. Naturally the usurocrat press supported the Loyd system of altering the value of the monetary unit, right along from the day the newspapers were invented. That is perhaps the main reason for having newspapers, especially large newspapers in usurocratic regimes.

Newspapers govern the world, remarked the Conte de Vergennes to Mr. John Adams. The American Bankers Association circular of 1877 reads: "It is advisable to do all in your power to sustain such newspapers, especially in the agricultural and religious press as will oppose the issue of greenback paper money, and that you also withhold patronage and favors from all applicants who are NOT willing to oppose the Government issue of money." Unquote. The quite exquisite spirit of illegality and treason in these manifestations of the usurers SHOULD need no comment.

It takes five million dollars to start a daily paper of any size in the U.S.A. One should have ten million to do so with any chance of getting a paper going. It is hardly safe to attempt it without twenty million, and in that case you must be willing to "CONSIDER" the views of your advertisers.

Hence the totalitarian states, hence fascism, and nationalist socialist revolution.

The American citizen can, of course, appeal to his Constitution, which states that: "Congress shall have power to coin money, regulate the value thereof and of foreign coin."

Such appeal is perhaps quixotic.

#73 (April 4, 1943) U.K. (C30)
LYRIC TENORS

A few faint voices have been raised in England to request a new order; but the speakers have possessed an unrivaled talent for avoiding any honest discussion of the means whereby a new order would be possible.

The men who had done some WORK toward that end, are either in jail or excluded from the microphone, and so far as one knows, from the press.

The supreme betrayal of Western civilization is manifest in the alliance with Russia. The perfect and swinish readiness to have all Europe destroyed in order to maintain the domination of all of us, the British people included, by a gang of extremely unpleasant monopolists, many of whom have moved their chief offices right over to Wall St., that is, to the new ghetto. Debt is the prelude to slavery. And neither Baruch, Lehman, nor any of their British bootlickers and servants says a word about freedom from debt. Or the freedom to keep OUT of debt. It is nine years since Jeffrey Mark published *The Modern Idolatry*.

Interest payments due on Western capital have been made possible by the creation of slavery conditions in Western countries.

In the past the progressive accumulation of debt claims has brought about the ruin of civilizations as single units. Nearly all the creations of the nineteenth century capitalists such as, for instance, the power loom cotton industry of Lancashire, have been broken by usury.

Forty years ago it was the habit to make much of Shakespeare and the styge [stage]: by people who seem never to have thought about the text, the meaning of the words used by Henry Irving and other darlings of the theatre public.

The daughter and ducats theme is familiar to many who have not meditated [*on*] the six lines that Mark uses to introduce the third part of his volume:

I hate him for he is a Christian,
But more for that in low simplicity
He lends out money gratis and brings down
The rate of usance here in Venice.
If I can catch him once upon the hip,
I will feed fat the ancient grudge I bear him.

I strongly suspect these lines have been omitted in more than one Jewish performance of Shylock.

There is something too near to nature, something too pertinent: "Brings down the rate of usance."

That just won't do; and the Times, Telegraph, Yorkshire Post, and the Beaverbrook papers are all there to keep discussion off that so dangerous topic. And Reggy McKenna and the big Five are there to deplore OUTSIDE interference. Discussion of usury, that is, banking as understood by Mr. Churchill and Mr. Eden, and I imagine Lord Lee would deplore the use of the very word usury in polite conversation. And yet the big FIVE are making higher profit now than they were before the war started.

France brought in the black troops. Churchill's England is allied to Soviet Russia. And the Times on September 12, 1933 spoke thus of Rumania:

Rumania can not make the payments (that was debt payments) in foreign currency until markets have been assured abroad for her surplus products.

The Times was quoting M. Modgearu.

This has not been done up to the present and to make things worse, prices of the products which Rumania exported have fallen considerably. Rumania cannot leave its officials, widows and invalids to starve in order to pay debts abroad which have become burdensome.

Just why England today has learned nothing from Rumania's position a decade ago would be a mystery if one didn't know how little the usual Briton cares for looking at ANYTHING. Yes, ANYthing that could serve to enlighten him. Mr. Mark observed pertinently at that time that Sir Otto Niemeyer had left a trail of economy, increased taxation, and a lowered standard of living behind him in every country he had visited. Twenty-six central banks formed since the other war to facilitate the service on internal and external debt. Note the title Sir, and the implications, racial implications in the name Niemeyer.

You have NOT had to learn harakiri from the Samurai. The Japanese do it with a difference.

To maintain the loan capital swindle, Britain has been ready to wreck all of Europe. That is the ONLY explanation of the alliance with Russia. There is no honor in it. And it does NOT serve the people of Britain. By liquidating your empire to the kikes and semi-kikes in N. York you are NOT conferring a benefit on the American people. You are doing nothing that will or should earn you the gratitude or tolerance of the American people. Basset Jones, writing to the editor of Electrical Engineering in December 1932, wrote:

Taxes and obsolescence included the fixed charge on debt are 34 billion dollars a year, practically half the national income.

England's forty million inhabitants by acquiescing in the debt swindle merely aid the bleeders and cheaters to keep on going and sink the Americans under the same imposition.

As Mark points out, Basset Jones was writing not of a debtor nation, but of the greatest creditor nation in the world. That ought to put a rock through the sham term NATION when applied to any particular section of the usury system. A Warburg, Sassoon, Beit, Goldsmid, Schiff or other potentate of the bleedery can get to N. York by plane in a very few hours. First the gold, then the Jews, then one helluva war in the place where the Jews are not.

According to the fashionable system of accountancy, the wealth of the American nation shrank from 36 billion in 1928, to 160 billion in 1933, Now just what do you think causes that sort of flimflam? Does it sound crazy? Does it sound as if something or someone MONKEYED with the account books?

I am not for the moment engaged in selling you the Axis, OR the European system, or the late desires of the late Napoleon Bonaparte. I am trying, still patiently trying to excite a little curiosity among my possible hearers in Britain. In 1943 one of those voices that sound like an advertisement for Bird's custard was complaining that the Germans use metaphor. In June 1932 more than ten million gallons of port wine was poured to waste by the wine growers and distillers of the Duoro district in Portugal as, quote, "the only hope of preventing wide misery and privation among the workers."

Oh no, it wasn't only in pore little Portugal. In Lancashire, nearer home to you, a proposal was made to dismantle or immobilize ten million spindles and 100,000 looms as quote "a means of restoring prosperity to the British textile industry."

When are you going to look into this? These statements are absolutely free from all trace of metaphor.

#74 (April 6, 1943) U.S.(C27)
FETISH

I am opposed! I believe that no American should kill or be killed in order to maintain the fetish value of metal, of ANY metal.

The pattern of the crime is known. The patterns of the various component parts of the major crime are known. They have been witnessed time after time.

A weak and cowardly nation invokes the aid of savages to crush a rising more honest power. England, inciting red Indians against ENGLISH colonists in America; France, in the grip of her usurers bringing black troops into Europe. London and New York inciting aid of the Tartar and Muscovite. And no man knows better than Churchill the meaning of the Stalin canal. NO literate man in Europe or America is ignorant of what Judeoslavic domination has meant and means.

Sheer terror and lust of greed, and no amount of evasion and hired propaganda will hide it. The governments of London and Washington have betrayed civilization and KNOW it. They fight for monopoly, and the American people have been betrayed into fighting for the gold bugs.

Throughout the ages it has been the favorite device of the creditor class first to work a contraction of the currency, which bankrupted the debtors, and then to cause inflation which created a rise, during which they sold the property they had laid hold of.

This alternate lifting and debasing the value of money is not accidental. When Kitson met Bryan, Bryan already knew that the silver propaganda was an implement or a camouflage over a major issue, that namely of the control of the national credit, or the national power to buy.

England makes war to HAVE war, war being the maximum sabotage. And without sabotage on this scale it was impossible by 1939 to create scarcity, and without scarcity no monopoly, and without monopoly of goods, or more particularly of money itself, extortion is difficult.

Samuel Loyd understood the use of the single standard, After Waterloo no effective power withstood the usurers until, by 1914, the complete usurocracy had been constructed. For fifty years or for seventy it had been almost impossible to get any large scale propaganda against the fetish value of gold save by ballyhoo about silver. By 1978 [*1878*] silver ballyhoo was already necessary to get in a motion to keep at least some of the NON-Interest bearing national debt in circulation as currency. Those words are Greek to most hearers. Bryan denounced the cross of gold, but needed support from the silver interests, and it was insufficient.

Most of the gold in the world is in the British Empire, in the U.S. and in Russia. And mankind is against dying to maintain the fetish value of gold. Thousands of Americans have already died for that metal. They have died for a fetish, a fetish used for more than a century to hypnotize mankind into accepting certain frauds inherent in the money system. In the CONTRACTION of the currency, periodically, in order [to] force other people (sometimes called the debtor class) to pay double for what they have had. But beyond that, to extort produce, wheat, cloth, natural products, and elaborated goods, from the producers.

Can you ever understand that the return to gold under Lloyd George and Churchill meant that 73% of the population of India had to pay up twice as much grain or farm products to meet taxes and interest charges? Seventy-five percent because that is the percentage of Indian population that depends upon agriculture.

And what goes for Indian agriculture in a case of that kind goes for agriculture all over the world.

Wars are made to make debt. You have already got quite a lot of it, and the judeophile N.Y. Herald is already howling to have it quadrupled by the simple device of returning to GOLD as the fictitious basis of bank loans, and currency. Willkie I take it is already being groomed up to work that betrayal on the American people. The wheeze was worked after the wars of Napoleon. It was worked after the American Civil War. It was worked by the Cunliffe Committee, after the last war.

Ships are sunk IN ORDER TO HAVE SHIPS SUNK. When ships are sunk, there is a greater demand for new ships. The sinking augments the MARKET for new ships. More ships are wanted because more ships have been destroyed. And LOAN CAPITAL, usurer's capital, money made by a stroke of the banker's pen is wanted for FINANCING new construction. Arabs are murdered to keep things lively.

Cities are destroyed IN ORDER that cities may be destroyed. The frontier means nothing to the financier.

The MORE houses fall on BOTH sides of the frontiers, the more loan-capital will be wanted so long as the usurocrat system endures; so long as the usurocrat system endures, the more loan capital will be required to finance reconstruction. The more simple people are ruined, the more bankruptcies, the more bankrupt concerns can be snapped up cheap by the owners of loan capital. Has NO one ever examined the reconstruction period, the period after the American Civil War? from this angle?

With race or without race, examine it. The more energy goes into destroying goods, the less will go into making them. The more energy goes into goods intended for immediate destruction, the less will go into goods made for USE. The faster you destroy goods, the faster superfluous money will mount up, unless you employ a Gesellite or similar mechanism to destroy the money as fast as the goods are blown to hell or sunk in the oceans. Without Gesell that means inflation; i.e. a dollar worth ten cents worth of potatoes.

Debt is already upon you. Some of you know that. But 99% of you don't see that the DEFLATION, the contraction of the currency, is already PLANNED. That the same banking houses that have worked the wheeze four times and more times are already waiting their moment to spring.

If there is a sane man or an honest man left in America, let him get out a new edition of the Bankers Conspiracy. A ten cent edition, an edition people can buy. Henry Ford or Firestone, or whoever survives of their generation OUGHT to have memories long enough to remember Olney and Cleveland, and the struggles of 1893. Hank Wallace betrays Martin van Buren. But there ought to be some college campus left where the local historian still has liberty to correlate the works of the American founders, and to put the works of Kitson and Brooks Adams together, DESPITE the new censorship, despite telegraph restrictions, despite, and I warned you of it, the interruption of inter-communication between one American and another INSIDE the U.S.

Your means of communication by your own automobiles have been curtailed.

#75 (April 13, 1943) U.S.(C29) VALENTINE

About St. Valentine's day the light broke on Steinie Morrison and he mentioned the word "collaboration."

No longer going to shut down on all European radios and suppress all discussion of vital topics, but England going to collaborate in a world system.

This after Iran or Persia had mentioned wanting to control its own banking and currency. The light of hither Asia? Perhaps.

On June 19, 1934 a gent, now I believe in jail in the U.S.A., wrote me from Ashville, after professing disinterest in European personalities as follows:

The working out of the problems of America is exactly along the policy of constructively eliminating the power of money as money (it is absurd that the medium of exchange should have value in itself); scrapping the banking system and the international warplots; and installing a currency which will provide an equal balance between the capacity of industry to produce and the ability of the public to buy.

If that be treason, go to it. My correspondent continued:

It is as simple as this, but will not be accomplished until the present time worn system, capitalized upon by the Rothschilds, Ginsbergs, Sassoons, Warburgs, etc., in their century-long plot (already fighting among themselves for the loot) collapses of its own worthlessness.

My correspondent believed in the American Constitution, and mistrusted Jefferson, retrospectively.

The ideal political prisoner, I suppose. And the Commonwealth Party. What is it? Is it a real party? Does it stand for the just price and the homestead, or is it just another fake opposition set up and financed by the financiers? Longnosed or shortnosed?

There is manifestly no freedom without economic freedom. Freedom to keep out of debt. In 1936 a discussion of Simonds and Emery's "The Price of Peace" appeared in London and contained a division of nations which seems to me inadequate. The first group, according to the criticisms of Simonds and Emery, consisted of status-quo powers, such as France and

England, who were "naturally satisfied with their enormous possessions" and desired to see no change.

The second group consisted of revisionist powers: dissatisfied powers, Germany, Japan, and Italy, who wanted the world to move. Otherwise their standards of living would sink, and national existence shrivel.

You will at once think of a third set of powers, namely, Roosevelt's Hebrew Republic, and Stalin's Russia, both possessed of vast wealth. No need to expand their borders, having vast need of clean sane and decent distribution INSIDE those borders. But rich beyond the dreams of anything but Rothschildean greed, and flagrantly determined to expand, grab and pervade.

And England certainly has entered some sort of plot, or gang, to betray Eastern Europe, to betray pretty much all of European civilization. There is no truce with Adam Zad, the bear that walks like a man.

That on the one hand, and W. Manning Dacey, in the Observer for January 10, telling you and the world that the profits of the Big Five (that is BANKS), the chief banks of your country, are for the first time above the 1929 level. *Cui bono*, whom doth it profit?

For gold I arm their hands
And for gold I buy their lands
and for gold I sell their enemies the yield
Their nearest fees may purchase, or their furthest
friends may lease.
Said, or as they say "sang," the late Rudyard Kipling in a poem called "The Peace of Dives," or dives.
Who grindest for thy greed
Men's belly pinch and need.

What hope have you in a Russian invasion of Romania and Finland?

I hear your Sunday parsons howling to Christ. It is unconvincing, YOU know, at least many of you know as well and better than I do, what the Soviet system has been for the past 20 years. For yourselves you do not believe in the communal ownership of gardens, bathtubs, a woman, you like a bit of promiscuity, but you don't run to the communal system.

You had a decent proportion of communal ownership of pasturage; village commons, common lands, and you would do well to get back to it, 150 ducal filchings, somewhat tangled skein, but you could untangle it. He who would make his own liberty secure must guard even his enemy from oppression. Tom Paine said it and died only partially honored. I repeat that, quote: "He who would make his own liberty secure must guard even his enemy from oppression." You don't appear to want to put that in practice.

You do NOT fight for world freedom, you are stampeded. You, some of you, had dislikes, quite proper dislikes, dislikes of being oppressed; and a great laziness, a very great laziness, especially in the head.

Even Lenin saw that the "easiest way to debauch the capitalist system is to debauch its currency." No, you don't exactly want the capitalist system either. Especially if it is to be somebody else's capitalist system, with you vainly trying to get back to the udders. And so this is the new opposition, the Commonwealth Party. [It] don't seem to have got to your microphones, not at the moments I have unhooked a receiver. It is said to be of Communist tendencies. That is suspicious, considering the presence of yiddo slays, and associates of the late Mr. Trotsky and the pressing desire of the Bolshies to get control of the Labor Party.

Why, God alone knows why they want to get hold of the fake opposition. But still they like to be as ubiquitous as possible.

I wonder, has the Commonwealth party said anything about money, control of the national power to buy? If so, of course a poll of ten thousand against eleven thousand votes for the Big Five, the City, the Gold exchange, is peculiar.

It might even be a real party ... but Lord alone knows ... can it be? Is it?

#76 (April 17, 1943) U.S.(C31)
J.G. BLAINE

I was highly diverted, along in January, to hear that American historical sense had got down to an almost invisible minimum. They were havin' a celebration or commemoration of the fiftieth anniversary of the death of Mr. Blaine, J.G.B. I couldn't quote the pertinent document, without a return to Rapallo, but I note that in late 1880 in August, August 27 to be exact, of the year wherein Grover Cleveland was elected, a stalwart Republican, state legislature 1864 and subsequent, Congress 1876 and subsequent, wrote to General E. Bryant a letter that was reproduced in a good number of papers western and eastern, includin' the N.Y. Evening Post.

The Philadelphia Times called it the most significant of many recent Republican protests. That is perhaps why Blaine's commemoration occurs during a Democratic administration, The Democrats owed him Cleveland's elections. It is a two-column letter and I don't think I can get it into my time. It began with reference to President Arthur, his integrity. Regretted that he had not been nominated for the subsequent term which, being the case, the writer supposed that the nominee should be a man of the highest type of political integrity, and republican principles.

He continued:

Mr. Blaine is not such a man. He embodies most in American politics that is menacing to public morals and INTEGRITY in government. [A] long public career distinguished mainly by a sort of declamatory and pugilistic statecraft, not the inspiration of a single valuable policy, or author of an important statute. Opposed good and supported bad legislation. Record clouded by suspicion and accusation of jobbery and corruption undefended. He brings to us personal antagonisms which have torn and weakened our party in the past, invading the administration of Garfield with demands of personal vengence so virulent as to inflame the spirit of assassination and culminating in the defeat of Judge Folger and the election of Grover Cleveland, Governor of the Empire State.

I skip some references to Roscoe Conkling, and continue re Mr. Blaine: A speculator, enjoying a fortune too great to have been acquired by honest industry. Legitimate business enterprise of his country's service at five thousand dollars a year, he sympathizes with and profits

[from] speculative stock jobbing and gambling methods of acquiring wealth, methods which have wrought ruin, disgrace and business disasters beyond computation, schooled youth and persuaded middle age to avoid honest and useful industry, made suicide and insanity commonplace, unsettled values, placed the fruits of honest toil in the power of Goulds and Armours, to bear down and bull up in the markets, as whim or interest may dictate, methods which gave us but an exaggerated illustration of their iniquitous consequences in the Grant and Ward 150 million dollar failure and robbery.

Reference to Blaine's Congressional record relating to subsidies, class legislation, corporate exactions, etc. will readily satisfy the honest inquirer of his uniform support of monopolies and indifference to the common weal.

Little wonder that he omits from his letter to refer to, or explain, the cause of the great disparity in the distribution of this marvelous increase of wealth accumulated during the period he chooses for comparison, that he fails to note the fact that one 300th of [the] 44 billion dollars is held by one man, while others rank little below, and his own palatial residence [at] a rental of 11 thousand per year suggesting more than an average per capita of wealth. Little wonder he is silent on the subject of interstate commerce, the regulation of which is demanded by all producers and legitimate traders. Great corporate interests demand noninterference.

Sorry to skip reference to people fed at public crib, Brother Bob etc. Nor will the citation of his pacific assurances to Mexico quite cover up his S. American policy and interference to protect the Landau Guano scheme. Death of his servant Hurlbut, etc. The disingeneousness of his letter of acceptance is further betrayed by its significant silence touching the events of the past three years (1881, 2, 3).

Bringing down his historic figure to the present would have revealed the fiction involved in his statements, would have shown a marvelous shrinkage in nominal values, would have noted the downfall of business prosperity and business morals and would have pictured as few can do so graphically as he, the furnace fires dying out, the wheels of factories standing still, wages reduced, beggary usurping the place of labor, bank and business failures, creditors and depositors wantonly defrauded, homes lost, and crookedness in public affairs.

Mr. Blaine is objectionable, furthermore, for the company he keeps, for the "friends he has made."

Will the chief promoters of his nomination be his chief advisors if elected? There's the rub. I need mention no names but will suggest that the least objectionable of his pet supporters are the Tribune supporters of Greeley in 1872, accusers of Blaine in 1876 and 1880, charging him with bribery and other penitentiary crimes. With no pronounced issues between the two great parties, we can safely afford to yield temporary executive control at this time.

It is vastly more important to good government that the Republican Party be restored to supremacy in Congress than that the administration of law be entrusted to an unworthy partisan surrounded by bad counsel. The N.Y. Times commented on the letter thus: that Blaine's advocate will be amazed to see how formidable is the list of his offenses and how small a part the Mulligan letters (sufficient in themselves) play in the arraignment.

You will say: why rake it all up? Hasn't Woodward summed it all up very neatly? It was an unfortunate choice. Blaine was thoroughly tarred with financial scandals. The worst of it was that the public knew all about his slippery doings. He declared during the campaign that his life was an open book.

It was, indeed, but it had been opened by somebody else. For the first time in our history a major political party nominated as its candidate a man who was known to be dishonest. All of which is, indeed, past history, and could have been let alone were it not that a Democratic administration, the Morgenthau-Lehman administration, has run a commemoration of a defeated Republican candidate. Now isn't that odd, just a bit odd? It is just part of [the] process of falsification of history.

I hope my little bit of reminiscence may shed a side light, and even back up Woodward's summary. He is sometimes laconic.

#77 (April 1843) U.K.(C35)
CANUTE

It is my considered opinion that the Canute Club, alias the BBC's Brain Trust, has not produced anything up to the level of Caedmon's Dream of the Road. Visionaries in retrospect, but placing their past in an unattainable future; I do not think the Continent attends to their gentle murmur. It needs a peculiar sense of the ridiculous, which I don't find here in Italy. Old buffers of my day, something of the period. Waverley novels, and divorce from reality. It takes so long to explain it to a non-English audience. All this pretense of free discussion with ALL the real issues barred.

Freedom to stay out of debt, for example. Imagine Masaryk and Doc Joad on THAT issue. Even if the more-enlightened load HAS got round to wondering how you would install a world bureaucrat without admitting at least a FEW of the indigenese of the European continent, for example. Now in 1919 England had a choice of curing one or the other of TWO economic diseases. Douglas having had practical experience, having a sense of justice, but no faith in the goodness of man, tried to cure possibly the lesser disease. At any rate the one with less popular appeal. He hit out against the swindle inherent in issuing all, or practically all the public's purchase power as interest-paying debt. That, as I think he saw it, would have allowed speculation to go on, would have needed if not a minimal of bureaucratic control, at least less, than guild socialism coordinated into a national central. He was probably out in his calculation, as he did not produce very detailed blueprints of HOW to control prices, toward the JUST price.

Hitler went to a deeper root with his "a great deal [of] purchasing power goes for something OTHER than labor, construction labor." All of which now sounds pretty mild. The irrealists go on murmuring and the tide of Moscovite chaos rises. It becomes more and more evident that the old gang in Britain does NOT want ANY social amelioration whatever. And in that position, I think they tend to overplay their hand.

Now it can't be said that England, via the ONLY medium still open for free (if you call it free) communication with the outer world, i.e., via the radio, it can't be said that England shows any very acute desire to understand or to communicate an understanding of what the Continent calls the "historic moment." What the late H. James called, seeing "where in a manner of speakin' we have got to."

No one praised the social order, slums, etc., in England before the war. "War was his only OUT," as an experienced American politician put it of Roosevelt. Most of the gold in the world is in the U.S., in the British Empire, and in Russia, and I reckon any attempt to diminish the power of them that have it will meet with pretty serious resistance. Voice of experience that, not of theory. When I talked Douglas and Gesell, he replied: what effect will it have on the price of gold? Gold has been mentioned in Brain Trust or Dumb Freedom forum, but not usury.

History will note, whether you like it or not, that Hitler came on a phrase of Feder's: "A great deal of purchasing power is allocated for reasons other than the performance of useful labor." Labor not limited to work of HAND, but would include work of head, organization, any act useful to the community.

In fact: damn well known that money, under the foetid usurocrat system was gained by speculation, rigging stock markets and by method of issuing so much of the nation's money as interest payin'—and how—interest paying debt, debt on which the whole community was welched for interest. And the minute Hitler opened his mouth on the subject he became *caput lupinum*. Target for assassination like Mussolini became *caput lupinum*, target for repeated attempts at assassination: minute he opened his mouth reconnection of New York Jew capitalists and the Russian revolution.

Just like Abe Lincoln became target for assassination when he got round to resisting the desire of FOREIGN Jew bankers to control the currency of the U.S.A. by means of the great debt; inducted, erected, by the American Civil War. In a case that has never been cleared up. Oh yes, we know Booth shot Mr. Lincoln, but the protection of Booth, the nature of the trial of his alleged accomplices, has NOT been cleared up. Booth's getaway, his capture due to accident of sprained leg, etc. and the hoods worn at the trial. Lot of past history to go into. The unwillingness of the Reds to GO into MONEY, to go into the question of money, of potential abundence, OF the English Reds to go into question of people who financed [the] Spanish Revolution. There we get to the raw, the things the bolos will discuss and the things they won't.

Lenin and Stalin at one stage, both clear about export of capital. The questions that are NOT discussed in certain circles. That is the use of THIS radio, of me on this radio.

The Beveridge Plan, a lame duck, a blind alley, a Aunt Sally, a target for metaphor. And the position of the laborERS. As apart from the labor/ites? The pie in the sky, the pie at the end of next century. The KNOWN and archi-known possibility of abundance in the U.S.A. before Mr. Roosevelt's war started.

The Church of England praying that a denser form of atheism than its own shall descend and engulf us. Now I repeat, England had economic diseases. Unemployment, distressed areas, slums, and the rest of it. Germany and Italy set out to remedy such conditions INSIDE their own borders. England did NOT.

Whatever was done, was done tardily, half heartedly. Nothing about justice or any of that darn nonsense from Mr. Churchill. Not a word.

The remedies vs. speculation made great headway in Italy and in Germany. Men of good will wished something similar might happen in England. Men of good will IN ENGLAND thought monetary reform would be preferable. BOTH exits were barred, by whom? For whom? War is the greatest form of sabotage.

The acute form of sabotage. Someone in England insisted on having a war. The devil's answer to the enigma of poverty amidst plenty is to sabotage plenty, to annihilate the PLENTY, so as to put an end to the problem. To enforce poverty, to enforce scarcity, to create scarcity, so as to enforce scarcity economics.

The system of scarcity, which enables monopoly, gives monopoly power to exact the UNJUST price.

And men in America NOT content with this one, already aim at the next one. War with Russia. The time to object is NOW.

#78 (April 20, 1943) U.S.(C35)
ZION

If or when one mentions the Protocols alleged to be of the Elders of Zion, one is frequently met with the reply: Oh, but they are a forgery.

Certainly they are a forgery, and that is the one proof we have of their authenticity. The Jews have worked with forged documents for the past 24 hundred years, namely ever since they have had any documents whatsoever. And no one can qualify as a historian of this half century without having examined the Protocols. Alleged, if you like, to have been translated from the Russian, from a manuscript to be consulted in the British Museum, where some such document may or may not exist.

What we know for certain is that they were published two decades ago. That Lord Sydenham wrote a preface to them. That their content has been traced to another sketch said to have appeared in the eighteen forties. The interest in them does not lie in [the] question of their having been, or NOT been concocted by a legislative assembly of Rabbis, democratically elected, or secretly chosen by the Mysterious Order of Seven Branched Antlers or the Bowling Society of Milwaukee. Their interest lies in the type of mind, or the state of mind of their author. That was their interest for the psychologist the day they first appeared.

And for the historian two decades later, when the program contained in them has so crushingly gone into effect up to a point, or down to a squalor.

What is interesting, perhaps most, to the historian is their definite campaign against history altogether, their declared intention to blot out the classics, to blot out the record, and to dazzle men with talk of tomorrow. That is a variant on the pie in the bait. As far as reality is concerned, as far as you and I are concerned it makes little difference whether prosperity is in heaven, or in the year 2300, or just round a corner that will never be turned.

A religious man might think his reward might be in heaven, but even a religious man ought to know that his reward will not be on earth in a hundred years time. In fact, the pie in the sky is a more reasonable proposition: an opium with more to it than Mr. Keynes' day after tomorrow.

I am not concerned with fixing blame retrospectively so much as with judging the present: those who are against the true word, the *protocolaires*.

Now Keynes whose fair is foul, foul is fair sentence can be taken as the quintessence of something or other, is the perfect *protoclaire*. It comes over me that on the one occasion I had the curious experience of seeing him, he managed to utter two falsehoods in a very short space of time. In fact never opened his mouth without doing so. First in stating that he is an orthodox economist, which he is not, second in saying that the then high cost of living was due to lack of labor, when there were millions of men out of work.

You couldn't have done much better in two sentences if you were out for a record in the falsification.

Protocol No. 8, second [paragraph]:

We shall surround our government with a whole world of economists. That is the reason why economic sciences form, etc. Around us again will be a whole constellation of bankers, industrialists, capitalists and the main thing, millionaires, because in substance everything will be settled by the question of figures.

Is it possible to arouse any interest in verbal precision? Is it possible to persuade more than six or eight people to consider the scope of crossword puzzles and other devices for looking at words for something that is NOT their meaning? Cabala, for example, anything to make the word mean something it does NOT say. Anything to distract the auditor from the plain sense of the word, or the sentence? Even to communism that is NOT communism. To communism of the episcopal sort, which they want in England. A Bolshevism that is to leave the archibishops and curates just where they are, each with his living or benefice. A revelation against capital, allegedly against capital, that attacks property and leaves capital setting pretty.

Lenin all out for making banking a state affair. And then twenty years during which it has seemed to drop decidedly into the background, when the world revolution was very busy about something else.

It should by now be clear that some people fear NOT the outcome of the war, but the END of the war.

Churchill, for example. Not defeat, not the ruin of the Empire that worries him, but the END of the war.

End of the slaughter, end of the war conditions.

Robert Clive has been clear enough, ex-British ambassador in Tokyo. Tells you and the world Japan can not be beaten. But the war must go ON, according to Churchill and Roosevelt. Churchill sees the end of monopoly and privilege, or at least a shift when the war ends, no matter HOW. That is the point you should consider. In regard to the protocols, either there is and was a plot to ruin all goyim, all nations of Europe, or some people are stark raving crazy. They want war to go on to certain wreck. WHO are they?

Mere cannon fodder. The American troops in N. Africa know they are not there thru any wish of their own.

The war was started for gold, to maintain the fetish value of gold. Plenty of other sidelines. Minor advantages have been COMMERCIALLY taken. Did the present regime in England WANT the troops to return after Dunkirk? Every move for reform in England is a fascist reform, or proposition along fascist lines.

The supreme betrayal of Europe is inherent in the alliance of Anglo-Jewry with Moscow. Debts rise.

That is one part of the war. It is a contest between STOPPING the war and going on with it. And only one side does any fighting. Namely the party that STARTED the war. They are for its continuance. Who are they?

BUT they are also for starting the next one. They openly proclaim that AFTER (that is IF) America finishes with Japan, she will have to fight Russia. IF Russia should break into Europe.

Only blindness and deafness can keep you unaware of these proclamations. The U.S. must protect the world? Why? Does the world want it? The U.S., once this war is over, must be strong enough to beat Russia.

The U.S. had a chance to maintain her prestige and unique position by staying NEUTRAL. Neutral while other powers exhausted themselves. And she DID not.

Who are the lunatics? Was there a deliberate plot? That is what should concern you. WAS there a plot? How long had it been in existence? Does it continue, with its Lehmans, Morgenthaus, Baruchs?

Proposals to send the darkies to Africa, to work for Judea, and the rest of it? And WILL you, after Japan is thru with you, take on Russia? In order to maintain the banking monopoly? With Mr. Wille Wiseman, late of the British secret service, ensconced in Kuhn, Loeb and Co., to direct you and rule you?

#79 (April 24, 1943) U.S.(C34)
CONSCIENCE

The Americans in French Africa have not a clear conscience. There are probably no Americans in North Africa with a clear conscience, tho' there may be some with no conscience whatever. An existence at gangster level, with no velleity above wanting to bust something or punish someone.

The American people have decency enough to know that they should NOT be attacking Europe from the East while Russia attacks from the West. And in the name of what? Of stealing French territory and British trade?

I have mentioned the small boys in Trenton N.J. who played at being Emperor of the World.

Infantilism in high places! And Madame Chek, on February 18, made a stirring speech to the American Congress speaking better American than Sol Bloom and half the assembled delegates, and with a better delivery than Mr. Roosevelt. I have no doubt the audience fell for it as leaves in autumn.

It was an appeal to one's sympathies. I should have been swept off my feet if I hadn't been lying down at the time, next to my radio. Bedside habit of radio. The Chinese have a very old saying, that it is an ill omen if the hen crows. *Canta la gallina.* Mme. Chiang's appeal was clear enough. Everyone wants their own country to be governed by their own people. But it is Wang Chin Wei and not Mons. C.K. Chek who has got back the treaty ports, the extraterritorial rights for his country.

And the grouped ideograms that are translated, "man of high character," indicate, unless I miss my guess, the men through whom and in whom one hears the voice of his forebears. Order at home. China with 400 millions IN ORDER would indeed be an element for world stability. But that order must RISE IN CHINA. In 300 or more years of history, in fact in all the history we have of that country, the order must rise inside. At no time has China been at peace in the hands of a government run from outside on loan capital. That is Mme. Chiang's error. Her aim is admirable, but she climbs a tree to catch fish.

When Mencius said that to King Huei, of Liang, the King said: "Is it as bad as that?" And Mencius answered: "Worse, for you would do no harm. You would not of course catch any fish. But you would do no further damage."

This loss of Chinese wisdom, under the smatter of Y.M.C.A. dogmatism, and occidental class teachings is not the answer.

I have heard from someone who knows him that Chiang himself did not want the war with Japan, but was worked into it, on sheer theory, sheer western nonsense. Kung is to China as water to fishes. Meaning Confucius, the Confucian doctrine is the true habitat of the Son of Heaven, and from the Emperor down to the common people, the duty or root is ONE. And that root is NOT to be found in an exotic government imposed in the interests of foreign loan capital.

If the Chinese ever get hold of a few copies of the Talmud, there will be even less room for the servants, Jewish or Goyim, of the doctrines therein contained. And if the root be confusion, the fruit cannot be order. Mme. Chiang appealing for help to a smaller nation may be a stirring figure. But the grab in French Africa in no way assists her husband in Chungking.

Japan is NOT the hereditary enemy of China. There are over two millenia of history wherein the two nations did NOT damage each other. Whereas the history of Anglo-Saxon relations with China is one record of infamy. One almost unmitigated stink. And the Japanese have recorded some of the more recent chapters in a work whose translated title reads: "The British Empire and British People."

Mme. Chiang arouses one's sympathies. BUT the error lies in this idea that a universal theory will govern the world WITHOUT local order. If neither Chungking nor Washington can bring order into their OWN country, what likelihood is there that a still looser and larger bureaucracy having still less definite responsibilities, and still less competent executive offices, would be able to do any better?

One of the key thoughts, the bedrock thought that the late A.R. Orage produced in 30 or 40 years ideological battle, was in an article on the recession of power, i.e., FROM the people. As soon as people get control of ANY organ of government, deliberative body or whatever, the real control seems to retire into something INNER.

The ballyhoo vs. fascism was all tosh, insofar as it objected to organization and control. What one sees after 20 years, two decades, is that Italy has the professed Jeffersonian ideal. That of governing LEAST.

That the Fascist ideal is well nigh unattainable; not from wrong direction, not from lack of aim toward organization, but from the natural chaos of man, the unfailing laziness of the average man, who WILL not be bothered to organize, who can not be persuaded to organize, save in moments of danger or of enthusiasm. Even co-directors have to be lured to board meetings by fees. Fifty dollars or whatever, to be bothered to go watch proceedings. Machiavelli Senior remarked: "Men live in a few, and the rest are sheep." The idealists struggle against that. An occasional miracle happens. In China men have set up a series of dynasties. Acts of heroic creation, 160 to build or continue, and 160 years to decline. NOT one of the great dynasties, the durable dynasties, was built on gangster grab. Kublai was a great Kahn, but the Ming came 89 years later.

The cheap half baked smattering of western half learning, the lies of half trained professors, shot into foolish young students have NOT been of use to China. If the ancient Kings are too far back to be counted, the Chinese would have learned more from Han, Sung, Tiang, Hong-Vou and Tai Tsong, than from Woodrow Wilson and the Sassoons.

No one can pronounce Chinese names so as to satisfy everyone. If you don't like my transliterations, that is, if any oriental auditor is puzzled, let me put the sentence: Chinese history itself contains more lessons, and better lessons, than have been learned by a scattered joblot of college students, hurled into jerk water colleges, or into the London Fool of Economics or Oxford.

That is perhaps Mme. Chiang's tragedy. Foreign loan capital is NO substitute for the tradition of Wen and Wu, for the lesson of pre-Christian dynasties.

#80 (April 27, 1943) U.S.(C37)
ON RETIRING

I think quite simply and definitely that the American troops in N. Africa, all of'em ought to go back to America: IF they can get there.

America ought not to be makin' war on Europe, and America knows it. I think it is time the American U.S. citizen studied Mr. Morgenthau's treasury reports, whether or not he is out in front proclaiming the coming of Zion or not. I think it is time you opened Kipling's memoirs "Something about myself." I think it is time more American Masons developed a curiosity about the possible relations of their order to Jewry as such, and to at least a sect or portion or selection of ORGANIZED Jews as a possible enemy of mankind, and of the American people, the British people in particular.

I think it might be a good thing to hang Roosevelt and a few hundred yidds IF you can do it by due legal process, NOT otherwise. Law must be preserved. I know this may sound tame, but so is it. It is sometimes hard to think so. Hard to think that the 35 ex-army subalterns or whatever who wanted to bump off all the kike congressmen weren't just a bit crude and *simpliste*. Sometimes one feels that it would be better to get the job done somehow, ANY how, than to delay execution.

A chair has been founded in the Sorbonne to study modern Jewish history, i.e., the role of the kike in modern history. It would be well to have similar chairs in ALL American universities, though Harvard and the College of the City of N. York might find it hard to get the necessary endowments. I don't think there is any American law that permits you to shoot Nic. Butler. It is a pity but so is it. No *ex post facto* laws are to be dreamt of. Not that Frankfurter or any other damn Jews care a hoot for law or for the American Constitution. But we are not here to uphold Frankfurter or the Jewish vendetta. In the midst of which YOU jolly well are. And every American boy that gets drowned owes it to Roosevelt and Baruch, and to Roosevelt's VIOLATION of the duties of office.

It is on the ground of those violations, those that occurred before Pearl Harbor, that you should impeach him. It is time that the matter was studied. It is time that the practical means for doing the job were made subject of study. It will be difficult insofar as your press and radio are mostly in Chewisch hands. It will be difficult to coordinate effort in our so all-fired anarchic country. Instinctively anarchic BUT controlled, by an organization. An organization well worth your study. Be you Mason or Non-Mason. You will have to form cells, nuclei, and communicate. You will have to maintain some freedom of the press and get radio stations somehow. Congress should go on the air. Failing that, state senates and legislatures should go on the air. And state universities in states not wholly run by their ghettoes should start a study of history of the Jew's role in history, of the role of usury, and currency control BY extraneous private bodies, all that should be made subject of study. You've got to start some time.

You have got to learn a little, at least a little about the history of your allies. About Jew-ruin'd England. About the wreckage of France, wrecked under yidd control. Lousy with kikes. Blum, Zay, and the rest of'em pushed France into war, when it was dead certain France would get beaten. Preparing ANOTHER. Oh, yes. ANOTHER ten or twenty years war between the U.S. and Slavic Russia to start just as soon as this one shows signs of relaxin'. Don't think the kike WANTS to stop wars as long as non kikes will go on killin' and drowning each other, in order to provide dividends for loan capital. And SOME capital. A part of loan capital is, mebbe you have heard this before, some part of loan capital IS really in chewish hands. Mebbe you haven't yet heard that. And some of the American dollars that went for gold, went OUT of America to buy gold, well some of that went out to KIKERY. And Heinrick ben Sloman, ben Soloman, ben Isaac, ben Morgenthau, son of his father, was the sheeny that sent it right out.

And you go on taking it, you go on being diddled, and listening to the Jerusalem synagogue radios from London and Jew York City. Gawd ellup you. Bags of money, offered thru fear or guilt, have been uniformly refused by the mobs, wrote Mr. Jefferson to John Jay from Paris, July 19th, 1789. Paris was lively. On September 6 Jefferson was blissfully dreaming an ideal republic as follows: But with respect to future debts would it not be wise and just for the nation to declare in the Constitution that they are forming, that neither the legislature nor the nation itself can validly contract more debt than they may pay within their own age, or within the term of 34 years?

Think it over. That was T.J. writing to Madison, from Paris, 6 September 1789. It is the famous letter containing the words: "the earth belongs in usufruct to the living." That theme he later repeated, in the form "the earth belongs to the living." And the "within their own age" was reduced to 19 years.

First, he thought of the "own age" as the period into which the average inhabitant of a nation would survive. Then he figured that children and those under age wouldn't have any say in contracting the debt.

So they ought not to [*be*] bound. That is, sold into slavery for its payment. These are fine points of the ethics. They won't appeal to Mr. Constantine Brown. They will have no effect upon those of you who are given over to the comforting (comforting if it comforts you) theory that devastation just doesn't matter and to whom.

Shakespeare and Bach are a bore. Architecture is dangerous. Sculpture is taboo. Mr. Brown wants a bright new world; and debt is after all only the prelude to slavery. One can conceive a regime in which there is NO economic liberty. I mean absolutely NO economic liberty for anyone. Not by accident, but by program. It is much easier, in fact, to conceive a slave state than a free state. A state wherein all men are slaves, and no man has any right whatsoever to life, liberty, and where even the pursuit—marvelous phrase that "pursuit" of happiness—would be illegal, or at least regarded as a grave misdemeanor.

A really severe Puritan like Eden or Morgenthau would probably tell you that the pursuit of happiness is on a level with chippy-chasing. I know you don't THINK you are ripe for a real revolution. You don't think YOU are ripe for the end of the capitalist system altogether. You would rather such revolutions occurred in the Punjab or in Bessarabia. But one thing leads to another.

And yet, Civilization was not yours to destroy.

#81 (May2, 1943) U.K.(C36)
ON THE NATURE OF TREACHERY

I should like tonight to get a little serious attention, yours, to a serious subject, or to several serious matters.

I have in fact been trying for over 20 years to get a little serious attention; persuade you to direct a little serious attention to a few serious subjects. Nature of money, and mode of its issue, and usury. Before that and during the interim I have perhaps been more successful in drawing attention to a few literary problems, and authors. As to my remarks on economics, my methods have been such as were possible. Nobody ever suggested that I should improve'em. When noticed, the reaction was in most cases merely a cordial invitation to join in the great betrayal. "La trahison des clercs," as Julien Benda called it. The cry was NOT, tell us more, perfect your own understanding of this knotty, or these knotty subjects. The cry was: be quiet, it is indecent for a man of letters to touch such a subject. And now you are in a mess. You are spiritually in the worst mess than you are in materially. Despite the loss of tonnage and markets, your loss of tonnage and markets.

I wonder if you have any concept of what Europe means by England's betrayal of Europe. I should like to sort certain things out. Your defense of your empire, for example, as distinct from the drive to START war. To keep the war going, to extend the area of the war. Both your attempt and that made by your pals in the U.S.A.

I should like to distinguish between war and mere violence. I should like to distinguish between valor on the field of battle, and the bombing of civilians, the sinking of hospital ships. I do not think the two kinds of activity are necessarily inseparable. And neither do you.

Nothing is without efficient cause. You can't beat Aristotle on that statement. Something causes the destruction of mosques, and museums. Something totally different from the will to die for freedom's cause: for King and country, for the defense of the homeland. The two activities are NOT identical; nor are they inseparable. Now, hospital ships have been bombed, and not by accident. And the typical American feeling is one of revulsion and the soldiers' is one of revulsion.

An American airman had been floating about the middle sea for some days on an inflated rubber raft.

He and his pals were at the end of their tether. They were picked up by an Italian hospital ship, put to bed, told they were patients for the time being but would be prisoners on landing. The hospital ship was sunk on a later trip, but one of the nurses who escaped tells this of one of the American airmen. She came to his berth to attend him; he said: turn out the light, I am ashamed to look at you. That is the soldier's feeling about baby killing, about bombing hospitals, the cad's feeling is possibly different.

The words "Palazzo S. Giorgio" probably mean nothing to you. A few art lovers, architects, may know what they refer to. The Palazzo was of no military importance. Neither were Gaudier-Brzeska's charcoal drawings. The Kensington Museum accepted some after Gaudier's death. The bulk of them were in a suitcase in Gertova, in a sculpter's studio. I knew that his father's flat had been burnt out, but was told the studio had not been hit. I thought it was time to remove the drawings. I found them. The suitcase covered ¼ inch thick with dust and plaster. A hole in the ceiling six feet away, a pile of sand on the floor. I used the cover of Dick's bookcase to dust off the suitcase. The concierge said: "Yes, fortunately we noticed the *spezzoni*; and put it out quickly." Gaudier gave his life in the last war, for France and England. I had shared the drawings with England. I suppose it is due to me that some of his sculpture is in the S. Kensington or the Tate Gallery. At least I believe no one will contradict that statement.

You came within an ace of burning up most of his drawings. Especially as the small abstract notebook was in the suitcase with the large charcoals. And a copy of Hughes and one or two other more or less irreplaceable objects. Another mark in Genova was the library [of] the S. Carlo theater.

"ONE spot of earth that is forever England." Dick's father used to be Anglophile. He was a friend of your late Admiral Martin. He had forgotten or forgiven [the] Caracciolo incident, a chapter in Nelson's life that is not emphasized in your school books or official biographies of the columnist.

This vandalism is perhaps the minor part of your treachery. By treachery I refer to the alliance with Russia, any Russia. It may be unwisdom ... eh; on your part. You meant, of course, MEANT to set the two great powers at each other's throats once again and to come in when both were exhausted. Might overdo it?

Might find yourselves in the grip of the new pincers? It used to be felt that the Americans would get more *soaviter in modo*, than the Germans *fortiter in re*. Half time score seems to be to American advantage. Not my place as a Yank to complain of the material advantages gained by American policy. And yet I deplore the American policy. NOT because it was *soaviter in modo*, with YOU. And I do NOT hold you responsible for it, save insofar as you tolerated the precedent and falsifications.

On theory, on grounds of program, I have perhaps said a few words for Lenin. When asked to criticize the Kharkov Congress, I did so with perfect good will. I went on writing in Communist papers. I have quoted Stalin's "Foundations of Leninism" over this radio. Not of course when expounding fascist doctrine. Merely from personal sympathy with various points made in 1922 by Joseph Stalin. In 1926 or whenever I got the brochure, it was not with Stalin's Bolshevism but with his backsliding that I should have quarreled. I disliked a year ago to see Stalin repeating the Czarist error, and sacrificing millions of Russians IN THE CAUSE of the usurers. The NON-slavic usurers. In fact one never does hear of Russian money lenders. I suppose Russians must have had jobs in banks, now and again, but one doesn't hear much of it.

I don't know that I should have any difficulties about accepting a REAL Bolshevik program. The artist does not, and never [has] been part of the bourgeoisie. I object to a pretended attack on captial, on usurocracy, that degenerates into a mere attack upon property and leaves the money lender, the pawnbroker, setting pretty and in full control of the exploitation system, milking the producer.

Producers of the world, unite. All right by me. The artist don't need to own property. Usually bores him. What he wants is to own his tools. NO, not even that, he wants the right to USE the tools of his craft.

Bolshevism has never by program denied this to him.

I should never go and get scragged on a theoretical issue as to whether farmers should KOLKHOZ, or own homestead. I believe that in general experience, the latter has better results on production. But it is NOT a principle. It is empiric observation.

If Churchill had accepted Bolshie DOGMA, one might not think him a traitor. But he has NOT. At least no BBC stooge has claimed that for him. What even a pink might query is the practical executive capacity of Moscow in WORKING the communist system. One has read reports to the effect that a hitch now and again occurs among the angels of the Soviet paradise. As realist one wonders whether a judaic bureaucracy on the Dimitrov system, with Dimitrov and Co. running it, is the most desirable regime for Finland, Denmark, Rumania, Switzerland, Warwick, Kent, and the Midlands.

World revolution, with LOCAL executive autochthonous is one thing, world revolution with a strictly Jewish and Moscovite control is another.

It is England's betrayal of SELF determination that ought to lie on the English conscience. Your alliance with Adam Zad.

#82 (May 4, 1943) U.S.(C40)
ROMANCE

Just why the campus Communist, the starry eyed idealist Communist, or realist Communist or Bill Bullit millionaire Communard, should suppose that Stalin is still leadin' a world revolution instead of playing power politics on the old Romanoff model; well, I leave it to you.

Back before the American young stopped reading Tennyson's *Idylls of the King*, or the *Morte d' Arthur*, or *The Tristan of Beroul*, or M. Hillaire Belloc's *Avril*, back then, I once called on old Harrison, sugar trust Harrison, and spoke of the S.P.C.A. Soc. Prev. etc. and he didn't question the aims of that society. He said, who administers, meaning who handles the funds of the society, and administers?

Well, do you watch the course of events? Of course most of you do not. But why should the proletariat dictate BY means of a secret committee of furriners? Why should the proletariat not dictate locally by means of itself? Why should it be administered by foreign agents, and men of alien race?

Yes, I know—those of us who are older [know?]—my meeting with Harrison was before a Jewish administration had provided the U.S.A. with an army for export. Points of arrival not designated. And George Washington said peace can not be founded on racial antipathies. So the BBC says you must hate the Germans, that is regular Semite logic. From the mouth of the babes and the suckers.

Well, DID you notice how quickly the propaganda for eugenics degenerated into birth control? And race suicide? And how quickly romanticism was replaced, well perhaps that was a slower rhythm, to get to the gang shag? First was Mme. Bovary, and Hedda Gabler; and the romantic hero was to rescue Mrs. Jones from the tedium. And then the bright young Communard was out to rape as many young ladies as possible, and health declined, and [there] was contagion. Well that didn't date from the Communist revolution. Was it a Communist revolution? Or are you all mixed up, as the pencil seller said to me in Washington?

And another case, the white haired boy of the American communists, cause perhaps he didn't think very clearly, and vaunted a Jewisch ancestor. Anyhow, when I tried logic on him, re his commrade, he said; "But did you ever know a Communist [to] think?" Meaning have you ever encountered a Communist who would think?

Well, in a way, and in a way NOT. First eliminate religion, and then eliminate thought from amidst the goym. Are they cattle? Do cattle think?

I don't know where to find a susceptible spot in the American or English brain, one whereinto one could inject a little historic curiosity? But what caused the antipathy between Christians and Moslems?

And the Crusades, to rescue the sepulchers of a Jew in Jerusalem? And were the Masons incited against the Catholics? [The] normal American Mason is the type of friendly fellow who says to you: "Shucks, I'm a Mason and my wife is Catholic and the kids going to Catholic school, and I think a man would have to be pretty small to allow it to have an effect on his politics."

That is the soil prepared. Some drop out or stop going to lodge meetings. Some feel bound by their oaths. And not one in a hundred thousand won ders about the central control. Penetration? Get into all parties. BUT why, if the auditor is a Communist, should he want a Communism administered by a foreign committee of plutocrats, whether of his own race or some other? It is the question about local control.

Communism has been tried, as one wearies of repeating, in America, under favorable conditions. But there is a gap, a sudden collapse from the idea of owning all property in common, and the effect of one's owning anything whatsoever but being constrained to work like heelll for the state. Ain't that funneee? Well, is Stalin leading a world revolution? And if so, why so? Or is he playing at power politics?

Why not revolute? Why should world revolution need a foreign secret committee? Why revolute at the command of Mr. Finkelstein? Is America unable to go Communist without Finkelstein? Is England, are the young saps of Cambridge unable to revolute without Maisky to help them? Or is there a touch of insincerity somewhere in the wangle? As a producer, I can go Communist, the artist can go Communist without trouble. But why all the trimmings?

[Just?] as I can accept the idea of some Catholic economists, but I can not accept all the trimmings, and so with Mr. Bullitt's Communist leanings. Undersell private business; sell the nation's industry short, go into national bonds, BEFORE the slump in industrial shares? Yes, yes, very clever, and when industrials have slopped from 100 to 3? Then you come out with the national money and buy'em up at the fire sale.

Dulce et decorum est. Lovely to die For the Prudential Insurance Co. which has the strength of Gibraltar. To be exported as so much dead meat in order to extend the Russian or Semitic control from Moscow down to the Persian Gulph? But is it sensible?

Debt is the prelude to slavery, and what about the freedom to keep out of debt? That dead fish Sumner Welles does not tell you about THAT sort of freedom. The yellow-livered traitor to the American honesty does not mention that sort of freedom. None of the Lehman-Baruch productions talk of that sort of freedom. Nor of course do your Jew-begormed British allies who will not certainly win this war on their character, not on the personal fascinations of Beaverbrook and the B.B.C. whiners and threateners.

WHAT are you doing in war at all? What are you doing in Africa? Who amongst you has the nerve or the sense to DO something that would conduce to getting you out of it, before you are mortgaged up to the neck, and over it? Every day of war is a debt day, as well as a death day. More debt, more future servitude, less and less of American liberty of any variety? Less liberty to ride in your cars: to post letters. Oh yes, censorship, when Rothschild got hold of the Austrian postal service in the time of Napoleon, censorship was used for commercial espionage. As nowadays, always the same bischniz houses, and the same leading chewish names, except when they change'em. The Freudian Jews, paralyzing the nucleus of will in his goyim victim. The unFreudian chewess eating like a boll weavil into the creative will of her victim. The psychology, well, do a few monographs on the psychology of mixed marriages. You needn't proclaim your object at first. You need not go far enough to lose your professorship. But you can at least do a little prospecting. In psychology, the aim at getting control, getting power over others, by personal contact. As distinct from the desire for competition. Not boxers but referees, who decide the contest in some cases, where the purse is heavy, or not, as the case may be. Well, is Mr. Stalin playing materialist idealism and idealist revolution against idealism and against ideology? Or is it just the same power politics? And isn't it lovely? And debt is the prelude to slavery. And freedom to keep out of debt will not be a tea table subject on the Jew radio or in Roosevelt s regime.

#83 (May 8, 1943) U.S.(C42)
PHILOSEMITE

Waaal, I reckon there must be something worse than Jews in America. At any rate there is one yellow livered snot that yawps over the Schenectady General Electric radio that I would like to take on personally when it comes to a clean up. As my part of the clean up, if there ever is or can be a clean up in the U.S. of A.

Now as for tyranous governments of Italy and Germany, as per the punk end of a codfish, well is the government of Russia a kid gloved democracy, with respect for individual rights? What about the habeas corpus in Churchill's plutocracy? As for the newspaper lies, every newspaperman in America knows what gets into print and what don't. Enough Americans know personally a newspaperman to know what he thinks about freedom to print, and what the advertisers have to say as to what is printed. My comments [of] April 21, 1939 are not likely to get past the copy desk.

That the American press prints news of war disasters means NOTHING whatever regarding freedom of the press. The news is bawled over international radios, so everyone knows it. And it helps to keep the war going, and keep open a market for munitions: why wouldn't loan capital want it printed? What do they care for BAD war news? More smash, more need of loan capital afterwards, to reconstruct devastations.

Tell the cod in Scheneckdety to sell his damaged goods elsewhere. Or bust him one on the puss, if you have a few shreds of decency left in your biceps.

There is not an ounce or atom of honesty in either Churchill or Roosevelt. Most of the reasons for England and America being in the war are unconfessable and indecent. Let us admit that some English and Americans disliked the reported touchiness or roughness of Nazi methods. That did NOT cause the war.

The CONclusive reasons for both England and America being at war are dishonest, basically and fundamentally dishonest.

Refusal of Eden's pimps to live with other powers. Everyone knows the League of Nations was a den of cheats. And the very honest effort of the International Labor Office to work out schemes for world justice or social justice was sabotaged. All this HAD and HAS not been told the American people justly.

England went to war needlessly, the whole war was NEEDLESS. A scheme as far as Roosevelt is concerned to grab world monopolies. What was inevitable after twenty or more years of preparation BY Russia, was a Russo-German war. THAT was on the cards. BUT the area of conflict could have been limited to those two countries. And the English and American governments know it. That is the sort of thing the American and English press and radio DO not reveal to the people. The American people have been betrayed by Roosevelt, and the inflators. And no amount of pi-jaw from Scheneckdety can alter it.

The history of the past 200 years has been kept a mystery. And the printing of a few military disasters or their broadcast by the Scheneckdety whiners will NOT make up for it. [FCC transcript: And it is almost impossible to get anyone to think consecutively or to hold observed facts in mind over a period of years long enough to get them to understand the various details. Straws in the wind they are called.

Now, years ago in a railway train, I talked to some technical robots being shipped into Russia. Russia wanted technicians, and got them. People who wanted a job, who could get lost in a job, people who had no general ideas, no aspiration about making money and no sense of civic responsibility. After all, the sense of civic responsibility is not born in slums or under the starvation lines. Nor is it born anywhere in the middle reaches of the population whose main anxiety from cradle to grave is to get a job and keep it.

Of such is the kingdom of sheep destined to be shorn and led to the slaughter. Technical kids.

Religions, the opium of the people, said Lenin. The late William B. Yeats countered that by saying, "Science, opium of the suburb."

Now, watch the birdy, deane, watch the B.B.C. and the pluto-propaganda transmission after transmission about the details of a job. Civil or even military. But not a word as to why the job is being performed at all. That is one line of hokum to watch, watch it, and also watch the attempt to revive the League of Nations.

Up to now I had thought Wallace an honest man, easily misled by kikes and shysters, but with decent intentions. But one must now face an alternative. Given, I mean, the mass of documentation as to the object, worthlessness and dishonesty of the League as you see, for example, by the reports of the International Labor Office—a man must be either utterly and absolutely irresponsible or else a crook to try to revive any such swindle. And the documentation is there, and no man in a responsible public office, even if he is only a vice president, is excusable for not facing the available evidence.

As for Wallace's talk about arranging a peace, it is time for political puppets, even for political puppets in the British and American government to realize they're in a minority. Until England and American delouse and get rid of her Jew gangs, there is no place for either England or the United States in the new world at all. The present English and American governments are regarded as lepers by most of the world. Ask any cheated Chungking Chinaman or a bamboozled Pole what he thinks of Churchillian and Rooseveltian honor. These sweepings of the various employment agencies are not the world's majority, they are— —. Bulldozed and black mulled South American countries do not support you, they are merely suppressed by you. Corrupted, with her politicians hired by Bill Bullitt's cronies and Donovan's gun sweepers. A clean England and a clean United States might collaborate in a new world, but it will take a hell of a lot of Sapolio to wash off the mess made by Roosevelt and Churchill.

I'm telling you, I'm not giving you the Axis point of view, I'm giving you a terrible estimate, and the news in case the— —who run your radio and most of your press haven't told you. And Russia's contempt for the present pawn brokers regimes in London and Washington is even more vigorous than that of the Axis. The question is how long will it take the clean men in England and America to find out what has happened. Or to get control of at least some of the minor centers of power inside their— —countries.]

#84 (May 9, 1943) U.K.(C39)
LORD BLEEDER

On February 24 Lord BLEEDER, for your pawnbroker's government, defending your pawnbroker's government, said the main purpose of the government after the war ... eh ... he was throwing cold water onto Beveridge's half plan, for giving half a boiled potato per week to the bleeding poor. Lord Bleeder said the main purpose of the government, after the war, would be to pay interest on debt.

I don't know why you don't shoot'em. The main purpose of your having a war is to have a debt to pay interest on. And Stalin like the bleeding Czar before him, killing off 12 million bloody Rhoosians, in order to help the pawnbrokers of London, and elsewhere. The British are mugs.

Now then, IF one had been feeling low after the Russian advances, and if one had been looking round for encouragement and indications of Axis strength, would one have noticed a difference between Berlin and London? YES.

If Germany has been in the hands of the yellow livered cheats and *escros* of your pawnbrokers' government, what would Germany have done? She would have yelled bloody murder for Japan to come hellup her, and attack Russia from the east.

THAT is what England would have done under similar circumstances. And the Axis published agreements are such as to have made the arrangement quite possible. And if the British socialists were anti-capitalists, they would have been attacking loan capital IN England, for the past 20 years or more years, and IF the British communists were real communists instead of the left hand of loan capital, THEY would have been attacking the capitalism of England, the U.S.A., the Jew capital, and the sub-Jew or yellow British capital in the interests of world revolution, instead of standing out.

And that is where the sincere young men who have been caught by socialist and communist ideology in England have been HAD. They have mistaken communist and socialist parties in England (and also in the U.S.A.) for honest parties wanting a world revolution and being out against the capitalist system; and, I repeat, they have been had, bamboozled.

And Mr. Dalton and the rest of'em are shown up for what they are: usurer's narks, undercover men for the bank swine, hollow shams, rank impostors, with no political principles, no social principles, only the old profit motive and lust after a job. Lackeys for a pestulent squirarchy, toadies, germ carriers for syphilitic banks. Wanting to set up a pink regime in England: furnish communism with a House of Lords, and remain the Vicar of Bray, sir. Yours truly, the vicar of Bray, yes, yes, yours jewly, the Vicar of Bray.

The men of principle in England are the men who have gone to jail. They were the patriots who wanted to save your empire. You knew, or should have known that the U.S. was casting lots for your empire, that Russia had more than a century old policy against you for the spoils of your empire. That Italy and Germany needed living space; a few men wanted you to keep out of the war, and to follow a policy of reform, not of atavism. The Jew is atavistic. Communism is not progress but a return to the Anschauung of the nomad, the Tartar tribe: living by rapine. Property is of agriculture. Responsibility, foresight, care of the crops, are agricultural products. The Jew is atavistic: the psychology, may the stink of your camp drive you onward. The herders, having no care but to let their herds browse and move on, when the pasture is exhausted.

So you are allied with your enemies. I don't say all men of principle are in jail, but that is what those who are in jail are IN for. For trying to save you. Will you EVER realize that the mere continuance of the war is a victory for loan capital, a victory for the lenders of money, or for the money monopolist, the controller of monetary issue? Usually foreign controller, or at least private, NOT public controller. Great debt to be made from war: that was [the] American Civil War, to be used to control the currency.

Producers of the world unite. But NOT under secret control of Semitic or any other finance.

What does war cost? Well, a lot of the COST to YOU is the stuff that is NOT made. All energy going to make explosives. All that energy subtracted from making things you WANT to eat and wear. That is part of the cost, irreplaceable. What is exploded, sunk and destroyed is a COST, on which loan capital fattens.

Revolute, revolution, from where to where? From one state of society to another? Never simultaneous all over the world.

But the administration? The control? Peasants prefer to own land. War between peasant and undifferentiated labor, [the] peasant has skill, has knowledge, not to be acquired in two weeks in a Ford factory. No, you don't think. You have, I suppose, a vague feeling that you don't want Bolshevism in England. But you want it to prevent farm ownership BY the actual farmers elsewhere. Now what caused that?

Savings. Another red herring. War savings. Illusion of savings! Saving tickets for something that isn't there. Theatre tickets for a show that never comes off, for a play that never opens? That is another hoax.

Pie in the sky? Pie at the end of the next century? And says Lord Bleeder, main job will be paying interest on public debt. Can you beat it? No social security, no living wage, no reward for labor that will permit two Englishmen, or two Aryans of any kind, to produce and bring up two kids. Well if they don't, the race dies. So you are told to oppose the race issue, and stop being English. No, not change your nature, be Englishmen, but don't BE. Cease to exist, die out. As the frogs did very largely. That is what Mr. Churchill and Eden lead to.

Follow Churchill and Eden and their owners a few steps further and you not only cease to exist as an empire, you will cease to exist as a race. One spot forever England. A lost island in the Aegean. What are you for? What does England exist for? For the upkeep of Lord Bleeder and a few Wall St. millionaires, of mixed origin, some of'em British émigrés, or at least émigrés from London and other parts of your empire.

In order, may we repeat to keep the Teutonic peoples out of the Teutonic city of Danzig, and sell up General Sikorski, in the name of self-determination. And to be able to pray.

You might pray for restoration of at least enough energy to follow your natural instincts, which were to KEEP out of the war, and which are to STOP fighting, now.

All of which is too simple for you to think of. You might stop the war now, at least your part in it. Let it die down. You are in a blind alley. Some of you know it.

#85 (May 11, 1943) U.S.(D1)
SUMNER WELLES

Sumner Welles' speech at Toledo was a carefully prepared indictment, which will hardly convince anyone here in Italy that Mr. Welles should be taken to mean literally what he said.

It is a speech which arouses, and yet almost quenches interest. What he says about America ought to be true. What he says against Germany could, many people will think, have been said quite as truly of Russia, in fact rather more so. Mr. Welles spoke of freedom from economic aggression. No nation has more soberly faced that problem than has Italy. Italy has done almost nothing else for the past twenty-one years. Mr. Welles admits that U.S.A. has not always refrained from economic aggression in the past. He says with some cogency that all the British empire trade preference policy was a form of economic aggression.

Olivia Rossetti Agresti over this radio has adduced a considerable array of data concerning the rather cold reception the idea of Italy's freeing herself from economic aggression met with from the American government, and continued to meet from that source for a considerable time.

Immunity from economic aggression means that nobody has to take stuff they don't want, merely because Russia, for example, dumps it onto'em. You probably did not hear Natalia Troubetzkoi telling you about Russian dumping. That was some months ago. Russia was dumping in the hope of creating industrial unrest.

Moscow was in fact sweating her workers unmercifully, and dumping the results on the rest of the world, according to the worst plutocratic methods. Hollywood and diverse other American sources of production were dumping their products on Europe, and threatening to make war on Italy if Italy didn't go on buying what she couldn't pay for. Of course Mr. Welles may have had a change of heart. His heart may have always been pure. But how can Europe know that? Mr. Welles' firm seemed for so long, so VERY reluctant to take count of Italy's efforts toward autarchy, of Italy's effort to keep out of debt.

Oh yes, autarchy is just what the Avv[ocato] Nicoletti defined it as, in a recent speech at Pisa. Autarchy is, among other things, the freedom to keep out of debt. That phrase is sometimes used here as a slogan. It isn't my personal slogan.

To aggress, economically to aggress, to aggress economically is, among other things to go out with a flock of cruisers and force someone to buy what they can't pay for. The whole of the past life of the S. American continent is one long record of economic aggression. That is one side of the picture.

Then he quite definitely and clearly mentioned the common man's desire to have a house of his own for his own family. That is what we believe national socialism stands for in Germany. It is what Italy stands for. It is quite emphatically what Communist Russia does NOT stand for, and would not stand for by program.

Mr. Welles has made a distinctly anti-communist and anti-Muscovite statement. And yet Russia is hurled upon Europe with the official consent of the American government and the connivance of England. The past record of these three countries on the issue of economic aggression is not such as to tempt any among their old acquaintance.

Do his own work, and get his own provisions. That is what the Axis is askin' for. There were plenty of Italians down there in Africa working their farms. Houses were improvin'. For twenty years we have seen people gettin' better houses, have seen straw covered shacks being replaced by brick houses, built to hygenic specification, curved edges to floors where floor joins wall, so as not to leave dust space for tuberculosis baccillae. Every man his own vine and fig tree. Mr. Welles ought to have spent more time here in Italy, goin"round as I have to Sicily, Apulia, and the Abruzzi. He ought to read Dr. Dietrich on German homesteads. Homesteads you can't lose by mortgage. Mebbe you better MEET Europe.

Now what I believe, war or no war, not waitin' till the war ends, or even putting it second to any military contingency, I believe that every social reform put thru in the Axis countries ought to be DEFENDED. I believe the American people ought to defend those social measures. I will say, as readily as the next man, that a good deal of opposition to the New Deal was due to the worst possible motives. But I have not heard of the New Deal gettin' down to the debt problem. And Mr. Welles' statement that he wants to avoid economic aggression comes as a novelty. I hope he means it. But the idea has not affected Russian policy in the past. It is very hard to see how Mr. Welles expects to believe that Germany wasn't encircled.

As to the "patient toil of centuries," seems like the U.S. was trying to undo as much patient Italian toil as possible. And if he wants bygones to be bygones, he certainly isn't being effective about preventing there being any more bygones. Italy was resistin' absolute slavery, had been doin' so ever since that treaty made at Versailles.

#86 (May 15, 1943) U.S.(D2)
ECONOMIC AGGRESSION

Mr. Sumner Welles' speech at Toledo was a serious matter. It is a great pity that even the majority of his listeners would have been unable to tell one at the end of it what he had said at the beginning. That is, it was a long and close exposition or argument. At the mercy of even minor misunderstandings. It is a pity that auditors do not more often examine the printed text of such a speech. The efficiency of the communication is further impaired when it falls to translators, for the minor shades fade out of language.

Who among the Toledo auditors now remembers whether Mr. Welles said that the subject "economic aggression" probably was, or whether it ought to be, in the minds of all of us. One Italian word translates *next to*, and *after*, I mean that is when a translation is verbally correct at one point, but does not take into account the whole paragraph.

Had I been making a daily or immediate comment I might [have] drawn rash conclusions, or no conclusions whatever. The man reporting on events of the day hasn't time to chew over a text and place it in a general scheme.

Probably few among you thought of correlating the Welles' speech with a talk made a week before by Mr. Agar, speaking from London on the BBC and allegedly connected with the American Embassy.

Had Mr. Welles been ready to make such a speech three years ago, this distressing war might have been quite well avoided.

Mr. Welles appeared to be renouncing dollar diplomacy. If the U.S. had renounced the more aggressive features of dollar diplomacy a few weeks sooner, a good deal of bloodshed might have been spared us. Mr. Welles also spoke of misapprehensions, of incomplete knowledge, of heedlessness, inconsideration. I am perfectly ready to take Mr. Welles' speech at its face value. If the U.S. has been ill-informed or tardily informed of the conditions of Europe, there is no reason for you to remain VOLUNTARILY in that condition, but it is now extremely hard for the people inside ANY country to get accurate impressions of the state of mind of people inside any other.

It has been for years extremely hard to get news INTO America. I have long held that MORE disinterested observers, American observers, should be let loose on Europe. I mean people whose news and view is not limited by what they can sell to the advertisers of a particular paper or group of papers.

Undeniably misunderstandings have arisen, and still arise, and will continue to arise until it is possible for people to talk without heat, and without attempting to read into other men's statement what the speaker or writer never intended to put there.

I mean there is the question of will, the question of good will, of being I; ready to hear what the other man says to you. It is not to be supposed even now that Mr. Welles would listen to me over a table. Or answer what I intended to say during the next five minutes. I have been trying to get news of Europe across the Atlantic for a number of years.

It is today my impression that Mr. Welles was speaking of a Germany which no longer exists. I know that for years the American people were incited against an Italy which was NOT the Italy that I live in.

Before all wars, before any war, there arises a tide of misrepresentation. That sort of thing did NOT begin in this century or the last one. In every country there are groups of people who aim at construction, who reform toil more or less consecutively to ameliorate living conditions. They are often considered impractical. Sometimes they get into office.

There are also in all countries destructive or heedless groups. Sometimes heedless, sometimes almost malevolent. Now to the outer world the American history of the past eighty years appears to be an uninterrupted record of economic aggression on the part of the U.S. The U.S. is the home town of the Rockefellers, Guggenheims, Morgans. The world has had on its newspaper stalls the works of Zischka (I suppose he is a Polish author). Anyhow he wrote the *War for Oil*, the *War for Cotton*, etc. We have heard of the wars for commodities, and the war for GOLD. We have heard much less of the secret war that the U.S. LOST in 1863, while the boys in blue and the boys in grey were obligingly dying and taking the spot light. Our Civil War was at that time a world record for carnage. And both sides were vanquished. The control of the national credit, control of the national currency, the national purchasing power, passed RIGHT away from the people, and right out of the control of the national, and responsible government.

That's why many of Mr. Welles' foreign auditors will think there is a nigger in Mr. Welles' woodshed.

Suddenly a coalition of the three most aggressive powers, economically aggressive powers on earth put forth not an official statement, but a statement by the most authoritative member of the State Department, to the effect that economic aggression is after all a factor in causing wars, and that to obtain a durable peace we must lay off it.

England, Mr. Welles tells us, is aggressive economically. The U.S. has in the past been aggressive, Russia has made up for lost time, and been extremely aggressive quite economically. It does sound to the European almost as if Legs Diamond, or Billy the Kid, or Jesse James had suddenly decided to change his habits. I mean economic aggression has been for so long considered the very breath of life of the American system, the bone of its bone, its inner and intimate fiber.

And then again, when a nation's INNER life is so palpably made up of the economic aggression of one class or group against the whole of the rest of the population, it is very difficult for any foreigner, or indeed for anyone not carried away by the political heat of the moment, to see why that particular nation should be entrusted with the latch key of any other.

I will return to this subject.

#87 (May 16, 1943) U.K. (C41)
ADMINISTRATION

Along about St Valentines day Fraser, what's his name, Fraser of the Breetisch bard ots consorzium discovered administration. With the voice of a sour bellied mongrel, he told us that Germany couldn't bring in the New Order because Germany hadn't enough trained administrators to keep the Soviet hell out of Europe and stave off the baby-killers and bombers of hospitals, and administer a perfect civil system all over Europe.

Q.E.D.

To take up various points seriatim: 1) the rancid hate of the BBC and the inability of Brits in general to recognize other races as human is no card in the British hands. 2) If ever a nation produced efficient bureaucracy, it has been in Germany. 3) Just as if ever a race could colonize and bring civilization and the benefits thereof into colonized lands, that nation is Italy, and that race is the Latin race of this peninsula.

SO THAT.

The reasons Germany's allies can not be pried off by the silly guff about uncertain allies rests precisely on the fact that Germany will need and *want* collaboration from men of good will, which the intelligent allies and several ex enemies recognize I may say that this line of propaganda was already spewed about in America before Eden and the Jews got the war going.

Secondly does Fraser, what's his name the London snarler, think that SOVIET Russia is indicated as the fountain of that perfect bureaucracy which will bring the amenities into all countries overrun by the Muscovites? According to the prayers of the Lamb of Canterbury and the other boot lickers of Britain?

Naturally Fraser being as much a coward as any other servant of Churchill and Jewry will not answer this query. The BBC never answers. And therein lies its damnation, and the damnation of those who tolerate its continuance. Mostly from sheer laziness.

Then again we hear the noble generals English of course Gibraltar the couchant lion, Prudential has the strength of Gibraltar and Gibraltar has the strength of Prudential; i.e., the Prudential Life Insurance Co.

And it is a pity that the noble traditions of the British Army (as distinct from the more obscure patches of English history) should be reduced to doing the dirty work for Moses Sieff and Baruch and the émigré Jews and others who have taken England's titular wealth over to Wall Street.

Generals, often notable for absence from battle fields, as the British Air Force has been absent from major engagements, but present when it comes to bombing civilians, with, until recently, little risk—that is Churchill's warfare. The bombing of civilians, for which his obscene name will stink into futurity.

It is not a man's war. No, bombing of hospital ships and of civilian quarters is not a man's war. And not even the lowest liar on the BBC has claimed that Germany started it. Plenty of sob stuff, but the facts on that line are too strong. Strong is the word. England is NOT making a glorious end. I know many Englishmen think the only way you CAN delouse is by losing the empire. But I am not sure the method is a wise one. I am not sure that the mere impoverishment and ruin of the middle and upper middle and upper English working class in the interest of Jewry, in the interest of loan capital that can migrate and that HAS migrated, is going to land you in that garden suburb desired by Joad, where he an'Uxley, Julian not Aldous, can pass their senility, making model houses for an extinct population and arranging the post-bellum world according to the stipulation of the late Sir J.M. Barrie.

I still almost marvel at the lack of any trace of justice, any demand for justice, BILATERAL justice, in the Anglo American propaganda. Any recognition that anyone not in the Jew Roosevelt, Churchill, Maisky ring, should receive ANY justice whatsoever.

References to Japan are even more idiotic than those to Italy and to the main body of Europe. In matters of civic rights, India remains the untouchable, naturally. It will take more than a few Guards' Uniforms and busbys to cover the basic causes of wars. Of this war in particular. No, Mr. Bull, your heart ain't pure, not by a damn sight. And your brain never was clear by profession. But some of the Bulls must by now recognize that their war was an unjust one, that they ought not to have gone to war for the aims that underlay the hostilities. War on France, France that could have by now recovered, as she did after 1870.

England, [the] worst foe to her allies and whose worst foes are allied to her now.

It is a choice between Europe and Jewry. That at least is clear and out in the open. And England is on the Jews' side, against the rest of humanity. And in a subservient position at that. It is not a glorious position, or even a glorious road to an exit from empire. And the way of life, the amenities, the Englishness of what gave England her prestige, will not be saved for you by Willie Bullitt, or Mr. Lemonface Welles, the silver tea urn, and the rest of it. The powery, the ghetto and Wall Street are NOT at war for the deer park, and the old line of London hatters and haberdashery shops. NOR for the traditions of the guards regiments. NOR for the Polytechnic and Dicken's Xmas Carol, and the garden suburb, the 100 towns of England resurgent. And every day you stick at it is a day FURTHER from freedom from debt. A day deeper in that servitude wherein your overlords had aimed to plunge Europe. How far have you lived your past life at the expense of Oriental cheap labor, of famines in the far Orient? One will never get those statistics.

The Jew is behind you, but you cannot blame it all on the Jew, though you are the Jew's most damned accomplice. Above all you can not blame [it] at all on the small Jew; for he is in most cases as damned a fool and as witless a victim as you are, [he is] the shock troop, the below the starvation line; starvation line, below which there is NO morality. Only the instinct for survival at the cost of whatever baseness, more often heedlessness than planned iniquity; milked by his damned kahal just as you are. Truly, you had great possessions.

And while the BBC was evoking or reconstructing Carlyle, for propaganda purposes they might have included that item from Froude's life of their hero. Carlyle stood opposite the Rothschild great house at Hyde Park Corner, looked at it a little and said: "I do not mean that I want King John back again, but if you ask me which mode of treating these people was nearest to the will of the Almighty about them, to build them palaces like that or to take the pincers for them, I declare for the pincers."

Naturally Monty Norman and Sieff won't have that sort of thing going over the British air. But think what a free radio might mean to England. Carlyle was a historian. Never till you kill off your Churchills and Edens, will you get your history without bandages.

#88 (May 18, 1943) U.S.(D3)
ECONOMIC OPPRESSION

I am going on with my comment of Sumner Welles' speech at Toledo. As I said last time, I think Mr. Welles' view of Europe is a bit out of date. I suffer under similar difficulties when I try to focus America. I have protested against the interruption of communications. I wish more Americans had been hard-headed enough to stay over here in Europe and try to speak to America. I wish that during the twenty and more sad years that followed the Versailles Treaty more Americans had had the patience to learn what was going on in Europe, instead of which, even the better class of journalists were told to HOLD down, hold down on even the rather superficial stuff they usually sent you, let alone on the stuff deliberately colored to suit the real or supposed prejudice of the American newspaper readers.

Now Italy was an open book. I have seen violently prejudiced partisans come to Italy and be much disappointed at not finding food for their polemics. Very few impartial witnesses visited these shores, or at any rate very few who made use of the pen and the typewriter. Serious correspondents, in particular one English correspondent of a highly esteemed British paper, now extinct, complained of the way his reports were doctored. He said to me: "I have to watch every sentence. If they find a single phrase that they can twist or cut out and use as a headline, they do it."

American views of Europe have, I think none of you will deny it—that is, you won't deny it if you stop and think over it—American views of Europe have been influenced, if not colandered thru British newsprint, and British magazine or weekly paper publications. Germany invited the young to come over.

Various people went into Germany and tried to report on factors of German life OTHER than those which Mr. Welles brought into his foreground. After the first flush of pure idealism, days of John Read and Linc Steffens, Russia notably ceased to invite careful inspection. Even Mr. William Bullitt began to have doubts as to the humanity of Russian state administration.

Now admittin' that I may have old fashioned views, admittin' that I may at this moment be speaking to an America that no longer exists, to a type of

American that is almost as extinct as the bison or buffalo, would it occur to any of you that Mr. Welles might be inveighing against a Germany that is no longer the country he visited? He said nothin' about the homestead reforms. There WAS the militarist Germany of the Kaiser, there was the Germany of Mr. Stinnes and Thyssen, but there also IS the Germany of the young fellows who now come down to Rapallo for holidays. God knows they have probably earned'em. No, no I have NOT spoken of Germany in the past. I tried to speak of the Italy that I live in. I tried to convey a knowledge of specific facts, which if not sufficient to prove my particular estimate of the DIRECTION of Italy were at least components that should have been taken into consideration by those responsible for the U.S. relations with Italy.

In EVERY country there are two or more forces; one dispersive or shiftless and, at least in a happy era, another constructive. ANY constructive or positive idea is now labeled propaganda. There is an enormous prejudice vs. what is called propaganda. Yet almost any valid and serious statement IS propaganda in the best sense of the term, The modern world has been fed narcotic. The deadly propaganda IS precisely the shiftless, is precisely the stuff that has built up the prejudice against ALL order, and all coherence.

It is the easiest propaganda to write, and to distribute. It does not have to preach at all. It says *nichivo*, it says, what does it matter, it says let's be funny, let's jitterbug. It is hard to be heard against it. Any tendency to discount it, anybody who makes any attempt to withstand it, gets called a blue nose. Liberty is not a right but a duty. Now what do you know about Italians who can read that on a wall? Nothin'.

A new concept of civics has been built up in Europe. The old mercantilist life went on, violently and unscrupulously. You won't look at the record. You won't count the cost of having your ideas after a TIME lag. Mazzini never got into the American curriculum.

The incidence of this war into a whole series of wars has had very little publicity. I wish to God I could meet Mr. Welles or any other American who wanted to get the thing straight. Mussolini and Hitler are not enemies of the people. You sabotage a constructive effort, the effort both of and for a new generation, by the process of going on with OLD wars. Yes, economic aggression OUGHT to be checked.

I don't believe it can be wiped out all at once, but it might be reduced to a minor tension, to a tension compatible with making trade agreements, such as both Germany and Mr. Welles advertise.

BUT there is the twin brother, or perhaps it would be better to say the PAST tense, the aorist, or continuing past tense, of economic aggression. Namely, ECONOMIC OPPRESSION. What about economic oppression?

Economic aggression IS the prelude to economic oppression.

Now what is the U.S. record for economic oppression of weaker nations? What is the U.S. record, or even Mr. Welles' own record in the matter of economic OPPRESSION of, specifically Italy?. Somewhere, and some time, we should go into this matter, if Mr. Welles or anyone else in the U.S.A. wants to clear up the tangle of political ideology, and of geopolitical tensions. Or if Mr. Agar be so inclined. Let them put their cards on the table.

There are other matters of detail: Does the destruction of the world's historic monuments constitute economic aggression? Does the scattering of explosive pens and pencils, to be picked up by three and five year old children, constitute economic aggression? Are these parts of a coherent program or do they occur in some world whereto Mr. Welles has been denied access? Are we to suppose that NO one is responsible for the marks of the non-aggressive style in Mr. Welles' cosmos?

#89 (May 22, 1943) U.S.(D4)
IN THE WOODSHED

Before paintin' the picture of the nigger in Mr. Welles' woodshed, I think we ought to be clear about Mr. Welles' intentions.

He was talkin' of economic aggression at Toledo, Ohio. That was ten days or a fortnight ago, so I suppose the American people have already forgotten it. Our U.S.A. memory is brief, it is fleeting. Hardly a man is now alive who can remember what Sumner said at Toledo. "Bitter experience of two wars, destroyin' so much which is beyond price, and which has taken the patient toil of centuries to create."

Sounds like as if he was talking of utterly irreplaceable historic monuments, which aren't really objects of warfare. NOT essential objects of warfare. They don't sink any merchantmen.

I want Mr. Welles or someone in authority to sort out TWO kinds of acts. Those having to do with this war, and those intended to embitter mankind, and make way for the next general massacre.

Who wanted the conflict, who has extended the conflict, who has embittered the conflict, for fear that the desire for peace might break out? I mean *out* might become effective too soon for the war makers' comfort.

A young Italian returned from America, knowing the race tracks, and stock exchange and various lines of hard business says to me:

Aw what is the use of your talking. Take a fellow gettin' four hundred dollars a month, and his wife two hundred and fifty, what do they want with peace? They might have been gettin' twenty eight dollar between'em. TELL them, there will be a crisis in ten years' time, and what of it?

That is undoubtedly the hinterland of several districts of the American mind at this moment. Bitter experience of two wars. Well, I remember the old Civil War veterans, the Grand Army of the Republic, settin''round the lobby of the old Mint in Philadelphia. Down there on Chestnut Street with the front of a classic temple. Before it went up to near Columbia Avenue, next to the Baldwin Locomotive Works, to be just one more factory among factories. But nobody talked THEN about the war that the United States LOST.

That is, I tell you, and I go on a tellin' you THAT WAR that the U.S. lost in 1863, and that was followed by the assassination of Lincoln. THAT war is the war that you ought to be winning. Right now.

NOT after, not next to, not waitin' till this war has destroyed the best mosaics in Europe, and shot up a few hundred more or ten thousand more school children, for the [sake] of getting' a bonus. That was the war FOR economic aggression, the war conducin' to economic oppression. And it got very little publicity, or rather it has had waning and paling publicity. Calhoun said something about it. Lincoln knew that it was in process. He said something about the internal enemy.

Now I think the U.S. has been hooked into sabotaging the clean forces of Europe, just as the North was hooked into hostilities against the States that stood out for state rights. I think Mr. Welles himself has been hooked by propaganda. God knows he had a chance to see things in Europe that perhaps I had not. I mean he had high and official contacts, but he didn't set'round for so long. He came the last time, on a mission. He learned, I mean he must have learned a number of things about England, that were not confided to me, for example. And yet, I don't think he has the full picture. I never much thought, until his speech at Toledo, that he was over here to get the full picture. The German capitalists whom he was a cursin' seem to me to be the very people who went OUT of power in Germany. I mean I think that part of his speech is out of date.

If you are trying to be fair, whatever facts you can heap up, I mean facts not mere rumors, to support Mr. Welles' thesis, you got to, I mean you should if you aim at justice, you should take count of another set of facts which I see as standing to total opposition to those Mr. Welles drug into his foreground.

Every social amelioration, every clause of the homestead laws in Germany, every act in Italy put thru [with] the intention of getting a better life for the mass of the people, ought to be sacred.

I mean that part of the Nazi revolution and of the Fascist revolution. Fascist revolution started it first, every part of that new social order, which is the continuation of the strife for the rights of man, of OUR own four revolutions, ought to be sacred. We ought to defend it, just as we ought to defend habeas corpus, and our right to life, liberty and the rest of it. No real liberty without economic liberty. And NO maintainable liberty that does not recognize that the free man has DUTIES. That was the bed rock of Mazzini's sainthood, or the key to his quite impractical historic opposition.

And when I cite "Liberty is not a right but a duty," as I did the other day to a young undersecretary, he opened up; he had been wondering what sort of an animal he had in front of him. And he said: "Yes, THAT is the real Mussolini."

It is NO use puttin' up false horizons. War is too serious. If war has a use, it might be that it destroys false horizons. It never destroys ENOUGH false horizons, and in the heat of the conflict other stage sets are rigged up. Meet Europe, meet Mr. Europe. Something has happened in Europe since Kruger was considered a Titan. But there is the question of TIME in these things, the question of times.

People in Italy ask WHY Mr. Welles chose that particular date to tell us about non-aggression. I can't look into his inner mind. There is in Europe a distinct memory of Mr. Welles as photographed in a French government office with several French politicians, in front of a MAP. Well now, many Europeans took that map at that TIME as indication of a distinct plan, or at least daydream of ... eh ... eh ... of aggression. Of course Mr. Welles may reply that the map didn't mean, or perhaps that it didn't STOP at ... economic aggression. We do need a clear terminology. To Europe, at that time, that map looked awfully aggressive.

Would Mr. Welles specify? At the time he said he just hadn't noticed the map, it was just part of French government scenery.

How, Sumner?

#90 (May 23, 1943) U.K.(D6)
SOBERLY

The moment is serious, just as serious for you as it is for anyone else. For twenty years you have fought against shadows. And now a real danger affronts you. In fact several enemies confront you. Quite solid dangers. You have been stirred up against a Germany that did not exist. For two decades your press has conducted a campaign of defamation against Italy. The campaign of lies does no good to anyone. You included. One expects you to be a bit up in the bottle. Perhaps it will be easier, or more nearly possible for you to *hear* in such a moment than when you are in the doldrums.

The moment calls for realism of a kind more real than you are accustomed to. Let us take down the stage set. It is very easy to fall into rhetoric. It is very easy for people to be swayed by cliché. No one is immune from THAT danger. Least of all men who write in a hurry.

YOU are threatened. You are threatened by the Russian METHODS of administration. Those methods are not theoretic. The theory of Bolschevism has never constituted a danger to England. Mr. Churchill knows quite as much about Bolshevik METHODS of administration as anyone else. Mr. Churchill has in the past expressed himself quite clearly on that subject. Nothing equivocal about Winston's words when referring to Russia under Bolshevik rule. The mass graves at Katyn surprised NO one.

BUT the Russian system of administration in Iran, for example, is not your sole danger. It is, in fact, so far from being your sole danger that I have, in over two years of talk over this radio, possibly never referred to it before.

Usury has gnawed into England since the days of Elizabeth. First it was mortgages, mortgages on Earl's estates; usury against the feudal nobility. Then there were attacks on the common land, filchings of village common pasture. Then there developed a usury system, an international usury system, from Cromwell's time, ever increasing. That system gave you your slums. It brought in that civic leprosy that has made England a byeword. It has taken the shock of this war, three years of war to jog your memory, to bring your slums up again into headlines.

The usury system does NO nation good, it does no nation any good whatsoever. It is an internal peril to him who hath, and it can make NO use of nations in the play of international diplomacy save to breed strife between them and use the worst as flails against the best.

It is the usurer's game to hurl the savage against the civilized opponent. The game is not pretty, it is not a very safe game. It does no one any credit.

A ruined Europe gives you no market. A ruined England will give no market to the new usury control.

Systems grow rotten and die. You have thrown Poland, had thrown half of Poland, to Russia, not in any attempt to save Poland. With the new Russia you have no longer any need of that particular dagger thrust into Germany's vitals. Russia constitutes a quite sufficient counterpoise to German force, now that they have a common frontier.

Let me interrupt myself at this point, to be perfectly clear as to my own convictions. EVERY social reform that has gone into effect in Germany and Italy should be defended. And the best men in England know that as well as I do. The time of calumny is past, and its passing should be seen very clearly. It should be seen very clearly IN England. Colonial empires should be administered by those nations who can best TEACH how such empires can and should be administered. That sentence perhaps needs a whole talk to itself.

The usury system rots the earth. It is a malady dangerous to ALL people. As your own slums can testify. The usury system has ruined millions of poor devils in England just as it has brought misery to millions in India. And that system is shifting its central. That shift represents NO gain to your American allies. It merely means an increase of vigor, it means a new and more violent infraction of America's 120 millions, and that infection will do YOU no good. Your middle class will be engulfed, London will feel the blow as Vienna felt the blow after the last war. That is to say, the glitter of scum, the feverish distribution of tidbits among a privileged few, and among the art world surrounding "society" will decline.

The nomadic parasites will shift out of London and into Manhattan. And this will be presented under a camouflage of national slogans. It will be represented as an American victory. It will not be an AMERICAN victory. The moment is serious. The moment is also confusing. It is confusing because there are two sets of concurrent phenomena, namely, those connected with fighting this war, and those which sow seeds for the next one. Your leading men ought to *see* that. You ought to see it.

It should constitute food for reflection. For YOUR reflection. You are between two very rough millstones.

#91, FCC Transcript
(May 24, 1943) U.S.[?] [TITLE UNKNOWN]

The Italians in America will have noted the American inability to understand what Italy is, the inability to acknowledge the American debt to Italy. The average American admits that the continent was discovered by Christopher Columbus. The more cunning are disposed to believe that Columbus committed a grave error.

But seriously speaking, how many Americans have you met who know that the constructive ideas to which is due the creation of the North American Republic, the United States, were an Italian product? Does one speak at Harvard and in the other great American universities of the Leopoldien Reforms? The Tuscan history of the 18th century is almost completely ignored by the Americans. I say, "almost," advisedly.

Have you met in America a man of politics who does know anything about 16th century Tuscany? Perhaps they have heard somebody speak about some painter or musician, but of the policy, the reforms—I wager—never.

The American is disposed or was disposed to acknowledge theoretically an intellectual debt to France.

Perhaps he believes that the American Revolution was due to the French revolution. This is to say that they are ignorant of the dates, also having forgotten that the French Revolution took place a decade after the end of the American revolution. The ideas of Leopoldo were largely experimented with under the Grand Duke Pietro Leopoldo, in Tuscany.

The errors of exaggerations, manifest in the materialization of ideas or ideals, were also known. And his son Ferdinand went about correcting them, aided by the very same counselors who had aided his father.

This movement of castigation was interrupted by the French disturbances and by the chaos brought about by the Jews, who took part in the French chaos.

One waited more than a century to continue the rectification, to continue the historical process, in the constructive sense. I do not tell you on whose part, because perhaps many among you are not yet ready to recognize these further manifestations of the Latin's genius! The more or less military gentleman Fiorello La Guardia is not possessed of the Latin spirit (genio).

The classical mentality differs from the Rooseveltian. And it seems stupid to me for one to entrust himself to a Lehman or a Morgenthau. None among these American officials possesses the Latin spirit. I would say that the Italians do well, every time they run true to their own spirit, the Italic, the Latin (spirit).

I would say that they are doing well to differentiate that spirit from the Gaelic spirit. I would say that you would do very well to investigate it a bit, to search, if possible, for the causes of the confusion.

I know that your situation is difficult. The American press does not guide you and does not help you, but rather admonishes you to forget your own culture, your Italic instincts, your language, the most beautiful daughter of the mother Latin (language). Do not yield! Persevere in reading your Italian books among yourselves. Those among you who have the opportunity to get into universities, must retain their Latin culture, not looking backward, but forward.

France did not create Latinism. And rather, I say to you, insist, persist! You are American citizens. The America of the Fathers of the Republic worshipped Latin wisdom. That America of the— —ones has almost disappeared, forgetting the Latin wisdom. That Latinism is preserved in Italy; it manifests itself anew.

I divide this short address into different parts. I say that the Americans around you ignore the Italian tradition. You ought to educate them, and first of all you ought to educate yourselves.

I say that in observing the Americans you will note that they are anarchic, profoundly anarchic, not organized, do not apply their own inventions. When an idea is born or seems to be born, in America, that idea does not sprout in America itself. When propaganda is made on a sound idea in America, something impedes its fertilization.

For instance, the battle against gold was fought half a century ago in the United States; it was fought by the Democratic party. William Jennings Bryan was a great orator—more or less an orator with a large popular following. But he cried out to the world that humanity was being crucified on a golden cross. But he did not speak with perfect frankness. He spoke of silver (sic) instead of speaking openly of money.

All the truth, or almost all the truth, about money had been known in the United States already for a century, but Bryan did not reveal it completely. Now the world all of Europe and a large part of Asia know that the monopoly of gold and the fiction of money based on gold is an infamy an instrument used to fool the people, to strangulate all the peoples. I say that this idea has had in the past, it has had great publicity in America. But the American is slow. He has not placed high the wisdom of his best men. And the same thing with electrical experiments. You probably do not know that in 1863, a certain Loomis succeeded in sending wireless electric signals, he invented wireless telegraphy. But the Americans did nothing about it.

He was considered a madman, a fool. The world was waiting for the Italian genius of Guglielmo Marconi, before putting into practice the possibilities of wireless transmissions.

The same thing is taking place in the political and economic spheres. And, if you wish to understand true economics, you must look outside the damned American press. You must read that which is being printed in Europe, in Italy. And for the moment it being difficult to obtain printed press, you ought to listen as much as possible to the European transmissions and the European addresses in this connection, in connection with money, with credit, with money on the basis of work, with work that you have—every one of you—residing in your brains and brawn.

Ezra Pound speaks from Rome, in a regime under which liberty is considered a duty; and where one knows that economic freedom carries with it the freedom from falling into debts.

#92 (May 25, 1943) U.S.(D5)
AND BACK OF THE WOODSHED

I am not going to go into the details of Mr. Welles' schemes; I can't in ten minutes get down to as many details as he put forth in an hour. And as for your international currency scheme, your allies in London and Mr. Keynes can, I'spose, be counted on to put up a much more audible howl. Though whether it will be loud enough, or have any effect, remains for the chroniclers of the future.

Economic aggression. Economic oppression. Economic oppression, the past tense, and the future tense of economic aggression.

Welles admitted that the U.S. had in the past participated in the aggression. Now does he propose, or does the State Department really propose to lay off certain forms of economic oppression after this war is over? If so, can the State Department really assure itself or anyone else that the American business man will consent to mislay or to lay off economic aggression?

England and America made ugly, England pretty well gutted by economic oppression? By the economic aggression that has reduced England so largely to a C-3 population to national health statistics that no British government bureau dares print. When you talk of economic aggression or oppression your European hearers say: My God, their whole life, the whole life inside both those countries is one compost of economic oppression. That was what we were resisting. That was what was held over us. God knows Italy wanted to work, and to EARN economic freedom. She didn't go round weeping and asking someone to give her the earth on a platter, or any slice of the earth on a platter. She sent out her roadmakers and plowmen. No, no, by right a colonial space, land space ought to be administered by the folks who will use it.

Italy's colonies never tried to hide living conditions. Which is NOT what Mr. Welles can say for America's strange ally Russia. *Vide* the Stalin canal, *vide* all those known liquidations which lead the Christian Science Monitor to say "the thing was not such in itself as to arouse incredulity" (or whatever the words were. I am quoting from memory, but that was the gist of it).

There is a great deal of undisputed and incontroversial evidence about Soviet Russia that makes many things "not impossible," not such as to'rouse incredulity.

For every honest word, for every constructive statement in Mr. Welles' speech in Toledo, Italy was and IS the United States' natural ally. She was England's natural ally UNDER any system that had even a tendency toward eschewing economic oppression. She was the natural partner and guardian of one of England's main trade routes.

Twenty years ago, when I saw Italy risin', when I saw the constructive work toward economic justice startin' in Italy, I had a wild idea, an impractical idea due to my ignorance of economic geography at that time. I say AT that time; I wish more men of my age would come out and admit that they once knew less than they now know. Mr. Welles has made a good step forward. He has talked of aggression of the selfish and unenlightened kind. Well, aggression is probably selfish, and as for economic cooperation, if Mr. Welles' little group had started thinking of economic cooperation WITH Italy ten years ago, we would most certainly not be now in bloody conflict.

And I don't think Mr. Welles is yet ready to make a dispassionate and thought-out, reasoned, analyzed, articulate statement of the fact about Italy and about Germany and about the corporate state.

I think a man in his position ought to make honest comparisons. There is, God knows, enough ground for friction, there are enough REAL contrasts of interests without building up false horizons. You don't need to slander an enemy, not when you are bombing his cities, his women and children, the noncombattants.

A man might think he had to lie about some foreign country in order to get a war started. But now the war is a goin' on. It will take more than a clear statement about either opponent to bring it to a conclusion.

Further slander or further misrepresentation of the nature of the Axis regimes is just so much waste motion. Economic collaboration. That is the front name and the last name of corporate organization. And the doin' away with the laws of God is part of the Russian program, not of the Roman program. Hang it all, a new ethics has grown up, an ethics of responsibility, of the responsibility of him that hath. The revolution goes on, under the fireworks and the polemics.

The corporate state is a state in which representation of interests have been revived, after its lapse in the parliamentary countries. I mean to say the division of the representation is programmed to be by trades; if America went corporate, I would be MORE represented in the confederation of artists and professional men than I would be as a citizen of Montgomery county, though I would or could also be a component of both articulations. And the YOUNG men in Italy, and the Hitler Jugend have nothing whatever to do with economic aggression. That ain't the way they are geared.

The Italians are, by the way, by temperament so full of the Renaissance tradition that you will know a man for two years without finding out how he spends his time. 1 mean he is autarchic, often to a surprisin' degree, whereas freedom in the anti-Axis countries has in many cases been perverted or watered down into the one freedom, namely economically to aggress onto everyone or anyone else.

Of course Mr. Welles was speaking interiorily. He wasn't speaking to the outer world as the representative of America's, of the U.S.A.'s foreign policy. He is merely part of the State Department and may have been speaking in propria persona, as part of some local political strategic plan. In which case, let us say, his aggression wasn't in the least economic, it was just political aggression directed against that soft egg Wendell Willkie, or something of that sort.

Has the State Department participated in Mr. Welles' view about ANY sort of aggression? The speech is of interest, but it hasn't exactly swept the world off its feet yet. And the root question subsists: How is the world to be expected to believe that any nation whose inner life consists, and has so persistently consisted for the past eighty years, or more years, in the absolutely unbridled, not to say, in the old sense, LICENTIOUS aggression of the rich against the poor, of the money lenders against those who do not print and coin money. How, I repeat, is the whole world to be led to believe that unbridled economic aggression in the home can in any degree whatsoever fit any country to acquire overnight a belief in international non-aggression?

England, Russia, America, certainly three outstanding aggressors.

#93 (May 29, 1943) U.S(C46)
SURPRISE

America is a surprisin' country. A SURprisin' country, anything can happen there, provided it isn't too good. Anything, except let us say a treasury, a national treasury without Jews, or government contracts with a rake off. Why, now people here think that bootleggin' of licker might be being followed by bootleggin' of petrol and nearly everything else: everything that is supposed to be rationed.

But I dare say it hasn't been. I dare say no one started high jacking sardines and pimentoes and canned tomatoes.

Mr. John Adams, whom I have mentioned before in these causeries, remarked that very few people in his time had studied systems of government. He was referring to LEGAL system of government. It might be remarked that in our time very few people have written seriously of definitely criminal or illegal system of government. About ten years ago a very interesting study of gangsterism, gang rule, appeared in Paris.

Had to be printed in Paris'cause anything unfavorable to Mr. Churchill's owners, the Rothschilds, is unlikely to get printed in London; has for years been very difficult to print in London, which was during all the grimy and filthy XIXth century the chief stronghold of kikery; with Paris a formidable rival in high corruption, monopoly, and financial swindles, never so decorous as the top-hatted Yidd rule in London.

Mebbe the book was printed a bit before 1933. My copy is labeled, 2nd edition enlarged.

However, not to raise undue prejudice, let us consider some habits of gangster, or the nature of American gangsterism.

Has it been observed that the head gangster occasionally takes steps to get some guy acquitted? Not of course by proof of the ruffian's innocence, but by "other means," let us say "other means." Has this a precedent? Have you looked into the history of crooked acquittal or an attempt at crooked acquittal?

Can you divide control into two sorts, open and secret? And if so, have you, or your professors, your teachers history, yet given sufficient attention to the history of secret controls, to the history of secret taxation?

Don't start with a parti pris, don't start with a prejudice. Don't assert that any one race has the monopoly of secret controls, or of a technique of secret taxation. Look into it. Think a bit about secret taxation. Then think of law. I know that is hard. It is antipathetic, unsympathetic, no American likes to think about law, let alone keeping it. But still, draw back a moment, think about law. What is the aim of law? And of law codes?

Is law there to preserve public order? Is it all like traffic regulations, designed to keep things moving more comfortably for the public? Or is there another kind of law, or code, or regulation, just made to give the beak a chance to shove FINES on to the public? And if so, can you distinguish it?

I should say it was fairly easy to distinguish the moment one starts looking at any law code from that angle. Code or hoax, or codification of fool regulations would be sought by the— —"cui bono," the old question, WHO gits the rake off? Where do the fines go? Who gets'em?

When you, those of you who are my age, and were old fashioned and read the Bible in childhood, when you did, IF you did, you did NOT read it with curiosity. Francis Train read it with curiosity. I remember him as an old man with white hair settin' tilted back, settin' in a wooden chair out in front of the Brevoort Hotel and being told as a seven year old kid, that is Francis Train, and wondering what that meant. A man who got jailed in our marvelous country for reprinting the Bible, in bit, and trying to distribute it via the postal system. I hear he was got on the charge of distributing indecent literature.

Is that history, or is it folklore? I have seen it printed as fact. But I don't assert it. But mebbe he did read The Pentateuch with curiosity. Ours is a marvelous country. I won't even swear it was before the Brevoort Hotel, but it was down in that part of town somewhere, I dare say Mencken would verify, or produce an accurate statement.

A hundred million dollars in TAXES were said to have been collected for the rebuilding of Palestine.

How were they collected? One malicious author, not German I think, said that Rothschild, I think it was the Paris Rothschild, GAVE 80 million for Palestine but cleaned up 100 million by selling real estate in the desert and parts adjacent. That, I take it, did not refer to the collection of "taxes."

Sampter in her guide to Zionism says that the League of Nations is an old Jewish idea. In practice the League at Geneva was certainly dirty, no prejudice was needed to see *that*. We saw it in London in 1918, I think, or shortly after. Long before the words antisemitism were widely current in my little entourage. The League was certainly DIRTY. And here is Rabbi, or mebbe not Rabbi Sampter, saying the idea is Jewish.

British mandate to the Holy Land, over which the Jews exercised complete control in practice, leaving the English taxpayer the expense of civil administration.

Well, you paid for that I suppose, in British defalcation on debts to America. But the AIM now, as it don't look as if the British would ever again pay up on anything, the aim, as for the civil administration pro tem in Persia, and anywhere else the loan capital percolates, the aim NOW is for the American taxpayer to pay the EXPENSE on all lands, eastern, western and central; Chinese (fading bet on the Chinese Nepalese) and West African, for all lands that the Jew is to control completely in practice. The AIM is to leave the expense of the civil administration to the American taxpayer. Along with the interest on billions of dollars, pesos, baksheesh, or other monetary units and denominations. Yes, the interest payment on ALL debts, ancient and modern, domestic and foreign, all debts contracted by friend and foe, inside or outside America is to fall on the AMERICAN taxpayer, along with the strain on all inflations and all deflations. You are to get into debt in CHEAP money. You are to have your canned goods controlled, your imports and exports cut off. And when you have got six hundred billion in debt, you are to be left with [the] debts of your Allies, and then will come Wee Willie Willkie or some other trump card from the left sleeve of Jewry, and quadrupple the burden, by putting you back onto a solid dollar, worth five or ten the one wherein you get indebted.

It is a marvelous country, yes, yes, the U.S.A. is a marvelous country.

#94 (June 1, 1943) U.S.(C47)
BIG JEW

Don't go for the little Jews, go for the big Jews, and study KAHAL organization. Fry says you can start with the betrayal of Jews: the sell out of Maccabaeus or whoever to the Romans.

Barral goes back to the split between Judah and Israel. Fry states that he was attemptin' to present a study of the "inner structure of a system that has produced and still foments racial enmity," and has "even" undermined certain civilizations and overthrown established national governments.

That was printed at least ten years ago. He seems to [have] been moved by the Balfour Declaration.

The Russian steamroller was to have crushed Europe, and then it exploded. The English exploited the Arabs. Dear Lord Rothschild, yours sincerely Arthur James Balfour. Certain Jews, not all Jews wanted a national home. And you all remember Mr. Wilson, most of you forget if you ever knew the Balfour Declaration took the form of a letter to dear Lord Rothschild, signed, as I have just quoted, "Yours very sincerely A. J. Balfour."

It was of course a lie as was pretty much the whole life of Balfour. It being clearly understood that nothing shall be done which may prejudice the civil and religious rights of existing non-Jewish communities in Palestine or the rights and political status enjoyed by Jews in other countries. Six weeks later Allenby entered Jerusalem He had been loafing about in the desert for four months before that according to some accounts Colonel Lawrence was not wholly satisfied by his country's role in or rather subsequent to, the adventure.

I don't know that Rothschild shed a tear when speaking to Balfour. But either he or some subsequent series of events aroused Monsieur Fry's curiosity, so he concluded that in studying the Jewish people, special attention should be given to Jewish *community*. Peculiar secret order that for 20 centuries had got itself disliked and talked of, administrated its own laws, often in defiance of the laws of the land it was lodged in.

Jewish history doesn't STOP with Josephus. It continued, but has been singularly neglected by people who disliked the Jews. This was just as dangerous for the mugs, or Aryans as some call'em, as to leave the evidence unstudied. The American school books have been wholly castrated. They say nothing of [how] Cromwell brought back the Yidds into England. They do NOT compare the dates of the Battle, of Newbury, Marston Moore, Laseby, execution of the English 1649, with the date of the foundation of the Bank or Stank of England, a bit over 1/2 a century later. Nothing about the embassy that the Kikes in Constantinople sent over to see [whether] Cromwell was really the chewisch Messiah (he possibly wasn't).

Mebbe he wasn't. There was blood shed in Ireland. There was ultimately a split between the English in America and the English and England.

My table of dates marks 1693, "The national debt begun." Well that is all an old story. Nicole's tables start with the year 200, so he don't mention the chews at all, not even Josephus. Fry on the other hand is interested in chewisch organization, the separated and Sadoc, "certain political clubs," the siege by Vespasian.

After which they were entrusted with imperial government and administration of Palestine. After the sack of Jerusalem, destruction of the temple and death of the patriot leaders, and all the family.

Erafman, Jewish Brotherhoods, I don't suppose there is an American edition? Or is there? It was published in Vilna.

Other agents were posted at doors of shops, hotels, business houses, lawcourts, and even in the private houses of government officials. These trained agents had each a special field to cover: police, export, import, exchange, government supplies, lawsuits, etc.

The duty of an agent assigned to lawcourts was to keep constantly in touch with the proceedings or with the officials, meet the petitioners, and when practical, fix the sum they must pay for a favorable judgment. Report on all this carefully filed. Don't think America is the true home of all novelties. All this is very old story. Don't go for the poor Jews. Don't pick on the amhaarez. Look into the system.

In fact the lone Jew is subject of study. He seems a good fellow, but is he in some way cut off from the organization? Has he declined to kiss the magic rod ... is he in exile ... is that why he has apparently no more luck than the goyim?

What the devil do YOU know, what the devil does anyone in America know of the Shulchan Aruk, or the alleged fights between Ginsberg and Herzl? The whole subject is so infernally boring. It is so sickening that we would rather pass over it. God knows, I don't want to go into it.

If you would run your own government properly. If you would think out a clean code of ethics. If you would make use of the machinery our respectable forebears bequeathed us, you wouldn't need to be bothered with Jewry, and the peculiar story of Jewry and its peculiar, oh VERY, organization.

But you have not used the machinery set up by our forebears. You have betrayed the national founders.

You have NOT kept the Constitution in force. You have not developed it according to its own internal laws. You have not made use of the machinery provided IN the Constitution itself, to keep the American government modern. The main protection of the WHOLE people is in the clause about Congress issuing money. But that is not the whole of the Constitution.

There is nothing in it to prevent an adjustment of, or progress from, LOCAL articulation; administration divided by geographic division, toward articulation by trade and professional organization.

BUT you have NOT wanted to maintain the Constitution. You have NOT wanted, that is, you have not had a WILL, to maintain the Constitution or to maintain honest just government.

And now I hear New York meat is slaughtered by chewisch butchers, or was a decade ago. Mebbe now there is of it to slaughter. Mebbe all American meat is slaughtered by Jewish butchers. Beef as wuz.

Long pig as may be. (Yaaas, long pig is what the cannibals call it.) But their preparation of it is for consumption, not merely as carnage.

Yes, Yes, and LINKS between the societies. Sir Moses Montefiore, D.I. Lowe, Rabbi Cohn, Strahun, Magnus, und Silberman, that was in 1864, and [?] lowitz, Times correspondent and Reuter. Brotherhood for enlightenment. Lernestein, Ginzberg, Lalischer: there is a lot to the story. And the worst of it is that, if you spend your time looking into it, it will prevent you from filling your mind with the light of the classics, and may tend to distract you from inheriting our cultural heritage.

#95 (June 5, 1943) U.S.(C48)
DEBT

Will you folks back in America NEVER realize that you are fightin' this war IN ORDER to get into debt? I mean just that, you have been dumped into the war IN ORDER to get into debt. To get in further, to get in up to the chin, the throat. To get into the morass up to your eyebrows and no man living can see WHEN you will get out of it.

Wars are made to make debt. The other reasons are hooey. It don't in one way matter who got you into it. In another way it matters a lot; because WHEN you discover who got you into it, you may begin to cast round toward, begin to wonder WHY you are in.

Debt is an implement for creatin' and enforcin' slavery. Your Rhoosian allies are slaves of an infernal state, life sentence. You have pretty nigh got a life sentence. Prosperity WAS just round the corner. Now it ain't, not by a darn sight. It is NOT just round the corner. And the LONGER you go on being at war, the further off it will be.

Lunacies, manias, collective hallucinations are abstract. They are general. They do NOT look at the FACTS in front of their noses. As for example Mr. Hopkins, dispeptic Harry.

Now Europe is fighting quite definitely for something concrete. Europe is also fighting for something avowable.

The ashes of his fathers and the temples of his gods? [Thomas B. Macaulay]

Those also are something worth fightin' for. Great odds were NOT against you in 1939. Nothing threatened your welfare.

You are NOT fighting for the bonnie blue eyes of old England. That much is at least, and at last pretty clear. England is getting indebted. She WAS indebted. She is now MORE so. Do YOU get anything out of it? I think most of you do not, and *will* not. You most certainly did not, last time. If Mr. Hopkins is to be believed, you are already constricted, and Harry hopes you will be more so.

Sadism is one form of mania. Do you NOTICE it, in particular cases, does it appear amongst ye, in any PARTicular instance?

Have you by contrast ever known a single case in which a mortgage did any positive GOOD to a farm? Have you ever known a case in which a debt benefited the debtor? In which the necessity to pay some interest per month or per year on a loan was of any positive use to the borrower? And if your personal interest payments on a loan or a mortgage exceeded your income, would it help you to sleep and eat? Your allies, the English, had the edge on you some years ago, but they are NOT very intelligent. Some of you see a net gain in things, mostly territory that used to be English, and that seems likely to belong to the U.S.A. someday, if somebody don't take it from you. It don't strike me that anybody in Europe ever had any intention of takin' it from you. But then there is Asia. Russia is largely in Asia. Russia and Japan are NOT at this moment at war.

Mr. Wallace foresees danger of war with Russia unless Stalin will eat angel cake and give you the icing. Mr. Stalin once spoke harshly of loan Kapital. He once upbraided the Czarist regime with having spent a lot of Russian blood in the interest of the loan sharks of Paris and London.

Why would he eat angel cake out of Wallace's kitty-bag?

Why wouldn't he be ready to divide up with Japan, say a sphere of influence in Alaska, while the men of Nippon went down to eat kangaroo meat and take a dip in the Australian wool trade?

Mr. Wallace's propensity to venture forth on the apple bough is such as would cause perturbation to any nation less acephalous than that now inhabiting the N. American continent.

Now lest you think I am making this up as I go along, or lest you think my view is tinged by opinion picked up in the Mediterranean basin, let me quote you one of your "allies" who wrote it back in 1931, in Mr. G.K. Chesterton's paper.

Let me be serious. Let me animadvert, or at least cite a few passages from J. Desmond Gleeson on winning the War. Oh no, not THIS war. The last war. Gleeson was writing in 1931 on winning the last war. They saw the golden sun setting in the West. They certainly did win the war and the losers stood about the shores of their ancient continent looking toward the newer continent where the world had begun splendidly again.

I prefer G.K. Chesterton's style to Gleeson's. Quote:

But though it seems a criminal thing to say the business men of America were not quite so business like as they should have been. They organized a scheme of debts due to themselves and appointed a chief debt collector, but neglected to close down all workshops in the U.S.A.

They piled up stacks of finished stuffs designed for every imaginary purpose. They anticipated the wishes and set a whole complicated and expensive process in motion that should FORCE individuals to own to the wishes that the big business man wished them to wish.

That is a rather florid prelude, a florid way of expressing the prelude to the present mass slaughter, but go back and read it.

There were, according to Gleeson, but two ways out. Either the manufacturers must distribute their goods free of all cost … or they must stop the incoming tribute at least for a space. By riddin' themselves of their goods without charge they might still go on with their production. Or by cutting off the gold stream, the gold might accumulate abroad and THEN be used for purchase.

That was the end of Hoover.

The process of buying the gold with dollars, thereby robbing the American people of THEIR purchasing power as well, was another ultimate flower in the Talmudic garden.

It is not, and has not been my purpose in these talks to speak of this war as an isolated phenomenon, a bit of meteorite fallen from some other planet.

My function is to arouse a little curiosity about a PROCESS. War is PART of a process. Some men would want to know what part of a process it is, and what process it is a part OF.

#96, FCC Transcript (June 12, 1943)
U.S.(C55)
[THERAPY]

Some of you are trying to save a rotten system of economics and get the Jews out of it. As in the case of a man who had syphillis and wanted to cure his left arm of it without curing his right arm.

Hitler exposed the wheeze practice in every war and post-war period and sometimes between wars; namely, of cheating the public by inflation and then making the debtors pay double. Simple swindle. Man gets into debt in dollars worth one bushel of wheat and has to pay in dollars worth two bushels.

And the Aryan shysters in Wall Street, lone wolves, have thought they could go on forever beating the organized kikes.

Well, there are sane basis of economics. There are sane basis of ethics. Henry Ward Beecher's religion probably wasn't one of them. That is, wasn't one of them. That is, wasn't a basis of ethics. Religion reduced to border speculation is not an ethical basis.

Shucks. We can say it in less pompous words. Can we? Maybe not, damn it. But as joyriding is said to be on the wane, amongst you except for the black market purposes, try force for a change. Diversion is not open to all, but the elite might try it on Wednesdays or on alternate Wednesdays. Instead of cross word puzzles, the last refuge to your British allies.

I shall have to annoy you by remarking on the advertising game. That is a nail in your coffin. But it is so much a part of your Sundays that it seems— —to suggest that it ain't all for the slickest and loveliest, in the loveliest streamlined world.

What would you do without advertisements? Good wines need no push. Many of you are cocked to the eyes with tobacco; liberty, liberty, liberty, to smoke. I'm not getting censorious. I'm only trying to get you to think about a few things, about anything that you haven't taken for granted, or that you have taken for granted.

How much advertising in the United States is devoted to smoke and synthetic liquor? Why? What started it? Advertising has [led] the American people away from the soda cracker at ten cents a pound.

Some could be worth two— —at the turn of the century, it has led them to the six ounce package. Six ounces of crackers and two ounces of paper wrapping. Oh yes, hygenic wrapping.

Nobody in 200 years of American history ever got poisoned by soda crackers. Hygiene is a— —on the unessentials. Oh yes, a few ounces of real stuff somewhere in the hygienic wrapping. The nation's booze bill and tobacco bill, the campaign seven years ago against alcohol and tobacco. There has never been a campaign against good wine in Europe, not so's you'd notice.

Artificial demand. Ruin of the nest. Ruin of the quality for sake of the profit. Raw nations, uncivilized, in the deep sense of the word. Contrast. No can— —said the old Chinese silk merchant to the traveller who wanted to know why a certain bolt of silk was so expensive.

I bought some myself in London in 1914 of an old firm; three lots, three different kinds for three pairs of pajamas. Result, one pair went with the first washing, I kicked and got it replaced. Second lot lasted normal time or a bit over. The third pair, I've got six of them left now, after 29 years.

What I am getting at is that we, as of Shakespeare, all the quality in the product pre-date the advertising— —which is at— —, an attack on the just price. I know it isn't a hundred percent attack on the just price, but if by any miracle two percent of the American spirit, or six men in Congress would start thinking things out from the bottom up, you might even discover Europe and know what is going on here in Europe.

German revolution, a revolt of the— —brothel against the— —. American mammas have not thought of it that way. And the intelligent— —has had 150 years of propaganda for the— —. Disguised as romantic literature and disguised because of a falsification. At first the Romantic literature was something sane. Then it got rotten. It began with a return to nature. Purity of nature is against the rottenness of artificial society. How come it went rotten? Oh, one thing leads to another. False standards of puritanism lead to revolt, quite properly.

It is now very hard to touch on such subjects at all without sounding like a Methodist elder or killjoy.

All I can say is that nobody with a knowledge of facts can claim that I have passed my life in gloom and without a fair share of the pleasures. This is not a Salvation Army meeting. I merely maintain that I have seen more pleasure loosed on the evening air at a marshmallow roast than in any— — de Nuit in Montmartre.

Dreary cafes, with a few worn out [hags] and the usual staff sitting around, hoping against hope that something will come in from outside and spend money; and hope dies hard. Hoping somebody will come in and entertain them or introduce a little variety.

Well, you can get Wyndham Lewis' book on what Germany was like before Hitler took over. Now just why have you had so much anti-German dope for the past 25 years? Why are you so bone ignorant of present day Italy? The advertisers, do advertisers advertise for the benefit of the public? What was being sold to you while you were being put off Europe? Why, you've been hornswoggled down the back lane into scarcity. I'm not trying to sell you anything, I'm not making a speech or delivering an argument. I'm trying to open up a chink for the light to come through. Italy has not advertised. Nobody in the United States knows anything about Italy.

What are Italians like, for example, apart from opera tenors? The Italians sit on their own base, they eat out of their own plate. You know a man here three years, suppose he is a journalist like any other. So he wrote the weekly paper over a pseudonym. Then you find out he had done a translation of Aeschylus, that is, the original. Clear as a pane of glass.

There is the Agamemnon in front of you, in front of anyone who can read Italian. You probably been put off [from?] Aeschylus with a bum English translation by a very— —. The— —, as Mr. Eliot puts it, has [erected?] between author and reader a barrier more impossible than the Greek language. No surprises like that can happen here in Italy.

What is the level of American general ignorance about the real nature of Italy? I leave it to you, brother. You have been misinformed about pretty nigh everything having to do with this old continent of Europe. That is why you would have done well to keep out of European affairs.

The depth of American ignorance about everything in Europe hallucinations is as bad as— —delusions, that Europe is what Sassoon and Warburg has represented it to be, in— —giving you cream with your oatmeal. Just like they made you [think?] the whole of Serbia was composed of a gang of Jews, Croatian Jews in— —and— —. And that is, they made you believe this gang of yids with New York connections represented the farmers in Serbia.

And that goes on for the whole shabingo. You know nothing of Europe and you go on believing what Roosevelt wants you to swallow, that is to say, supposing even he knows what he wants you to swallow.

#97 (June 13, 1943) U.K.(C44)
TO THE MEMORY

You do not, not officially, YET know what the war is about. And you have singularly failed to listen to the voice of reason. I don't mean to my voice. I don't mean to reason as conceived exclusively in Rapallo. I mean you have been such golthunderin' asses that you have NOT, for 40 years listened to any Englishman (or alien critic) who told you anything sensible.

I mean when I was last immersed in London, I don't want to anticipate, I don't want to claim that I possessed more judgment, or perception when I left you in 1920, than I had AT that time. Liberty is not a right but a duty. That is an Italian saying. I don't claim that I had anything more than a strong personal taste for personal autarchy. American anarchy and Italian Fascism, being in perfect accord about the desirability of personal autarchy. Not a right but a duty. That may be exotic, it may be alien to the British bullheadedness. You were better off when the school boys recited Macaulay and meant it. Your sense of values was probably better in those days.

But so recently as 1931, there were still voices: in fact right up till the war broke loose there were still voices, and AUDIBLE voices in England, and no one ever called Mr. Chesterton an exotic. I may in my hot youth have called him various other things. But I got over it.

Now in 1931 Mr. Chesterton was telling you, (November 21, 1931, in G.K.'s [weekly]) Mr. Chesterton wrote:

The press is a machine for destroying the public memory. When it is called the daily press, it means that it exists entirely to wash out the popular recollection of yesterday.

Public Opinion left to itself would have the proportion of perspective. It would see certain events as big, even when they are no longer new; ... It would naturally recognize old friends or foes, the man who has figured in these affairs— —The great strikes and the great war, that refers [to]. He is talking of a dirty bit of work now forgotten, namely Ramsey MacDonald.

MacDonald ought to be called Mr. MacNab when he is a Bolshevik robber stealing all our goods, and then called Mr. Mackintosh when he is our beautiful shining protector against the storm of Bolshevism in the state.

The principle implied could be applied otherwhere. I don't want to divagate into flogging the dead horse MacDonald. I would willingly spend several evenings trying to get you to concentrate on the depth and import of G.K.C.'s opening statement.

The press, your press, is a machine for destroying the memory, the public memory. For effacing, for washing out the memory of yesterday and the day before yesterday.

Now what causes that? I mean why does the press exist for that particular purpose?

It is a great pity more people aren't isolated—as I believe you call it—aren't in some way left once a year, for a week, with a stock of old periodicals. Just to find out what did happen, or what was written AGAINST the current, or with the current, a decade ago. No one supposes Chesterton was writing Axis propaganda in 1931 and 2. Big business depends on big bankers (*Vide* G.K., Two Views of England, September 26, 1931). Big bankers who govern England as a dependency from New York, though they themselves are something non-American enough to get into a club there.

By 1931 G.K.C. had attained a concision of phrase which, had he possessed it 20 years earlier, would have prevented my juvenile rage with his views about poetry. He continued: "These people are the dependents of dependents of dependents; and nobody is independent but a few foreign financiers working from the other side of the Atlantic." And then with bitter irony he finished the paragraph: "This is an assurance that we shall always be masters of our destiny." Perhaps irony is a sin, or at least a peccadillo.

Perhaps Chesterton's phrase shot over the head of his readers. It seems to have shot over the top of British intelligence. "Indifference to fact," said G.K.C., he tries to distinguish that from stupidity. "Our weakness in politics. By refusing to face the facts the English had let themselves in for being ruled by Jews, or Americans." G.K.C., 1931, I add "and/or Americans."

But as my compatriots are now ruled by Jews, and by the dirtiest dirt from the bottom of the Jew's ash can, I suppose it comes to the same thing. The Anglo-Saxon race in both its cousinly branches is bloody well hog tied by Rothschild. More is the pity, Goyim or cattle, milked, skinned alive, hog tied, sent out to the slaughter or drowned like blind mice in the steerage, to keep up the usual swindles. Usury at 60% being the quietest. Control of national credit by sheenies, silver wheeze, and the gold sheeze. The gold or the silver, what does the corpse care for the nails in its coffin, made of amethyst, make'em with ruby heads, and nail shafts of platinum? Or dole'em out in the market, like de Beers pebbles.

The point is Chesterton was writing in England, for England ten and twelve years ago. He was not writin' Axis propaganda. He may have been writin' mankind propaganda, withstanding the all engulfing filth from 2 Little Essex Street from which rock, or lighthouse, it would seem like as if the light no longer shines. At any rate it don't get quoted: not on the B.B.C.

Now it would be a pity if all that was England, all that made England worth being England were to be submerged by the Kikes of New York. By the filth that you have bred in your bosom, for over a century you have caressed, and encouraged this syphilis, you have bred up this bubonic plague, and shipped it over to Wall Street. You did NOTHING, nothing what bloody ever to cure it. It infected the world and made England's name accursed from Pretoria to Singapore and Calcutta. And then its centre shifted across the Atlantic. So we owe you no gratitude if it is now gnawing American vitals.

Still it would be a pity if you sank under an order that has completely lost all classic culture—all that was best of England—as proof that the British press has succeeded in its mission of effacement.

#98, FCC Transcript (June 15, 1943)
U.S.(C58)
[OBSEQUIES]

The final, ultimate, not penultimate but terminal, definite and definitive demise of the Republican Party was announced by Heinrich Ben Cohen and Solomon Morgenthau sometime ago. The absolutely last and ultimate unwill and distestament of the corpse of the Republican elephant was published to the listening but inattentive world by little Hymie, the mute kike of our treasury. And that today Willkie is now out of a job, the job of sitting on the curbstone waiting for Jehovah to call him to a place (Henry Wallace summit) as a Jew's jockey in Washington, has evaporated.

The demi-kikes are going to deflate on their own. The Republican Party is not. As long expected by the lone wolves of Wall Street, the Republican Party is not going to be called in to officiate at the return of the holy banner. Hymie will look after that for his patrons, with no need to change office holders. Gold, gold, not a mere cross this time, but a whole grill full of dozens of crosses, a grating guaranteed to close any— —is going to be provided right in the Democrat's home. Isn't it wonderful? And the new Unity, the universal monetary unit will be called the Tekel Upharaim, so that all Sunday School boys will feel comfy.

It will be stabilized. The world's money will be the little gold dollar. No allusion to the well known brothel in— —. The sacred name will be Unity.

Gold does not fluctuate. Uh, doesn't it? Well, there are some tiresome tables but you can [bet] your boots, if you have any boots by that time, you can bet your automobile tires and underwear in perfect safety, that everything else will. I mean, the prices of every other goldarned thing on the market or off the market or in the highjacker's van will fluctuate, right up and down, and there will be a B.O. such as never— —in the American sky. The advantages of a one standard system were understood years ago, a century and more ago, by Samuel Loyd. And this time there will be no competition. The price of farm products will go up and down. There will be plenty of people out of work, so that you can get people to work for nothing or near it. There will be plenty of strike-breakers' unions, the vulgar people who work, the rustic folk who toil in the fields, the Polish folk who [go?] down to an office and work over [ledgers?]

will have nothing, nothing what-bloody-ever to say about the wage to be paid for their labor, or the relation of the wage to the price of what they buy, or what they can buy, or what they would have to buy if they wish to eat and wear clothes. There will be plenty of men out of jobs to replace them. Ain't that what Mark Hanna wanted? The Republican principles will have been saved, but the party, the old ghost of an elephant, will not be in on the reception. Of course, some of its components will have been spared. A Scandinavian once said to me, "There aren't any Scandinavians who would put his money into gold mines." He said to me, "Republican Party, hell. 14 Jews on their committee." If there were six, they would be running the whole of it. And some members would have been satisfied, perhaps like Knox and Stimson, they would be burned on the seats of the cushion. But the old equine members, the old horses of battle, the lesser orders of the Republican Party will be way out in the cornfield. The Demi's will deflate on their own. And the name of the new [abattoir?] will be called the world's uniform currency. To be managed on the interests of whom? The Republicans are not the sole goat. England is one goat. Thirty-two other nations are being sheparded toward shearing field and the slaughter house. Gold and more gold. Those among you who sold business short and went into national bonds will come home again. The dollars that were sent abroad to buy gold will come again, worth twice or more than they were at the rate of export, and Democracy shall be holy.

Mr. Morgenthau or Bill Solomon-Isaacs Smith may replace Mr. Wallace as the white-haired, the oncoming darling. You may at least have openly and avowedly at last have a full-blooded circumsized kike in the White House to celebrate annually the defeat of Jim Blaine. Mr. Hoover will be given a post of honor as bellboy's assistant [maid?] in the Senate or something, as a reward for long and infamous service to financiers. But the old party will be no more. Ham Fish will be reduced to the status of a Shindwell in England. Mr. Vandenburg will retire, and the universal gold standard, the price of foodstuffs, and clothing fluctuating in Fall River and Sweden will reign from Kentucky to Cawnpore, if you are still in possession of Cawnpore. And the war with Russia will be imminent and stay imminent until it breaks out.

But in the meantime there will be hot money to be made in providing Russia with the latest tanks and armaments. But there is or should be grief in Republican circles, because the banker's conspiracy, the— —wheel, the control of currency wheel, is a game to be manipulated right in the Democratic circle, right in our Democratic party's home circle, and perhaps Hymie has his eye on the White House. After all, between one Henry or another, what does it matter? Henry the seventh, Henry the eighth, both of them Tudors, both of them in the tradition. Henry or Hank, the Vice-President Hymie or Henry, the Vice President Henry or Henry Heinie Ben

Morgenthau ben Solomon Isaac, what does it matter? Both parties have sinned. And now the Republicans are in for another skin deal, but it is their pelt that is up at auction. All hail the Soviet Paradise. The American slave state is to be elected on gold, under gold, and there will be still more unemployment, more than anything else you've been used to, only less of it, while the leading Republicans who are elderly men may find it hard to adjust themselves to a rapid and wicked world. Perhaps it's— —that they should stear toward their graves. They did not hear the engine squeal. Perhaps [Ford?] will be your next President.

#99 (June 19, 1943) U.S.(C43)
WAR AIMS

You do not know WHAT you are fighting for. Europe considers you complete swine to be making war on Europe at all; and considers you utter asses to be diddled by the Morgenthau, Lehman combine, Seligman, Rosenman and the rest of it.

And you lose your OWN liberties faster than you deprive Europe of hers, or at least that's what it looks like.

Prosperity, American prosperity was just'round the corner, and American prosperity has gone down the drain. Hasn't it? Mebbe your press tells you different; but in that case why is it so hard to get American papers? One bit of paper still has some life in it. I don't want to exaggerate. But looks like as if somebody out in Colorado (ColorAAAdo) had a brainwave. AMENDMENT. Three fourths of the states have to amend it. Is there a part still left of the old machinery that hasn't been rusted and rotted by Jews? Five states, very little. Straw in the wind. But I heard Illinois was amongst'em. Mebbe it is just Schenectady hooey. Five is a long way from 36. Mebbe it is just a display of emotion. Locking the door after the blighter has got into the stable and taken out all the bran, oats and barley.

I could suggest a whole flock of amendments, as well as enforcements. In fact it is difficult to see how an amendment would be able to act where the text itself doesn't. I say difficult, not impossible. The text is known (to those who have the patience to read it, possibly one 1/100th of the denizens). They forget it, save in a few western states. I think somebody in Dakoty once read it. The Constitution. However that don't mean that a new amendment wouldn't get enough publicity to prevent a vast movement to suspend the amendment in favor of Trilby. Yes, yes, his middle name is Trilby, he writes it Franklin T. Roosevelt.

However, the removal of one hypnotized lunkus, for the sake of inserting another hypnotized lunkus or rabbit, might not bring total salvation, might not bring sudden salvation.

And prosperity was just'round the corner, and now it is out guarding Persian railroads, Iran, used to be Persia. Now it is part of the Soviet Russia, with American troops guarding the railways in order to bring the good life to Arkansas. Looks like Montana had slipped into Texas, and the American people ate loco-weed, in default of canned goods from Mr. Armour.

Do you YET sigh for the good old days, when you could write letters uncensored, or telegraph to Mama, without having a permit? I told you, I dun told you communications would be difficult. No American boys will be sent to die on foreign fields. O Ma, O American Mama, did you hear your beloved Franklin Trilby singing that operetta?

Now I repeat to you, I go on repeating to you that when Bryan, W.J.B., met Mr. Kitson, he said that the silver was ballyhood, to cover a deeper issue? A more basic issue, namely control of the national credit.

Well if credit is a mystery, shall we call it the power to buy? You know what the power to BUY is?

And second justice is measured by the way that the power to buy is divided between the citizens or inhabitants of a nation And the idea of having a Congress in the beginning was that the Congress should keep an eye on JUST that component of the life, they meant it to be the GOOD life, of the nation.

And they sought out many inventions. That is history. They, that is, a gang of'em sought out ways to diddle the people. And for 80 years the AMERICAN people resisted the wangles, in one way or another.

And now you certainly should vote for that amendment. No president to sit for more than eight years Robbing the people or presiding with a wealth of blather and falsehood over the depredations committed by the Jews in his treasury and the various other highly odorous swindles. The chief noise, the chief blather should be altered at least once in eight years but that ain't the arf of it deane. You need several amendments. And if Congress won t go on the air let the State Senators go on the air let the State Legislatures go on the air to compensate for the difficulties of communication, difficulties of communication by rail, by automobile, by gasless carriages, that were called horseless carriages once. You need a whole flock of amendments. You need state rights IN ACTION You need state rights put into effect put into practice UP TO the absoloot limit. I mean up to any length that don't mean dissolvin' the Union.

I say dissolvin' the Union, I don't mean the exclusion of Iran, Nepal, Bungalore, and Rhodesia from the benefits of Morgenthau's administration. One continent at a time. When you can trust the kahal, the Baruchs, the Rothschilds, Lehmans, Seligmans, Sassoons, and other importations ancient and modern from the sewers of Pal'stine, and the Ghettoes of Cawnpore, when you can trust the high kikery, high kahalery in Washington and the Bowery, and Fifth Avenue. What, only ten million yidds in America, said the American lady, why surely, why from 50th Street to 59th Street on Fifth Avenue, you hardly hear English spoken. She was a recent arrival in Rome, kicked out with her husband, who was

European. Still IS European. Well, when you can trust these big noses to govern America, without enslaving and bleeding the Aryan population, mebbe it will be time to send your sturdy sons to die in the foreign desert and to collect dividends for Kuhn Loeb and Co., in East Africa.

But in the meantime pass the amendment, pass a whole flock of amendments: let the individual states take a hand in governing and allotting the purchasing power of their OWN inhabitants. Let the producers eat of their produce.

Just'round the corner, pie in the sky. Where ARE your pathologists? Henceforth, as it can be retroactive, as you did not put him away, henceforth, grow wise by experience, and when any man refrains from, when any man eschews peace IN the present tense on the excuse that he wants to prevent his great grandchildren having a war, send for the DOCTOR, don't send for Rosenman, send for the doctor, for a responsible doctor.

And study the development of criminal process, say from the time of the Dreyfus case to the present.

Where, for example, did the gangsters get their system of getting criminals OUT of quo.

That is no novelty. Which of you has studied the development of the technique of gangster organization?

#100, FCC Transcript (June 20, 1943) U.K.(C45) [ON BRAINS OR MEDULLA]

They murmured of money. It wasn't very enlightening. It was almost as if they wanted to free themselves of the reproach of never having mentioned the subject. And they also mentioned the universal language— —name has been breathed into the ambient British air. I miss it. Wealth had something to do with the bread price. Perhaps England is waking. Perhaps certain persons and topics were apparently out of the silent zone into the zone of calumny. That is the usual kindly process. First ten or more years of silence, then the decade of calumny. So in twenty years one can collect on the invested capital and when the hoax has been exposed, Mr. Ike— —is already in some other line of business. They call it business. Now Esperanto and Basic English are both unsatisfactory. Any language is unsatisfactory. Any language is unsatisfactory if you have to cut down the thought to fit a very restrictive means of expression.

If the Brain Trust or any other group of permitted persons is serious on the subject of intercommunications between the different peoples, people who use different languages, they might, however, let bygones be bygones and consider the scheme which I broached in the JAPAN TIMES, on May 17, 1940 (or was it '39?): Namely, the trilingual system. The JAPAN TIMES gave good display to the article.

It was certainly above the conflict. The Brain Trust scheme seems to ignore the Orient altogether. My scheme was impartial. It contained one Axis language, one anti-Axis language, and one Oriental language, or other means of communication.

I was considering civilization at large, and a means of full communication, not merely a commercial stenography. I believe it would be about as simple to learn to write in a foreign tongue as to restrict oneself to Ogden's basic English vocabulary. That may be because I have written in French and Italian, and have not worried about keeping inside a restricted vocabulary.

My proposal was, as I say, tri-lingual. Italian, English, and ideogram. That is, Chinese ideogram used as a written tongue, but with Japanese pronunciation. That gives you the languages of Confucius, Shakespeare, and Dante. There is no sentiment in this selection. You say the Germans would never accept this. That is, you don't say so because you are quite crazy in talking of re-educating nations which are far more educated than you are. I believe our Germans would place unsentimental reasons first, the Germans are more diligent than other men, great numbers of them habitually— —. Secondly, my opinion is— —I omitted the German language, because that language retains more inflections than the three languages I selected.

I say, ideogram with Japanese pronunciation, because almost no foreigner can pronounce Chinese properly, let alone manage the tones, because the pronunciation varies with the different regions of China, and because I find no agreements as how the sounds, such as one can understand, or really hear, should be transcribed in our alphabet. Whereas the Japanese is phonetically simple as the Italian, whose sounds in many ways they resemble. I say Italian, not French, not merely for political reasons. French is hell to pronounce. You have to screw up your nose for the nasals. Apart from the political, Italian is spoken like she is writ. No monkey business. Every letter is pronounced in the same way wherever it occurs. The only apparent exception is the c and ch before a and o. Before a and o, c is hard and before i and e it is soft. The hard sound is written ch before i and e. But the spelling is uniform and follows in all cases and there are no— —. I would suggest that the Japanese sign for the syllables, for the sound of the syllables, be transliterated to the Roman alphabet when they accompany the ideogram. Let me explain. The written Chinese is common in both Japan and China. All those written signs are the same for Japan and all China. Anyone who reads them in one place knows what they mean in another. It is the common tongue or common written tongue for all those millions.

As English, with its variants is common to England, and the United States, and is a lingua franca for India. I take into account distribution. The number of people who already know each of the languages mentioned. It is as easy to learn Italian as to learn Esperanto. It does not cut the fingers and toes off any one's thought. And that can be borne out by anyone of the hundred Englishmen who have studied with Professor Morelli. It is high time you looked into his methods. But apart from Morelli's methods, based on words almost identical in the two languages or at least perfectly recognizable as from English to Italian or from Italian to English, Italian is the simplest descendent from Latin.

Latin, the universal stronghold of European snobs for nearly 2000 years. Italian is clearer than Latin, you might say maturer than Latin. They boasted— —translated— —using fewer words in his Italian version than are used in the Latin original. Intelligent auditors can go on with his talk— —. The intelligent auditor ought to be able to think of objections and answer them. The Brain Trust, if it weren't utterly frivolous, would take up the subject. It is a non-political subject. It is outside the conflict. It has to do with the possible future. It does not set out any advantages of Basic English to those who choose to go on from the start Ogden made. But Ogden is too lazy to think of any developments, on his first outline. He hadn't even got the— —or to the introductory notes on the [Fenollosa?] essay notes on the written character.

I offer this as a challenge. If the Brain Trust is just one more part of the present system, as Chesterton has defined it, an instrument to blot out the public memory, an instrument for destroying the public memory, said G.K.C. when he wrote——December, 1939, in his weekly. Blotting out the past so that people shall not learn from it, distracting them from present realities with a mirage of an impossible future.

Well, the break from Italian to English is very short if you follow Morelli, or from English to Italian. That makes the universal language for Europe, a double language, not only of commerce but of culture. The fear of the ideogram is due largely to ignorance. I have followed Fenollosa and the tract is most thorny. He needs more printed manuals such as I have begun to print here, in my edition of The Great Learning, the Testament of Confucius.

And anyhow, when you people talk of a one language system, you mean mostly one language for Europe and America. Very few of you think of the rest at all.

#101 (June 22, 1943) U.S.(C64)
STALIN

"The first contradiction is the antagonism between labor and capital," wrote Stalin 21 years ago.

"Imperialism is the export of capital to the sources of raw materials," wrote Mr. Stalin, 21 years ago, in his highly vivacious little brochure, "The Foundations of Leninism."

Tsarist Russia was an immense reserve force for western imperialism, not only in that it gave free entry to foreign capital which controlled decisive branches of Russian economy like fuel and metallurgy, but also that it could furnish millions of soldiers to the western imperialists.

Russian army, 12 million strong; shed its blood on imperialist fronts to safeguard the staggering profits of Anglo-French capitalists. Tsarism was the agent of western imperialism in squeezing hundreds of millions from the population by way of interest on loans floated in Paris, London, etc., faithful ally in partitioning Turkey, Persia, China, etc. Was not Russia an essential factor in this war? Joe is speaking of the war that had occurred before he wrote his little brochure. As to this war: some estimates give 30 million as the cost to Russia, 30 million human lives.

The Leninist theory of the proletarian revolution is based on three fundamental issues.

First thesis, the domination of finance capital in the advanced capitalist countries, the issue of stocks and bonds as the principal operation of finance capital, the export of capital to the sources of raw materials, which is one of the bases of imperialism, the OMNIPOTENCE of a financial oligarchy, a consequence of the dominations of financial capital. All these reveal the crudely parasitic character of monopolist capitalism, make the yoke of the capitalist trusts and syndicates 100 times more burdensome.

Perhaps Col. McCormick had better get the pamphlet and read it. Tenth anniversary edition, International Publishers, 100,000 copies at 10 cents, probably reprinted dozens of times during the past decade, as they will have already celebrated a 20th anniversary.

The Col. has heard recently, i.e., in the course of the early spring of this year, of the American Constitution. I dunno whether he has yet passed the stages of his beardless youth, eh, the MENTAL stages.

If he had been a serious character SOONER, he would have used his enormous printing space for the reprint of the thought of the American founders, Adams, Jefferson, Van Buren, and the distribution of the works of the Adams descendents. BUT he omitted it. And I don't'spose he listens in to Rome radio. So somebody better tell him.

Twenty years ago Stalin was talkin' about self-criticisms within the proletarian parties, their education and instruction on the basis of their own mistakes. The proletariat, wrote Mr. Stalin, can not retain power if it does not possess adequate educated administrative cadres, ready for and capable of organizing the administration of the country. It's the question of the advance with seven-league strides to raise the cultural level that gives one pause. Instead of educatin' and teachin' the party true revolutionary tactics from a study of its own mistakes, we find a studied evasion of thorny questions, which are glossed over and veiled. "Left wing communism, and infantile discord," the words are not mine, but Lenin's.

Mr. Stalin said in regard to slogans and resolutions that it was enough to recall the history of the famous watchword "war against war," to realize the utter falsity and rottenness of the political processes of these parties which veil, etc. There really seems to have been little doubt as to Stalin's direction in 1922.

His mind appears to have been remarkably clear.

The main query to be raised at this moment, when Mr. Stalin is undoubtedly as victorious INSIDE the U.S. and Britain, as U.S. particular interests are being in absorbing the flesh pots of Empire, (British empire first), the main query is as to the nature and direction of the evolution of revolution in the United States. I know it is exceedingly difficult to get a general idea into, let us say, Co. McCormick's head or Hamilton Fish's. Do we move toward REVOLUTION, as from man toward the amoeba, or do we move, or even desire to move toward an integration of the individual AS component of the general social scene?

Do we want to be taken to pieces, separated into spare parts, quite spare and utterly separable, at the rate say of 30 million a shot, functioning at a lower level, or do we wish to maintain that complexity to which the human organism BIOLOGICALLY, BI/O/LOG/ICALLy has evolved during millennia, or however it did evolve?

Does the infantile disorder recognize that the homestead works better, or even might in certain conditions work better, function better than the kolkhoz? That is a superficial query. If the homestead displays a higher mechanical efficiency than the kolkhoz, how far should it be opposed? Can it be opposed as a matter of principle? In short, how protean is materialism anyway? Can it take on so new an aspect?

Are the cadres gettin' educated seven-leagued enough for the circumstance? And after all, is a theory about the mutability of materialism any more binding than a signed contract?

I'spect if the Colonel, Col. McCormick, is listening, or if anyone is kind enough to stenograph this discourse, the Col. is by now about all bawled up. Mebbe he is trying to ride on a party that just AIN'T guided by an advanced theory. What can one do with a country in which NEITHER party is literate? All this should hook onto S. Welles' pieties about economic aggression. But I am at the end of my time.

#102 (June 26, 1943) U.S. (C65)
MATERIALISM

An idea is colored by what it is dipped in. Take for example the more or less Teutonic idea of materialism.

Marx and Engels get to foolin''round with Hegel's philosophy, or something, and evolve or devolve what is called Marxian materialism, and it gets toted off into Russia. And after 25 years, what do we have? We have these howlin' Slavs: gone off on a purely metaphysical, typically Russian crusade. As crazy as any excess of the middle ages. Utterly OB/liv/i/ous of the material facts. That is to say, I suppose anyone will admit that the German workman is MATERIALLY better off than the Russian opposite number. Materially speakin', the factory reforms proposed by Robert Owen and the ideas of Hobhouse that Marx so approved of in fact all the British aims that caused Marx to write his Xth chapter Best chapter in Das Kapital so far as I am concerned. Well all that AIM, to get the workin' man decently fed, and clothed, and housed, and given decent livin conditions and hours of labor has we believe gone further in Germany than in Russia.

Despite labels and programs.

I have heard it said that Germany has gone communist but nobody can accuse Europe of havin' gone RUSSIAN, or Germany of havin' gone Russian. Marx looked at England, and thought about Germany, and something got set loose in Russia into which country inspection has long been denied. For years nobody was supposed to LOOK at what actually happened. It was all metaphysical. Nice programs and dire results.

And Russians certainly in ignorance of living conditions of working men elsewhere. What causes that?

Maybe it is the material nature of the slavic animal or of the Tartar fanatic.

However look back at some of the words in the program Materialism: what does it mean? Are you for it? Are you for WHATEVER it means? Or do you on occasion like to know what you mean, or what you are shouting for? Are you a materialist WHATEVER it means, or are you a materialist only on condition that it means something in particular, something rather than something else?

George Santayana calls himself a materialist. It rather shocked old William James. Ole William told young George, he was younger at that stage of world history, that his, Santayana's philosophy was organized rottenness. I can not agree with fuzzy old James. It appears to me that George Santayana rather agrees with Thomas Aquinas. I mean the materialist Santayana ends up by writin' a book called The Realm of Spirit. I occasionally plunge into the work to calm my heated mind. I mean when I am not up to Confucius and Mencius. And Thomas Aquinas says somewhere that the soul is the first ACT of an organic body. Well, I ask George Santayana what THAT means. And he says entelechy, which seems to me to be dodgin' behind a Greek word. But anyhow, a materialist definition of the soul seems to be that it is the first act, or first action, or first condition of an organic body. Don't ASK me. I am merely trying to show how far the word or idea materialist can be stretched by people who play with abstractions. Marx's theory of value always seemed to me metaphysical.

But to get down to brass material tacks. Does a Marxian materialist prefer human conditions for labor to inhuman conditions? Do the actual material advances in the conditions of German working men count for anything in a material universe? Or does the Marxian materialist prefer the Russian enwarped and metaphysical state, wherein no one has a room of her own?

I think it matters. I think it is a question of administration, material administration. I am all for local control. The principle of local control has made some advances during the past weeks. I mean on paper, and in the aerial discussion. On paper, or in the air, the comintern has declared for local control or administration. But is that material or metaphysical? I think it matters very much WHO administers. I think the future of any party, communist or other, in the U.S.A. depends very greatly on the men, on the personality of the men who CONTROL it. I am all for responsibility, personal responsibility. I fail to see what PRINCIPLE of materialism or metaphysicality has to do with the machine gunning of three year old kids. I fail to see where the invasion of one country by another hitches up to the program of any set of idealists, whether Moscovite or Democratic, i.e., plutocratic. Does the dissolution of the Comintern mean that Moscow proposes that every nation should be administered by members OF that nation or race? That would be an interesting line of inquiry. The suppression for all material and practical purposes of nearly all South American government seems rather out of line, with this dissolution of international aspirations on the part of the comintern.

The nipping, not in the bud, but in the decayed and gangrenous remnants on London's usurocratic grasp on large parts of most continents is of course a spectacular play against the economic oppression (past tense of economic aggression) of the London plutocracy. That might be all to the good, if the U.S. hadn't decayed into something very like, or possibly worse than the British methods of the late 18th century, impression of seamen included.

But in the oedeniatous decomposition of the U.S. plutocracy and usurocracy, what assurance has anyone, or what assurance is anyone in the U.S. trying to get, that the New Steal in the U.S.A. will be under local control?

There is really so much to say that I find it difficult to divide it up into ten minute samples. Are you heading for a RUSSIAN control of the U.S., the U.S. of A., or the U.S. of Europe? What assurance is anyone in the U.S. trying to obtain that Kansas and Illinois will be controlled in ANY way by denizens of those geographic parts of the American union?

Yes, I know, people are being sent out FROM the U.S. to take over control in ex-Persia, now labeled Iran, etc. and vast tracts of the ex-British oppressed dominions are fallin' under Wall St. control. But what is it MATERIALLY to the folks who have mortgaged their farms to the Milk Trust?

#103 (June 29, 1943) U.S. (C67)
COMMUNIST MILLIONAIRES

Is Mr. Roosevelt a Communist? Is Mr. Lehman a Communist? Is Mr. Morgenthau a Communist, is Mr. Bullitt, or Sir V. Sassoon, and if not why not? And what becomes of their millions, what becomes of their private fortunes when Communism takes over control of the U.S.A.? And if not, why not? And is the American Communist Party, now freed from the apron strings of the comintern, is the American Communist Party governed by Wall Street? And if not, WHY not? And if not, why this continual export of capital to places abroad?

And then there come these proposals, these money proposals, these starvation proposals, these restriction proposals. Of course any scheme to take control of the nation's money, to take the control of ANY nation's money away from that nation and vest it in Mr. Lehman or any other private shyster, or gang of shysters, resident either at home or abroad, is a booby trap. Such a trap was sprung on the gullible American people in 1863. And they have never recovered, not really. Not in 1943, such a booby trap can not be sprung on the outer world without at least someone in the said outer world's being made aware of it.

Even that Skinner of Rabbits, Prof. Keynes or Lord Keynes, the British proletarian specialist, has smelt the dead fish in the proposal for unitas, as the continent can smell the dead eels in Mr. Keynes' banker or bunk/or, what will you. And this question of who CONTROLS the central; of who wingles the wangles is of importance. There is no need to transport the problem onto the international checkerboard.

When the people of Nebraska lost control of its money, i.e., when Congress ceased to function constitutionally, and every state ceased to have a voice in the control of the national currency, that was a booby trap.

The nation did not react effectively. There were some voices uplifted in protest. When I was a boy, when your fathers were children, there were still voices uplifted in protest. But why suppose the whole world is as naive as the U.S. was at the end of the American Civil War? The bank game is simple, it is run on what are called classic lines. It is run on what Lord Keynes, the British proletarian specialist, used to call the lines of ORTHODOX economics. Meaning that the bankers collect 60% interest on the actual money, or that they collect interest on 90% of everyone's money, which they create out of thin air, wild phantasy, and a few bits of engraven paper.

OH, that they vary the currency, the purchasing power of money. When the bankers have money, it is of very great value, you have to pay for it thru the nose. But when you get a bit of it, its value evaporates.

The game is as old as Aaron, it was denounced in the time of Thucydides. "Banish your dotage, banish usury/that makes the Senate ugly," remarked the stage character, Alcibiades, in Shakespeare's Timon of Athens, Act. III, scene 5. Shakespeare is not my favorite author, but he occasionally bangs a nail on the head. That side of Shakespeare's dramatic writings is NOT given due prominence. It is not what gets large poster publicity. For decades the public in England and America has been FAR more interested in the private lives of the actors, of Henry, Irving and in Ellen Terry. "I come to bury" Caesar and all the rest of it, "not to praise him."

Well let's be MATERIAL, since you are lined up with the materialists. Let's see where we are, ideologically. Or in other words let's see what cards have been put on the table. Mr. Stalin says LOCAL control. That is to say, he says he disbands something or other, and the local communist parties must run their own local shows without daily orders from Moscow. Up comes Mrs. Trotsky, widdy Trotsky, and says that means SHE is to run the world revolution from Mexico City. Just what Nebraska was hoping for.

World communism governed from Mexico city. But was that JUST what Stalin meant by his maneuver?

Has Mr. Welles joined the local communist party? Not officially. But he put a few cards on the table (the joker face down amongst'em). Some rash bohunk said Sumner had COINED, coined mind you, the phrase "economic aggression." But what does Sumner mean by aggression? Let's not rake up everybody's past skeletons. Even Sumner admitted that the U.S. had aggressed. Let's look at his program, or as that is pretty vague, let's ask for a definition.

WHO according to Sumner's bright plans for tomorrow, WHO is to DUMP what on WHOM? And is the fellow that has to take what he don't want going to be forced to pay for it in money controlled by a gang of shysters in Washington, in Wall Street or in Mexico? And who, according to Sumner, is to be allowed to get what? And who is to be allowed to GROW what they want to eat in their own garden? That would seem to be one whale of a question. Aye, aye, sir, very like a whale or an octopus.

The agricultural districts hardly ever start wars. Lack of food may start people roving. It may in the last analysis provoke nomadic migrations. BUT people living in abundant farmland very seldom start out to raid someone else's bare fields. And then this problem of bilaterality. This question of justice having two sides. Where does Sumner get THAT subject? How much local control does Sumner allow to the local communist party or to the LOCAL party of any kind?

Europe seems rather inclined to have a bit of local control. It seems to me the seven league advance, which Lenin advocated toward the cultural attitudes, might rather include this idea of local control.

Especially as Stalin understands Senator Vandenburg and Mr. Welles so much better than they understand Mr. Stalin. Mebbe that is because he was so much more moral. I mean in his earlier writings. Why, 20 years ago Stalin was writin' about foreign imperialism "devoid of all moral authority and deservedly hated by the oppressed and exploited masses of India." I suspect the local parties in Washington are as ignorant of Stalin's past life, as they are of Europe, of European life during the past 20 years.

#104 (July 3, 1943) U.S.(C68)
COLORING

Ideas are colored by what they are dipped in. There was a young Chinaman the other day, nearly accusin' me of havin' invented Confucius. He had been UNeducated by contact with half-baked occidental ideas.

Lost his own cultural heritage, didn't think Confucius was so modern, that was because he hadn't read him, of course. Mencius was also accused of having brightened up Confucius, but he knew better. He knew he hadn't.

Formerly, when Kung died, the disciples after staying together three years, packed their baggage and returned to their homes, but Tzu Kung went back and built a house on the altar ground, and lived there alone for three years. And the disciples thought Yew Jo might serve as teacher, but Tzu said: Washed in the waters of Kiang and Han, bleached in the autumn sun.

After that, no. There is nothing to add. Nothing to add to that whiteness.

Mebbe the difference between the Greek flash in the pan, and the Chinese persistence is due to Kung's having got the answer. Mencius following and enforcing it. Whereas in Greece, Socrates gunned'round.

As Aristotle says: "Socrates was the first to see that thought hinges on definitions." But Aristotle had to put the guesses in order. He didn't take Socrates or any of the other Greek philosophers as a solid basis. And spent a lot of time talking about abstractions. Tho' he did say that the general statement must be based on a lot of concrete data. And he did study the different constitutions of states, i.e., different political systems, and regulations. All that of course OUGHT to be the basis of senatorial training, of congressional training.

And it drags me a bit away from the simple text I meant to enforce, or suggest. When I said ideas are tinged by what they are dipped in, I was thinkin' of widdy Trotsky. Down there in Mexico, speakin' evil of Stalin, in fact blamin' Joe for the war, and saying she was to fix it all up, and conduct the world revolution.

Now we all like revolution, except when we are settin' too easy. And a considerable revolution has occurred during most of our lifetimes. Though Senator Vandenberg mayn't have heard of it YET.

Mr. Marx, Charlie, went to England, went there at a time when England had a sort of a lead over less favored nations. And he heard about Hobhouse. And I reckon about Mr. Owen, Robert Owen. And he wanted to start something in Germany, but the ideas got switched off onto Russia, a less favored country.

A backward country, full of Tartars and Muscovites, and Cossaks and Nomads. And the result has been in many ways UNsatisfactory. In fact Owen's ideas about factory reform, etc. have gone a lot further in Germany, under the Führer, whose writing you probably haven't read. In fact you and Vandenburg and these sachems probably haven't read EITHER Stalin, OR Hitler, or Mussolini. So you decide to take over an old shirt of Lenin's, at least that passage about training a staff of administrators, and you send a lot of unbreached kids down to the University of Virginia to learn how to administer. Which is looney. I mean if you think a kindergarten can administer its parents, or infants officiate over adults.

The idea takes color from what it is dipped in. The idea of treating work men like human beings, favored by Robert Owen, etc. has progressed in Germany. I reckon for model factory conditions, etc. you would have to go to Germany NOW, thought the Burgomaister of Worgl, [who] had Henry Ford's life or ghosted autobiography on his bookshelf. But for the Senator's information, before he gives way to nostalgia for a lost era, and consents to puttin' up a stooge, or pseudo General Grant, to initiate a new era of pillage and public scandal. I mean by having a man, or wanting a president who knows NOTHING about public administration, but covers the graft by a military aureole, more or less.

Let the Senator READ a little Stalin, Hitler, and Mussolini. Of course you can GET Stalin for 10 cents in America, and you probably can NOT get the works of the Axis leaders. Or if so, I suspect they would not be in authoritative translations.

Well now, what in Stalin's Foundations of Leninism? And where was the error, if error? Was it in program or was it something that happened later, in petrification of program? Or in Russian inability to act on exotic ideas; and the general drop or droop or subsidence of the exotic ideas into the mire of Slavic chaos (with condiments: oh yes, with condiments, according to some unkindly critics)?

But supposin' the widdy Trotsky DOES drag the program OUT of the Slavic ambiance, out of Russia, into the American hemisphere? Already AT it in fact, get a humanitarian coloring. Not having been able to shoot Mr. Stalin, Mrs. Trotsky now decides war is wicked, or at least an error. The kindly U.S.A., Y.M.C.A. circumjacence coloring Mrs. Trotsky's susceptible mind. What would American communism finally come to? Where would it land? Or for the matter of that, where would the British episcopal Lambeth Palace, curates and mitre brand of communism finally end? What effect would the British dislike of the nosey parker have on Weishaupt's latch for universal and close range espionage, every brother spyin' and telling on everyone else?

Is Mrs. Trotsky ready to color, or to paint up to the point of seeing the homestead as something more germane to the American temperament than the kolckhoz or factory farm? That would be something to ask her. Since you are head in' for communism, lickety split, hell for leather, or mebbe hell with a shortage of leather, certainly with a shortage of pigskin and Japanese cherry trees.

And in conclusion where does she stand or SET on the matter of economic aggression? On the matter of dumping? On the matter of those seven league strides toward a higher cultural level than Lenin wanted to shove onto the Muscovites?

And the desired self-criticism inside the party? Has the American Communist Party yet opened up to the self-critics from the inside? Probably Will, or rather Kumrad William Williams was a bit pessimistic on that subject, when I was last admitted to his acquaintance. Certainly Messrs. Churchill and Roosevelt do seem to represent pretty much all that is worst in the plutocracy. So widdy Trotsky may git a run for her money.

#105, FCC Transcript (July 4, 1943)
U.K.(C57)
[TITLE UNKNOWN]

Reports to the Congress Commission, reports to the MacMillan Commission protesting against the ruin of China and India by Churchill's return to gold.

You would not listen, you would not listen, nothing would make you take the faintest trace of a half possible interest in Hitler's warnings, in Major Douglas' warnings, in the writers of McNair Wilson, Professor Stoddard— —. Those were the symbols.

A fine symbol, a holy synod, a rock on which such as Lamb— —, of ample— —upheld for their church. When I mention Mr. Morgenthau to you, you turn off the radio, the subject is so disagreeable. Mr. Morgenthau is returning to gold so that— —as soon as he possibly can.

That is, as soon as it will mean the highest possible profits on monies lent to humanity, on the debts made by the war which is to be used according to ritual to control the currency after the war, the world currency return. No small— —by mere manipulations by kikes of the money of your little empire or of the American continent, but the world currency is to be stabilized and you are old with 3 jockies in livery.

And that livery will not include coat and pants. You will go out in your underwear. It will be the livery of the new— —, of the new— —against which the prices of wheat and clothing will fluctuate.

I'll say they will fluctuate, but the money will remain fixed and— —and there will be no boys on the board of directors. Shop dressing, window dressing has prevailed up to the present. There always have been a few Lord (Windrums and Dindrums) on the board of directors to bamboozle the soft hearted public.

Oh, but the new money will not be measured by labor. The Morgenthau prices will most certainly not take into account the value of labor. The price of foodstuffs, fuel and clothing in Morgenthaudia, the new Soviet Paradise, will most certainly not be regulated so that the working man, nor the office worker can feed, clothe and house his family on the fruits of his labor, or by wearing a clean shirt to the office in the hope of getting good marks.

Lord, love you, no, the money is going to be stable. There'll be plenty of men out of work, millions and millions on the dole and of the dole so that the labor market may remain open. If there is any uncommunist district left where the worker is not slave of the plebe, where he is not conscripted to do sixteen hours a day in the factory or fifteen in the mines for the Soviets, for the Soviet Order, for the sacred Christian community of the Seligmans of the all holy, trinitarian no-God republican Paradise of the lenders of non-money at a somewhat higher return than is now asked by the— —, fifty percent.

Let us not look for help from democracies because there just won't be any democracies in that sense of the word. The war was made for the sake of doles, you were told that; it was made to make debts, it was made to impose the gold standard.

In other words you were the— —end; you were told and the gullible in Europe believed that the British working man sided with England because he got a share in the profits; he profited by the misery of India and of China; that his working conditions were better; that he could buy more copies of — —, see more pictures, read more— —news printed on more pieces of paper, see more Hollywood products and then his poor benighted brother the Hindu.— —

Now this poor brown underling who after the return to the gold standard paid two bushels where he before that had to pay one bushel and one in honor of the Queen. Well, now next time it might be that the receiving end will be over in [Goonland?], over in [Cleveland?], over in the new Roseman Paradise where blooms the— —in the new stabilized unity, with no non-Jews on the board of control, with no English control whatsoever, though a few British names may appear as representatives of the Canadian people so-called, and a few London agents of the golden Republic of Soviets may fly back and forth to see that the rent is paid promptly.

But at any rate you can now go to sleep again. You've been told what the war's about. You've been told what Rabbi Wise and Mr. Wiseman, your [Sasson?] are having a war for.

It is inconvenient: well, you've got used to it now and, when it's over, everything will be just as it was before. No, not quite as it was before, you won't have to worry about any novelties, there'll be no innovations. You'll not have to readjust yourselves to horrible novelties that threaten you from abroad. The money will be stabilized. You will have returned to sound money.

Perhaps you will be able to get some employment but that isn't necessary; you're used to not being busy so that will not disturb you. You will not have to think about anything. That will be a comfort to your penury. You never did like to think about anything. And the war will be over. That is, there will be a few— —interruptions before the next one gets going and you will have killed off some women and children and you'll feel proud of being conservative.

You will be told that the— —based on gold brought you prosperity. You will be told that it's really for England's benefit that her money should be controlled from abroad. I'll repeat that,— —. It'll relieve England of all that bookkeeping, trust Mr. Morgenthau to look after all your accounting; it is much simpler.

Mr. Keynes will explain. He will have had his little fling in the drawing room; he will have uttered the minority murmur and said that it will not quite be the millenium promise, by the prophet Isaiah. But that after all the old system of economics, the orthodox system, was the basis of Cambridge and that you have at least preserved the ideals that he stood for, and, of course, prices of foodstuffs will fluctuate, so someone can still make a little money by speculation, a little more money by speculation than they could by productive labor, which is, of course, another aim of the war.

#106 (July 6, 1943) U.S.(C69)
CREDIT: LEGALITY

John Adams won the American Revolution as a law case before the peculiarly venal and squalid government of England at that time had recourse to arms.

The 1770's were possibly imbued with a much more sensitive and active sense of legality than can be found today in the Anglo-Jewish countries.

We saw the United States flooded with quite squalid ballyhoo, telling the simps that they can make more in the army than in civil life. A level of baseness in some of these articles quite such as to turn the stomach of what was once considered the plain honest man, but will today be counted an hyper-sensitive by Hollywood standards.

Besides the offers of high pay for the army, such as appeared before America had OPENLY entered the war, are probably out-of-date by now. I am merely contrasting the venality of this purely mercenary disposition with the Italian state of mind or that of our American forebears.

Adams HAD a public to whom law and justice, equity, meant something. He could arouse indignation.

He had also the moral courage to stand up for law AGAINST the popular passion, as shown in his defense of the British soldiers in Boston, the implements, not the fount of the tyranny exercised against the people of Boston.

Today one HAS no such public. One has no law court. One can only insist that, IF there WERE a court, the line of justice COULD be demarked, and that from the European, continental side, there is an appeal to such equity.

And in contrast to the jitterbug state of mind DELIBERATELY induced in the American public by years of foetid press propaganda and demoralization, I have cited and shall continue to cite Franco Rusconi, now in military service, one of the four editors of Il Barco, a student paper issued in Genova, three of the four editors being in military service and the fourth carrying on the editing. Rusconi calls not only for peace WITH justice, but for peace AS justice.

That may be a fine and delicate distinction, a demarcation of the idea beyond the general grasp. I doubt if it IS beyond the general grasp. It is a profound distinction.

Highbrow stuff if you like. And Marshall Field and Colonel McCormick are possibly responsible for the lack of such highbrow stuff in America. When you start tearing down, there is no saying where it will end. The contempt for intelligence, the contempt for equity was not an overnight product.

YET there is no government with the consent of the governed UNTIL the governed believe that government includes at least SOME sense of justice. It is precisely on that ground that the majority was once respected. I mean that there arose in the U.S.A. in the time of Miss Harriet Martineau and President Madison a general feeling that the majority should rule.

That idea was DEFINED, it wasn't just plopped down like a poached egg, to break in its flop. The idea of majority rule implied that the majority should have the facts at its disposal. Just as Liberty in the program of the Droits de l'Homme was defined as right to do anything that don't HARM someone else.

Pardon me, if I seem to make a complicated statement. I am really working round to Mr. Welles, yes again. Sumner's speech BEGAN with an IDEA, with an appeal to some sort of reality. NOT Germany's military force, but Germany's commercial or economic energy was therein proclaimed the cause of Anglo-Judaic nervousness. Economic aggression.

The joker showed toward the end when Sumner wanted to leave the capacity for economic aggression in the exclusive control of ONE side, and of a hidden and irresponsible congerie of commercial and usurious interests. I know that's not what Sumner called it. He wrapped it up in a free-trade palaver. His essay was promptly debunked by every European economic observer. It was automatically debunked, or almost, and so quickly that it hardly got to the radio posts. I am almost the only radio commentator who gave the speech DETAILED attention. And I go on doing it because of the opening paragraphs. A lot of hooey WAS swept away. Sumner, despite the American time lag, got rid of a lot of pretense. And a LOT more, oh a LOT more, went west from Virginia Hot Springs.

If a man appeals against economic aggression, he appeals TO economic justice, or at any rate he takes ground from which appeal to economic justice can, one would say from which appeal to economic justice MUST, be eventually made. What is economic justice? Is it based on property? Do the communists answer that in the negative? Is economic justice material justice?

In modern society I think the answer must be: economic justice means an equitable distribution of purchasing power. It means a living wage for labor in all places where the means of subsistence exist.

WHO is to administer that distribution? Churchill, Roosevelt, and the filth of Judea? Answer US, us exclusively. Tear away the verbiage, and that is the Morgenthau-Roosevelt war aim.

And there being NO indication that Roosevelt, Churchill, or Morgenthau have in the past EVER for five minutes cared a damn about justice, the rest of the world demurs. Demurs with cannon.

All that we have got to—it has cost three years of war—all that we have got to is the collapse of a certain number of hoaxes, designed by the London Times, Eden, and the rest of the press swine TO conceal the basic issue.

A sane world, or an honest debating club, would take up the matter from there. And from that point I shall attempt to proceed in my next conversation or monologue.

#107 (July 17, 1943) U.S.(C71)
AUDACIA/AUDACITY

I reckon my last talk was the most courageous I have ever given. I was a playin' with fire. I was openly talking about HOW the war may be prolonged by the fellows who are scared that the war might stop.

I mean they are scared right out of their little grey panties, for fear economic equity might set in as soon as the guns stop shootin', or shortly thereafter.

The stage scenery fell with a flop, simultaneous with some anti-Axis successes. Mr. Welles tread on delicate ground. But DID make a step forward, I mean when he spoke of economic aggression. How do you prevent economic aggression INSIDE a nation? If you can't prevent it inside a nation, how do you expect to prevent it on the world base? How do you expect to prevent it internationally if you can not prevent it internally inside the territory already squashed and defiled by the plutocracy, by the usury system, by the rump end of the mercantilist system, which has been diseased and worm eaten by the cancer of usury (at 60 PER cent) and by the wheeze of varying the purchasing power of the government money, at the airy whim of the kikes and financiers? And if you won't, or if a given gang of profiteers, sometimes called politicians, WILL not even try to prevent it INSIDE their own countries, how the Sam Hill do you expect the rest of the world to expect'em to do anything about preventing it OUTSIDE the borders of their own oppressed and unhappy countries?

London slums and the rest of it, as proofs of Churchill's misanthropy, of his contempt for ALL social justice, his loathing of the ideas of justice or equity. Of the three murderers, Churchill, Roosevelt, and Stalin, conscious or unconscious, Stalin is the more open. I think he has never tried to deny his hand in mass murders, assassinations, etc. He would argue that it is just part of his business. Roosevelt would try to say that a murder today is committed solely in the hope of preventing murder by his great grand children's nephews. Mr. Churchill who is an arrant coward and clever scene shifter has never faced Mencius' question: Is there any difference between killing a man with a sword, and killing him with a system of government? Hence the pink popularity of Bolshevik propaganda amongst Lord Prof. Keynes' students in Cambridge, England, the seat of hermaphroditic aesthetics.

Parts of the world prefer LOCAL control, of their own money power and credit. It may be deplorable (in the eyes of Wall Street and Washington) that such aspirations toward personal and national liberty still persist, but so is it. Some people, some nations, prefer their own administration, to that of Baruch and Lemanthau and the Sassoon, and the problem is: how many more millions of British, Russians, and Americans of both the northern and southern American continents, plus Zulus, Basutos, Hottentots, etc.

and the lower, so-called lower races, phantom governments, Maccabees and their sequelae, are expected to die in the attempt to crush out European and Japanese independence?

Oh yes, I want it to stop. I didn't start it. I should like to conserve a few art works, a few mosaics, a few printed volumes, I should like to shore, or bring to beach what is left of the world's cultural heritage, including libraries, and architectural monuments. To serve as models for new construction.

I hear you are spending 45 billion dollars to keep this nasty little kike in the Treasury. It seems a high price to pay for one mangy Hebrew, but American taste is peculiar.

The American people ONCE knew what it wanted to buy with its money, but it looks as if that time was a passin', or had been poured out with the bath water at the time of Roosevelt's second election, I say second not fourth election. I wouldn't spend 45 billion dollars, not if I had it, I wouldn't spend 45 billion dollars, to keep Heine Morgenthau, wormy son of his biosophic father settin' there in the Treasury, spending the American people's purchasing power, in the attempt to bottleneck Ukraine wheat and Iranian petrol. And paying two or more dollars instead of one on purty nigh everything bought by the government in the hope of extinguishing the human lights of humanity. But there is no accountin' for the peculiarities of the American people, or for their lack of coherence, They seem to LIKE spending their money on war, destruction, and inedible metal. Perhaps the biosophists or other American votaries of the infinite will IN TIME produce some sort of diagnosis of the neurosis of the American ethos.

In the meantime, how do you EXPECT to emerge from the shindy, where do you expect it to END?

Do ANY of you, except Mr. Welles, Sumner, and Mr. Agar expect the American, or the British or Yittisch mind to collaborate in reformulation of a workable plan, for international equity? Does Mr. Welles expect the eschewment, the laying off, the desistance from economic aggression (or its more stable state, economic oppression) to be BILATERAL in the postwar world? And if so, why don't they or he step on the gas.

A lot of old card tricks have been published. They do NOT allure the world. The cheese in the free trade trap is too stale to cause the tremor of any exotic whisker. Have we got to wait for a new (possibly pink, or milk white) American generation to SHOW up, and demand local administration? Demand a government with the consent of the governed and NOT by a secret Committee of irresponsibles?

#108 (July 20, 1943) U.S.(C77) OBJECTION (PROTESTA)

I object quite as much as the next man to the loss of American life and to the misfortunes of the American people. I don't know how far I am makin' this clear. I have perhaps two other objections NOT shared by my hearers, or by those who turn off the radio at the sound of my protests.

The American gangster did NOT spend his time shooting women and children. He may have been misguided, but in general he spent his time fighting superior forces at considerable risk to himself. But not in dropping boobytraps for unwary infants. I therefore object to the modus in which the American troops obey their high commander. This modus is NOT in the spirit of Washington or of Stephen Decatur.

I also object to the misuse of the American army and navy. I mean in view of a long term policy. It is known, and should be known better, that an empire to be solid, to be a goin' concern has to be able to stand the expense of policing its trade routes. Now I see Roosevelt and his Jews and his monopolists setting out on a scheme that implies very expensive trade routes, i.e., routes that will require police expenses much greater than would be the case of trade routes maintained by amicable agreement with other nations.

The trade route to the Orient, via the Pacific Ocean, has become very costly. After one-fourth of a century, American plus Rooseveltian methods have generated a degree of friction that has become suddenly quite expensive. The U.S. has irritated Japan. Now I see very considerable likelihood that the methods, and their intensification as registered during the last unfortunate decade, I see, I repeat, a very considerable likelihood that these methods of grab and extortion and bottleneck will in time irritate other eastern and near-eastern peoples. And all that will go into the bill, as it has gone into England's, and the U.S. will have either to pay or get out. There is an old motto about the inutility of winning wars militarily when they have already been politically lost.

What about wars that are economically lost? To win a war, economically, as distinct from merely carrying out an incursion, the subsequent system, the subsequent peace system, or pacification system must bring with it at least a temporary economic stability. Stability enough, that is, to permit the trade routes to pay for their upkeep, that upkeep including the cost of maintainin' order along them.

It was suggested in the American Congress in the 1870's that "as it costs the government 20,000 dollars per head to kill off the red warriors" (i.e., American Indians), it might be humaner and even cheaper to educate. But you were there dealin' with a very sparse population of improvident scattered tribes, NOT with millions and millions of, say, Mohammedans, proud with age-old tradition, thousand and more years of unified doctrine, traditions, customs, and a dislike of the Anglo-Saxon disposition, let alone their feelings toward other races. Now I have no doubt, any more than you have, that one Dupont or whosis or Vickers tank can make a good deal of head way against a bevy of Bedouins. But you have to get the tank there, you have to feed and maintain its incumbents, you have to feed it with petrol. Of course you can make a desert, or make two deserts where before had been one, one desert and one oasis. BUT then again, you have to take into account the cost, the cost of life and convenience to the incumbents, of your Dupont or Vickers tank as well as the taxes falling with increasing weight on the home population, in Kansas and Missouri, for example. To say nothing of the mental and spiritual degeneration of troops used against half-armed opponents under the airs of the Orient.

What sort of old age do you picture for the boy who is sent off to machine gun women and children?

Supposin' he has one? And what sort of bill is the American people expected to foot for the attempt to control Persia and Mesopotania in concurrence with hordes from the Urals? Your English loolahs spent a good deal of air on telling Germany about Napoleon's invasion of Russia, the winter campaign and the rest of it. Now wouldn't it be better to stop and consider for a moment Mr. Henry Wallace's projected invasion of Russia from the Potomac? Wouldn't those arguments apply with still greater force?

I think you will be successful in kicking the British Jews out of Persia. You have already the Bahrein Islands, which you reach via the Cape of Good Hope. BUT Mr. Roosevelt wants also to police the more direct route via Suez. Which has become rather costly. And WILL remain very costly unless you precede it by a complete absolute and permanent crushing of France, Spain, and Italy. I say permanent, not merely spasmodic. If you put a permanent garrison into Europe, to hold down, 20 million Spanish, a few MILLION Portuguese, 45 million Italians, 80 or whatever million Germans, the Scandinavians and the Russians who now wish liberation from Stalin. Just how large a garrison would it require, and WHAT would the annual cost be to the taxpayers in Kansas, and Californy? To say nothing of your Pacific commitments which England shows no sign of wishing to share, having kissed goodbye to her strongest bases, and having handed over such commercial prestige as she possessed in Australia and New Zealand.

And showin' no real hope of competing successfully with the New Orient, it being now generally believed that the Japanese troops are quite ready to die, after having killed off per man three Americans, or done equivalent damage to the instruments of Roosevelt's police squads.

Of course if some Santa Claus is going to come along and pay the bill for you, that is a different matter. But just what far planet, or comet do you expect Santa Claus to descend from? The interstellar spaces have not yet yielded to the Pan American Airways. You can not feed American garrisons on inedible metal, even if it has been bought by the American Treasury. You are already projecting curtailment of Europe's supplies of grain, in conformity with the plow under policy, which was said to have ruined the morale of American mules. IS it intelligent? Does the project inspire confidence on the Stock Exchange?

#109 (July 24, 1943) U.S.(C79)
CIVILIZATION

If we were in normal times, that is to say if it weren't for this tiresome war, I should be writing letters to a small number of people, say 10, 20, a dozen, two dozen, on what some of you would call rather special subjects.

For example, I should be writing to Mr. Otto Bird: I suppose he is now Doctor Bird, Ph.D. He was up in Canada, I forget which university but he was a studyin' with Etienne Gilson, who has writ in French among other things an admirable history of medieval philosophy. And I had sent Dr. Gilson some very pretty photos of the manuscript, unique manuscript, containin' Dino del Garbo's commentary on Cavalcanti's canzone "Donna Mi Prega." Cavalcanti, a friend of Dante's and that poem of very great interest. I spent a good deal of time translatin', and editin' Cavalcanti's poems with paleography, I mean reproductions, of the manuscript so as to show what we really do know and can know, about one of the finest poets that ever lived, sortin' out what is ascertainable from what is not ascertainable. How the stuff was first written down. No autograph stuff, but the earliest copies, and then the later manuscript editings: some of'em under the general supervision, or stimulus, of Lord Medici.

All this may seem very specialized. However I found it of interest, and were it not for this tiresome war I should be writin' to Mr. Bird, now probably Doctor O. Bird, as he was adoin' his thesis on the above mentioned comment by del Garbo's (no relation of Greta's), to point out that whatever I said about Guido's genial thought, his probably having read some Avicenna, and the general ideas entertained by the better minds of his time on the subject of LIGHT. That needed some attention to terminology. I should now want to add to what I printed, and to correlate it with Aristotle's Metaphysics, I mean Aristotle's particular treaties [*treatise*] called "Metaphysics," and that Guido Cavalcanti might have taken his terminology from it, almost entirely. Del Garbo refers to Aristotle and to the treatise. So mebbe Bird has done so in any case. But the matter is interesting at least to a small number of people who think that precise terminology matters; and that that poem and comment give one a very nice chance for ascertainin', gettin' your idea clearer and more precise, as to the likenesses and differences between 18th century thought and our own. Have we got better at thinkin'? Do we think with greater clarity? Or has the so-called program of science merely got us all cluttered up mentally and pitched us into greater confusion?

No, the comment on a medieval poem don't just stop there, any more than Frobenius' research just STOPS with some bit of African sculpture, or with some prehistorical drawin' on the side of a rock.

Grosseteste writin' on light, hooks up with the ideogram of the sun and moon at the start of Confucius' testament. Incidentally, if medieval bishops in England were anything like as intelligent as Robert Grosseteste, it would look as if the standards of English episcopacy have declined. I'll say DEclined since that date. Of course Bird wouldn't be my only or even chief correspondent, I am just taking the point most recently come up in my personal business. Wars interrupt this sort of thing. They mostly lower the level of livin', of the good life. Now as far as I am concerned, you have lost some of my contributions. I don't say that matters much, but the sum of such European contributions to the good life, or the life of the American mind does matter. You got to lump'em in with the deterioration of some of the American human material.

My edition of the Great Learning is in Italian, not in American, as was my first edition. And it has the Chinese text facin' it. And I know a good deal more now than when Glenn Hughes printed my first version in his University books. And you haven't got my translation of Pea's novel Moscardino. Carta da Visita is written in Italian. I believe something special was done about Geo. Santayana's manuscript or proofs of something or other. But other voices are silent.

You say I also am losin' something, I don't deny it. I don't hear from Mr. Eliot or Mr. Cummings. If they write anything, we got to wait for it. You've got to multiply that. After all immediate contacts probably count less for a man of my age than for a young man. One understands'em more, but they probably incommode one less in one's mental business. Eighteen or however many years ago S. Putnam was askin' me about Italian writers, livin' writers: and I knew considerably less. I finally got round to mentioning [Morelli?] (I mean of writers not known like Pirandello. And Basil Bunting). Wanted to translate Tozzi, but no English or American publisher had sense to let him. I now see some sort of clearance: clearin' up in Italian style. Carlo Scarfoglio whose political notes you sometimes hear on this radio, did a preface that pretty well coincides with my views on writin' (no collusion). Two men headin' from different quarters, come to the same main conclusion. He startin' with translatin' Aeschylus, and doin' it beautifully. Clear like a piece of glass. And his version of the Hymn to Demeter, homeric Hymn to Demeter. You may remember that Doc. Rouse calls Greek a necessity of civilized life. IT IS. So is Latin.

Take time to go into these matters. I was layin' for to point out the difference. The European and specifically Italian SENSE of these things. It shows in my bein' here at this radio. That is due to [the] Italian sense of civilization, sense that special work like mine, and like that of other writers, Carlini, for example ought to go on. That communication OUGHT to be kept up war or no war. Like they go on having picture shows. Go on holdin' up and improvin' criterion in the arts. NOT universal in any country.

But a field where competition is healthy. And I have before now said that from England and America I do not HEAR any indication of a similar sense of civilization. The best writers in England and America do NOT get to the microphone, which is the only way of communication left open. The American microphone descends to the level of Hollywood.

I could trace that back a good way to the decay of integrity in the BETTER American magazines.

Decay of sense of responsibility, to and FOR the thought of the American nation. Sedgewick and other blights that I started objectin' to 36 years ago. I got no time tonight to be political. I meant to be political, but nobody here ASKS me to be political. I wanted to make a little list of lies and swindles that are breakin' down, not catchin' coneys (that means catchin' suckers) so plentiful. The swindles England put over on others; that she don't like you puttin' over on her. Mr. Welles bein' pious, and trying to resell us the free trade hoax. And up jumps the Bolshevik threatenin' to DUMP like all hell, according to the most rabid pluto Bolshevik methods.

All that is instructive but on a more popular (mebbe I ought to say in a certain sense less popular) plane.

#110 (July 25, 1943) U. K. (C74)
LOST OR STOLEN (PERDUTO O RUBATO)

A friend of mine once entitled a poem "Attys or something missing." I wonder if any of you realize, or could by an effort arrive at realization of the degree of detachment that I feel at moments or if you, on your own, ever do try to see the present historic moment from the outside.

The thing in my case goes beyond an effort of will, I simply find myself outside, observing. *Le reconnaitre et le savoir*. There is a poem of Guy Charles Gros that does not end in the same manner, for he ends: "Ai-je cru un seul instant a la realité du monde ..." That is French poetry, and Buddhistic detachment.

But I do not make out what has become of those Englishmen, or of that English tradition that led one to believe in the existence of Englishmen who protested against the drift of their governments. Mebbe they are too old, the ones I remember, or too young, the ones whom I have not met. Certainly the few dozen voices that rose from the printed page in Britain, before this war, demanding justice, social justice INSIDE the borders of England, and comprehension, or at least some degree of attention to fact outside the borders of England, those voices are silent, or smothered. Or at any rate they are inaudible here.

Lord knows you have the equipment, as contrasted to what I have available. You have your BBC with your archives. And I have not one disc, not one phonorecord available. And perhaps those past records are the BEST that you have. But your use of them is deficient.

You know, the most flatheaded among you knows that your press has lied, and that your BBC is not impartial. And no one expects it to be impartial. But there are degrees in all things. And some of you must perceive that from the difference between a howl for monopoly and dominion and a demand for justice. Or at any rate I am not yet brought to believe that that type of man is wholly beaten, is wholly extinct in England.

Some of you MUST stand back now and then, and sift out what you hear on your air. What you read in your papers. Must perceive that most of it is flimflam, that is, stuff poured out to get your mind off the fact, and to KEEP you from reflecting on the facts, and keep you from thinking at all of a sane order. There are plenty of flights of what Lenin called derisively "revolutionary inventiveness." Meaning schemes detached from reality and possibility. Plans divorced for [*from*] true data.

All right. Where have we got to? You don't know. Perhaps no one does know. But at any rate in the debating club, the international, mondial world wide, etc. academy of the air, certain points have been made. In fact nearly all the points I have been arguing these past few years HAVE BEEN made. And made so thoroughly that your official world just has to pretend they aren't there. Just as the press always did ignore certain facts for as long as possible.

Your parliament does discuss points that were smothered for decades. Gold for example. Even Monty Skinnergue Norman knew that the value of gold is not stable. It fluctuates. Tables of its fluctuations were printed. A few bright lads deplored a gold standard simply because it did not recognize the mutable value of gold. Didn't let it rise and fall on the market according to the law of supply and demand.

Irving Fisher's arguments about its fluctuability were, I suppose, used to help in the greatest gold brick swindle (I suppose it was about the greatest of all time). Gold fluctuates, Its price today is as never before a fancy price. It has gone out of use, it is not necessary as is oil or wheat. Nations can live for years without it. They could live without it altogether IF they were not attacked from outside. Its price is a fancy price.

Not a fancy price such as is paid for a Rembrandt; not a fancy price as is paid for an old painting by a great master. Say there are only a dozen or ½ dozen Giorgiones, mostly in museums, national property, and, if there is one for sale and you can get six or eight millionaires all to think that they want it, you run up a fancy price. But gold is not even like that. There is more of it. AND its value is mutable: and the need of it or the want of it was declining, has in fact declined; could decline to almost zero, no, not quite to zero, but to dental etc.

Well the answer was not to lower the price on the market but to put UP the price, and to sell it to the American boobs, the great American public, in what was probably the greatest gold brick wheeze of all time. When the boobs have it all, the price will come down again rapidly as is usual, when the boobs have obtained possession of anything, but during the course of the present unpleasantness: old wheezes HAVE dwindled, as the Virginia hot air conference showed. The sham about money flopped. The wheeze of 60% interest has been ventilated. The wheeze of varying the value of any national currency has at last had some publicity. At the Hot Springs all the sham and the scenery fell, there was nothing left but the stark evil desire to extort and monopolize. Flash lit from a dozen capitals, "corner the world's grain market," said one Rome commentator A half dozen voices from

Berlin, at once denouncing the swindle. AND also a few voices from England. Aware that the British farmer will be better off if he has an INTERNAL market in England, at a just price, for what he can grow.

But that is NOT in itself a desire for JUSTICE. That does not constitute in itself a willingness to DO justice. It does not constitute in itself a perception of justice. Let alone a will to support it, to support justice or even to permit justice to others.

There was a murmer on the BBC air about unfairness; but it wasn't of unfairness extending outwards; it was a complaint that somebody had said you hadn't imperial confraternity, or solidarity. God knows you have EXPLOITED Australian sentimentality about the mama country. And probably will exploit it still further. That don't mean that a new Burke has risen amongst you. Row after row of pretenses has fallen, but the sense of equity? What was at one time, or was at one time supposed to be your sense of equity? Has it been lost, mislaid or stolen? And if stolen, by whom?

Part II

10 Miscellaneous Scripts

#111 (early 1941)
HOMESTEADS

What will remain from this struggle is an idea. What spreads and will spread from the determination to have a New Europe is an idea: the idea of a home for every family in the country. The idea that every family in the country shall have a sane house, and that means a house well built, with no breeding space for tuberculosis bugs. I have seen the details of some of these houses. It means that every family's house will have land enough, fields enough to support the family. It means that these houses will not be burdened with mortgages. They will be inalienable, and indivisible. The eldest son if he likes, or at any rate one son or daughter will keep the farm, but above all the farmer will be guaranteed a sale for his crop AT A PRICE that will cover his needs.

You may have heard that Andy Jackson OPENED the American lands to the settlers. As against John Quincy Adams who had what might be called a more communist idea, not that he was read, but he wanted at least some land reserved to the nation and its proceeds used for schools, and more highfalutin' branches of education. He was "out of time." Jackson beat him. Jackson's policy was a bit sketchy. American homesteads in great part passed into great estates very quickly grazing in place of farms etc , etc. My grandmother and great grandmother lived on claims, land claims. The boys of 20 in New York now know very little of such affairs. My father still has 80 year-old cousins living I take it on claims in Montana They do not represent the majority life of America.

But Jackson's land policy was called DEMocratic. The New Europe is in that sense DEMociatic, and if you folks rush out to SMASH this New Europe history will NOT give you ANY medals whatever for saving DEMocracy.

Italy does NOT confiscate the farmers' crop. I have seen that lie along with 200 others. Italy has not set up Utopia in XIX years, but the farmer here knows he will be paid for what he grows. He knows what he will be paid for it. Nobody will get an option on it and grab excess profits. Get it quite firmly in mind that war mongers are asking you to prevent and smash this idea of a solid and clean well built house with land for each family. Look into it before you decide to go out and die for something or other, without quite knowing what.

Let me remind you that Brooks Adams was seen shortly before his death, an old man of 80 in running shorts and sweater, pulling the weights in the gym of the Boston Athletic Club and prophesying a 30 years' war, an IDEO LOGICAL war. And let me remind you that the notion of ideological wars is FORWARD, not backward. Our American forebears, given an empty continent, sketched in a civilization. Rough draft without very great attention to detail. Settlers rushed onto the land, they had hunger, land hunger, each man to be free: Free of RENT, free of mortgage. Reflection came later. A new idea rises in Europe, it is not confined to the continent. You can not confine it. No amount of postal thieves, censors, examiners, can smash it or swush it. There arises the idea that a man may own all he can use. But that he may not own what he can't *use*. And especially he may not use this surplus to starve his neighbor, he may not prevent farmer Jones selling his corn. The millionaire may NOT rush in and undersell Jones till he has ruin'd him, taken a mortgage on Jones' farm, turned out Jones' children the day the interest isn't paid to the full. I will get round in time to the flimflam of a past kind of pacifist, the suppression of news, the gyrations committed by the Carnegie so-called Peace Foundation, their failure to get thought into America.

Wars are made to make DEBT. Our Civil War had a relation to DEBT. Christopher Hollis knows this.

Read his book, the TWO NATIONS, debts of the South to the City of New York.

Greece spends 54% of her income paying the interest on DEBT. Until you know who has lent what TO WHOM, you know nothing whatever of politics, you know nothing whatever of history, you know nothing of international wrangles.

I wish Hollis hadn't taken to silence and solitude just when he did. But on the other hand has ANY man in England now the power to speak out or communicate with his fellows?

Little Red Riding Hood, better look out for Wilikie's false teeth! Is Wendell saving DEMocracy? Is Wendell selling the New Deal to Winston? Or is Wendell trying to shovel a few million farm boys into the trenches?

And SO soon after headlines "It's War OR Willkie"? Is Wendell now for it at all costs; just to prove not having elected him, war is the consequence? Is Mr.'Opkins selling the New Deal to London?

My venerable friend Doctor William C. Williams roars with laughter when I suggest that people might THINK. "Ever see a communist THINK?" writes ole Bill. I been told the process ain't nacheral. Waal, the Doc. is their white-haired boy. Will even he notice that one group of people has steadily tried to EXtend this conflict and to SUPPRESS all kind of intercommunication between Europe and the U.S.? The other side (my side) has asked [for an] investigation. Now what CAUSES that?

Did this war start for Danzig? Did this war start for POland, and if so why such silence re the half of Poland that has been et [eaten] up by Rhooshy? You people don't believe those sad tales? Or do you?

Some people want to make money. Some people want to keep on with a racket that has paid'em and their papas large dividends. There may be six or eight rackets. Debt interest, gun selling. Is American youth expected to run out and die for debt interest and gun selling? If that is what the war-wanters WANT, let'em say so.

In England for years it has been KNOWN that the English war plant could NOT produce the goods. Is it to be supposed that a lover of England pushed his country into war, KNOWING that country could NOT produce the goods?

It has been declared in England for years that there was a plot on to bash out the WHOLE of Europe for the profit of Russia and the moneyed in America. It now appears that England has been caught in the tweezers of the attempt but that continent largely has NOT French *bon sens* showed itself at the last minute They declined to have Paris completely coventried in order to hold off the German advance for six days or whatever.

The English are not so quick on the uptake. My Hollis has ceased to talk about "the debts of the South to the City of New York being 200 million."

I have been 20 years on this job, but you will not read. The new generation will not read AFTER it has been bombed to blazes or buried by high explosive. It may be your last chance. I suggest that you try to read Hollis' *Two Nations* and read pages 206, 207 to learn what the Civil War was ABOUT, who and what caused it.

Then you may see who and what is trying to get you yet again into the trenches, and to KEEP British men UNDER fire despite the fact that they did NOT vote for this war. The gombeen men's idea is that the MORE of England gets smashed, the higher the rate of interest, and the MORE of it, they can change the survivors. What [does] the farmer in West Africa get out of this war? Who now owns THEIR government, for example? If Mr. Hull means to say: I hate the English, I hope there will be in England not one stone left on another. I hope the Stone of Scone will be smashed into powder and made into portland cement. I don't want ANY life left in Britain.

All right, let him express himself. If he means: let's grab all, positively all the British assets, let him say so, but in that case why dress up as a friend of Britain? And in the meantime let me remind Messrs.

Roosevelt and WALLACE of the Report of the National Survey of Potential Product Capacity, published by Hodson, Chairman of the Emergency Relief Bureau and Post, *idem*, New York Housing Authority in 1935, one of the greatest glories of Mr. Roosevelt's administration which has also been somewhat neglected both by administration and its opponents. As to the Academy of Social and Political Science, I keep wondering when they will start a serious study of ANYthing whatsoever that is vital to American welfare. A bunch of playboys.

#112 U.S. (1941)
MARCH ARRIVALS

All the world knows that Mons. H.E. Matsuoka arrived in Rome last evening. I also arrived in Rome last evening, at a different station, through no intentional disrespect on my part toward the Orient's first rank diplomat. The events quite naturally received different degrees of attention; after all I arrive here more often, and have not come from so great a distance. At the present moment I see no chance whatever of breaking into official circles and discussing with his Excellency my proposals for PEACE in the Pacific.

I do not know that even the rank and file of our own leaders would take the plan, treat the plan with due gravity, I do not know whether either they or my present auditors will follow my meaning. The plan is simple but even that may not recommend it. I should quite plainly propose to give Guam to the Japanese in return for one set of color and sound films of the 300 best Noh dramas.

The films could not be delivered all at once, so we would not need to give up Guam all at once.

We Americans are, or were, as you probably know, considered a set of soulless roughnecks, by most of the outer world. Of course we are not, but fact and opinion differ so often in this imperfect world.

Of late there has been added to our portrait a touch, a, eh TOUCH of hysteria. Old blokes like me begin to wonder where all the Dan'l Boones and Davy Crocketts have got to.

Americans are supposed to run wode at reports of Martian invaders. Well now, I don't suppose more than two or three chaps ran out and committed hara-kiri at the news of those parachutists from Mars.

You may think I am joking about this Guam proposition. I am not. I ask the impartial auditor whether the individual American citizen wouldn't get a great deal MORE out of a set of such films as I saw, the one I saw in Washington two years ago, than he would out of a few tons of tungsten, with possibly a few family coffins thrown in. It would mean, and I admit it would mean, getting educated up to the point of knowing what is meant by Kumasaka and Kagekiyo.

The film I saw was of Awoi no Uye. The Japanese would be truly grateful to us, not for Guam, but for prodding 'em on to make a complete high grade record of these plays before the tradition gets damaged.

Umewaka Minoru is dead. I have heard discs of Noh music that did NOT seem to me up to the mark.

It is never too soon to start on such records. And for the American auditor who doesn't yet know what I am talking about, let me say that half a century ago an American professor with a Spanish name went over to Japan and brought back the news and some notes on a number of remarkable plays, said to have been kept unchanged in their stage tradition for 4 or 5 centuries. Centuries. And after a lapse of years W.B. Yeats said it was the form he had been seeking all his life in an attempt to write drama that should be also high poetry.

And in the play Kagekiyo we have, I think, the soul of Japan. As its delicacy in Nishikigi, and its epos in Kagekiyo, which contains so far as my very imperfect knowledge extends, the one truly Homeric passage in such of their literature as Fenollosa brought back to us, or other of our translators have come on.

That is the JAPAN we WANT. That is the Japan that could mean something to us, and be in the high sense of some use to us. We have most material things inside our own borders, though in a bull market for means of murder we may want a little more tungsten etc. We do not need Indian opium.

I don't know about taking a plebiscite. Probably the bulk of the population would not understand it, but given time to know what I am driving at, I believe this proposal would come nearer the normal American wish, a wish after all for the good life, than any of these dinimiteros and earth hoggers have any idea of.

Is there any need for the whole earth to run mad because two-fifths have gone beserk?

The American people WANT civilization. Get under their skin and even that crack about the 5-cent cigar does NOT move the American deep. We like a wisecrack some of us, including the high bracket writers aim to be TOUGH, I say TOUGH and HOW when appearing in public. But in private they lay it off.

That old phrase about clarifying one's intentions is not worked nearly enough. In trying to give the American people what they WANT, I mean WANT, no one can offer them blood and destruction. The sob stuff aimed at getting 'em into trenches is all based on NOT getting into the trenches. It is all based on how wrong it is for anyone to get into trenches. Which being the case, why not move DIRECT toward the goal?

Why has so little been done in and FROM North America to stop the war or before that to prevent it, or at any rate to keep it from overflowing the whole of the earth?

I gather that if I am to go on with these talks, I shall have gradually more to say about letters and less about international politics. I might even say a word or two about Joyce, but before I get onto that subject, I shall one of these days read you a letter from Mensdorff, Count Mensdorff Dietrichstein-Pouilly, containing a few ideas on peace, and how to attain it, written in Vienna back in 1928. Just to show how long it takes to get ideas into action. Then again they asked me here a couple of weeks ago what I thought about one or two American writers, handin' me samples. And I wrote out a couple of comments, which I will also read you one night, if the spring advances, and rain lays off and the spirit of man takes on a little normality.

You probably still think I am joking about those cinema records of Japanese plays. I am not. You spend millions a year on education. Young men go to colleges to get education. You spend MONEY and time to get education. I am telling you how to get some. I have knocked'round Europe for 30 years, I have seen some fairly good dancing, I have heard some music, Mozart, Janequin. I have even been paid for writing down my opinions on music. As to dancing, Russian or whatever, I have never seen anything that could touch the movement of the tennin in the Hagormo dance that Tami Koumé did for me in his London studio 25 years ago. And as to music, a couple of bars of modern Japanese film play, after 25 years, hit me straight in the midriff. You couldn't mistake it for any one music in the wide and blinkin' world. And it was worth hearing.

You've got land, when you don't let it go to hell with erosion. You've got God knows what in the way of material wealth if you'd only learn how to USE it, how to get about from one part of the U.S. to another, and not starve the share croppers. Sanity in foreign relations means getting IN what you haven't got, you haven't got any Japanese classical plays or anything like'em. Yeats merely wrote some plays more or less in the form of the Japanese non-libretti. The Noh is made up of words, dance movements and music, as well as great acting. Think in terms of the individual. What does the American individual get out of such and such IMPORTS?

#113 (1941) U.S.(68)
AMERICA WAS PROMISES

I do what I can to keep an even tone of voice; now when I drop my voice, they turn on more current. As to the tone, there are times to speak mildly and there are times to speak with asperity, and as to American war makers ALL thought of America going to war is bunkumb, it is hogwash, bug wash, unmitigated b.b.b. [?]; and I will tell you WHY it is hogwash, and why we should not give way to the gibes of pink tea females, and their soupheaded consorts.

There has even come up the term "UNamerican" used by asinine females and tinhorn employees of Jewsfelt to define ANY man, woman, or child who isn't ready to chuck away and destroy every last vestige of the American heritage.

They git that way reading Jew papers for 40 years. They git that way hearin' kike radio, and I propose to use the word KIKE regardless of race. Use it to cover honorary Jews, AND TO EXCEPT honest Jews when we find'em.

Talk of America enterin' war is sheer DIRT. And it is ignorant dirt because it HIDES a hundred years of American history. It forges and falsifies the WHOLE aim and purpose of the American national foundation. The colonists went to the stem and rock bound to get away from dirt, and start fresh.

The Union of the 13 Colonies after the Revolution was founded to efface certain differences and, whatever one may think now of the meltin' pot theory, it has had this effect. The U.S.A. is NOT formed and organized INTERNALLY to participate in foreign quarrels. It can't be done without a lot of small dirty meanness to millions of American citizens and that means appeal to the smallest and dirtiest human instincts. It is babyish, it comes from the natural akussed tendency of two or three kids to pick on some other one. A meanness which their mammies and pappies try to wipe out if there is any decency in the family. Anybody who will draw back a minute and look at the way people pick on minorities, can see what I mean by this statement.

When things are scarce, or fearing fear, when people git scared and make a run on a bank or a grocery store, there is a scramble and, when things go slower, there is a conspiracy, to shut out someone or other.

Starts as a joke: ends as a monopoly. The only old style relation of emigrants IN America to aliens was in their Indian wars. They are over. As to how much dirt was done to the Injuns, as to how far the Injuns wuz fractious, I refrain from pronouncin'.

The Injuns were an alien race. Our other troubles came FIRST from or trying to git out from UNDER the rump and boot of money lenders and stinkers in London, who thereafter tried to bust us. Look up the history of our relations to London during the Civil War. I am not lookin' backward for the sake of rousin' a rancour. I am telling you something about the way the U.S. are built up inside for PEACE, and NOT for takin' sides in European combat. Our Civil War was wangled. Read Christopher Hollis on the DEBTS of the South to the City of New York. Also read Overholser, on the DEBTS to BE CREATED by that war so [that] London kikes and American traitors could control the American currency.

It is not today a case of being DARED to fight part of Europe. It is a case of getting rid [of] the whole snot and dung of usury propaganda, which conduces to slaughter. The British who are in part a softhearted, in part a dirty and brutal race, have been had. They have shown docility in fighting for their owners and masters. And these owners and masters have gradually become Jewish; but are not yet wholly so. When we did something clean, Europe honored us. Europe even longed for a U.S. of Europe. Toward which Europe is now movin', offered now only by the usury centrals.

It is such UTTER buncomb, this talk of America being menaced by FINLAND. And it is such utter buncomb, this alliance with the Bolshevik government. Fruit of utter hysteria. Fruit also of readin' periodical crap for the past 50 or 80 years. And these ninnies, these pimps, and shysters who now have the gall to use the words American and Unamerican with NO reference to the fiber of the American nation.

Most of'em have never read anything but magazines.

The extent of the betrayal, whereof Roosevelt is part, whereof he is an excrescence: a protuberant nose is indicated by the fact that there are NO handy volumes of the writings of the men who MADE and kept up the American Union from 1750 till 1864.

What does Mrs. Jonas Keikenbaum mean by "American"? These chicken-headed fat mammies have never given a glance at our history. They are wholly unaware of the purpose for which we are existin'.

Clever Kikes runnin' ALL our communication system. Simple-hearted Wallaces and Wickards, trying to do good to the farmer; without gittin' down to bedrock. OF course there are scandals about Army contracts, and for defense of the Volga and the Yangtze-Kiang River in China. Where the WHOLE system is founded on fraud, fraud will crop up in the details. Does any man of my age reflect on the theory prevalent when I was in college, namely that you GOT TO BE dishonest to git on in business? What caused that theory at the turn of the century?

It warn't there in 1776. I'll say it WAS NOT. When you git a minority of Americans, that is, a large enough minority, to KNOW why it is tommyrot to issue all national purchasing power as INTEREST payin' debt, the nation will lay off so doing, and thereafter men can live, and carry on business without being told to run crooked. Without young men being advised to run crooked. You got to define your terms, define your words, think what money will BUY (as that constitutes the value of money). All that is part of a nation's INTERNAL structure.

But in the immediate foreground, get it into your block that the U.S.A. has not been livin' for a thousand years NEXT door to ALIEN races, formed, compacted with relatively clear national or tribal frontiers. We are all intermixed, interwoven, livin' next door to each other. We do NOT need more land, we may need land improvement. If you go on destroyin' and urging others to DESTROY, you will need more production. Don't believe me if you don't want to, but do at least look into facts of American history.

Why was the U.S. founded? How come we had any colonial architecture, any American craftsmanship?

What part did local colonies' groups of different European races take in the development, in the foundation of what made our life worth livin'?

You look into that, before you go shootin' Frenchmen at Dakar, or keepin' up dope sales in the Orient.

You can't go to war without small meanness to SOME of the neighbors. You get het up over the sorrows of Mrs. Ikestein, the tailor's wife; you can't DO anything about it without doin' dirt to Giovanni the grocer, and the Hungarian livin' next door, or the grandson of R. Schuz's old friend who sells delicatessen.

#114 (1941) U.S.(50)
ARISTOTLE AND ADAMS

Johnnie Adams, the first, the real father of his country, the man who picked General Washington, George, to lead the Colonial armies against a damned, stinking and cheating British Government, no better than Roosevelt and Morgenthau, or Churchill or any other set of enemies of the people and thieves of the public purse, was on the trail of Aristotle's studies of constitutions, constitutions of a lot of Greek states. In fact Johnnie wanted to know what really was the best form of government. And more than any other man, not excludin' Jim Madison and Thomas Jefferson, he got on the trail. And it is a damn pity that the only known copy of Harry Stotl's brochure on the Athenian constitution was then lying on an Egyptian dump heap. In fact the back side had been used as a farmer's account book, and if Mr. Didymus, farm bailif, hadn't akept his accounts on the back of the sheets, that admirable work might have been lost to mankind altogether, near the Egyptian town of Hermopolis, in the year '78/'79 A.D. in the time of Vespasian. Well, Mr. Adams would have enjoyed readin' it; but as he didn't, you can.

At any rate it might broaden the mind, especially it might inconvenience some of them 4,000 paid liars attached to the British legation or embassy in Washington, and graduated from that sink of hell and bog of iniquity, the London Pseudo-school of Pseudonomics.

For years economics professors have been lying, even going so far as to deprecate loans BY THE STATE, when the fleet that won the battle of Salamis was BUILT with money lent by the Athenian state to the ship builders, INSTEAD of morgagin' the whole nation to kikes, Biddies, swine, and enemies of the people as has been done in damn near every nation ever since the Stank of England was founded.

Well states have lent money, and the Pennsylvania Colony lent it. And the French frawgs are lendin' it. So the British fire on their late allies. And every damn possible thing is done to prevent the American in Utah or Montana from learning economics or history.

And our Constitution DOES give Congress the right to determine prices, though it is worded, "right to determine the value of money," which is the same thing. If you can determine HOW long a yard stick is, you can determine how may yards there are in a piece of linen. Well, ole Harry he noted some features in that model DEMocratic and Republican constitution, along with regulations fer not having balconies overhanging roads, and conduits overflowing into the roads; he mentions market controllers. Blame it on me and on Mussolini. Go on, blame it on us. Athens was a light amid ancient civilizations. There was superintendence of merchandise, to prevent the sale of spurious and adulterated articles. And there were also the corn wardens, or wheat wardens, to see that unground grain was in market at a FAIR PRICE, and next, that millers sell their barley meal at a price corresponding with that of barley, and the baker women at a price corresponding with that of wheat, weighing the amount fixed by the officials.

HENCE, the Catholic doctrine of the just price, which, roughly speakin', built the cathedrals, and assured European civilization from the time of St. Ambrose to the time of St. Antonio. Sure, blame it on Hitler! blame it on Mussolini. And don't, don't learn anything of WHY there was a French revolution.

What abuses it set out to correct, what abuses it failed to correct, and hence all the flimflam.

Even Marx KNEW what the abuses were. In fact he is pretty good at diagnosis of evil. Waaal, then there is also a very pretty little passage in Harry Stotl's li'l book labeled Politics. And if you had read it Franklin Delano might not have got so far away with HIS politics.

ληρος είυάι ςοχει τό υόμισμά
Times when money is humbug
μεταδεμέυωυ τε τωυ χρωμέυωυ

People go alterin' the currency, and somebody is played for a sucker.

In fact a classical education WOULD be useful if the universities didn't wrap it in cotton wool, and keep the stewdents from reading the more vital passages.

In fact a little Greek of the right kind or even readin' some with a crib IF you have the real curiosity would be useful. It would put you wise as to WHY Keynes and Guggleheim alias Gregory, and the scientific departments have managed to get Economics, so called, studied so COMpletely separate from any general education, classical education and general culture, so that they can LIE and not get caught out, and ball up the simple facts about money, and what it is. Without havin' the student ask inconvenient questions based on a knowledge of HISTORY, of the salient facts in our history or Greek history, or Demosthenes law cases, or Lincoln's fight for a national currency, or the Pennsylvania Colony's loans of PAPER money to the Colonists, to be paid back in ten lot, one tenth per year, as brought prosperity to the colony, and was the admiration of

Europe, till the sons of bitches in London cracked down on it, and tried to sell the 13 colonies into slavery as the same bastids succeeded in doing after the great betrayal of 1863, Ikieheims, Vandergould, Sherman, playin' stinky with Rothschild, and betrayin' the American people.

Like Roosevelt is doin' with Morgenthau's able assistance, down underneath, down at BED rock, and quite apart from using war as top dressing to keep your minds OFF the American Treasury.

When will American college students realize that almost ANY bit of real knowledge would keep'em from being dead rabbits? Aristotle, Demosthenes, Mencius or Confucius, all antidotes to bein' suckers.

And of course it would be a revolution, and INTERlexshul revolution if college students would be wondering what they spend four years in college NOT learning!! Which would be both an adornment in the conversation and of use in their business. Business of LIVIN', I mean, cent per cent, 100% livin', gettin' something out of life by the process of puttin' their interest, mental interest, into it. Instead of being played for a sucker, by an ex bank tout and international swindler, a specialist in inflation and devaluation.

And of course it is a mere matter of opinion, but it WAS Aristotle's opinion, expressed in the 5th book of his Politics, that the three qualities which supreme magistrates ought to possess are loyalty to established constitutions; secondly, great capacity for the duties of the office; and thirdly, virtue and justice.

In each the sort of justice suited. It seems a bit hard on Franklin Delano, but so it is in the Greek ably translated by Mr. Rackham, and verified by the present speaker.

#115 (1942) U.S.(27)
TO CONSOLIDATE

If anyone takes the trouble to record and to examine the series of talks I have made over this radio it will be found that I have used three sorts of material: Historical facts; convictions of experienced men, based on fact; and the fruits of my own experience. The facts go back to the opening of a copper mine by Tching Tang in the year 1766 B.C., they mostly antedate the fascist era and can not be considered as improvisations trumped up to meet present requirements. Neither can the beliefs of Washington, John Adams, Jefferson, Jackson, Van Buren, and Lincoln be laughed off as mere Fascist propaganda. And even my own observations date largely before the opening of the present hostilities, as do those of my grandfather expressed in the U.S. Congress in 1878.

I defend the particularly American, North American, United States heritage. If anybody can find anything hostile to the Constitution of the U.S.A. in these speeches, it would greatly interest me to know what.

It may be bizarre, eccentric, quaint, old-fashioned of me to refer to that document, but I wish more Americans would at least read it. It is not light and easy reading but it contains several points of interest, whereby some of our present officials could, if they but would, profit greatly.

Or, considering the jack in office, of less importance than the whole people and the whole nation, I should say the nation would greatly benefit if the literate citizens would attend to the document, both it its more important details and in its spirit. Even if Charles Beard does think it a barrier against real democracy. I would remind Prof. Beard that Adams studied republics. Even Beard now knows less of the Constitution than did John Adams and Madison. The treasure of a state is its equity. That is to say, its capacity to give every man a square deal. Teddy used to say square deal. There is no sane economics, without a sane ethic at its base.

And certain kinds of honesty have been known for 5000 years. Certain kinds of dishonesty are equally well recorded in history; and the capacity, anybody's capacity, for fooling all men ALL the time is, as Lincoln remarked, limited.

A considerable force, in some cases a force of inertia, has been espoused to my views, to my perceptions, to my patient collecting of data, ever since I had any views, or perceptions, or started collecting data. I have in the main been confined to papers of very small circulation, but not invariably. As I can not AT ALL count on the present hearers, if there are any present hearers, [not] having read a line of [my] writing I have, for the sake of clarity, to repeat things I have said before.

Sometime the DATE at which I emitted my beliefs adds, or should add, a bit of weight or interest, to the fact shown, or the conviction presented. This is not in retrospect, but in prospect. If I had always been WRONG, as nine tenths of the people to whom you listen, I should have less cause to rake up old articles printed, or old statements made when I have been interviewed, now and again often by reporters who did not expect their copy to get past the editor's desk. New York Sun, April 21, 1939: "We don't think that much will be heard of it since many of the author's comments ... aren't likely to get beyond the copy desks."

Most of the lads kept their notes simply as curiosities ... and so forth, referring to remarks by present speaker, my own conclusion being that an American newspaper can occasionally print something useful, but can very seldom do so TWICE. American editors and newspaper men having a perfectly well grounded terror of the power that rules by night, and strikes mercilessly at the pocket. I did, however, suggest, and it is in print in the files of several N.Y. papers, that there was on April 21, 1939 a group of people *in America* trying to get a war started, there were people doing so. Mr. Wallace, now Vice President, in a definition of the Democratic body of faith, started off with demanding action based on the will of the majority AFTER the people have had an opportunity to inform themselves of the real facts. Mebbe he has changed his view since 1938, when his book was printed? The real facts about British bank agents in America, Mr. Ikleheimer, etc., during the past 80 years have NOT been very amply revealed to the citizens. The real facts regarding the connection of at least ONE of Kuhn Loeb's directors, with the British Intelligence Service have not, so far as I know, had the publicity they deserve.

One of the Roosevelt cabinet, in 1939, asked me where I thought the link was? I told him. Mr. Dies hadn't been quite as diligent in looking into the activities of British financial agents in the U.S. as some of his own committee would at that date seem to have wished. What opportunity has the people had to get information regarding gold purchase by Morgenthau's department? What facts of American history are widely available? Not only of past eight years' sins against the whole people, but of the record of the past 80 or 100 years? Munitioneers? Speculations in war material? Speculation in other materials made scarce by diversion of work FROM sane activities in production [?] of food and clothing to war material.

WAR IS THE MAXIMUM SABOTAGE. Nothing so helps the creators of artificial scarcity as a condition wherein goods are rapidly destroyed without doing direct good to ANYONE. There seems today to be at least an audible minority of people who think NOW, as I did in 1939, that some group or groups of interested persons in the U.S. desire and then desired war. My remarks on gold at that time seem to have a considerable confirmation within the past few weeks. In an interview printed on June 15th, 1939, I stated that "A war on Germany in our time would be a war against an honest concern of money." I cited Schacht's remark about money issued against goods. I might have cited Mr. Zubly in one of the earliest sessions of the American Congress. I should be glad, I should be very glad indeed, if Mr. Wallace and his friends would get busy and give the people an ADEQUATE opportunity to inform themselves of the real facts. "Paths to Plenty," lovely little title for a booklet, but is your gasoline going to be rationed? I can't read you the whole of Wallace's booklet. What I don't make out is how, having written that booklet, Mr. Wallace has been got at—HAD in the interim—and is now out yelling bloody murder ALL on the side of the loan sharks, the munitioneers, the despoilers of agriculture and murderers of the working man. And what the Sam Hill he thinks a ten years war would do toward attaining the very ideals he was preaching in Californy three years ago? He can't believe in the filthy hell of Geneva, he can't believe in the infamy of the League of Nations with its 20 year record of refusal to make ANY move toward social justice constantly working for the international swine and bleeders and scarcity makers, monopolists. Churchill and company represent usury they represent tyranny oppression, greed, unrestricted exploitation of humanity, by the most contemptible batch of egotists the world has seen in our time. Betrayers of their allies, public enemies of their own people. Suppressors *in excelsis* of those FACTS which Mr. Wallace was three years ago suggesting as necessary for majority opinion. Not even the wildest jungo denies that Churchill is a phenomenal liar. Not even that canting nark Halifax would sustain publicly that Churchill gives the poor deluded Britons the facts, or ever believed in ANY of the main points of Wallace's doctrine.

The men with whom Wallace could agree are in Rome and in Berlin. They are not all of'em in the limelight. They are DOING the things Wallace asks for. How the heck he has got over onto the other side of the fence needs some explaining.

A new order means a world where every man has the chance to work and GET PAID enough to feed and clothe at least four people, himself, wife, and two kids. Roosevelt's 10 million employed are men employed ONLY on condition that cannons are being made and goods sunk. They are NOT promises of a world ORDER. They are proof of the present DISORDER, based on Keynes, Baldwin, Salter, and all the other bleeders and liars who refuse to let facts into print.

#116 (1941) U.K.(20)
TO ALBION

I have hesitated several months before asking Rome radio to let me speak TO England. I have been exercising my native right as an American to speak to my own compatriots, but I have not considered it suitable to meddle in the internal affairs of another country.

I did as much as the foreigner of good will could do, to keep you OUT of this war. I am convinced that every honest Englishman did likewise. I am convinced that the minority who got you into it are utter fools, but they are also that particularly unpleasant KIND of fool, the dishonest fool who thinks other men will be taken in by his inept trickery.

For a decade or more, everyone NOT wholly blinded and hoodwinked has been remarking on the peculiar stink of your press, the mixture of dung and saccharin dished up each morning in your newspapers. Everyone not fed directly BY a putrid and decrepit system has been filled with an increasing DISesteem of your chief politicians, particularly with Baldwin, and in minor degree with his epigones. The various tricks whereby the British Empire has fleeced the world were already threadbare. The Rothschild trade espionage, etc. All old, all stinking, all decrepit, all worn out. Months ago I typed the draft of a radio talk, and destroyed it. I advised you to bump off Churchill before he bumped off all the rest of you.

That appeared to be out of order. It was not my place to advise civic violence in a foreign country, especially as it might cost some clean and decent young lad his life.

Still you had better get rid of Winston. Put him OUT. Get a few sane men into your government somehow.

I am speaking these words in PITY for the decent men left in England. Many of'em saw Winston coming. Many of'em prayed to God, or whatever else they invoke, to spare England the final calamity.

Only a nation as moderate as Italy would allow me to speak over its radio in this vein and from these motives.

As to right and justice. Your unspeakable government of worn-out pantaloons and senile commedians has NO right to ask MY relative, decent young man from Montana to fight for the scum of the earth and slime of your millionaire ghetto. Sassoons, Beits, Sieffs, and their fellow Christians, the Astors, the owners of your lying and slimy news sheets. That I stand on and am ready to fight. If profiteers in America cheat you out of your eye teeth and betray you, it is no more than you as a nation have done to every one of your dupes and allies.

You can not wipe out the past. You can not undo your lies, and your cheatings, and your pretenses, from the question of Danzig onward. But you CAN STOP. You can dissociate yourselves from the fools and knaves, who have made you ridiculous by their inefficient deceits, their caddishness to the French dupes, and so forth. You haven't, historically, a leg or a peg to stand on. You lied as to causes of war. You suppressed truth. But that had already become a habit, with your Mendes, Edens, Jecketts, your ape faced Beaverbrooks, and your stock jobbers. It all falls back on your own heads. Your island is being cleaned OUT, you're cattle slaughtered. "As barren as her deck. /My sons shall see the land I am leaving as barren as her deck," wrote the greatest of your living poets, Basil Buntin'. You have silenced your honest authors, or you have [flooded?] out their speech with the sewers of Fleet Street. Your cranks have stopped their ears with cotton wool, and now it is too late to help it. You refused to hear your soldiers. You put aside all good council. You covered over the facts. A year, nine months, ten months, you can not go back on it.

Your Tommies have been sent to the slaughter. Your leaders have lied, and kept silent. The little cheats are no alternative for the big ones. You had better clean out the lot. I could have found you a better government when I was in London in 1939. I had even then the wild idea that I ought to try to TELL Chamberlain what he was headed for. I missed a phone call. It is probably BETTER for Europe that you were governed by fools, it is probably better for Europe that you cheated, and lied, and dragged in worse fools from Washington to settle the Balkans. But your government of idiots has probably served its turn and it has probably done all the good that it can do. And you had better get out from under, while there are still a few tons of beef left in England, and a few hens to lay eggs for your population.

I am of set purpose writing this a few weeks before speaking it. I wish to set down nothing in haste or in excitement. People who dislike you were saying months ago that, if the U.S.A. came into the war, so much the worse for England, as Japan would absorb American products, especially in munitions.

Few nations have ever made a worse showing that you have. France in 1870 did NOT drag down a half dozen innocent countries before her debacle. Twenty years of your reformers' warning were insufficient to turn you from infamy. Many of you do not YET know your sin; or the sin wherein you permitted your loathsome overlords to entangle you. All you can do is to LAY OFF IT.

Stop shooting Frenchmen, and flogging Hindoos. Stop trying to extend the war into still further regions. Lay off it, while there are still a few loaves of bread left in England.

In 1939 I said: in wartime one farmer is worth more than forty lenders of money.

As far as I can recall, no one in England would print that.

Some day you may know it.

#117 (1941) U.K.(65)
TWO PICTURES

On the 20th of November, two days after the anniversary of SANCTIONS (52 nations vs. Italy), I said to the couple at the next table: Would you say there was a difference of FEELING, I mean FEELING, not thought? I said, would you say there was a difference of FEELING in your country, difference in the way you FEEL about this war and about the last one?

I was in my humble caravansary, the Albergo Rapallo, and they were a pair of John Everyman. I should say PLAIN folk from Germany, of a bit less than my age, but well on, past the middle. The waiter had a try at making 'em understand octopus sauce, which is DElicious. I was havin' rice, with octopus sauce, little octopi, young and tender, and before the pair had come in, I had fished all visible bits of octopus out of my sauce dish so as not to lose any tidbits. However, my persuasions were to no avail, once they knew it was octopus. They had some other kind of sauce with their risotto. After that I put my question, saying I shall probably go to the microphone; can you tell me?

Then the lady said: Very ... First place, *sicher*. We were using my broken German as medium of communication. First place, no worry about the outcome. And in the second, i.e., in 1914 our old government MADE the war, started the war. This time our government did all it could to avoid it. It might be time to recall that even in England reliable parties admitted that Mussolini had done all any man could, to avoid an armed outbreak.

Whatever you still think were the facts, I report this conversation. It at least proves a point of view.

None of your war muggers have, so far as I know, adduced any evidence to the contrary. There were doubts, fears, lies, but NO evidence. None of your spoutin' pets has ever lined up to a SINGLE ONE of my statements. Not for six years so far as I can remember. That goes back to before the war. And I have told you what Chamberlain's chance was, AFTER he staved off one war, and WHAT occurred in your dirty press within 48 hours, according to my lights, thereby dishing England's chance to regain her prestige.

Chamberlain could have had a European triumph of prestige, and England could have jogged on for 40 years, and built up her own inner structure.

Which is exactly what some folk figger out, the usury central DID NOT intend that she should do.

God knows I began noticin' cracks in that structure about as soon as I got to your island in 1908. And nobody has yet even accused me of ONE subversive act during the interval. I am still stickin' on with brother Gibbs in these monologues. It may take me a month to get thru with him. And nearly everything Gibbs openly loves is loved, I should say, more or less by most human beings. I say THINGS cause when he gits to PERSONS I differ. And I haven't yet wept pink tears at a coronation. I have observed certain dates, such as that on which W.S. Landor departed from England. I have observed that Landor wrote a poem to Andy Jackson, which puzzled me no end when I first read it. I have observed that Byron, Shelley, and Keats lived partly in Italy, NOT with the idea of being hauled up by a pair of counter jumpers like Percy Loraine and the late Lord Lloyd as national advertisements.

I have heard of an Earl of Oxford, I think it was, already farmin' out his rents in the time of Elizabeth.

Subversion was not invented in the days of Disraeli. I have told young Englishmen to read Cobbett. I have heard of Tories and WHIGS, and been told that Whigs were the fathers of Liberals. I got out of London slums, that is to say in 1908 I passed thru Islington; I spent seven days in Islington, and that was ENOUGH. I got into Kensington Church Yard, and during 12 years I took occasional bus rides, but I did NOT go slumming. And the term "distressed area" was not widely current till I had moved over to Paris.

So I can't wring anyone's heart.

You got your own native born statisticians to tell you who is not fed. You got your own writers to tell you dole rots the morale of a nation.

My second picture is one Gibbs ought to like. Before my British demise, or whatever it's listed as, it was my privilege to go up a tower. That is, I went up stairs in a manor, where there are some I believe 14 century or thereabouts cloisters. And I crawled over the roof beams of an attic, and thence into the top of a tower, where they conserve a Charter, not Magna Charter, but I think it is Henry II's guarantee or confirmation of what John had pledged to the barons. And I believe her late Majesty Queen Mary, or one or the other, went over the same set of rafters about six weeks later.

It's not my period, and some specialist in English history may correct me, but that is what I recall of the charter. It is the STATE of the manor that mattered to me as an observer of England. Some of the best pictures had been sold, the library was not in working order, there had been some restoration, about Walpole's time, I should imagine, but the ECONomic system of THAT time hadn't permitted FULL restoration. What had been done when England had far LESS money, was not to be done; and now the place, that OUGHT to have been a center of life, that would have housed 80 guests splendidly was as far from action as you might say Carcassonne or St. Bertrand de Cominges. Then, we drove some miles across country for tennis, and an amiable man explained to me how hound's feet ought to be formed.

I asked something about a hound in a sportin' print or perhaps it was a water color of the— —sportin' print period, and he said the hound was, as I recall it, a bit long in the pasterns, if that is the word. And all of this, as far as it was ALIVE is, I suppose, what Sir P. Gibbs was upholdin' in his liberal way. In 1938 and before that. But as an economist, I say god damn, here you have the scene, you have the SHELL of the plant (to use a commercial term), you have the perfect setting. You have the OUTSIDE of the picture, and you go on from decade to decade, for hundred years or more years, eating the VITALITY out of it. And this is the work of the USURY system, you have done that with the adoration of PROFITS, you have done that with SLOP in your politics, and the JEWS have NOT saved you. Whatever they have done, they have not saved you and they have not helped you to SAVE IT. And by IT I mean all of your welfare. I mean all of your yeomanry. Jew Rothschild and his fellow Jew Goldsmid and his fellow Christian Baring have NOT helped you to save it.

And I now ask you and Sir Philip WHAT CAUSES that? I will leave one of the regular lecturers here in Rome to talk to you of slums that he knows better than I do. I will merely ask about a FEW rural scenes in England. What caused'em? Or a few friends from the English country, or a landlord of my room in Church Walk, or some of the humbler GOOD people that I met at one time or another, who are the right sort of English, WHAT have THEY had from your system? Or takin' it a grade or two further up, when I was last over in London after a lapse of ten years, about the time Gibbs was writin' his book, a good poet motored me out to a suburb and looked at the shoestring building and said "Jerusalem in England's pleasant land" with FULL understanding of usury, and the dry rot and wet rot. And then went into the Army the minute this was got going, knowin' what started it, but wantin' his own hands clean from the beginning. What do these people, who are the BEST of England, expect from the union of Mr. Churchill and Mr. Gollancz's book club?

#118 (1941) U.S.[?] QUISLING

Mr. Roosevelt seems determined that England shall not get out of this war alive, and that there shall be no end to the war until the English have been Dunkirk'd out of Cape Town and the Americans had a try at Dakar and the Azores.

It's a hard life, but we have an Italian proverb "chi la dura la vince" [he who holds out longest, wins].

Similar proverbs doubtless exist in other languages. But on the supposition that the war may end sometime, either before or after the collapse of Western civilization, in either case it will be necessary either to continue civilization or to start another, and Mis-INFOR MATION or policy based on ignorance is not recommendable for either purpose.

Several American publications have mentioned the UNWILLINGNESS of their political bigwigs to learn facts about Europe. If their editors are sincere in these expressions, it might be well to start on the case of Quisling. No man has had more mud and slime flung at him from the sewers of British newsprint.

Mr. Roosevelt used up about ten pages of his twelve-page speech of May 27 with what might have been questions from the particularly low London Daily Mirror, from any issue printed during the past six or eight years. But at one point it appeared that he spoke not merely from prejudice (unconscious or other) but from plain ignorance. We ask what does he know of Quisling.

Norway, like other countries in 1936, had at least varieties of inhabitants. The lowest and vilest of human types represented by the international, and possibly non-aryan financier Hambro, an exploiter of the people, a money lender, who in time of crisis quite naturally fled the country, taking his bonds with him.

This is to be expected whether these leeches are Jew or Gentile, whether they are millionaire socialists like Blum and Bullitt, or puppets or larger financiers.

And Norway had also men who wanted a better Europe. Now Italy has no debt to Mr. Quisling, but in the interests of truth and fair reporting we suggest that before America accepts an estimate of Mr. Quisling based wholly on reports from what might be called Harnbro sources and sources allied to Hambro, namely London Jewish and Aryan papers, controlled by Ellerman, Mend alias Melchett, Eden's friends, the Astors, et cetera, some one should go back and look at Quisling's plan for a north European federation, and then decide whether or not the real Quisling corresponds with the London distortion of Quisling. Quisling based his position on the belief that "an old world falls, a new is being born." This is anathema to the unholy trinity Baruch-Roosevelt and Moses Sieff. NO conclusions drawn for a belief in or a desire for a better social order could bring favor from the Jew-Beaverbrook-Astor press.

Quisling not being in England, and not being dependent on British editors could not be starved directly, starvation being the financiers' FIRST and main mode of attack. There remained only vilification, and President Roosevelt is merely the last recruit to dirt-slingers emergency corps.

SECONDLY: Quisling observed that the Jewish international had had some effect on the affairs of Soviet Russia. How unfortunate! What an error this would have been had Mr. Quisling wanted favorable publicity in the Sieff-Mond Guardian-Eflerman papers!!

THIRDLY: Quisling regarded the League of Nations with suspicion, thereby forfeiting the support of the Keyneses, Welleses, Streits, and other bootlicking agents of the Bank of International Settlements and its then Paris, and still London affiliates; in short by all these three positions, he dissociated himself from the Mandels, Blums and Stavitskys.

Quisling's position against Bolshevism was to him a position against "universal materialist republic under Jewish dictatorship," a position analogous to that taken by Finland. But Quisling owned, so far as it appears, no nickel mines, and therefore the publicity controlled by "Anglo-Canadian nickel (alias, Melchett, etc.) would hardly give him a "build up" in "Time" or other Jewish-owned American organs. At the time of Sanctions, Quisling's party was for Norwegian neutrality. This of course showed the cloven-hoof from the Morgenthau point of view. Quisling was and is, however a Norwegian and judged the matter in its relation to Norway's interest. His movement however took NO sides. He was worried by the Soviet participation in the League of Nations and by the Jewish factor in Russian politics. It annoyed him that the lives of people IN NORWAY were dominated by foreign policy and not by home politics.

The idea that the citizens of a country should consider their INTERNAL affairs does, of course, render Quisling incompatible with the Roosevelt way of life; but even so it was scarcely high treason on Quisling's part to observe the 1936 situation IN Norway. Quisling was capable of the magnificent axiom:

"The influence of a state in foreign politics always corresponds to the degree of development of its INTERNAL strength."

How unlike the Roosevelt technique of raising hysteria, both for personal and national use. In fact Quisling advocated autarchy, rather than GRABarchy. Autarchy for Norway, and co-operation BY Norway and foreign states. He saw Czechoslovakia bucked by international Jews. He saw the Brito-yitto attempt to encircle Germany was provocative of unpleasant tension. AND he observed the GE-O-GRaphic position of his own country in case of Germano-Russian unpleasantness. "Norway, the cross-roads between Russia, Germany and England."

BUT he did NOT turn against England, as the British Jews would have wished him to. He saw a RUSSIAN attempt to use Norway in a flank attack on Germany AND on England, and advocated a union of Norway with ENGLAND and Germany. A nordic world federation. Why do WE in Italy mention this?

Quisling was not pro-Mussolini, the Axis was not yet in being. Contrary to the Edens and Churchills WE in ITALY do not believe that continual lies about everyone will help to a new and better world order.

QUISLING considered that peace between England and Germany was vital to Norway. Therefore the Beaverbrook and hog press have for the past four years denounced him as a traitor to Norway. Which is what we expect from Lord Beaverbrook, Sieff, and the Astors, and why the prestige of the British press has during the past years notably declined on the continent of Europe, in Asia and in South America, though apparently NOT in the Morgenthau circle.

To Quisling, "peace and conciliation between Germany and England" was the one way in which Norway could escape from war and chaos. With no tenderness for the Latins, Quisling went beyond this conciliation of Germany and England and wanted a Nordic federation containing these two great powers, plus the Scandinavian countries, plus Holland and Flanders.

OBVIOUSLY such a union would not have been as advantageous to Italy as the Axis. However it is not the Rome end of the Axis which is demanding Quisling's head. It is our opponents who have done their utmost to turn his name into a common verb and make him a synonym for anti-national activity whenever and wherever.

OBVIOUSLY Quisling's plan would have been to the benefit of the English. They would not have lost so many American bases, nor would our position in the Mediterranean have been, by that plan, at all improved. We might still be where we were in 1937. What is absolutely and uncontestably apparent is that Mr. QUISLING'S OWN country would not have suffered invasion, and this from the patriot's view is of chief importance. The present war would probably not have occurred. At any rate it could not have started as an Anglo-German conflagration.

In any case, what is ABSOLUTELY incontestable is that Norway would not have been invaded; and this from Mr. Quisling's point of view, that is from the patriot view, must be considered as important.

History will possibly decide whether Quisling's attempts to avert war or the efforts of Kuhn-Loeb and Co., and the yitto-brito financial agents IN the United States to get the war started, and of their American colleagues, half-breeds Bullitts, et cetera to GET the war started, that the American effort to START war in Europe, in order to pick Europe's pocket, and ultimate[*ly*] to drive the American people into the shambles will have proved to the advantage of England.

At any rate, as indicated in our brief earlier comment on the Quisling paragraph in Roosevelt's speech of May 27th, we believe Roosevelt's allusion to Quisling was due, as are so many of the President's outbursts, to his reading the positively, the WORST type of newsprint, until it obscures his world outlook.

To sum up, Quisling's plan might have averted war. It would in any case have kept war out of Norway. Hence the abuse of Quisling in the usurocrat, monopolistic, mercantilist press both Jew and Gentile. But the heads of states should not be wholly subservient to the lowest and yellowest papers.

#119 (1943) U.S.(14) PHILOLOGY

I have mentioned Brooks Adams in these talks? I hope I have mentioned his name often enough for it to have sunk in. I know of no better introduction to American history or the understanding of the historical process than Brook Adams' two volumes, *Law of Civilization and Decay* and *The New Empire*.

Of course you need collateral readin', other history books, general history of the U.S. No better introduction than Woodward's. Can't trust it at all points but will give you an outline. Unjust to Van Buren and the Adamses but clearly intended to be fair and not a mere smoke screen.

D.R. Dewey's *Financial History*. Lot of facts, doubt if student ever remembers any of'em. No key, no clue, nothing in the whole book to help the reader understand "what it is all about." Nacherly it is THE standard work in the universities. Universities for the past 80 years, increasingly for past 50 or 40, have inculcated respect for lucre. Adoration of money grabbing, bred taste for luxury, called standard of livin', above what student is likely to attain, and told him the great man was the man who got MONEY, no matter how. Religion fadin'; religion, church buildin', a branch of the real estate business. All churches mortgaged. Church buildin', a means to get community groups to borrow money.

Pete Larranaga, *Gold Glut and Government*, tells you something. Kitson a bad writer in many ways, piles up obstacles for the reader, possibly *knew* more than any of'em. Even Woodward does NOT give the clue. He gives some clues but not the debt clue. In course of long desultory readin', the FIRST book I ever struck that would lead the student to an understandin' of the whole historical process in the U.S. was Overholser, in 64 pages, published by Honest Money Founders of Chicago, now I hear; at least they would know where to find it.

Doc. Ames, H.V., at University of Pennsylvania, in 1902 was already gettin' interested in reconstruction. The *"Tragic Era"* as C. Bowers calls it, period after the Civil War. But he hadn't got down to the debt component. And without study of debt and usury NO history of the U.S. can be written save as a smoke screen, consciously or unconsciously. I don't mean that historians haven't written with intention of tellin' the story, of writing true history, but those that did mainly had NOT found the clue, the pattern in the carpet. And don't run away with the idea that I told you Brooks Adams was the last will and testament of God Almighty. His books are merely, as far as I know, the best introduction. It is written from a mercantile position, with amazin' lucidity and power of synthesis, as you can see if you compare'em with some of his very rare followers who have written BEFORE having so thoroughly digested their data.

I doubt if you will understand the full imbecility, the absolute squalor of the Knox-Roosevelt (F.D. Roosevelt) Baruch administration till you have read Brooks Adams. He writes about trade routes, the dislocation of trade routes, the FLOP of empires consequent on the dislocation or loss of trade routes. What Frankie and kikie have DONE to you NOW. No author can get the whole history of mankind into one book, or two books. The spectacular drama of history has, let us say, been consequent on the shift of the trade routes, caused by new discoveries of minerals, caused by magnetic compass, or new modes of transport, sometimes ruined by excess charges of administration, such as usury, and false accountancy, false accountancy having corroded all Mr. Adams' nice mercantile systems, though he don't put his main emphasis on that component. Wars rise from commercial competition, BUT to have that competition, down under it is the production, production system.

That is what Brooks Adams was not writing about. God knows he had enough to write about. Enough history that hadn't been sorted out in men's minds, in ANY man's mind. Over and above the books I have mentioned at the start of this talk are the actual papers of statesmen. John Adams and Van Buren and so on.

Woodward suggests that the explanation of the Adams family is to be found in glandular secretions. I would say mebbe it was due to John Adams, the founder of the line, gettin' spliced to Abigail Quincy, that might explain some of that problem. However, one point that Brooks Adams more or less passes by is noted by Woodward and will do to fill in the chink of the story. Just to keep from introducin' Europe, and foreign systems, topics on which you run ravin' mad out of prejudice. Will you note that John Quincy Adams and Henry Clay worked out in theory what was called the AMERICAN system? Meaning that the U S was to be self supportin'. At a time when there was one party, [the] idea was broached that all sections of the country were to be harmonized, North East to develop manufacturing, supported by protective tariff to keep out European competition; and that the industrial towns would provide a market for the agricultural products of the West and South; and the rural sections would provide customers for goods produced by the factories. Nothing in it that is not plain commonsense. Of course most American prosperity rose from the application of those ideas, partial application. But still the good life in America has been due to'em.

Well now Europe has GOT that idea. There is nothing fancy or new about THAT idea. It is just horse sense and intelligence. BUT it don't produce war. It don't produce gallopin' usury. It is not romantic enough for the sheenies. And you will never understand American history or the history of the Occident durin' the past 2000 years unless you look at one or two problems; namely, sheenies and usury. One or the other or BOTH, I should say, both.

And dear ole Bill Woodward does NOT give you clearly the answer. He is not stallin', at least I don't think so, but some things escape him, or remain in penumbra, probably his own penumbra. For example, he notices that in the Quincy Adams-Jackson campaign a change came over American political method. For the first time there was a wild outbreak of vituperation in the press: wild slanders against both of the candidates —.

Shall we say that something had bust? TWO candidates, Quincy Adams and Jackson, who did not belong to the banks. Of course John Quincy Adams might not have disturbed'em, but he was so gol' thunderin' honest, and his father had SO seen thru the bank swindle.

I don't mean that that is all of the story. And let's not get lost in retrospect. I tell you. FIRST, you can not understand American history without digging down into the problem of debt and usury. Up to now no American history has been written. Takin' due count of the personnel and the component of Jewry. Brooks Adams seeing that the Kike triumphed in England, after Waterloo, and Overholser givin' you the clue (along with Col. Lindbergh's papa)—the CLUE to the betrayal of the American nation, the American Government, the American system in 1863, the sellout to Rothschild.

But Brooks Adams havin' his limitation, at least the exposition in the two volumes mentioned, has the limitation of dealing with wars and the decline of empires—wars from economic competition. BUT down under that, if the thing for you to study if you be lookin' forward, is the production system. Possibly about to be reinforced ON the U.S.A., as consequence of the squalor of Knox, the ignorance of the governing oligarchy. You may be too dumb to do it until you are forced. Seiff's embargo was a protective measure.

On a basis of autarchy and collaboration a peaceful world can arise. And on NO other basis. The mercantilist system, mercantilist disposition, or an Anschauung, never brought peace. Monopoly, megalomania, reading the Jewbrew texts never brought peace honor or decency, or the good life, neither did neglect of the Latin classics.

America declined. The whole tone of American life went down, slopped, grew foetid, step by step as the Latin classics went into the discard, and the reading of the Hebrew superstitions continued to be tolerated in the American colleges. Out of Sallust and Cicero a man might LEARN something useful. Out of Demosthenes he might git a line of the habitual human swindles that would help him understand the second bank of the United States, oh, ably described by Woodward, as to its personal habits, BUT not exposed in its perspective as it is exposed in the autobiography of Martin Van Buren.

Go on, read the Brooks Adams and then go on to the study of contemporary Europe. In the light of the Clay Quincy Adams project. Don't die like a beast, I mean if you are dead set to be sunk in the mid-Atlantic or Pacific or scorched in the desert, at least KNOW why it is done to you.

To die not knowin' why is to die like an animal. What the kike calls you: goyim or cattle. To die like a human being you have at least got to know why it is done to you.

#120 (1941) U.S.(142)
CHURCH PERIL

I am speaking as promised to the students of Fordham, and professors, and other Catholic universities.

When I was a young man in America, one heard a good deal of talk about the union of the churches. It was very nice and humanitarian on the surface. And one heard less of a more bizarre proposition, namely, that of Anglo-Israel, all dressed up with the Stone of Scone on which Scotch's King's were recrowned, now it is in Westminster Abbey, and about the prophet Isaiah, and the rest of the stage set, "hast given us the gates of thine enemies" and so on. Well, comin' to Europe I thought nothin' about either of these movements or drags for the next 30 years and very probably you didn't either, those of you who are old enough to have heard of the phantasies of the year 1900. But that is not the end of the story. A few weeks ago in London there was a powwow between the Archbishop of Canterbury and a Catholic Archbishop, or Cardinal, and a high Rabbi. And if I were a Catholic, I should want to know more about what that meeting was up to. I should want, quite seriously, to see that conventicle in historic perspective. That perspective is very clearly outlined, or indicated in a book called La Sibille, by Zielinski, a Polish writer who seems to me to be imbued with sincere piety. But who sees Judaism in direct contrast, spiritual, theological contrast, with the Christian faith.

Many other writers have written on the gift of earlier Mediterranean philosophers to the developments of the Church dogma. Zielinski calls this the MATERIAL influence of Hellenism on Christianity. But he takes what is, to me at least, a new angle of analysis. He speaks of the psychologic preparation for Christianity that was there in the Greek and Roman religions, both the religion of Delphi, that is of the cult of Apollo and in that of Ceres Demeter, Mater Dolorosa, and in less degree in some of the more— —cults.

Few of us know that the Mithraic religion identified their saviour with Love. As in the gospels we read: God is love, so in Mithraic worship, or in at least one praise of Mithra, we find the same words: is Love; Mithra is love.

Zielinski offers a fairly complete list of prototypes, of the essentially Catholic beliefs, I say essentially Catholic because they are quite patently

NON-Jewish, and ANTI-Jewish, and they are specifically the features of Catholicism which Protestantism has wiped out.

E="font-size: 11pt">I think you should consider these things. The Jews do not honor the Virgin, they do not honor the Mother of God in any form. Neither do the Protestants. Mother Mary gets a look in at Christmas, that is, on the anniversary of our Lord's birth, on about the same footing as the Sheperds and Magi, just as the Catholic Church notices the Semitic period once a year in the prayer for the perfidious Jews on the anniversary of the crucifixion.

And Zielinski's term for Protestantism is "REJEWdiazed religion." But I am not so much intent on the theology as on the immediate ecclesiastical polity of the enemies of faith. He points out, I think uncontradictably, that the people who got converted to Christianity in the early centuries were, as Zielinski points out, the pagans, and the people who most pertinaciously opposed the new religion of Christianity were the Jews. Various attempts at syncretism preceded the Conversion of Constantine, and the formulation of the Catholic or general church and emperors of other empires had felt the need of a single religion for all their people. The Tarquins were converted to Apollo, there was a fusion of Delphi with the Persians, Ptolemy First wanted a single cult for his subjects, and Seleukos held out against Ptolemy and Lysimacus. In short, there is nothing essentially new in an emperor's wanting a synthetic and inclusive religion for political ends.

And remains of these syncretisms persist in great beauty in Christian ritual, and in the Catholic disposition. Isis, Demter Mary, the fans in the Easter Mass at Siena. The Greek church held out against Rome in calling itself orthodox and not the General Church. The Greeks by that time were not a people ruling an empire. Given the Roman empire there was a political need of a general or universal religion for the whole empire, which claimed more or less to be the circle of lands, the whole world.

As to the seriousness of the Anglican church, Brooks Adams sums that up fairly completely when he remarks with perfect accuracy, the relation of Christ's blood and body to the bread of the sacrament was changed five times in the course of a life time, by royal decree or act of Parliament.

The Brits are a theatrical and not a religious people. And the last meeting in London was not wholly religious in nature. The Anglican church is a national church. The Church of Rome was an imperial church at the outset. A Protestant sect is by definition cut off from universality. But today we are faced by a new INTERNATIONAL empire, a new tyranny, that hates and bleeds the whole world. I refer to the empire of international usury, that knows no faith and no frontiers. It is called international finance, and the Jew and the Archbishop in London are at work for that tyranny trying to draft a universal religion in defense of the infamy of the usurers. It is DEMOCRATIC in principles and I think the Catholic representative is ill-advised to put his head into the noose. As a democratic and usurious combine, the Catholic is in a minority of ONE against TWO. He will always be outvoted, and I can not see that this conduces to Catholic welfare.

A universal church of the usurers would be very poor substitute for religion.

Already published

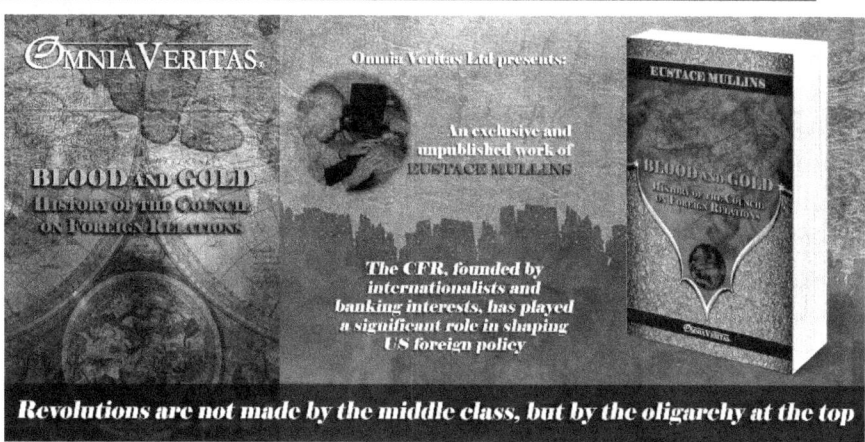

Revolutions are not made by the middle class, but by the oligarchy at the top

Ezra's interest in money as a phenomenon, in contrast to the usual attitude toward money as something to get, is a legitimate one.

Omnia Veritas Ltd presents:

EZRA POUND
THIS DIFFICULT INDIVIDUAL
by
EUSTACE MULLINS

An illustration for his own monetary theories...

THE STORY OF THE MEDICAL CONSPIRACY AGAINST AMERICA

Omnia Veritas Ltd presents:

MURDER BY INJECTION
by
EUSTACE MULLINS

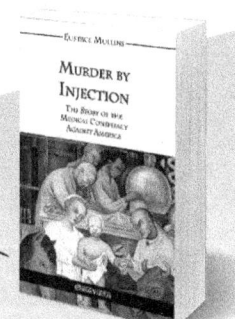

The cynicism and malice of these conspirators is something beyond the imagination of most Americans.

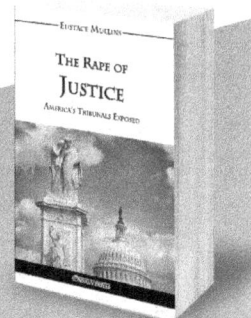

Omnia Veritas Ltd presents:

THE RAPE OF JUSTICE

by
EUSTACE MULLINS

AMERICA'S TRIBUNALS EXPOSED

American should know just what is going on in our courts

Omnia Veritas Ltd presents:

THE SECRETS OF THE FEDERAL RESERVE

by
EUSTACE MULLINS

HERE ARE THE SIMPLE FACTS OF THE GREAT BETRAYAL

Will we continue to be enslaved by the Babylonian debt money system?

Omnia Veritas Ltd presents:

THE WORLD ORDER
OUR SECRET RULERS

A Study in the Hegemony of Parasitism

by
EUSTACE MULLINS

The peoples of the world not only will never love Big Brother, but they will soon dispose of him forever.

The program of the World Order remains the same; Divide and Conquer

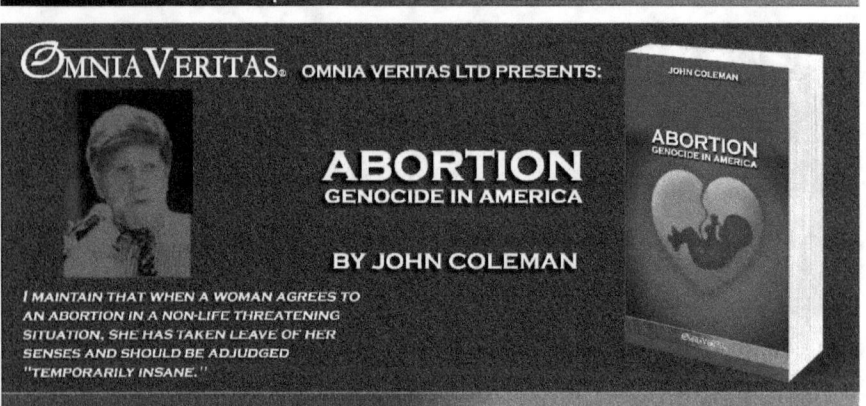

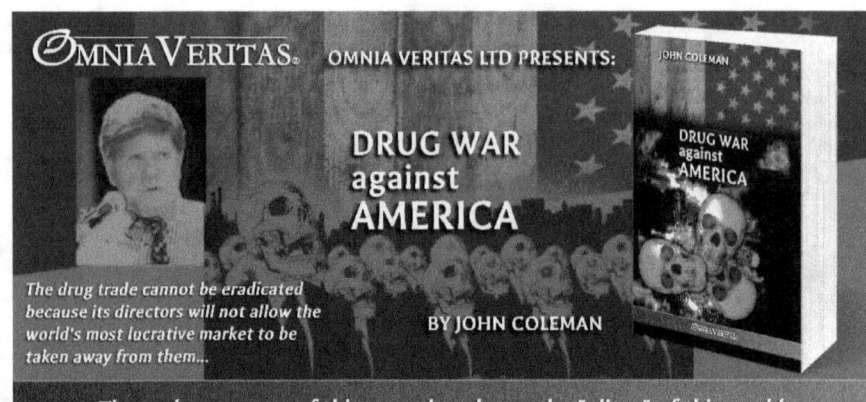
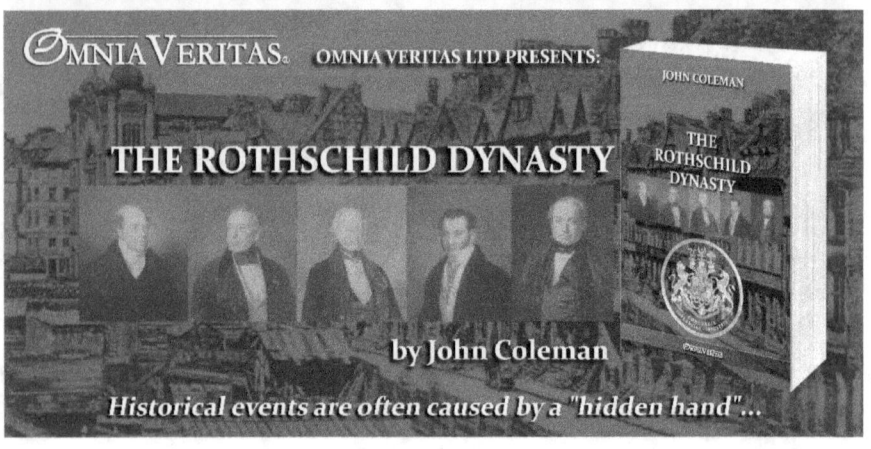

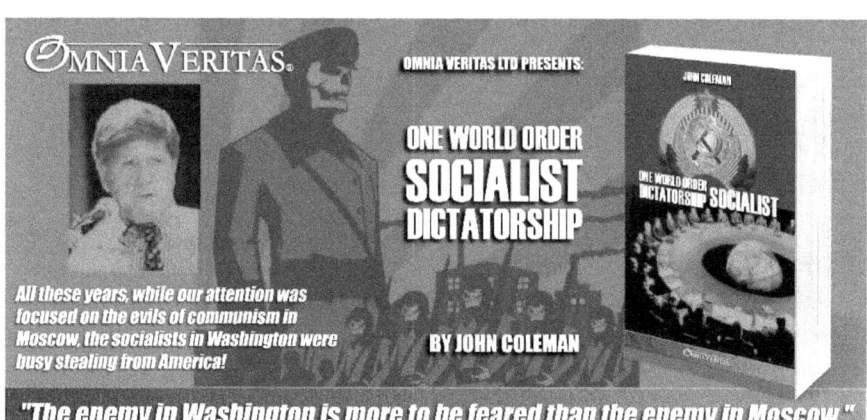

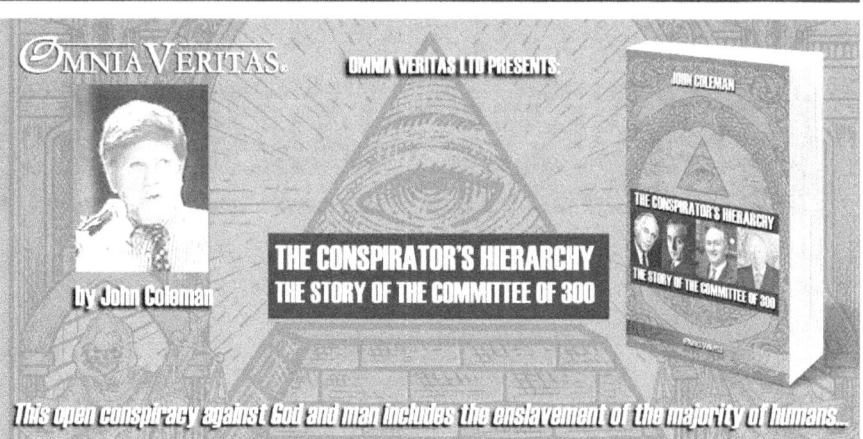

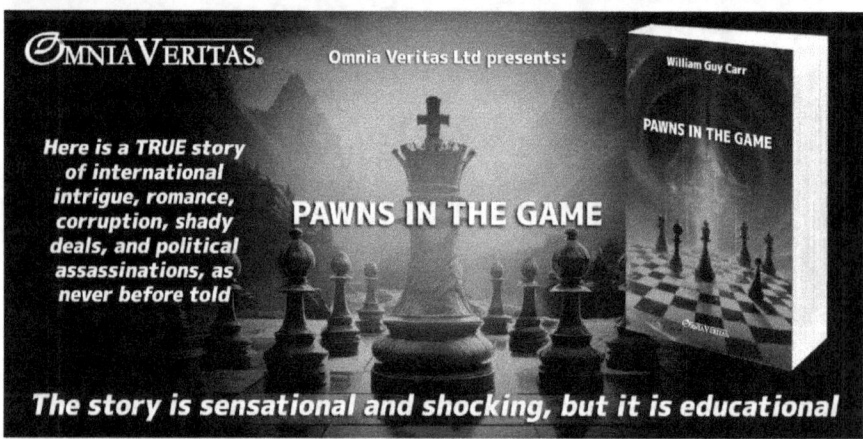

www.ingramcontent.com/pod-product-compliance
Lightning Source LLC
Chambersburg PA
CBHW071940220426
43662CB00009B/934